THE GLOUCESTERSHIRE
REGIMENT IN THE WAR
1914–1918

LIEUTENANT-GENERAL THE RT. HON. SIR F. C. SHAW, K.C.B.
COLONEL OF THE REGIMENT

THE GLOUCESTERSHIRE REGIMENT IN THE WAR

1914–1918

THE RECORDS OF THE 1st (28th), 2nd (61st),
3rd (SPECIAL RESERVE) AND 4th, 5th AND 6th
(FIRST-LINE T.A.) BATTALIONS

BY

EVERARD WYRALL

WITH A FOREWORD BY

Field-Marshal Sir G. F. MILNE
G.C.B., G.C.M.G., D.S.O.

WITH FRONTISPIECE AND TWENTY MAPS

METHUEN & CO. LTD.
36 ESSEX STREET W.C.
LONDON

First Published in 1931

FOREWORD

THE history of the Great War abounds in examples of the heroism and stubborn fortitude displayed by the County Regiments. These old regiments of the line received too little attention in the press and were at times forgotten by the general public ; but though they were deprived of the stimulus of popular recognition they were to be found in every theatre of war steadily and unpretentiously bearing the heat and burden of the day. That the Gloucestershire Regiment may, even in this gallant company, be proud of the part it played will be clear from a perusal of this book. It is a record of patience and determination, of self-sacrifice and bravery, common alike to regular and territorial battalions of the Regiment, and should prove in the future an inspiration to the men of Gloucestershire and to the youth of the country as a whole.

G. F. MILNE,
F.M.

4th March, 1931

CONTENTS

LIST OF MAPS

From drawings by John S. Fenton

ix

THE GLOUCESTERSHIRE REGIMENT IN THE WAR 1914–1918

CHAPTER I

THE CALL TO ARMS

RUSHMOOR BOTTOM, Aldershot, was well known to most officers and men of the British Army of 1914, and there, at the end of July of that year, the 1st Battalion Gloucestershire (the 28th) Regiment, with other units of the 3rd Brigade, 1st Division, was engaged in annual training when rumours of war reached the camp. This annual training was the culmination of the year's exercises. During the winter months the soldier was trained individually in physical exercises, route marching, bayonet fighting, musketry, signalling and scouting ; in the spring individual training gave place to training by units, and, finally, in the summer, brigade and divisional exercises were carried out. When, therefore, on 1st August the 3rd Brigade was suddenly instructed to ' strike camp ' and move back to its own station at Bordon, the situation was regarded as serious and war almost certain.

The Gloucestershire Regiment (28th and 61st Foot) at this period consisted of six battalions, the 1st and 2nd Regular, 3rd (Royal South Gloucestershire Militia) and 4th (City of Bristol), 5th and 6th Territorial Battalions.

The 1st Battalion (28th) was stationed at Bordon and, as already stated above, formed part of the 3rd Infantry Brigade, 1st Division. The Battalion was commanded by Lieut.-Colonel A. C. Lovett and was brigaded with the 1st Royal West Surrey Regiment, 1st South Wales Borderers, and 2nd Battalion Welch Regiment. The 1st Division was in the Aldershot Command and, with the 2nd Division, eventually formed the 1st Corps of the British Expeditionary Force.

The 2nd Battalion (61st Foot) was abroad, at Tientsin, under the command of Major R. Conner.[1] The 3rd Battalion (Lieut.-

---

[1] Colonel A. C. Vicary adds the following note :—

' Lieut.-Colonel Tulloh did not take command till the 61st reached Port Said on its way home at the end of October 1914. Lieut.-Colonel

1   1

Colonel G. H. Burges, commanding), who had finished their annual training on the 27th June, were at this period disembodied. The Depot of the Regiment was at Bristol : Major R. P. Jordan commanded the Depot.   The three Territorial Battalions had their Headquarters as follows : 4th (City of Bristol)—Queen's Road, Clifton, Bristol ; 5th—The Barracks, Gloucester, and the 6th—St. Michael's Hill, Bristol.   Lieut.-Colonel J. B. Butler was in command of the 4th, Lieut.-Colonel S. S. Marling, of the 5th, and Lieut.-Colonel H. C. Woodcock, the 6th.[1]

The series of political events which led up to the Great War form no part of Regimental History, but overt acts of a military nature which ultimately precipitated the struggle are of interest. At 12 noon on the 1st August the German ultimatum to Russia (which stated that unless Russia ceased mobilization within twelve hours she also would mobilize) had expired without the Tsar's Government giving the necessary undertaking, and a general conflagration became inevitable.   It was this situation which forced the British Government to put an end to the Army manœuvres and training and the Territorial annual training, and order all troops back to their stations.

On the 2nd the Germans demanded a passage through Belgium, which request was promptly refused, the Belgians appealing to the Powers who were signatories to the Treaty guaranteeing the neutrality of Belgium.   On this date also other important events of a military nature had taken place : German troops had crossed the Polish frontier, had broken into France at four different points, and had entered the territory of Luxembourg, though Germany had guaranteed the perpetual neutrality of that State. In Great Britain the Territorial Force was embodied and the Naval Reserve called out, but still mobilization had not been ordered.   On the 3rd of August Germany declared war on France and completed her arrangements for the invasion of Belgium.   On the morning of the 4th two of her cavalry divisions passed the frontier and in the afternoon the heads of German infantry columns also entered Belgium.   The British Ambassador in Berlin was then instructed to ask for his passports unless a

Tulloh picked us up there, having gone to India and back to Port Said. The 61st in Tientsin, shortly after the outbreak of War, had orders for Sialkot, India, then for Tsing Tau to take part in the siege of that port with the Japs.   We actually put our kits on board labelled Sialkot for it.   At the last moment we had orders to embark for " destination unknown ", which turned out to be England for Flanders.'

[1] The Honorary Colonels of the Territorial Battalions were : The (then) Lord Mayor of Bristol of the 4th, Colonel Earl Bathurst of the 5th, and Field-Marshal Earl Roberts of the 6th.

satisfactory answer was given regarding the observation of Belgian neutrality by 12 midnight. At 4 p.m. the British Government gave orders for the mobilization of the Army, and at 12.15 a.m. on the 5th August the Foreign Office issued the following statement :

'Owing to the summary rejection by the German Government of the request made by His Majesty's Government for assurances that the neutrality of Belgium will be respected, His Majesty's Ambassador at Berlin has received his passports and His Majesty's Government have declared to the German Government that a state of war exists between Great Britain and Germany as from 11 p.m. on the 4th August.'

Headquarters of the 1st Division at Aldershot received orders to mobilize at about 5 p.m. on the 4th, and the 1st Gloucesters very shortly afterwards.[1] The 5th was named as the ' first day of mobilization '; everything was to be completed by midnight, the 7th August.[2]

The Battalion was much under strength and two captains, seven subalterns and about 600 men were required to bring it up to war strength. The order to mobilize was received at the Depot at about 4.30 pm. on the 4th August and reservists poured in during the next two days. The first reservist to report was Corporal Minahan, who arrived from London on the 4th. This non-commissioned officer was wounded with the 1st Battalion on the 9th May 1915 during the abortive attack on the Aubers Ridge and after returning to the 1st Battalion was killed during the Somme battles in July 1916, just as he was about to receive a commission.

The mobilization of the Regular reservists was completed and the required number had been dispatched to the 1st Battalion by Friday, 7th August. On Saturday, 8th August, the 3rd Battalion mobilized and proceeded on that evening, together with the surplus Regular reservists, to its War Station on the marshes at Abbey Wood, where it encamped and started on its duties of guarding the Arsenal, and training reinforcements.

On the 7th, also, the War Office issued orders to each battalion to send one captain, two subalterns and fifteen sergeants or corporals to their Depot for duty with the 3rd Battalion.

By midnight, with the exception of some twenty men still required to complete the Base Details, the 1st Gloucesters were fully mobilized and ready to move.

Although a prodigious amount of work had to be carried out

---

[1] The Diary of the 3rd Infantry Brigade H.Qs. does not begin until the 12th August.

[2] The mobilization of the Territorials will be dealt with later.

everything had gone splendidly from the very first day—a tribute to the Battalion Mobilization Scheme, worked out mostly by the Adjutant.   Peace equipment was handed in and war stores issued, the doors of the Quartermaster's Stores being thrown open to all who needed replacements or new issues.   Swords and bayonets had to be sharpened, pay books, conduct sheets and other documents prepared, medals collected and handed in, personal kits packed either to accompany the Battalion or to be stored in England until the end of the War.   From the Remount Depot draught horses were received on the 6th and riding horses on the 7th.   The breaking-in of these was no easy matter, for the transport personnel were new to their job.   The harness and equipment, issued from the mobilization stores in small pieces, had to be put together, softened and fitted to the various animals, and these, being accustomed to civilian harness, did not take kindly to the rather tight military impedimenta, with the result that when out for a first and short trial route march there were certain episodes which lent comic relief to an otherwise serious business.

During the summer there had been a practice mobilization at Aldershot, the 2nd Division bringing its units up to war strength by absorbing temporarily personnel from the 1st Division in order to save calling up the general reserve.   This trial mobilization undoubtedly assisted the troops and staff when the time came in August for a rapid calling up of men and animals.

On the 7th instructions were received that the first day of movement was to be Sunday, the 9th August, but it was actually the 12th before the 3rd Brigade left Bordon.   These extra few days were invaluable to the reservists who had to be initiated into the mysteries of the new short rifle : some of the men had not served with the colours for many years and their knowledge of drill had to be brought up to date.   But once a soldier always a soldier, and in those few short days the reservists soon fitted themselves for service in the field.   On the 10th a further batch of thirty reservists to complete the Base Details arrived.

On the 11th Brig.-General H. Landon, the Brigade Commander, inspected the Battalion, and during the day preparatory orders for entraining were issued to companies.

It was still dark in the early hours of the 12th when the 1st Gloucesters, without bands playing or any of the flag-waving usually associated with the departure of troops to take part in an overseas war, paraded and marched to Bordon Station where they boarded two trains, the first of which arrived at Southampton at 5 a.m. and the second at 6.30 a.m.

And here for a while it is necessary to digress in order to

give the composition of the Expeditionary Force which Great Britain was sending to France.

The Regular Army, before the outbreak of war in 1914, consisted of 6 divisions of all arms and 1 cavalry division. Each of the 6 divisions comprised 3 infantry brigades (12 battalions of infantry in all) with divisional mounted troops, artillery, engineers, signal service, supply and transport train and field ambulances. The total strength of a division was some 18,000 troops of all ranks.

On the 5th and 6th August two meetings of the Cabinet, including Lord Kitchener (who on the latter date became Secretary of State for War) and leading members of the Staffs of the Navy and Army, were held to consider the conduct of the war. The main military question was the employment and disposition of the Expeditionary Force. At the meetings it was decided first that the 1st, 2nd, 3rd and 5th Divisions and the Cavalry Division should embark for the Continent, the 4th and 6th Divisions being retained for the present in the United Kingdom in order to reduce the chance of a German landing in force interfering with the transport of troops overseas to the assistance of France and Belgium.

The 1st and 2nd Divisions formed the Ist Corps [1] under the command of Lieut.-General Sir Douglas Haig, the 3rd and 5th Divisions the IInd Corps, commanded by Lieut.-General Sir James Grierson : [2] Major-General E. Allenby commanded the Cavalry. The Commander-in-Chief of the British Expeditionary Force was Field-Marshal Sir John French.

On reaching Southampton the 1st Gloucesters went aboard (curiously enough) the S.S. *Gloucester Castle*, which sailed at 12.10 p.m. on the 12th. In Sandown Bay the vessel stopped and dropped the pilot, then at about 3 p.m. put out to sea again.

Thus, almost unnoticed, the 1st Gloucesters, in company with other units, all of that

> 'little mighty Force that stood for England ',

set sail for an ' unknown destination '. Never had Great Britain sent a better-trained or more perfectly equipped force into the field :

> ' They went forth first a little Army,
> All its men were true as steel.'

---

[1] The adoption of Corps was in accordance with the formation of the French Army and was not in vogue in the British Army before the War.

[2] General Grierson died in a train in France on the 17th August and was succeeded in command of the IInd Corps by General Sir Horace Smith-Dorrien.

CHAPTER II

ARRIVAL IN FRANCE, CONCENTRATION AND MOVE TO THE MONS POSITION

THE 'unknown destination' for which the Gloucesters were bound was the French seaport town of Le Havre, but it was 11.30 that night ere the dim outline of the coast of France was sighted by the excited watchers aboard the *Gloucester Castle* : for all ranks felt they were embarked upon a great adventure—perhaps the greatest in their lives.

Slowly the vessel approached the port and nosed her way into the docks, and between 12 midnight and 1 a.m. on the 13th was berthed. The Gloucesters were amongst the first British troops to arrive at Havre, and disembarkation preparations were somewhat scanty, for with the exception of a few French infantry reservists no labour was available.

Disembarkation began at 1 a.m., but it was a tiresome business, especially in unloading the transport, all the animals having to be slung. Meanwhile the men were disembarked and assembled in a large cargo shed where they were allowed to lie down and sleep until the transport and Battalion stores had all been taken ashore.

Between 5 and 6 a.m., however, the Battalion fell in and Colonel Lovett read the King's message to all ranks, which drew thunderous cheers. A copy of Lord Kitchener's letter to the troops was also distributed to each officer and man.

The Battalion, with transport, cookers, water carts and maltese carts, marched off for No. 1 Rest Camp, near the forts at St. Adresse, some 4 miles from the docks, on the high ground north of the town.

None of those who formed part of the original Expeditionary Force are ever likely to forget the wild enthusiasm of the French people on the arrival of the first British troops on the historic shores of France. As the Gloucesters swung along the road their going was like a triumphal march : cheers and shouts, smiles and handclapping, and not a few tears from the more serious-minded, greeted them, receiving in reply loud cries of 'Are we downhearted ? ' to which the troops gave their own reply in many

6

a thunderous and long-drawn-out ' N-o-o-o ! ' Flowers, fruit,
cakes, cigarettes and tobacco, and even beer and wine, were
pressed upon them, while here one woman cried out, ' Oh, but
they are brave to go laughing,' and there, another pressed her
handkerchief to her eyes for the memory perhaps of a husband,
brother or son who also had marched away to war : for every
Frenchman of military age had already been called up.

The ' Rest Camp ' was somewhat of a delusion, for it proved
to be a large flat stubble field where stood a vast number of bell
tents, one hundred of which were put at the disposal of the
Gloucesters. Here another day was spent most profitably in
further exercises in fire control and discipline, for in 1914 the
British soldier's marksmanship was incomparably the finest ever
witnessed in the Armies of the Nations. Not only was he a fine
shot, but the wonderful ' 15 aimed shots a minute ' was at once
the admiration and dread of his enemies when he first met them
in battle. Such rapidity and accuracy with the rifle had, however,
only been brought about by constant practice.

By the 14th August the 1st Division had completely landed in
France and the 3rd Brigade received orders to entrain and proceed
to the concentration area on the 15th. The night of the 14th/15th
was broken by a violent thunderstorm which blew down many
tents and drenched the unfortunate occupants. Reveille sounded
at 4 a.m. and no one was sorry to leave the Camp, which by now
had become a mud patch. At 8 a.m. the entraining point at
the docks was reached. Here trains bearing on the coaches the
legend ' hommes 30-40, chevaux 8 ', which in the future was to
become so terribly familiar, awaited the Battalion. Four hours
had been allowed the Battalion for entraining, but the Gloucesters
did it well under the hour, including transport. It was, however,
12.39 p.m. before the train moved slowly out of the siding,
carrying the Battalion on the next stage of its now-historic journey
into the unknown. Again the same wild enthusiasm greeted
the troops as their train ran through town and country. Everywhere there was flag-waving and when a stop was made gifts
were showered upon them. Rouen was reached at about 5 p.m.,
where an hour's stoppage enabled the men to wash and obtain
food and drink. To say that officers and men received a hearty
welcome from the French people is to put it in mild terms !

The journey was continued via Amiens, St. Quentin and
Wassigny, all of which in the future were to mean much more
than mere names of places. The main railhead at Le Nouvion
was reached between six and seven o'clock on the morning of
the 16th August. On detraining, the Battalion moved into a

field west of the village and cooked breakfast, marching off south at 10 a.m. through the Forest of Le Nouvion to the 3rd Infantry Brigade concentration billets in the Leschelles area.

And here for a while it is necessary to digress in order to explain the position in the Allied line allotted to the British Expeditionary Force, and the French plans which resulted in the Force finding itself on the left flank of the Armies of France.

In pre-war days the French General Staff, believing that in the event of war with Germany the Germans would respect the Treaty of Neutrality with Belgium, had prepared plans for an immediate offensive from the eastern frontiers of France against Alsace and Lorraine and on both sides of Metz. On the declaration of war between France and Germany the former, having massed her Armies along her eastern frontiers from Belfort to Longwy, attacked the enemy and made some progress, until news reached the French Commander-in-Chief, General Joffre, of the German advance through Belgium. The offensive from the eastern frontiers of France was then stopped and the Fourth and Fifth Armies (in that order from right to left) put into the line on the left of the First, Second and Third French Armies, continuing the line from the left of the latter Army to Sedan and Hirson. The British Expeditionary Force was then to concentrate on the left of the Fifth French Army. Concentration of the French left and the B.E.F. completed, the left of the Allied line (with the Belgian Army on the left of the British) was to advance and turn the right of the First German Army advancing through Belgium. In the meantime the French centre was to attack the enemy with the intention of breaking the German centre.

Such, briefly, were the Allied plans when the British Expeditionary Force arrived at its concentration area between Maubeuge and Le Cateau, east of the Forêt de Mormal, the IInd Corps east of Landrecies and the Ist Corps east of Bohain, with the Cavalry east of Maubeuge, Jeumont, Damousies and Cousolre.

Up to the 20th August units were either arriving or, having arrived in their concentration area, were engaged in making final preparations for the move-up, the troops being exercised daily in route marching.

The Gloucesters, having arrived in the Leschelles area with other battalions of the 3rd Brigade, went into billets in two small hamlets, Le Tilleul and Dohis on the south-west border of the Forest of Nouvion.

As in Havre and on the journey to Le Nouvion, the French inhabitants of Le Tilleul and Dohis gave the British troops a hearty welcome and did all they could to make them comfortable : in a farm in which A Company was billeted the farmer presented each man with a pat of butter—a small gift perhaps, but it was an instance of the kindly disposition of the French people towards the British soldier.

In the meantime the Fifth French Army, on the right of the B.E.F., had been rapidly concentrating, and by the 20th August both had completed concentration. In several ways the 20th was a day of note, for on this day the Germans entered Brussels, the main Belgian Army had retired into Antwerp and the enemy was within decisive range of Namur.

General Joffre now gave orders for a general advance—the Fifth French Army to the line of the Meuse at Charleroi, with the B.E.F. on its left.

During the evening of the 20th Sir John French issued orders for the advance of the B.E.F. northwards, the movement to be completed by the 23rd, when the Army would be aligned on a front facing roughly north-east from Estinne-au-Mont, near Binche, to Lens, about 8 miles north of Mons, the Cavalry Division being on the left and the 5th Cavalry Brigade on the right front.

On the 21st the IInd Corps (3rd and 5th Divisions) was to advance to the line Goegnies—Bavai, the Ist Corps (1st and 2nd Divisions) to the line Avesnes—Landrecies ; on the 22nd the IInd Corps was to move north-west to a line from Mons westwards to Thulin, Ist Corps north-east to a line from Hautmont to Hargnies ; on the 23rd the IInd Corps was to wheel eastwards, its two divisions being one in rear of the other, with its front east of Mons between Spiennes and St. Denis : the Ist Corps was to incline north-east and come up on the right of the IInd Corps, occupying a line from Estinne-au-Mont westwards to Harmignies. All these movements were to be covered by the Cavalry.

Preliminary to the move of the 1st Division orders had been issued to 3rd Brigade Headquarters on the 19th to move on the following day to the area Beaurepaire—Le Sart—Bergues and Barzy.

Reveille on the 20th was at 5 a.m., and at 8.45 the Gloucesters, at the head of the 3rd Brigade Column, began the march northwards towards the Belgian frontier. The distance from Le Nouvion to Beaurepaire (in which area the Gloucesters were to billet) was 8½ miles—really only a short march. But it was one which found out the weak spots in the Battalion. The abnormally hot weather and the hard, dusty roads proved too much for some of the reservists who were still suffering from sore feet and the natural strain experienced in passing from civilian to army life once more. The result was that ten men had to be sent into hospital. These were, however, trifling casualties ; otherwise the Battalion was in splendid fettle.

On the 21st the 1st Division, marching along two roads, with the 2nd Brigade acting as right flank guard, moved to the area Avesnes—Landrecies. The 3rd Brigade marched at 8.30 a.m. and reached Doulers, where officers were billeted in the inns and houses and the men in outbuildings.

On the British right the Fifth French Army was in contact with the German Second Army along the whole line of the Sambre, on both sides of Charleroi from Tamines to Pont-à-Celles, and hard fighting was expected on the 22nd.

' The concentration was practically complete on the evening of Friday, the 21st ultimo,' said Sir John French in his first despatch, ' and I was able to make dispositions to move the Force during Saturday, the 22nd, to positions I considered most favourable from which to commence operations which the French Commander-in-Chief, General Joffre, requested me to undertake in pursuance of his plans in prosecution of the campaign.'

At 2 a.m. on the 22nd, 3rd Brigade Headquarters issued orders for the march to be resumed at 5.30 a.m. via Maubeuge.

The Brigade Group was formed up on the road at 5 a.m. and moved off until 5.30 a.m. in the following order : Brigade Headquarters, Welch Regiment (less one Company and machine-gun section with the vanguard), Gloucesters, 26th Field Company, R.E., South Wales Borderers, Queen's Regiment, Brigade Reserve of S.A.A.[1] carts (two carts per battalion), brigaded cookers and water-carts, and 43rd Brigade R.F.A.

In the early days of the War only the S.A.A. carts and the machine-gun limbers accompanied the battalions. Two S.A.A. carts per battalion were taken from units to form the Brigade S.A.A. Reserve. The remainder of the battalions' first line transport (tool-carts, cookers and water-carts) were brigaded, the supply and baggage wagons marching well to the rear with the Divisional Train.

Soon after starting the Brigade Group struck the main Avesnes—Maubeuge—Mons road, and at about 10 a.m. Maubeuge was reached. The town was full of French troops busily completing the defences. The latter consisted of nine forts with intermediate fixed and mobile batteries. The whole perimeter was being

---

[1] Small arms ammunition.

surrounded by triple belts of wire. The town was also circled by a moat and ramparts : in the centre was the citadel.

At midday the Brigade Group halted in a cornfield north of the town, but at 3.15 p.m. marched off to occupy billets just south of the Belgian frontier—the Gloucesters to Villers-sire-Nicole. Here, tea had already been taken when sudden orders were received to turn out and dig trenches north of the village. German cavalry had been encountered at Bray, some 8 miles farther north. The Battalion had, however, barely got to work when fresh orders came to hand (at about 6 p.m.) : General Landon's [1] advanced guard was ordered to push on and occupy a line Peissant—Farœulx—Haulchin—Givry and hold it for the night. The Welch were to hold the right of the line about Peissant and Farœulx, the Gloucesters, with the 26th Field Company R.E., Haulchin, and the South Wales Borderers, Givry. Brigade Headquarters were to occupy Croix-lez-Rouveroy.

Tired out after a long day's march (it was 22½ miles), units of the 3rd Brigade reached Croix-lez-Rouveroy at about 10 p.m. ; the 2nd Brigade did not reach Villers-sire-Nicole until 12 midnight, and the 1st (Guards) Brigade did not march into Grand Reng until 3 a.m. on the 23rd August.

The 2nd Division occupied the line La Longueville—Hargnies —Pont-sur-Sambre, its head some 6 miles south-west of the rear of the 1st Division.

The IInd Corps had meanwhile reached its allotted position, the 3rd Division the area Nimy, Ghlin, Frameries—Spiennes : the first outpost line taken up by the Division was from Givry north-west to Mons, but later in the afternoon the outpost line had been pushed forward in a wide sweep eastwards through Villers-St.-Ghislain, St.-Symphorien, the bridge at Obourg and the bridge at Lock 5 to Nimy ; the 5th Division occupied the line of the Mons Canal from Mariette to the bridge at Pommerœul.

' For the moment the line of the Mons Canal, now held by the outpost of the IInd Corps, was the left of the British front, and with the Ist Corps front formed a salient angle, not a straight line.' [2] The IInd Corps alone held a line round Mons of over 20 miles. The 2nd Division had yet to come up on the left of the 1st Division.

The 22nd August had, however, witnessed dramatic events which entirely altered the course of the operations and the intentions of the Allied Commanders-in-Chief.

Aerial reconnaissance during the afternoon had discovered

---

[1] Commanding 3rd Brigade.
[2] *Official History (Military Operations) of the War.*

that at least two German corps were attacking the French on the line of the Sambre, and in the evening observers returned with the grave news (confirmed by British and French liaison officers) that the French centre had been driven back and that only the XVIIIth Corps of the Fifth French Army remained in its original position echeloned to the rear between Marbaix and Thuin. The French Cavalry Corps (Sordet) had also moved southwards from Binche and was halting for the night 9 miles south of that place, well to the rear of the British Army.

The British Expeditionary Force was therefore some 9 miles ahead of the main French line, and the 1st Division, when it reached its destination about Grand Reng, would be fully the same distance from the left flank of the French XVIIIth Corps. There were no troops to fill the gap—only the 5th Cavalry Brigade. Moreover, the British line from Rouveroy to Mons, another 9 miles, was held only by a brigade of infantry—the 8th of the 3rd Division.

The enemy, in considerable strength, was now reported at various points in dangerous proximity and action could not long be delayed. Early that morning British cavalry had been in action with German cavalry patrols at Soignies, and at several other points along the front later.

As the situation became clearer Sir John French, still hoping that offensive action would be possible, began to realize that the B.E.F., isolated as it now was, must be prepared either to advance or retreat.

During the evening of the 22nd Sir John held a conference at Le Cateau and the dispositions of the enemy, as then known, were explained and discussed. At the conclusion of the conference the Commander-in-Chief announced that owing to the retirement of the Fifth French Army the British offensive would not take place. A French staff officer brought a request from General Lanrezac at about 11 p.m. asking the British to attack the flank of the German columns which were pressing the Fifth French Army back from the Sambre. To this request it was impossible for Sir John to accede, but he agreed to remain in his position on the Mons Canal for twenty-four hours.

The Ist Corps was then ordered to take over by 6 a.m. on the 23rd that portion of the outpost line of the IInd Corps which lay east of Mons. The 2nd Division, which was then in its original billets in La Longueville, Hargnies and Pont-sur-Sambre, was ordered to move forward at 3 a.m. for that purpose, and come into line on the left of the 1st Division, but was too late to relieve the IInd Corps before fighting began on the 23rd.

Meanwhile the Gloucesters, having reached Haulchin, set to work to dig trenches round the northern outskirts of the village. Tools were commandeered from the inhabitants, doors and shutters (to loud expostulations from the civilian population) were taken down to help make revetments and head cover.

By the time these defences were constructed dawn had broken on the 23rd August : the British Army lay waiting for the enemy.

CHAPTER III

THE BATTLE OF MONS: 23RD AUGUST 1914

THE position taken up by the Gloucesters was north and north-east of Haulchin, and about half-way between that place and Estinne-au-Mont. Three Companies were in the front line, i.e. D, C and B, from right to left : A Company was in support with Battalion Headquarters, which were in Haulchin. The Battalion had the 2nd Welch on the immediate right at Farœulx, the 1st South Wales Borderers being on the right of the Welch at Peissant. On the left of the Gloucesters was a battalion of the King's Royal Rifle Corps, thence the line of British troops could be seen stretching far away towards Mons. The fourth Battalion of the 3rd Brigade— the Queen's Royal West Surreys—was in Croix-les-Rouveroy.

The Diary of the 3rd Brigade Headquarters has the following entry concerning the Gloucesters : ' The Gloucesters are pretty strong, but the whole position is very extended and not at all ideal for defence (not half so good as the line we were on last evening).' The line of the previous night had been round Villers-sire-Nicole, too far back, for the 2nd Division had not then come up into line on the left of the 1st Division. Indeed it was between 11 a.m. and 12.30 p.m. on 23rd before the 6th Infantry Brigade and part of the 4th (Guards) Brigade of the former Division, tired after a long march, moved into the line between Haulchin and Harmignies, by which time the battle had already begun and the 3rd Division, holding the line from Harmignies northwards, and around the Mons Salient, was heavily engaged with the enemy.

The Battle opened with attacks early in the morning against the Middlesex and the Royal Fusiliers, holding the bridges at Obourg and Nimy, respectively. For the First German Army was still engaged in wheeling south and on the Mons Salient the first attack naturally fell.

All day long, the Gloucesters, listening to the heavy gun-fire coming from the north-west, waited in their trenches without firing a shot. About noon the 9th Battery (16th Brigade) of the 2nd Division galloped up and came into position in the open

14

just behind the brow of a ridge about 800 yards in front of the Battalion's trenches. Word was passed round that the Battery would open fire at 1 p.m. In considerable excitement the Gloucesters awaited that hour for, so far as they were concerned, it was the first shot they were to see fired in the Great War.

Precisely at 1 p.m. the Battery opened fire and was almost immediately replied to by the Germans. For three hours the duel went on until at last, outnumbered by the enemy's guns, which were firing from concealed positions, the Battery was forced to cease fire. It was of course impossible to see the results of the British fire : the 9th Battery lost 2 officers and 10 men killed and wounded.

After the Battery had ceased fire the German guns swept the valley in front of the Gloucester's trenches with shrapnel, but did no damage and caused not a single casualty.

Although the enemy was reported to be holding Binche, nothing was seen of his troops by the Companies holding the front line. Back in Haulchin the support Company had spent the morning in disguising the village by discolouring the white-washed houses and in removing all signposts.

The only information obtained of the movements of the enemy came from cavalry scouts, but the British positions were constantly reconnoitred by German aeroplanes.

At dusk the enemy's artillery ceased firing and along the front of the Gloucesters the night passed quietly, though far away on the left heavy rifle and gun-fire continued long after darkness had fallen.

Thus, so far as the Regiment was concerned, passed the 23rd August—a momentous day in the history of the British Army. The Gloucesters had had none of the excitements of battle, indeed the infantry of the Ist Corps as a whole had not encountered the enemy, only a few shots being fired by troops of the 2nd Division.

Into all the details of the Battle of Mons, in which the IInd Corps and Cavalry were practically the only troops of the Army engaged, it is impossible to go, for this history concerns primarily the Gloucestershire Regiment. But a general outline of the fighting is necessary in order to show how it came about that a retirement was ordered.

The heaviest fighting had taken place in the Mons Salient, where troops of the 3rd Division had first made a magnificent stand against the hordes of the enemy flung against them. The attack had spread gradually westwards along the Mons—Conde Canal to the extreme left flank held by the 19th Infantry Brigade.

At nightfall the general situation was approximately as follows :
the 8th Infantry Brigade of the 3rd Division held a line just in
rear of the Harmignies—Mons road ; the 7th and 9th Infantry
Brigades of the same Division were established between Nouvelles
and Frameries, 3 miles from the Canal. Of the 5th Division,
on the left of the 3rd, the 13th Infantry Brigade still held the
southern bank of the Canal, but had received orders to retire to
Wasmes at midnight. Of the 14th Infantry Brigade, on the left
of the 13th, the East Surreys opposite Les Herbières, and the
remaining units of the Brigade were in the act of joining the 1st
D.C.L.I. in the second position south of the Haine River : the
19th Infantry Brigade, on the left of the 14th Brigade, was still
on the Canal.

At British G.H.Q. there was little anxiety, though events
farther east were disturbing. But at 8.40 p.m. Sir John French
had sent a message to the IInd Corps that he would stand the
attack (expected on the following day) on the ground then held
by the troops, and instructions were given the latter to strengthen
their positions by every possible means during the night.

However, during the evening and just before midnight further
information led the British Commander-in-Chief to the conclusion that his position was untenable, for the B.E.F. was now
in advance of the general line. He therefore decided to fall
back to a line running westwards from the fortress of Maubeuge
through Bavai to Jenlain. The Ist Corps was to cover the
retirement of the IInd Corps and for this purpose a special rearguard, composed of cavalry, a battery of Royal Horse Artillery
and two Field Artillery brigades, and the 4th (Guards) Brigade
of the 2nd Division, was to concentrate at Bonnet and make a
demonstration at daybreak on the 24th so as to delay the advance
of the enemy. The 1st and 2nd Divisions were also to fall back
under cover of this rearguard.

All unconscious of the impending retirement the Gloucesters
snatched what sleep was possible on the night of the 23rd, fully
expecting to attack, or be attacked by, the enemy on the morrow.

CHAPTER IV

THE RETREAT FROM MONS

WHEN dawn broke on the 24th August the British Army occupied a line facing north-east and north, roughly 17 miles long, with its centre some 3 miles south of Mons. Of the Ist Corps on the right, the 1st Division held Grand Reng, Croix-lez-Rouveroy—Haulchin ; the 2nd Division, Givry, Harmignies, Harveng and (with troops of the 5th Division) Paturages, with one battalion also at Bougnies. The IInd Corps occupied a line extending from Nouvelles—Ciply—Frameries (3rd Division) and Paturages—Wasmes—Hornu—Bois de Boussu (5th Division). The 19th Infantry Brigade and the Cavalry Division held Thulin, Elouges, Audregnies and Quievrain.

Throughout the night 23rd/24th there was desultory firing along the front south of the Mons Canal, and as dawn approached on the latter date the rattle of musketry became more intense : at Haulchin the sound of troops in action could be heard by the Gloucesters, for the Battalion Diary records : ' After midnight there was a good deal of rifle fire to our left ', i.e. in the direction of Mons.

As late, however, as 3 a.m. on the 24th the Gloucesters had no intimation of an impending retirement : ' 3 a.m. Orders were received to hold our position at all costs, so we made all preparations to have ammunition, water and food in the trenches.' But it was not to be, for two hours later other orders were received : ' Send the transport to Croix-lez-Rouveroy and be prepared to retire at short notice, as a general retirement of the British Force has been ordered.'

About 7 a.m. a delayed order to retire in conjunction with the King's Royal Rifles of the 6th Brigade on the left reached the Gloucesters.

' This order,' records R.Q.M.S. Brasington in his narrative, ' was received with great disappointment by all ranks, as they had so eagerly looked forward to a fight and showed the dissatisfaction usually shown by a British soldier at anything in the nature of a retirement.'

But in the meantime the main bodies of both the 1st and 2nd Divisions had already marched off unmolested, excepting by

2   17

a little ineffective shelling and a few small bodies of German cavalry, who were so roughly handled that they soon fell back.

The Gloucesters acted immediately on their orders, though they found no troops on their left, as the K.R.R.C. had retired at least an hour earlier, leaving that flank of the Battalion uncovered. Patrols of Uhlans, however, had already gained touch with the Gloucesters' outposts, and the enemy's cavalry in force was within striking distance of the isolated Battalion.

'One of the sentry posts saw a hostile cavalry patrol advancing towards it, the first of the redoubtable Uhlans which had been seen. Such was the excitement of the sentry that he prematurely disclosed his position with the result that he lost the chance of drawing first blood. The patrol galloped off towards the right, but here they came under the fire of another sentry post and paid their toll.' [1]

Captain Shipway's Company (B), on the left, was the first to retire, and being most exposed it was spotted by the enemy and came under artillery fire, but had no casualties. The Company retired according to the first instructions received, parallel with the Bavai—Binche road, and got detached from the rest of the Battalion. The other three Companies, taking a less exposed route, fell back on Croix-lez-Rouveroy where the Queen's were entrenched. They were closely followed by a hostile patrol of six cavalrymen. When the Gloucesters had passed through the Queen's the latter opened fire on the patrol (now only five hundred yards away) and only one escaped, the others being shot down.

From Croix-lez-Rouveroy the three Companies of Gloucesters marched back through Villers-sire-Nicole to Bettignies, where the 3rd Brigade had been ordered to assemble. They were lucky in getting away from a dangerous position without suffering casualties, for a body of German cavalry, certainly no less than a brigade, was seen not a mile away before the Battalion had cleared Haulchin.

A small incident, but characteristic of the British soldier, took place as the Battalion Transport was bumping across country. One of the Companies' issue of meat fell off the cooker. The enemy was quite close, but the rations were precious, so the cooks calmly took off their coats and set to work to reload the carts with the day's rations, and then made off without further trouble.

From Bettignies the 3rd Brigade marched at 5.40 p.m. on Neuf Mesnil, and all ranks were extremely fatigued when finally

[1] Lieut.-Colonel (then Capt. and Adjutant) A. H. Radice, 1st Gloucester Regiment.

the village was reached at nightfall. They had marched via Gognies Chaussée and Feignies to Bettignies where, under the guns of one of the forts of Maubeuge, they billeted. For over sixty hours they had had little rest, the country through which they had moved was close and confined and the heat was oppressive. The labour of entrenching and marching had worn them out. Yet withal they were cheerful, having swallowed their disappointment of the morning in being deprived of a fight with the enemy.

At Neuf Mesnil B Company rejoined the Battalion.

The total march of the Gloucesters on 24th August was roughly 17 miles.

The Ist Corps had withdrawn without serious opposition or interference from the enemy, and on the night 24th/25th occupied the line Feignies—La Longueville (1st Division)—Bavai (2nd Division). But the IInd Corps did not get away so easily. First at Frameries and later at Elouges the 3rd and 5th Divisions and the Cavalry had heavy engagements with the enemy : the British losses on 24th were greater than at Mons on the previous day. At nightfall, however, the IInd Corps occupied (or its units were marching to occupy) roughly the line Bavai, St. Waast (5th Division), St. Waast, Amfroipret and Bermeries (3rd Division) : it will be observed that the 3rd and 5th Divisions had, during the day, crossed over, the latter being now on the right and the former on the left. With the assistance of the Cavalry and the 19th Infantry Brigade the IInd Corps had triumphantly parried von Kluck's attempt to envelop the western flank of the British Army.[1]

' The flanking battalions to the east and west had, it is true, suffered much, but only one had been overwhelmed, not a single gun had been lost and the enemy had been very severely punished. Our troops were still confident that, when on anything like equal terms, they were more than a match for their opponents : the one trouble that really oppressed them was want of sleep.' [2]

The endeavours of the First German Army to envelop his left flank and press him back upon the Fortress of Maubeuge and surround him, had not been lost upon Sir John French who, not to be drawn into the trap, issued orders on the night of 24th/25th for a retirement to the Le Cateau position where the IInd Corps was to occupy the line Le Cateau—Caudry—

[1] The 5th Cavalry Brigade at Feignies covered the rear of the Ist Corps, and the Cavalry Division and the 19th Infantry Brigade at St. Waast, Wargnies, Jenlain and Saultain, the western flank and rear of the IInd Corps.

[2] *Official History (Military Operations) of the War*, Vol. I.

Haucourt, and the Ist Corps Landrecies—Dompierre and the neighbouring villages. The former Corps was to march west of the Forêt de Mormal and the latter east of it.

A 1st Divisional Preliminary Order stated that the retirement would be continued at 5 a.m. on the 25th to the area Noyelles —Landrecies, but this order was cancelled and orders issued later on the 25th stated that ' the Division will move at 6.30 a.m. by Marbaix and Le Grand Fayt to near Favril, ready to support the left of the 2nd Division which is at Landrecies '.

At 5.15 a.m. the 3rd Brigade H.Q. Diary has the following entry : ' Got the column started with most, but not all of the train in front.' The Brigade] formed the advanced guard of the Division, the Gloucesters being in rear of the column.

Overburdened by an extra 100 rounds of ammunition per man, issued at Haulchin for the defence of that place, the Battalion set out in the cool air of the morning. The ammunition could not be collected as the Small Arms Ammunition cart had been immediately replenished and was already full. A big country cart with its team of three horses, harnessed tandem, was eventually requisitioned and the men relieved of their extra weight.

As soon as the sun was up, however, all ranks began to suffer from the heat and glare : the dust was also horrible. But, marching in fours, the Battalion trudged along and reached Marbaix, where dinners were prepared and eaten in a field by the wayside.

At about 5 p.m. the march was resumed. A storm had broken during the afternoon and had for a time cleared the atmosphere. But soon after the march was resumed the intense heat again made itself felt and many began to show signs of exhaustion.

Le Grand Fayt was reached about dusk. Here apparently there was considerable congestion :

' There are crowds of wretched people on foot and in carts, going south, all over the place. Brigade left Marbaix, except Queen's who had preceded it, and reached Le Grand Fayt. Here, what with the " Convoie Administrative " of the 53rd Division de Reserve, the Heavy Battery and Divisional Ammunition Column of the 2nd Division all coming in the opposite direction to assemble, there was a pretty good muddle.' [1]

Billets were allotted to the Gloucesters and the men were just turning in when there was a wild alarm given by a mounted man galloping down the street shouting : ' The Germans are on us ! '

The Battalion at once fell in and advanced to the north-western outskirts of the village only to find eventually that there was no

[1] Extract from 3rd Brigade H.Q. Diary, 25th August 1914.

prospect of an immediate attack, the report being false. With the exception of C Company, which formed part of an outpost screen protecting the village, the Battalion marched back to billets to snatch a few hours' sleep.

There is another interesting note in the Brigade Headquarters Diary on this date :

' Held a conference of Os.C. Battalions, 14.30 ' (2.30 p.m.), at Marbaix apparently. ' They all said their men were pretty tired and wanting to know why we are coming back to where we started from. But then this knowing nothing is inevitable, and they were all warned that the officers must not do or say anything to admit that the men can do no more.'

On the night 25th/26th August the 4th (Guards) Brigade and 6th Infantry Brigade of the 2nd Division were attacked by the enemy at Landrecies and Maroilles respectively, and C Company, posted on the outskirts of Le Grand Fayt, could hear machine-gun and rifle-fire, and even cheering, in the near distance. Both attacks had been beaten off, but they disclosed the proximity of the enemy.

During the night, in order to reduce the weight carried by the men, all packs were handed in and loaded on to motor lorries. What eventually became of them no one knows, but it was rumoured that they fell into the hands of the enemy, for they were never seen again by their owners. The men only retained their waterproof sheets.

Soon after midnight (25th), in view of the unsatisfactory position of the Ist Corps, Sir Douglas Haig had ordered the 1st Division to take positions near Favril, 1½ miles south-south-east of Landrecies, in order to cover the withdrawal of the 2nd Division. The latter was to retire, part to the right rear and part to the left rear of the 1st Division, i.e. the 5th and 6th Brigades to close in upon Le Grand Fayt, 4 miles east of Favril, and the 4th (Guards) Brigade to retire as soon as possible on La Groise, south-west of Favril. The 5th Cavalry Brigade was to cover the western flank of the Ist Corps between Ors and Catillon.

As already stated, the Guards Brigade from Landrecies retired very early on the 26th, and at 5 a.m. the 1st Gloucesters, as advanced guard of the 3rd Brigade (the latter having been ordered to cover the retirement of the 1st and 2nd Brigades), left Le Grand Fayt and marched towards Favril.[1] On approaching the latter village two Companies were extended in fan-like formation from Rue du Bois—Point 173—Croix Hainaut, and finally moved

---

[1] The 3rd Brigade H.Q. Diary has the following note of that march : ' We were nearly blocked on the way by motor lorries which had dumped supplies for to-day (preserved meat, biscuits, jam, Oxo cubes for iron rations) on the roadside. We picked these up as we passed.'

on taking up positions astride the Favril—Landrecies road. C
Company (Captain Temple) was posted on the right of the road
and D Company (Major Gardner), with the machine-gun section,
on the left of it. A Company (Captain Rising) was in reserve
200 yards up the road in rear of C and D. B Company (Captain
Shipway) was posted out in front of C and D as a covering party.
A section of the 54th Battery, R.F.A., under Lieutenant Blewitt,
had come into action actually in the firing-line on the right of
the road. The Battalion then dug trenches along a line of hedges
covering the exits from Landrecies.

About noon horsemen were observed moving across the front
of the Gloucesters, down the road towards Le Cateau which ran
from north-east to south-west on the farther side of Landrecies.[1]
Doubt existed as to whether these troops were British or German
as only their heads and shoulders were visible as they passed gaps
in the distance. But whoever they were it was evident they
were in considerable strength, for the column took three-quarters
of an hour to pass. At 1 p.m. a second column was observed
on the western side of the Sambre River, but these troops were
unmistakable, for they were wearing ' Pickelhauben '. Lieutenant Blewitt then opened fire with his gun and appeared to
make good shooting, for the Germans scattered. Two shells
burst right over a party of about forty of the enemy before they
could disperse. But it was not long before the German artillery
also opened fire, the majority of their shells falling in a field short
of C Company, one or two men of the latter being wounded and
a pack animal killed. Just about this time an aeroplane, bearing
French colours, flew low down [2] along the whole length of the
trenches. Almost immediately the enemy's artillery ranged
their shells accurately on the trenches held by the Gloucesters
and there were a number of casualties—all wounded. It is
certain that the aeroplane was German.

Hostile infantry then debouched from Landrecies and opened
fire from the left of B Company, who were thus enfiladed. The
Company was therefore withdrawn. Unfortunately Captain
Shipway who, with C.Q.M.S. Brain, was out in front of his
Company trying to locate the position of the enemy in order to
send back information, was mortally wounded by a sniper firing
from a house in front. He was brought back and taken to
Etreux in an ambulance, but died the same evening : the first
officer lost by the Battalion.

[1] They belonged to the IIIrd Corps, First German Army.
[2] Colonel Radice places the height of the aeroplane at 40 feet : the
Battalion Diary says 200–300 feet.

B Company fell back slowly—all but one gallant old soldier —Pte. Lander. Although twice wounded, Lander continued to fire on the enemy, killing several Germans and bayoneting seven before he was himself bayoneted by them and left on the field for dead. During the evening, covered with bayonet wounds, he was brought in, but died the next day. He was buried by a party of the 4th Field Ambulance, which had been captured in Landrecies, with wounded men of the 4th Guards Brigade. It is interesting to note that the burial service was read by Padre O'Rourke, who had been with the 3rd Brigade at Bordon. Together with his servant, Pte. Whyman, he had returned to Landrecies to do what he could for the wounded and was taken prisoner. Whyman, an old Gloucester man, belonged to B Company and had been left behind in England as it was considered the campaign would be too much for him. Before the War he had been servant to the Rev. O'Rourke, and when the latter accompanied the Guards Brigade to France, Whyman volunteered to accompany him.

An R.A.M.C. captain, some years after the War, mentioning the aeroplane incident, said they could not make out what the Germans were shelling, as the presence of British troops in any strength near Landrecies was unsuspected by those who were prisoners in the town. He also described how he had seen a party of about half a dozen men of the Gloucestershire Regiment strung out along the road south of the town. These men were apparently a patrol from A Company sent out to reconnoitre the outskirts of Landrecies, who failed to return. The patrol, losing its way, eventually found itself in rear of the German lines. The men then split up with the idea of trying to break through and rejoin their Regiment. Sergt. Walsh and Pte. Habberfield got as far as Prisches, south-east of Landrecies, where they were cut off, Habberfield being killed and Sergt. Walsh captured : the remainder also were captured eventually.

By 5 p.m. the action was over, as the enemy seemed not at all anxious to approach the main position of the 3rd Brigade and, covered by the artillery, the rearguard was able to retire south through a position prepared and held by the 1st and 2nd Brigades at Erruart—La Groise—Catillon.

The casualties suffered by the 1st Gloucesters in this, their first, encounter with the enemy were 1 man and 1 horse killed, Captain G. M. Shipway (who, as stated above, died of his wounds later) and 29 men and 1 horse wounded.

On the night of the 26th the Battalion bivouacked near Oisy where, in the dark and rain, the men obtained some straw to lie on and the officers found their valises awaiting them.

On the 26th August the Battalion had marched 15 miles, not counting deployments.

The general dispositions of the British Expeditionary Force on the night 26th/27th August were : Ist Corps—1st Division about Étreux, 2nd Division Oisy ; IInd Corps—5th Division and 19th Infantry Brigade Estrées, 3rd Division Beaurevoir, 4th Division Vendhuille.

From the battlefield of Le Cateau the IInd Corps had slipped away in broad daylight when by all the rules of warfare it should have been defeated, and that it was not was largely due to several gallant detachments which, not having received orders to retire, fought and held the Germans at bay until they were finally overwhelmed, or were able to slip away after darkness had fallen : the ' Contemptible Little Army '[1] had again foiled the enemy.

It was about 11.30 a.m. on the 27th August when the 3rd Brigade, the main column of the 1st Division, set out on the road to Guise : the 2nd Brigade was flank guard and the 1st Brigade rearguard to the 1st and 2nd Divisions. The delay in starting was due to the fact that the 2nd Division had to move off first from Étreux. But eventually the column started and for the first mile or two marched in fours in single column of route. The ' Chaussée ' was, however, exceptionally wide and good, so in order to economize road space the Brigade closed up, two battalions abreast, and in this formation proceeded on their way to Étreux. On passing through the latter place the column again opened out but there were many checks before reaching Guise. The road discipline on this day was good : no unauthorized vehicle was allowed to impede the way of the Ist Corps, and the owners of all private vehicles overtaken were

---

[1] There has always been considerable controversy as to whether the ex-Kaiser actually issued the orders containing the words ' Contemptible Little Army '. The following printed copy of the original order was issued with 3rd Divisional Routine Orders of the 23rd September 1914 :

' The following is a copy of orders issued by the German Emperor on the 19th August : " It is my Royal and Imperial Command that you concentrate your energies, for the immediate present, upon one single purpose, and that is that you address all your skill and all the valour of my soldiers to exterminate first the treacherous English and walk over General French's contemptible little Army . . . Headquarters."
Aix la Chapelle, *August 19th*.'

The 3rd Divisional Routine Orders then add the following words :
' The results of the order were the operations commencing with Mons and the advance of seemingly overwhelming masses against us. The answer of the British Army on the subject of " extermination " has already been given.'

forced to drive into fields or ditches on the roadside while the troops were passing.

Guise had already been left behind when news was received that the 1st Brigade (the rearguard) had been heavily attacked north of Étreux.[1] The 3rd Brigade accordingly turned about, retracing its steps through Guise, but before it had got very far north of the town a message was received that the 1st Brigade had (with the exception of the R. Munster Fusiliers) shaken off the enemy. The 3rd Brigade, therefore, turned south once more and, passing through Guise, branched off south-west along the St. Quentin road for five miles, then turned west, crossed the River Oise at Bernot and there billeted for the night. Earlier in the evening the Regimental Transport had arrived at the village and as there were rumours of German cavalry in the neighbourhood outposts had been put out and the streets barricaded.

The Gloucesters did not reach Bernot until nearly midnight, and when at last they marched into the village all ranks were dead beat, having marched 23 miles that day.[2]

Reveille on the 28th was at 5 a.m. (indeed that hour had now become usual), but it was 7.30 a.m. before the Battalion was on the road. The 3rd Brigade had been ordered to continue the retreat along the eastern banks of the Oise towards La Fère. The Gloucesters, however, on this day (until the afternoon) marched in two parties. One, consisting of A and C Companies, under Colonel Lovett, detailed as right flank guard, marched south along a ridge on the western banks of the river. The other (B and D Companies), under Major Ingram, followed the Brigade and, passing through Neuvillette, crossed more to the east of the Oise and marched through Mont d'Origny where preparations were being made for a stand against the enemy.[3] At mid-day the column halted for several hours in an orchard near Sery— a cool shady spot on the banks of the Oise. There was very little depth of water and most of that was dirty and very muddy, but it enabled all ranks to get the first real wash since leaving Havre, nearly a fortnight previously.

During the afternoon the Battalion was once more united and at about 5 p.m. the march continued along the Oise valley as far

[1] The Rearguard Affair of Étreux.

[2] The 1st Division on the night 27th/28th was disposed as follows : 1st Brigade Jonqueuse, 2nd Brigade Hauteville, 3rd Brigade Bernot : the 2nd Division was in the Mont d'Origny area. The 5th Division and 19th Brigade were at Ollezy, the 3rd Division at Ham and the 4th Division on its way to Voyennes.

[3] The 1st Corps was now in close touch with the French on the right, who later fought the Germans in the Battle of Guise.

as La Fère, an old fortified French town. The Battalion was, however, not quite at the end of the day's march, for the 3rd Brigade passed through La Fère and went on to a small village, Bertaucourt, where some units billeted and others bivouacked. Thus ended another long march of 21 miles.

Although unharried by the enemy the day had been most trying. The roads were crowded by a swarm of refugees and often the troops and transport had to be ' double banked '. Choked with dust, with scarcely a breath of wind, and on a hard road the Battalion had a severe gruelling, but all ranks were becoming hardened to it and fortunately their good spirits and the irrepressible optimists kept them going.

Owing to the number of refugees continually breaking through the column the First Line Transport and cookers were cut off from the Battalion during the evening's march and spent the night marching about the roadways and tracks through the Forêt de Gobain, hopelessly lost, and expecting at every minute to run into the enemy. But nothing so serious happened and early on the 29th, having found out the whereabouts of the Battalion, they rejoined, little the worse for their night's adventure.

On the night 28th/29th August the two inner flanks of the Ist and IInd Corps were still 11 miles apart, the former being south of the Oise and La Fère, and the latter with the 4th Division north and east of Noyon with one Division south of the Oise.[1]

In Bertaucourt the Gloucesters were allotted a large chateau with good outbuildings which accommodated most of the men. Those who could not crowd into the buildings slept on bundles of straw in the orchard or under walls.

All ranks slept comfortably, for orders from G.H.Q. issued that night had contained the following sentence :

' It is the Field-Marshal Commanding-in-Chief's intention that the Army should halt to-morrow to rest, but all formations must be south of the line Vendeuil (4 miles north of La Fère)—Jussy—Ham—Nesle, and will take steps for local protection.'

---

[1] In greater detail the dispositions of the B.E.F. were as follows : Ist Corps, northern edge of the Forest of St. Gobain and Coucy, from Fressancourt to Amigny ; 5th Cavalry Brigade at Sinceny. IInd Corps and Cavalry Division, 1st, 2nd and 3rd Cavalry Brigades, Berlancourt, Flavy le Meldeux—Plessis and Jussy respectively ; 3rd, 4th and 5th Divisions from Freniches, south and east through Genvry to Pontoise ; 4th Cavalry Brigade, Cressy (3 miles south of Nesle), north-west of the 4th Division ; 19th Infantry Brigade, Pontoise.
Von Kluck gives the line of the First German Army on the night 28th/29th as roughly Pontru and along the Somme at Epanancourt, St. Christ, Peronne—just south of Maricourt. He was then north-west of the B.E.F., still continuing his advance in a south-westerly direction.

By this time the B.E.F. had shaken off the weight of the enemy's pursuit. Indeed, the First German Army was still advancing in a south-westerly direction on Paris, while the British Army was moving south.

But the ' rest ' ordered for the 29th was something of a snare and a delusion, as the following shows :

' Apart from the general cleaning up and overhauling of arms and kit, etc., so essential after the last two weeks of incessant marching and fighting, the chateau grounds had to be put into some state of defence. The walls surrounding the place were loopholed and the various companies given tasks to carry out in the defence. Later in the day the Gloucesters were required to make secure the northern and north-eastern approaches to the Brigade bivouac. Companies in turn were then ordered out to construct trenches on a slight rise outside the grounds, to cover the open country towards La Fère and also to barricade the roads.'

After which, it is presumed, the men had the rest of the day to themselves ! A poor sort of ' rest ' day ! Possibly the Staff Officer of 3rd Brigade Headquarters, who wrote the Brigade Diary for that day, had his tongue in his cheek when he said : ' It is a fine, sunny day so they [the men] can appreciate their rest.'

At 7.30 p.m. B Company was ordered out to take up an outpost line half a mile outside the chateau and to get in touch with the brigades on the flanks : the other three Companies remained in billets.

At 9 p.m. G.H.Q. issued orders for a further retirement on the 30th to the line Soissons—Compiègne, behind the Aisne. The 3rd Brigade, with artillery, R.E. and 3rd Field Ambulance, was to act as rearguard of the 1st Division : the Gloucesters were to form the rear party of the Brigade. The march was to begin at 4.30 a.m.

In a thick mist the Battalion marched off, proceeding along side roads and lanes, up hills, and through the Forest of St. Gobain. The first part of the march was slow and continuous checks were necessary in order to keep up communication between units. When the mist lifted the sun beat down upon the ranks of marching men. In passing through Septvaux many of the men gave the inhabitants letters to post, but they probably fell into the hands of the enemy. In the next village through which the Battalion passed (Premontre) some English nuns of a large convent brought out buckets of lemonade and fruit for the troops, for which all ranks were exceedingly grateful.

Early in the afternoon the Brigade Group reached Brancourt and there billeted after a hot march of 10 miles. Of this day's march, from a regimental point of view, there is little to record.

There was practically no interference from the enemy throughout the 30th August, and at nightfall the 1st Division occupied an area about 8 miles north of Soissons with its head about Allemant, the 2nd Division being on the left and south-west about Pasly, the IInd and IIIrd Corps [1] just south of the Aisne, 3rd Division at Montois, 5th Division at Croutoy, 4th Division at Pierrefonds, and 19th Infantry Brigade at Couloisy.

The right of the Fifth French Army was north of Vauxaillon (south of La Fère) and the left of the Sixth French Army about 5 miles north-west of Compiègne in the direction of Crèvecœur and Quiry.

On the previous day the Fifth French Army had counter-attacked the enemy at Guise and, although dealing the Second German Army a sharp blow, the result was not quite satisfactory. General Joffre had asked Sir John French to co-operate in this attack, but the latter deemed the B.E.F. hardly fit to take part in the operations. The French Commander-in-Chief, therefore, came to the conclusion that he must yield further ground before delivering the enemy another and more decisive blow. The Sixth French Army was ordered to fall back to the line Senlis, Clermont, Beauvais, and Sir John French was requested to fill the gap between the Sixth and Fifth French Armies, which he agreed to do.

At 5.15 p.m. on the 30th orders were issued to the B.E.F. to continue the retirement on the 31st, the Ist Corps and 5th Cavalry Brigade to the area about Villers-Cottérêts, IInd Corps (west of the Ist Corps) to the area Feigneux—Béthisy St. Martin—Crépy-en-Valois, IIIrd Corps St. Sauveur—Verberie, and the Cavalry Division to the line of the Oise beyond Verberie.

These dispositions are not without interest, for they show how on the 1st September von Kluck's Army, which had changed direction, came into contact with the B.E.F.

Ist Corps Operation Orders, issued at 8 p.m., stated that the march on the 31st was to be continued in a south-westerly direction, the 1st Division by Crouy and Soissons to the area Vaux Buin—Saconin—Breuil—Missy-aux-Bois : 2nd Division to the area Pernant—Laversine—Cutry—Cœuvres-et-Valsery.

Again in a thick mist, the Gloucesters left Brancourt at 6 a.m. and took the road to Soissons. They marched via Pinon (full of French transport), then on past the bivouacs of the other brigades of the Division, through Crouy and down into the valley of the Aisne at Soissons. There were then plenty of civilians

[1] The 4th Division and the 19th Infantry Brigade were formed into the IIIrd Corps on 30th August.

in the town, but the Battalion saw little of the place—only one long, very narrow and cobbled street along which they tramped until they emerged on the other side, where there were more hills to climb. About 3 miles from Soissons, near Missy-aux-Bois, the Gloucesters halted and turned into a field by the dusty main road to Villers-Cottérêts. It was a poor spot in which to bivouac, without water or fuel within three-quarters of a mile. Fortunately the two French interpreters with the Battalion had assisted in purchasing extra provisions during the march through Soissons, but the want of water was badly felt, for the carrying parties could only bring a very limited supply. Another 18 miles had been marched that day—a gruelling test under the same trying conditions of the previous days.

From a regimental standpoint the 31st August was not of particular interest, but so far as the general situation was concerned it was a day of great importance. For it now became apparent to General Joffre and Sir John French that the First German Army had changed direction. Instead of making a wide sweep which might have enveloped the Sixth French Army and possibly the British Expeditionary Force, von Kluck, in response to an appeal from von Bülow (German Second Army) to help the latter exploit the supposed success in the Battle of Guise, had wheeled his Army in a south-easterly direction towards the Oise in an endeavour to roll up the left flank of the Fifth French Army.

There is no doubt that von Kluck's action in changing the direction of his advance affected the campaign decisively : the move was fatal, as the events of the next few days showed.

During the afternoon of the 31st two German cavalry divisions had reached the Oise and by nightfall had pushed across the river. The British Commander-in-Chief was aware of this, also of the fact that the First German Army, which from the 26th August had practically left the B.E.F. alone, was now closing in upon the British Army in great force.

G.H.Q. orders, issued on the night of 31st, contained the following information :

' The enemy appears to have completed his westerly movement and was to-day pivoting round to the south, large columns having been observed advancing in a general southerly or south-easterly direction on the front Noyon—Compiègne from about Roye—Montdidier. This advance is covered by at least two cavalry divisions who reached the Oise this afternoon.'

The Army was therefore ordered to continue the retreat on 1st September—the Ist Corps to the La Ferte Milon—Ivors—

Betz—Mareuil area, IInd Corps to Villers St. Genest—Manteuil—Silly—Brégy—Bouillancy, IIIrd Corps to Bois du Val—Baron—Montagny : the Cavalry Division to Montepilloy—Mont L'Evêque.

At 6 a.m. on the 1st September the Gloucesters set out on the march to Villers-Cottérêts. Dawn had again broken in a dense mist, foreboding another day of intense heat. But the march appears to have been uneventful. The route lay partly through a large wood where German cavalry patrols had been seen and the Battalion marched with fixed bayonets. No man was allowed to fall out except those suffering from extreme exhaustion, when they were picked up and brought along in a country cart which had been commandeered for the purpose.

On reaching Villers-Cottérêts at about 11 a.m. the whole of the 3rd Brigade halted and closed up in the station yard, which the Brigade Diary describes as ' a nasty dangerous place, as there was artillery fire going on opposite the rearguard '. However, all water-bottles were filled here and dinners cooked, but about noon heavy firing was heard, and when at 12.30 p.m. the Brigade again resumed the march everyone was glad to get clear of the place ; by that time the firing had died down. The Ourcq was crossed at La Ferté-Milon, and at 3 p.m. the Brigade arrived at Mareuil, where it was to bivouac, the Gloucesters resting by the roadside. They had marched 19 miles.

Three encounters had taken place during the day, at Néry, Crépy-en-Valois and in the Forest of Villers-Cottérêts.[1] They were the outcome of von Kluck's change of direction and the result should have shown him that the British Army was anything but a defeated force, as he imagined it to be, for although chance encounters and casualties had been suffered by both sides, the enemy had received a sharp check and at Néry alone he had lost eight guns.

No operation orders were issued from G.H.Q. on the night of the 1st September, but the enemy being close behind, the British Army was ordered to continue its march before daylight to the villages between Meaux and Dammartin, Ist Corps on the right (or east), IInd Corps in the centre, IIIrd Corps on the left.

At midnight, therefore, the Gloucesters were roused, and somewhere about 1 a.m. the Battalion marched off down the long road for Meaux.

[1] The Affair at Néry, the Rearguard Action of Crépy-en-Valois and the Rearguard Action of Villers-Cottérêts.

' We seemed to go miles in the dark, up hills and down valleys, but always on. Distances always seem greater in the dark, but judging from the halts it couldn't have been more than 15 miles. At dawn we were told we were going to take up a defensive position, and even marched back a short distance, but nothing came of it and on we went again, on, on, on, always on.' [1]

The 2nd Brigade was acting as rearguard and it was to lend assistance that the 3rd Brigade at 6 a.m. ' marched back a short distance ' but was not required.

Without a halt until daybreak the Gloucesters tramped along the road, but then a fifteen minutes' rest was called. Another halt for half an hour was made at 9 a.m.

The roads, as usual, were crowded with artillery, ambulance wagons, transport columns and infantry, and blocks were frequent, but about midday the congestion eased considerably and the march was less impeded. Nevertheless, it was sufficiently trying. The march of the early hours of the morning had been carried out without water or rations, and it was not until later that in passing through a village the men were able to fill their water-bottles, while later still, during a long halt by the roadside, a few tins of meat were given out.

When 2 or 3 miles from Meaux the Battalion turned west and reached Crégy and there billeted. The village was deserted, all but one small shop, which remained open and was soon sold out of everything which could be eaten. Poultry and vegetables were also discovered in considerable quantities and that night the Gloucesters fared sumptuously.

The march on the 2nd September was between 16 and 18 miles.

On the 3rd, Reveille was at 2 a.m., and by 2.45 a.m. the Battalion was once more on the road. Retracing their steps of the previous day for about 4 miles the Gloucesters eventually turned off at right angles from Chambry and crossed the Marne at Germigny L'Evêque, thence up a steep hill through the Bois de Meaux, down again and along the straight road south of the river to the neighbourhood of a lake near Perreuse Château, east of Signy Signets, and south of La Ferté-sous-Jouarre, where they bivouacked.

The day's march (about 16½ miles) had been uneventful.

Still obsessed with the idea of attacking the left of the Fifth French Army and rolling it up, von Kluck was rushing headlong into the net spread for him by the Allied Commanders-in-Chief : the hour was approaching fast when the French and British

---

[1] From the private diary of Captain R. M. Grazebrook.

Armies were to turn about and deal the enemy a blow which almost ended (for him) in disaster. But at present a little more ground had to be given and so at 11.50 p.m. on the night of the 3rd September Sir John French issued orders for all the bridges over the Marne in the British area to be destroyed and the Army to continue its march southwards on the 4th to south of the Grand Morin.

Reveille on the 4th was at 4 a.m., and after the Gloucesters had paraded they marched off at 4.50 a.m. The first part of the route lay across country until, striking the La Ferté—Coulommiers road, the Battalion turned south and, after a march of 11½ miles, reached Moroux, a village west of Coulommiers, at about 11 a.m. Here the 3rd Brigade expected to remain throughout the remainder of the day and the night of the 4th/5th September. There was very little accommodation in the village and the troops who could not crowd into the houses bivouacked in the orchards, being ordered to keep under cover of the trees in order to escape detection by the enemy's aircraft.

Dinners had been eaten when B and C Companies and the Machine-Gun Section, under Major Ingram, were ordered off to the high ground near Bois la Ville, north of Moroux, to dig a line of trenches to fill a gap between the right of the 2nd Division at Giremoutiers and the left of the 2nd Brigade (1st Division) at Aulnoy. C Company put the Bois la Ville into a state of defence while B dug trenches along the ridge to the east. The 2nd Brigade was shelled during the afternoon, otherwise there were no signs of the enemy.

At about 6.15 p.m. the Brigade moved further south and bivouacked on the high ground about Limosin, the two Companies of Gloucesters on outpost duty coming under the orders of the O.C., 1st Black Watch (1st Brigade): they rejoined the Battalion next morning.

The 5th of September was a day long to be remembered, for it was the last day of the Retreat.

At about 4 a.m. B and C Companies, who had been on outpost duty, withdrew and marched back to Moroux only to find that the Battalion had already started off south, via Mauperthuis to Rozoy. The two Companies, however, caught up Battalion Headquarters and A and D Companies about 3 miles away.

Between Rigny and Ormeau a longish halt was called where, under cover of outposts found by the Welch Regiment, all ranks had a meal. On resuming the march the Battalion pushed across country and soon after 3 p.m. reached Rozoy-en-Brie where the 3rd Brigade was to bivouac.

The distance marched on the 5th was 15 miles.   During the last part of the journey an almost endless stream of refugees crowded the roads—a pathetic sight.   In every description of vehicle they were making their way south-west, for they knew the enemy was close behind.   Cumbersome French farm wagons drawn by white bullocks jostled perambulators, hand-carts and even wheel-barrows, piled up with every conceivable kind of household treasures, mattresses, cooking utensils, clocks, umbrellas, chicken coops full of fowls, and even fodder for the animals.   Old men and women, children and priests were in that sad procession, fleeing from the terror which they feared might overtake them.

The Gloucesters bivouacked in a field and in the evening the Base Details arrived, about one hundred fresh reinforcements, which brought the strength of the Battalion up to War establish-ment, even slightly over.   But what was almost more important they brought with them a small supply of shirts, socks and boots, the first since the Battalion arrived in France.   By now many of the men's boots were in a broken and practically useless con-dition, they were walking on their bare feet : some were without socks at all.

The position of the Fifth French Army, the B.E.F. and Sixth French Army (in that order from right to left), and the enemy, on the evening of the 5th September is interesting, for during that day General Joffre had interviewed Sir John French and informed him that it was his intention to take the offensive, for the right flank of the German Armies, i.e. First German Army, had advanced to such a degree that it was in a dangerous position.

' The time has come,' states General Joffre's Order to the French Army on the 4th September 1914, ' to profit by the adventurous position of the German First Army and concentrate against that Army all the efforts of the ·Allied Armies on the extreme left.'

Sir John French in his despatches states that :

' In the meantime the enemy had thrown bridges across, and crossed the Marne in considerable force and was threatening the Allies all along *the line of the British Forces and the Fifth and Ninth French Armies.*'

Neither General Joffre nor Sir John French mentions the Sixth French Army which was the ' extreme left ' of the Allied Armies and to which von Kluck's right was now dangerously exposed.

The Retreat from Mons was over.   For thirteen days (from 24th August to 5th September inclusive) the Gloucesters had been on the move and during that period had marched 200 miles at least, to say nothing of the three days' approach march from Beaurepaire to Haulchin (20th–22nd August inclusive), another 44 miles.

3

The following table shows the daily marches of the Battalion during the Retreat :

24th August.	Haulchin	to	Neuf Mesnil	. .	17 miles.
25th ,,		,,	La Grand Fayt .	.	15½ ,,
26th ,,		,,	Oisy	. . .	15 ,,
27th ,,		,,	Bernot	. . .	23 ,,
28th ,,		,,	Bertaucourt	. .	21 ,,
29th ,,		at	,,	. .	—
30th ,,		to	Brandcourt	. .	10 ,,
31st ,,		,,	Missy aux Bois .	.	18 ,,
1st September.		,,	Mareuil	. . .	19 ,,
2nd ,,		,,	Crégy	. . .	18½ ,,
3rd ,,		,,	Signy Signets	. .	16½ ,,
4th ,,		,,	Moroux	. . .	11½ ,,
5th ,,		,,	Rozoy	. . .	15 ,,

There are no records either in the Battalion Diary of the 1st Gloucesters or in the private diaries of officers of the Regiment of the effect the news that the Army was to advance on the 6th September had on the rank and file, for although Sir John French's orders for the advance are timed at 5.15 p.m. on the 5th, the only order mentioned in the first-named diary is one which came to hand at midnight to continue the retirement towards Guignes, which was subsequently cancelled early on the following morning.

The Retreat from Mons was in every way honourable to the British Army. The Expeditionary Force had been hurried up to the line and by force of circumstances compelled to take up an extremely unfavourable position. Attacked by vastly superior forces, the Army had inflicted on the enemy serious casualties and there was not one officer or man who was not confident that they could have more than held their own on the 24th August. They fell back and began the Retirement reluctantly, without being able to understand why they did so. Thereafter whenever the British had come into contact with the enemy they had given more than a good account of themselves. Their pluck, their endurance, their discipline during the Retreat was wonderful to see, and when, on the night of the 5th September, their retirement was over, they were still an Army, and a very formidable Army too. The Gloucesters, it is true, had very little fighting to do, but they went through the same gruelling torture which had fallen to the lot of their comrades in arms, and had come through it magnificently, for, as the Official History says : 'They were never demoralized, for they rightly judged that they had never been beaten.'

CHAPTER V

THE BATTLE OF THE MARNE, 1914

THE dispositions of the Allied Armies and of the First German Army on the night of the 5th/6th September 1914 are interesting in the extreme, for they show how completely von Kluck had advanced into the net spread for him by General Joffre.

The British Army occupied approximately the line Rozoy—Vilbert—Fontenay—Chatres—Tournan—Ozoir la Ferrière : the 1st Division holding the Rozoy area, the right of the line. The outposts of the First German Army in front of the B.E.F. were at Vaudoy, Montcerf and Villiers, i.e. south of the Grand Morin. On the right of the British the Fifth French Army held a line from Sezanne westwards to about half-way between Villenauxe and Chenoise, faced by von Kluck's outposts from along the northern portion of the Forêt de Jouy to Villiers St. George and Chatillon. The Sixth French Army, with its right at Meaux and extending in a north-westerly direction to about 5 miles west of Nanteuil, lay north-west of the Marne and the Ourcq, von Kluck's IVth Reserve Corps opposing the French from just north of Meaux to Nanteuil, his right covered by a division of cavalry.

Thus it will be seen that the First German Army was now practically in a semicircle, its right flank in considerable danger from the envelopment movement planned by the French Commander-in-Chief.

Operation orders issued from British G.H.Q. at 5.15 p.m. on the 5th September stated that the enemy, having apparently abandoned the idea of advancing on Paris, was contracting his front and moving in a south-easterly direction. The British were to advance on the 6th with a view to attacking the enemy. The left of the B.E.F. was to be covered by the Sixth French Army, also moving east, and the right linked to the Fifth French Army marching north. These directions show the intentions of the Allied Chiefs. In order to carry out the part allotted to it the British Army was to make the following moves on the 6th : 1st Corps to take up a position with its right on La Chapelle Iger and left on Lumigny, the movement to be completed by

35

9 a.m. ; IInd Corps with its right on La Houssaye and left in the neighbourhood of Villeneuve, movement to be completed by 10 a.m. ; IIIrd Corps to the neighbourhood of Bailly, facing east, movement to be completed also by 10 a.m.   The Cavalry were to cover the flanks.

The Ist Corps was to move by the route Guignes, Chaumes, Fontenay and Marles.

The 3rd Infantry Brigade, preceded by an advanced guard, moved off from Rozoy at 7.20 a.m. on the 6th.   The direction was south to the village of Courpalay where a halt was called and the Brigade held in readiness to support the 1st Brigade which was engaged with the enemy to the north-west.   The outposts had been instructed to remain out until the 1st Brigade arrived, and D Company of the Gloucesters did not rejoin the Battalion until about 10.30 a.m.

The halt at Courpalay lasted until 4 p.m. when the Brigade once more took the road, but in a north-easterly direction until Vaudoy was reached, in the neighbourhood of which Battalions bivouacked, the Gloucesters in a stubble field.   The total distance marched on the 6th was only 10 miles, but frequent halts during the last few miles had tired everyone out.

Nightfall on the 6th showed a decided change in the dispositions of the opposing forces.   The British Army had reached the southern bank of the Grand Morin at Faremoutiers (head of 3rd Division), Courtry (head of 5th Division) and Villiers (head of 4th Division).   The Ist Corps held the line Vaudoy—Touquin with the cavalry on its right at Le Corbie.

The B.E.F. thus faced north-east.   On the right the Fifth French Army had reached Sancy, Montceaux and La Noue.   But the greatest change had taken place north-west of the Ourcq where the Sixth French Army had advanced to the line Penchard— Bouillancy, pressing the right of the First German Army back upon the river.   Von Kluck had, however, perceived the danger to his right and had hurriedly withdrawn his corps northwards, leaving only cavalry to oppose the British Army.

Although it was well after dark before the Gloucesters reached their bivouacs, and they had had a most tiring day, all ranks were nevertheless greatly elated.   The news circulated during the day that the enemy was in hurried retreat before the B.E.F. was a splendid tonic for the troops, who for the previous fortnight had themselves been in retreat.

It was on the 6th also that Sir John French issued a Special Order of the Day to the British Army, the text of which was as follows :

' After a most trying series of operations, mostly in retirement, which have been rendered necessary by the general strategic plan of the Allied Armies, the British forces stand to-day formed in line with their French comrades, ready to attack the enemy.

' Foiled in their attempt to invest Paris, the Germans have been driven to move in an easterly and south-easterly direction with the apparent intention of falling in strength on the Fifth French Army.   In this operation they are exposing their right flank and their line of communication to an attack from the combined Sixth French Army and the British forces.

' I call upon the British Army in France to now show the enemy its power, and to push on vigorously to the attack beside the Sixth French Army.   I am sure I shall not call upon them in vain but that, on the contrary, by another manifestation of the magnificent spirit which they have shown in the past fortnight, they will fall on the enemy's flank with all their strength and, in unison with their Allies, drive them back.'

The 7th September (so far as the Gloucesters were concerned) was not unlike the previous day.   The Battalion did not parade until 11.30, but at that hour moved off again in a north-easterly direction.   The morning was spent in the blazing sun, which had a tiring effect upon all ranks.   Some amusement was caused, however, by the discovery in the early morning that the Battalion had bivouacked on a spot which had evidently witnessed a cavalry action, for lances, saddle-bags and other odds and ends were found which had been left behind by the retreating enemy.   These were promptly seized by the souvenir hunters who, however, had to throw them away when the march was resumed.   The march route was by way of Dagny and Chevru.   As another column was using the main road to Choisy the 3rd Brigade marched via Leudon and cart-tracks to a point just east of Choisy-en-Brie, where in a field just abreast the village the Gloucesters bivouacked, with other units in the neighbourhood.   It was a poor spot as there was no shelter from the wind and no water close at hand.

The distance marched on the 7th was 13½ miles.   It was, as an officer of the Gloucesters records in his diary, ' not really a long march but we were all pretty glad to get in '.

Nightfall found the B.E.F. occupying the following positions : the head of the 1st Division was at Jouy on the Grand Morin with the 2nd Division on its left at St. Simeon : on the left of the latter the head of the 3rd Division was at Chauffry, 5th Division at Boissy and IIIrd Corps from Giremoutiers to La Haute Maison. Thus the left of the B.E.F. was well north of the Grand Morin. The enemy held the line of the Petit Morin, and west of the Ourcq von Kluck's right wing was still fighting hard against the Sixth French Army, but the German right flank (First and Second German Armies) was in a precarious position, for during the day the commander of the First German Army had sent frantic messages to von Bülow (commanding the Second German Army), asking where his IIIrd and IXth Corps were as their assistance on the Ourcq was ' very urgent '.

THE PASSAGE OF THE PETIT MORIN

Operation orders issued from British G.H.Q. on the evening of the 7th September stated that on the 8th the advance was to be continued against the line of the Marne from Nogent L'Artaud to La Ferté-sous-Jouarre, the cavalry to push on in pursuit, keeping touch with the Fifth and Sixth French Armies on the right and left respectively. But before the Marne could be reached the Petit Morin had to be passed and, although the latter was really little more than a stream, it ran through a narrow valley with steep wooded sides which were only approachable by way of close intricate country, studded with copses and villages : only six known bridges spanned the river. The River Marne ran through a valley similar in character, so that the country was well adapted, from the enemy's point of view, for the fighting of delaying and rearguard actions.

The Ist Corps (1st Division on the right, 2nd Division on the left) was detailed to follow the route St. Rêmy—Rebais (eastern road)—La Tretoire—Boitron—La Moue—Pavant—Charly to Breuil—Sablonnières—Hondevilliers—Nogent L'Artaud road : the IInd Corps was to march on Saacy and the IIIrd on Jouarre.

The cavalry were early astir and at 4 a.m. were out ahead covering the Ist and IInd Corps. At 5.30 a.m. the Gloucesters (forming part of the 3rd Brigade Group) marched off in a north-easterly direction, crossing the Grand Morin at La Ferté Gaucher. On all sides there were signs of the hurried flight of the Germans —stores, rifles and ammunition had been left behind in their endeavours to get beyond reach of their pursuers. At La Ferté a small detachment of reinforcements (forty other ranks) joined the Battalion. Here also water-bottles were filled and a short rest given the men before pushing on towards the Petit Morin and the Marne.

The 3rd Brigade Group then moved north via Le Jariel on Sablonnières, but before reaching that place information was received that the 1st (Guards) Brigade, the advanced guard of the 1st Division, was held up near Bellot. With all speed therefore the 3rd Brigade pushed on, but at Sablonnières word came to hand that the 1st (Guards) Brigade had succeeded in driving the enemy back.

The 3rd Brigade then continued to push on along the Nogent L'Artaud road, passing through Hondevilliers (already captured by the cavalry) to Bassevelle, in which area the Brigade bivouacked at about 5 p.m., the Gloucesters in a cornfield at Ferme de L'Ile in the open without the least scrap of shelter.

Most of the day's march (about 17 miles) had been across country and by field paths. During the late afternoon a heavy thunderstorm broke over the country, drenching the marching troops to the skin—an unwelcome reminder that greatcoats had been thrown away or left behind. But despite their discomforts everyone was in the best of spirits, for as the Brigade Major records in his diary, ' We seem to have got the Germans pretty well on the run, but they will probably make a big stand on the Marne to-morrow.'

Although throughout the day firing seemed to be going on all round the 3rd Brigade the latter had had none of the excitements of battle.

' We got our first issue of fresh meat to-day,' wrote Capt. Grazebrook in his private diary, ' but by the time the cooks had a chance of stewing it, it was no longer fresh and had to be thrown away.' Hard luck !

A Company found the outposts at night and succeeded in capturing a German officer and nine men who seemed pleased at their capture, for they were half starved.

The operations of the 8th September resulted in the capture of the line of the Petit Morin and the pushing forward of a line north of the river to within striking distance of the German position on the Marne. The enemy had put up a stout resistance and in places had been driven back only after stiff fighting : the B.E.F. had lost about 600 killed and wounded, the enemy at least an equal number, besides 500 prisoners and about a dozen machine-guns.

The British line on the night of the 8th ran from Bassevelle to Hondevillers and Boitron (Ist Corps) : Les Feuchères—Rougeville—Charnesseuil—Orly (IInd Corps) : the heads of the IIIrd Corps were at La Corbier and Signy Signets. On the right of the B.E.F. the Fifth French Army had also crossed the Petit Morin and, moving in a northerly direction, was turning the right flank of the Second German Army, between which and the left flank of the First German Army there was now an ever-widening gap. Von Kluck, on the Ourcq, had for the moment arrested the advance of the Sixth French Army, for he had now his IIIrd and IXth Corps, nevertheless he was still in a dangerous position.

Again on the evening of the 8th September G.H.Q. orders directed the advance to continue on the 9th : the enemy's rearguards were to be attacked whenever encountered : the cavalry to maintain touch with the flanking French Armies as before. Ist Corps orders stated that the 1st Division was to lead the Corps. The 3rd Brigade was to be the advanced guard of the Division and the 1st Gloucesters the leading Battalion of the Brigade, one platoon of B Company out in front as a patrol.

The Passage of the Marne

As on the 8th the cavalry were early astir, and by 5.30 a.m. the 1st Cavalry Brigade was in possession of the bridge over the Marne at Nogent, and the 3rd Cavalry Brigade seized the bridges at Aizy, 3 miles from Château-Thierry. The two Brigades then moved about 3 miles north to Mont de Bonneil in order to cover the passage of the infantry.

At 5 a.m. the Gloucesters, as advanced guard of the 3rd Brigade, left their bivouacs and pushed on through the woods to the high ground overlooking Nogent, which they reached without any alarm or checks.

'Here we halt for some time : down below us on the far bank we could see the town of Nogent to our right and Charly on our left front. Our cavalry had crossed earlier and now report that all is clear.' [1]

The 2nd Division was to cross at Charly.

Accordingly the Battalion marched down the slopes and crossed the Marne by a single bridge which had been prepared for demolition by the enemy, but after 1½ hour's unsuccessful work he had been forced to abandon it, indeed the British cavalry actually entered the town before the Germans had left it. The doors of all the houses in Nogent were chalk-marked, for they had served as German billets : shops had been broken open and looted and through the windows of the houses it was evident that they had been ransacked and turned upside down.

By 10.30 a.m. the 3rd Brigade had pushed on to near Fermé Beaurepaire without having come into contact with the enemy.

The advance guard of the 2nd Division had, however, to drive off a party of Germans who were preparing the bridge at Charly for demolition, but by 8.15 a.m. that Division also had won the high ground north of the Marne.

No further advance was made by the 1st or 2nd Divisions until about 3 p.m., when both moved forward again until the heads of the column reached Le Thiolet and Coupru respectively.

At Le Thiolet the Gloucesters turned into a field by the side of a wood and there bivouacked after a 13-mile march.

During the night another welcome supply of boots and socks came to hand and were distributed immediately to those most needing them.

Thus the Gloucesters had crossed the Grand Morin, Petit Morin and the Marne without firing a shot or without encountering the enemy.

[1] Captain R. M. Grazebrook.

CHAPTER VI

THE PURSUIT TO, AND BATTLE OF, THE AISNE, 1914

IN order to take advantage of the successes already gained General Joffre directed that the enemy should be pursued with energy and allowed no rest. At 8.15 p.m. on the 9th September, therefore, Sir John French ordered the British Army to continue its advance northwards at 5 a.m. on the 10th.

The Sixth French Army was to continue its endeavours to envelop the German right flank. On the extreme right of the B.E.F. the cavalry pushed forward to the high ground north-west of Bonnes, but came under heavy artillery fire from Latilly : on the left of the cavalry the 1st Division set out from the Le Thiolet area, marching north by north-west upon Courchamps, the 2nd Infantry Brigade leading, followed by the 1st and 3rd Brigades in that order.

The 3rd Brigade began its march at 9.30 a.m. via Torcy to Courchamps and Priez. At the latter village the 2nd Brigade had been in action, and when the Gloucesters passed through it a heavy battery of artillery was seen in action and a field ambulance at work.

' Along the road on the other side of the village we pass for a mile or so the results : on either side of the road the remains of rifles, equipment and ammunition, graves of various men killed in action, spots where German shells had burst on horses and wagons, fearful messes in places, broken telegraph poles, dead horses, and further piles of German equipment, etc., equally spread about.' [1]

The 3rd Brigade was, however, not engaged with the enemy and pushed on to Sommelans, which was reached at about 6 p.m., the Gloucesters bivouacking for the night in very exposed country.

' This was most certainly the coldest night we had had, the only protection we could get was from a wall built up of bundles of straw from a rick in the fields.' [2]

The Diary of 3rd Brigade Headquarters on the 10th September has an interesting comment on the enemy :

[1] Captain R. M. Grazebrook.   [2] *Ibid*.

' The general impression gained by all those who had been actually
in touch with the Germans is that we have nothing to fear or learn from
their infantry or cavalry, who both are said to shoot very badly, but that
their artillery and machine guns are very good and very well handled.'

The following note on aircraft during the early days of the
War is also contained in the Diary :

' One of the results of aircraft seems to be that it is very hard for an
army to bring another to battle.   One of two armies knows that it is not
in as good a position to fight as it might be and *through aircraft it knows
this in sufficient time* to enable it to move off to try and fight later under
what it hopes may be more favourable circumstances.'

Apart from cavalry actions, the 1st and 2nd Divisions of the
Ist Corps and the 3rd Division of the IInd Corps appear to have
done most of the fighting on the 10th September.   The British
casualties on this day were about 350, but some 1,800 Germans
had been captured as well as a battery of guns by the 1st Lincolnshire (3rd Division) and the sight of so much abandoned German
transport and of so many German stragglers raised the enthusiasm
of the troops to the highest pitch.   The general advance had been
about 10 miles and at nightfall the heads of the three Corps of
the B.E.F. occupied the line Latilly westwards through Rassy to
Monnes (Ist Corps), Dammard, St. Quentin, Chézy (IInd Corps),
Vaux-sous-Coulombs and southward through Coulombs to Cha-
ton (IIIrd Corps) : the cavalry were at Breny, Rozet, Macogny,
Marizy, Passy and Mosloy.

On the 11th the B.E.F. was directed to continue the pursuit
in a north-easterly direction between the boundaries Fère-en-
Tardenois—Bazoches (on the east) and La Ferté Milon—Long-
pont (on the west) : Conneau's Cavalry and a French corps were
on the right and on the left the Sixth French Army was to change
front to the north, wheeling up its right flank (which was approaching La Ferté Milon) practically level with the left of the B.E.F.

The events of the 11th September are thus related in the
Battalion Diary :

' Sommerlans.   The Brigade Group left its billets at 5 a.m. and
marched second in the Division.   The Battalion marched second in the
Brigade via Latilly, Grissoles, Coincy to Villeneuve-sur-Fère, where the
Battalion bivouacked, but as the weather became very wet we moved into
billets, all except A Company for whom there was no room.'

The distance marched was about 11½ miles.
The weather changed on the 11th September—very much for
the worse.   Rain fell in torrents and the temperature dropped
considerably, all ranks shivering without their greatcoats.   To

make matters worse, when the Gloucesters arrived at Villeneuve-sur-Fère they were told they were to bivouac ' in order to become hardened ' ! Hardened ? The B.E.F. had already endured the hardest tasks to which soldiers can be put and had come through them triumphantly. Was that order given by some officer fresh out from home who had not gone through the Retreat from Mons ?

The advance on the 11th was made without encountering the enemy and at nightfall the B.E.F. (heads of divisions) held roughly the line Bruyères (1st Division), Beugneux (2nd Division), Grand Rozoy (3rd Division), Hartennes (5th Division), La Loge Fme. (4th Division), Marizy (19th Infantry Brigade), with the cavalry holding a line in front from Loupeigne, on the right, to Ville-montoire on the left : the B.E.F. was abreast with the French Fifth Army on the left and the Sixth on the right. The enemy was now definitely in retreat in a northerly and north-easterly direction towards the River Aisne.

G.H.Q. orders, issued during the evening of the 11th, directed the pursuit to continue on the 12th. The cavalry were to harass the enemy, who appeared to be in full retreat north and east. The Corps were directed to move on Bourg and Pont Arcy (Ist Corps), Vailly (IInd Corps) and Bucy-le-Long (IIIrd Corps) : the crossings over the Aisne were to be seized and columns to reach the high ground overlooking the river. The boundaries of the British advance on this day were to be Bazoches—Craonne on the east and Soissons—Laon on the west.

Of the 1st Division the 3rd Brigade was now the advanced guard, the 2nd Welch forming the vanguard and the 1st Gloucesters heading the main guard.

Billets at Villeneuve were left at 5 a.m. and the column took the road in a north-easterly direction. The weather was again beastly. Rain fell heavily, turning the roads into seas of mud; both observation and movement were, therefore, difficult. The route lay via Fère-en-Tardenois, Loupeigne and Bazoches. On nearing the latter village the enemy was reported to be holding the high ground near Perles. At 1 p.m. the Welch were sent forward to reconnoitre and the Gloucesters were ordered to deploy and advance west of the road leading up the valley from Bazoches to Vauxcèrè. A and B Companies formed the first line with C and D in support. But no trace of the enemy could be found. A and B Companies were, therefore, ordered to form the outposts, C and D billeting in Vauxcèrè, resting in the caves which abound in that part of the country.

Sickness began to show itself during the day, for many men had fallen out during the march (about 18½ miles) :

'Up to now we had not had many cases of dysentery or other sickness,' records an officer of the Battalion, 'but the cold of the nights after day's heat, together with the wet, the repetition of tinned meats and insufficiently cooked food and the large quantity of only half-ripe apples and pears, were beginning to affect everyone.'

The day's march had brought the B.E.F. to approximately the line Longueval, Dhuisel, Brenelle, Serches and Septmonts, the heads of divisions (1st, 2nd, 3rd, 5th, 4th in that order from right to left) being at those places though the 4th Division, long after darkness, was still advancing : it was, indeed, the only Division to cross the Aisne on the 12th/13th, the 11th Infantry Brigade pushing on ahead and making good the northern bank of the river at Bucy by 3 a.m. on the 13th.

There was as yet no sign as to whether the enemy's intention was to make a definite stand north of the Aisne, or whether he would merely delay the Allies in their efforts to cross the river, in order to cover a further retirement of his troops which, by all accounts, were disorganized and undoubtedly weak. Nor were there any indications as to how much farther the B.E.F. and the French Armies, on its flanks, could push their successes of the past few days.

The Passage of the Aisne

Time reveals most things and now we know that the enemy had not only determined upon making a stand on the heights north of the Aisne, but had prepared positions on which to accept battle.

The battlefield-to-be is thus described in the official despatches :

'The Aisne Valley runs generally east and west and consists of a flat-bottomed depression of width varying from half a mile to 2 miles, down which the river follows a winding course to the west, at some points near the southern slopes of the valley and at others near the northern. The high ground both on the north and south of the river is approximately 400 feet above the bottom of the valley, and is very similar in character, as are both slopes of the valley itself, which are broken into numerous spurs and re-entrants. The most prominent of the former are the Chivre spur on the right bank and Sermoise spur on the left. Near the latter place the general plateau of the south is divided by a subsidiary valley of much the same character, down which the small River Vesle flows to the main stream near Sermoise. The slopes of the plateau overlooking the Aisne on the north and south are of varying steepness and are covered with numerous patches of wood, which also stretch upwards and backwards over the edge on to the top of the high ground. There are several villages and small towns dotted about in the valley itself and along its sides, chief of which is the town of Soissons.

'The Aisne is a sluggish stream of some 170 feet in breadth but, being 15 feet deep in the centre, it is unfordable. Between Soissons on the west and Villers on the east (the part of the river attacked and secured by the British Forces) there are eleven road bridges across it. On the north bank a narrow-gauge railway runs from Soissons to Vailly, where it crosses the river and continues eastward along the south bank. From Soissons to Sermoise a double line of railway runs along the south bank, turning at the latter place up the Vesle Valley towards Bazoches.

' The position held by the enemy is a very strong one, either for delaying action or for a defensive battle. One of its chief military characteristics is that from the high ground on neither side can the top of the plateau on the other side be seen except for small stretches. This is chiefly due to the woods on the edges of the slopes. Another important point is that all the bridges are under either direct or high-angle artillery fire.

' The tract of country above described, which lies north of the Aisne, is well adapted to concealment and was so skilfully turned to account by the enemy as to render it impossible to judge the real nature of his opposition to our passage of the river, or to accurately gauge his strength, and I have every reason to consider that strong rearguards of at least three army corps were holding the passages on the early morning of the 13th.'

Of the villages and small towns mentioned in the despatches, there were many which were to become familiar to all in the Ist Corps : Villers (just south of the River Aisne and Canal and the extreme left flank of the B.E.F.), Bourg (just north of the Aisne and in the south-eastern angle of the four cross roads formed by the Fismes—Laon—Vailly—Neufchatel roads) and Pont Arcy (west of Bourg and on the southern bank of the river). Just east of the Bourg—Laon road lay the small villages of Œuilly, Pargnan, Genly, Moulins, Passy and Troyon, while west of the road were Vendresse, Chivy, Beaulne, Braye, Verneuil, Moussy, Soupir and Chavonne, the last-named village being nearly 3 miles east of Vailly.

North of Troyon, and running east and west, was the (now) famous Chemin des Dames beyond which were the villages of Cerny, Courtecon, Lierval, Chavignon and Terny.

Uncertain still of the intentions of the enemy, Sir John French ordered the B.E.F. to continue the pursuit on the 13th, the heads of Corps being directed on the three last-named places—Lierval (Ist Corps), Chavignon (IInd Corps) and Terny (IIIrd Corps).

The advance was to begin at 7 a.m.

At the time these orders were issued (7.45 p.m. on the 12th September) there was a gap of about 13 miles between the right of the Second German Army at Berry-au-Bac and the left of the First German Army at Ostel. This gap was filled only by three cavalry divisions, and towards it were advancing the left of the Fifth French Army, consisting of at least two corps (one of which was Conneau's Cavalry) and several divisions, the British Ist Corps, and Allenby's Cavalry Division.

The *Official History (Military Operations) of the War* thus describes the extraordinarily interesting situation on the night 12th/13th September :

' The first and most insistent problem for O.H.L. (German General Headquarters) was how to fill the gap before the Allies could reach it in force and pierce the German line of battle by separating the First and Second Armies.   It is not too much to say that the fate of the German Armies on the Western Front turned on the solution of the problem.'

If only the weather had been more favourable for aerial reconnaissance, the dispositions of the Germans and the gap between the two Armies might have been discovered, but the skies were dismal with low clouds and continuous heavy rain, practically blinding the eyes of the Army, i.e. the aeroplane observers.   But the gods were against us, for when early on the 13th the cavalry pushed forward patrols to the crossings over the Aisne at Villers and Bourg, rain was still falling and dawn broke grey and miserable.   The bridges over the Aisne were found destroyed, but not those over the Canal south of the river.   Rifle fire was opened on the cavalry as they approached the crossings, the Germans firing from houses on the northern bank or from entrenchments, but by 8.30 a.m. the 2nd Cavalry Brigade had occupied the outskirts of Bourg.

The 2nd Infantry Brigade, the advanced guard of the 1st Division, then approached the village, but found that the enemy's snipers were picking off the cavalry as they drew near the bridge. A party of the 60th Rifles were, therefore, sent eastwards to cross the river lower down and endeavour to enfilade the snipers at Bourg.   The Rifles made the passage of the river by 10 a.m. and reported that the only crossing was by an aqueduct which carried the canal across the river south-west of Bourg, a circuitous and unsatisfactory route bound to cause delay : but it had to be used.

The cavalry, having made good the high ground north of Bourg, the 2nd Infantry Brigade followed and had reached the spur north of the village when the 2nd Cavalry Brigade, which had advanced as far as Moulins, was checked by the enemy holding the ridge north of Troyon.   Other German troops were reported moving on Bourg from Chivy, while a mile or two north of Courtecon still more of the enemy appeared to be concentrating.   The 1st and 3rd Infantry Brigades were therefore ordered to advance across the river as quickly as possible.

But the slow and devious route which the troops had to follow was responsible for considerable delay—delay which had an important bearing on the general situation. It was 2.15 p.m. before the 3rd Brigade moved off from Vauxcêrê and 4 p.m. before the actual crossing at Bourg began, and 5.30 p.m. before the last unit of the Brigade was across the river.

That night the 1st Division held approximately the following positions, all troops being in billets or bivouacs : 1st Guards Brigade Paissy, 2nd Brigade Moulins, 3rd Brigade Bourg. So far as the 1st Division was concerned the northern bank of the Aisne had been made good with little fighting and without any great opposition from the enemy, whose principal resistance was more westwards.

When darkness fell on the 13th, however, the gap of 13 miles which had at dawn that day existed between the right of the Second German Army and the left of the First German Army had been closed—the last opportunity of penetrating it (though no fault of the B.E.F. or French) had gone. Wellington at Waterloo is said to have prayed for darkness or Blücher : at German General Headquarters on the night of the 12th/13th September the precarious positions of the inner flanks of the Second and First German Armies can hardly have produced less fervent desires. For with all the means at their disposal, all the urging possible, the VIIth Reserve Corps, which until the evening of the 7th September (upon which date the Fortress fell), had been investing Maubeuge, had been ordered to march southwards. The first order to the Corps was to move to La Fère to form the nucleus of the Seventh German Army. But when the critical position on the Aisne became known the Corps Commander was ordered with all speed to push on and fill the gap. At 8 a.m. on the morning of the 13th the Corps was 5 miles south of Laon, by 9.30 a.m. it was on the march to Cerny and Braye-en-Laonnais and by 2 p.m. part of the Corps was in position along the Chemin des Dames, north of Braye, ready to oppose the further advance of the Ist British Corps. These were the troops which the cavalry reported as marching on Bourg and Chivy, whilst others were observed concentrating in the distance. By the narrow margin of two hours only the gap was filled, for other German troops on arrival carried the enemy's line still further eastwards until there no longer existed a vulnerable point between the inner flanks of the two most westerly German Armies.

If only the heavy clouds and rain, and the mists which hung continually over the Aisne valley, had given our aeroplane observers an opportunity, the gap might have been observed by the absence of German troops. But the Fortune of War again favoured the enemy.

Still all unconscious of the arrival of the German VIIth Reserve Corps and other troops, Sir John French, with a view to clearing up the situation in front and in an endeavour to discover whether the enemy intended making a stand, or was merely fighting a rearguard action whilst his main forces continued their withdrawal, ordered a general advance to take place on 14th September. The heads of the three Corps were to reach the line Laon—Suzy—Fresne.

The Ist Corps was to cross the line Moulins—Moussy by 7 a.m. and seize the crest line of the heights north of the Aisne, which included the famous Chemin des Dames.

The 1st Division began to move forward before dawn, the 2nd Brigade leading. North of Troyon and just short of Cerny stood a sugar factory, strongly held by the enemy, whose position also ran on both sides of the factory, i.e. along the road to the east and the road south-west to Chivy. In spite of gallant efforts the position proved too strong for the three battalions of the 2nd Brigade which formed the firing-line, the Loyal North Lancs were therefore hurried up from Brigade Reserve to lend their assistance. Simultaneously the 1st (Guards) Brigade was ordered to take part in the attack on the German trenches along the ridge. The 1st Coldstream were sent off to the right, the other battalions continuing the line of the 2nd Brigade westwards.

In spite of very heavy resistance and having to advance up a glacis, with rain driving in their faces, the Loyal North Lancs captured the sugar factory—a splendid piece of work.

In the meantime the 3rd Brigade had set out from Bourg at 7.30 a.m. along the road leading northwards to Vendresse. Just before reaching the latter place the Queen's were sent off to the right to protect that flank of the Division, while the remainder of the Brigade hurried forward through Vendresse to the Troyon Spur in order to come up on the left of the 1st (Guards) Brigade. The Welch and South Wales Borderers were sent forward to link up, if possible, with the right Brigade (6th) of the 2nd Division. But the Gloucesters were kept back in Brigade Reserve and sheltered under cover of the south-western end of the Troyon —Chivy ridge. Despite a good deal of artillery fire the Battalion was well protected. D Company, the first to arrive, was sent off under Major R. M. S. Gardner to the right flank of the Brigade to fill a gap between the South Wales Borderers and the left of the 1st Brigade. But the whole of the Battalion had not come up when a heavy German counter-attack threatened the left flank. A and B Companies were therefore ordered to support a Company of the Welch. The counter-attack was, however, broken up and the enemy repulsed by the front-line troops, ably supported by the guns.

At about 12 noon the 1st (Guards) Brigade was again heavily engaged and B and C Companies under Major J. O'D. Ingram were sent up as reinforcements. These two Companies reached a quarry and three platoons were sent forward to fill a gap in the line. Fire was opened on the enemy as he retired up the slopes opposite the position. The German guns then shelled the Gloucesters and, as there was no hostile infantry movement in front, the three platoons were withdrawn to the quarry, having suffered some casualties.

A general advance took place at 4 p.m. which ended in a decided success for the Ist Corps. The Gloucesters were not engaged, and at 6 p.m. the three detached companies were ordered to rejoin the Battalion. A and D Companies (under Major Ingram), however, moved back to Vendresse, while B and C reported to the C.O. at original Battalion Headquarters at the southern end of the Chivy Spur.

As dusk was falling the Welch and South Wales Borderers made another short advance which brought them to a position just short of the Chemin des Dames, the former Battalion taking many prisoners and two machine-guns.

The 3rd Brigade was then ordered to move forward to the line of the Chemin des Dames. B and C Companies of the Gloucesters advanced through Chivy and eventually entrenched immediately west of Troyon.

A and D Companies were, throughout the night, in Divisional reserve at Chivy.

The advance of the Ist Corps on the 14th September resulted in gains of ground which were never lost throughout the whole period the B.E.F. remained on the Aisne. At nightfall the general line of the Force ran, from right to left, as follows : The Ist Corps held Villers — Moulins — Troyon — Chivy — Beaulne — Soupir. There was then a gap of about 3 miles between the left of the Ist Corps and the right of the IInd Corps, i.e. the 3rd Division which held Vailly and a semi-circle round it. Another gap of about 5 miles still existed between the left of the 3rd Division and the right of the 5th Division at Missy. The latter division, with the 4th Division on its left, carried the line to just east of Crouy, at which point the left of the B.E.F. joined up with the right of the Sixth French Army.

From the general situation on the night of the 14th September it was evident that the enemy had arrested his retirement and was determined to dispute any further advance of the Allies.

4

Indeed, it is now known that von Bülow (under whose orders the First and Seventh [1] German Armies had been placed) had issued orders that the British and French were to be attacked and thrown back over the Aisne.

But it was far easier to issue those orders than to get them carried out. The First German Army was exhausted, and what attacks were made on the B.E.F. by von Kluck on the 15th September were only of a half-hearted nature. Indeed it was the British who did practically all the attacking on that day.

Along the front of the 1st Division the enemy made a futile attempt to advance, but was easily beaten off. Four men of the Gloucesters, posted at the corner of a wood, had a most successful day at sniping and scored many a hit. Dawn that morning had brought with it the ghastliness of the modern battlefield : " All round us are lying a large number of dead and wounded of the 1st (Guards) Brigade. They suffered heavily yesterday.' [2]

Dawn also showed that the trenches dug by the South Wales Borderers during the night were useless, and others had to be dug farther to the front. B Company of the Gloucesters was sent forward as soon as daylight broke to fill a gap between the Borderers and the Welch.

The German attack began between 10 and 11 a.m. and the Welch were slightly driven back. A Company of the South Wales Borderers and B Company of the Gloucesters were therefore sent forward and, by midday or soon after, the situation again became normal. With the exception of a few posts left out on the ridge for observation purposes B Company then withdrew into the cover of a quarry : they returned to the line in the evening.

During the day Lieutenant R. K. Swanwick was killed, whilst Lieutenant the Hon. N. F. Somerset was wounded in the head, and Lieutenant D. Duncan received a slight wound in the arm. The losses in N.C.O.s and men for the two days (14th and 15th September) were 10 killed, 72 wounded and 2 missing. [3]

[1] The Seventh Army had filled the gap between the right of the Second and left of the First German Armies. The VIIth Reserve Corps from Maubeuge had joined the Seventh German Army.

[2] From the Battalion Diary.

[3] The following message was received by 1st Corps Headquarters from Sir John French : ' I want to express my warmest appreciation of the conduct of the 1st Army Corps under General Sir D. Haig throughout the last two days' battle on the Aisne. It is owing to their intrepid advance and splendid resistance to all counter-attacks that we are now able to secure the passage of the river. I heartily congratulate Generals Lomax and Monro and their gallant Divisions upon their splendid behaviour.'

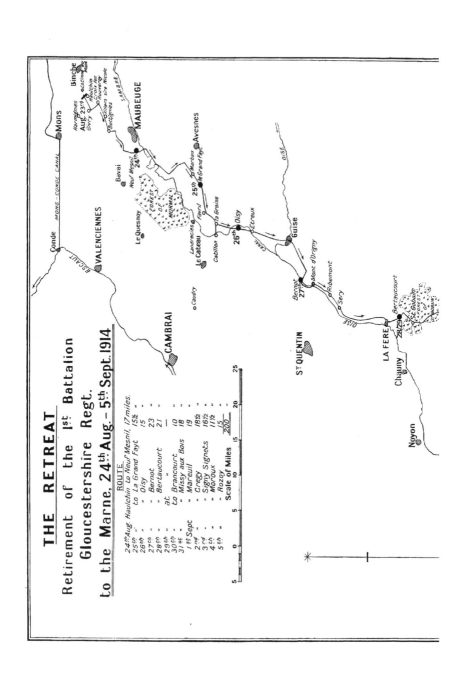

THE RETREAT

Retirement of the 1st Battalion
Gloucestershire Regt.
to the Marne, 24th Aug – 5th Sept. 1914

ROUTE

24th Aug.	Haulchin to Neuf Mesnil, 17 miles.
25th "	to La Grand Fayt, 15½ "
26th "	Oisy, 15 "
27th "	" Bernot, 23 "
28th "	" Bertaucourt, 21 "
29th "	at "
30th "	to Brancourt, 10 "
31st "	" Missy aux Bois, 18 "
1st Sept.	" Mareuil, 19 "
2nd "	" Cregy, 18½ "
3rd "	" Signy Signets, 16½ "
4th "	" Moroux, 11½ "
5th "	" Rozoy, 15 "
	200

Scale of Miles

0   5   10   15   20   25

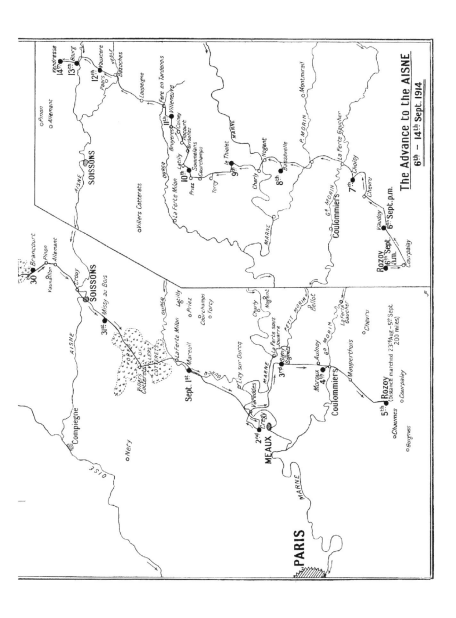

The Advance to the AISNE
6th – 14th Sept. 1914

Farther to the west of the Ist Corps the 3rd and 5th Divisions had been in action with the enemy, the latter Division at night having completed its passage of the river. But, speaking generally, there was little change in the general situation. The Ist Corps alone held a firm footing north of the river, for both the IInd and IIIrd Corps held at the best a precarious hold on the northern banks of the Aisne.

Operation Orders for the 16th September ordered the line held by the B.E.F. to be strongly entrenched and also contained a statement that it was the intention of the Commander-in-Chief to assume a general offensive at the earliest opportunity. No such opportunity offered itself, and the above orders eventually proved to be the official notification of the beginning of trench warfare.

CHAPTER VII

THE BEGINNING OF TRENCH WARFARE AND TRANSFER OF THE BRITISH EXPEDITIONARY FORCE TO FLANDERS

PUSHED forward as it was, farther north than either the IInd or IIIrd Corps, and in closer contact with the enemy, along the front of the Ist Corps the change from action to inactivity was more gradual.

The positions which Sir Douglas Haig's Corps had established north of the river were more threatening to the enemy than those held by the two other Corps of the British Expeditionary Force. From time to time, therefore, the 1st and 2nd Divisions were attacked by the enemy or made attacks on him. Yet, strategically, the situation had changed from a war of movement to static warfare.

On the 16th September there was a decided lull along the whole front, though it may be noted that on this day the opposing forces began those heavy bombardments of their opponents' trenches which were to become a daily and nightly feature of the War during the long years which followed. Rain again fell heavily and mud and water increased in the trenches and bivouacs to a most uncomfortable degree : the whole country-side was gradually becoming a quagmire.

At dawn A Company of the Gloucesters relieved B in the front line, the latter moving back under the bluff behind the trenches and digging in. The soil was chalky so that digging was not in itself a difficult task had tools been more plentiful and adequate. D Company moved down to the head of the valley and dug itself in, in a deep ravine. C Company dug in alongside the road. Thus early the value of ' digging-in ' as a protection against the enemy's shell fire was recognized. At 6 a.m. the German guns opened fire : they appeared to have a battery near Courtecon, from which guns fired all day in all directions, A Company's trenches receiving special attention—3 men were killed and 9 wounded. Towards evening the British guns opened fire in retaliation, but at this period our artillery suffered great disabilities. Whenever it came to a duel between field-guns the

British were generally superior, but where high-angle fire was concerned we could only pit the 4·5-inch howitzers and the 60-pounders against the enemy's howitzers and heavy guns with a greater range and throwing a much larger projectile. We had nothing to match the huge howitzers firing a shell which on bursting made enormous craters and threw out black volumes of smoke, so that our men dubbed them ' Black Marias ', ' Coal Boxes ' or ' Jack Johnsons '. These German howitzers had demolished the steel cupolas at Liége and Namur (deemed almost impregnable before the War) with demoralizing ease. With what may be termed siege artillery the Germans were well armed, whereas (except for the 60-pounders) our principal armament in artillery was in field guns and 4·5 howitzers. However, some 6-inch howitzers arrived from England during the latter part of September and were at once brought into action with marked results.

During the 16th, 2nd Lieutenant Baxter, Sergt. Durham of A Company, and No. 9714 Drummer C. Fluck did especially good work. The N.C.O. handled his platoon in a conspicuously brave manner when his men came under a heavy enfilading artillery fire. Sergt. Rickards (also of A Company) carried out most useful work in an observation-post, continuing to send back valuable information even when the enemy was making an attack on his Company's trenches. The Drummer carried messages to and from the firing-line under shell-fire in a most gallant manner.

The morning of the 17th was peaceful, but during the afternoon heavy rifle fire broke out further to the east. The Germans had launched another attack against the right flank of the 1st Division. The attack fell most heavily on the 2nd Brigade, which for a while had to give ground. A counter-attack, however, restored the situation.

At about 4.30 p.m. the Gloucesters were ordered to move in support of the 2nd Brigade. B Company, having been relieved by the South Wales Borderers, joined the Battalion which assembled in Chivy. At 7.15 the Gloucesters moved off towards Troyon and, after an hour's march, reached the 2nd Brigade area. C and D Companies were then got into position along the Chemin des Dames, filling a gap between the Northamptons and the Queen's, A and B Companies remaining in support 200 yards in rear of the front line, sheltered under banks.

Later B Company was sent a short distance out in front of D Company in order to fill in some German trenches. Two attempts had to be made, but eventually the work was carried out, though Lieutenant B. F. R. Davis, who was in command of the covering-party, was wounded in the arm during the work.

This incident is recorded in the official despatches : ' On the 18th [1] the Gloucestershire Regiment advanced from their position near Chivy, filled in the enemy's trenches and captured two maxim guns.'

The Battalion buried many dead Germans in the trenches, also three machine-guns, bringing in a fourth, and a German drum.

On this day the Battalion Diary records that : ' The mud is simply awful, the weather still raining.'

Heavy hostile shell-fire all day, most of it ineffective, characterized the 18th September. At 10 p.m., owing to a report that the enemy was advancing, the Gloucesters stood to arms, but no attack materialized. About midnight, however, the enemy made a weak attack on the left of the 2nd Brigade, but retired without pushing it home.

Until 7.30 p.m. on the 19th the Gloucesters remained in occupation of this position, but at that hour two companies of the Durham Light Infantry [2] arrived and relieved the Battalion, the latter moving off to the left and taking over the trenches of the Sherwood Foresters in the quarries on the ridge west of Troyon. The Battalion now came under the orders of its own Brigadier and formed the right of the 3rd Infantry Brigade line. Before leaving the 2nd Brigade area Privates Orr and Law, both of D Company, distinguished themselves by going out and bringing back a wounded scout. They crossed an open belt of ground, a hundred yards wide, swept by shell-fire. Both were awarded the D.C.M.

On the 20th the enemy's shell-fire began at 6 a.m. and continued throughout the day. At about 4 p.m. the Germans delivered a heavy attack [3] against the junction of the 18th Infantry Brigade and the French : the latter were Colonial troops. Having practically lost all their officers the French troops temporarily were driven back and the right of the 18th Infantry Brigade had likewise to give ground. The 4th Cavalry Brigade, however, restored the situation. Along the front held by the Gloucesters all was quiet and at night the Battalion patrols reported that there were no signs of the enemy : one of these patrols, under Lieutenant Wetherall, did specially good work.

---

[1] The date should be the ' 17th ', *vide* above narrative.

[2] The 2nd D.L.I. belonged to the 18th Infantry Brigade, 6th Division, which had arrived from England and had been sent forward to relieve troops of the 1st Division who badly needed a rest.

[3] Actions on the Aisne Heights.

The next few days were uneventful. More and more the struggle between the opposing forces was definitely taking on the character of siege warfare, and at first the British Army was not armed for such tactics.

On the 25th the Germans were reinforced by troops from Brussels and Verdun and more ' liveliness ' was expected. It came the next day.

At 4 a.m. on the 26th the 2nd Brigade (which had again come up into the line on the right of the 1st Division) was heavily attacked.[1] But although two platoons of D Company were sent off to support the South Wales Borderers upon whom the storm had broken, and the other companies also saw German troops in large numbers and at one period opened fire with terrible effect on the enemy, who were simply mown down, the Battalion was not actually attacked, though it came in for a good deal of shell fire. One shell fell just in front of the Gloucesters' trenches, behind which a group of officers were standing. An R.E. officer was killed and 2nd Lieutenant Watkins slightly wounded in the shoulder. Major R. M. S. Gardner, Captain Rising and Lieutenants Caunter and Duncan were all knocked over by the shellburst. About 7 men of C Company were also hit. Altogether the day's casualties numbered 27. On the 27th the Gloucesters were relieved and companies marched back independently to Bourg, where they occupied billets vacated by the Cameron Highlanders.

' Thus ', records an officer of the Battalion in his private diary,[2] ' came to an end a fortnight of continuous hard fighting, constantly exposed to hostile shelling and bad weather, and although the Battalion had suffered heavy casualties its morale was never higher.'

The rest at Bourg was, however, of short duration, for on the 29th the Battalion moved off to Pagnan, a little village hanging on the slope of the valley just below the plateau.

Following the attack of the 26th September the position on the Aisne slowly turned to stagnation. Realizing that it was impossible for one or the other to advance, both sides had taken to digging themselves in more securely and providing protection not only from shell-fire but from the weather, which was gradually growing worse. Patrol work was constant and the opposing forces frequently indulged in artillery duels, but of infantry attacks there were none. It is unnecessary, therefore, to dwell upon the closing days on the Aisne.

---

[1] The Action of Chivy.   [2] Lieut.-Colonel A. H. Radice.

On the 1st October greatcoats and packs arrived and were issued to the men immediately, who were now in great need of them. On this day also the Battalion marched off to Moulins, in Divisional Reserve, but on arrival in the village A and D Companies and the machine-gun section were sent forward to the head of the valley, north of Moulins, to fill a gap between the right of the 2nd Brigade entrenched on the Chemin des Dames, and the left of the French line. Two platoons held the front line by night and the remainder of the two companies were in close support. By day, however, so quiet had become the front line that only an observation-post was required there. The remainder of the Battalion billeted in Moulins.

Until the 16th October the Gloucesters held this position and one diarist records that ' The most exciting event during our stay at Moulins was the arrival at Battalion Headquarters of a solitary German shell which did no damage.'

On the 15th the Battalion had received orders to hand over its trenches to French troops, who were to arrive that night. ' This ', records Lieut.-Colonel A. H. Radice in his diary, ' was the first intimation it [the Battalion] got that the British Army was being transferred to Flanders.' But a portion of the Army had already left the Aisne and by this date had arrived on the northern flank of the Allied Armies, where the ' race to the coast ' was in progress.

That phrase—the ' race to the coast '—aptly describes the movement on the left which had been in progress whilst the B.E.F., with the Fifth and Sixth French Armies on the right and left respectively, had been holding the northern banks of the Aisne from the 16th September onwards. For the French had not given up their endeavours to outflank the right of the German line nor had the latter abandoned his attempt to turn the left of the Allies. The French had put their Second Army into line on the left of the Sixth : this was parried by the Germans putting *their* Second Army on the right of their First. Our Allies then brought up their Tenth Army on the left of the Second, the Germans replying by extending *their* right with the Sixth Army. By the end of September the opposing forces had reached Lens, the enemy holding that town and the French west of it. Early in October the ' race ' began again, still in a north-westerly direction, and by the 8th the French had reached a line between St. Omer and Hazebrouck, with German cavalry operating in the neighbourhood of the latter town.

By this date also the British Army was on the move from the Aisne, for as Sir John French states in his despatches :

' Early in October a study of the general situation strongly impressed me with the necessity for bringing the greatest possible force to bear in supporting the northern flank of the Allies in order to effectively out-flank the enemy and compel him to evacuate his positions. At the same time the position on the Aisne . . . appeared to me to warrant a with-drawal of the British forces from the positions they then held.'

It was natural also that, as the IVth Corps had already landed in Flanders and was engaged in attempting to relieve the Belgians in Antwerp, the British Army should be concentrated so as to act as one body : also the left flank of the Allied line was the natural position of the British Army, which would thus be nearer England, with which it was necessary to keep open the lines of communication.

The plan, therefore, for the transfer of the B.E.F. from the Aisne to its new positions in the Allied line was as follows :

' The IInd Corps to arrive on the line Aire—Bethune on the 11th October, to connect with the right of the French Tenth Army and, pivoting on its left, to attack in flank the enemy who were opposing the Xth French Corps in front. The cavalry to move on the northern flank of the IInd Corps and support its attack until the IIIrd Corps, which was to detrain at St. Omer on the 12th, should come up. They were then to clear the front and to act on the northern flank of the IIIrd Corps in a similar manner pending the arrival of the Ist Corps from the Aisne. The 3rd Cavalry Division and 7th Division, under Sir Henry Rawlinson, which were then operating in support of the Belgian Army, and assisting its withdrawal from Antwerp, to be ordered to co-operate as soon as circumstances would allow.'

The Ist Corps was thus to be the last of the B.E.F. to leave the Aisne.

The relief of the Gloucesters, which began after darkness had fallen on the 15th, occupied most of the night. At 6 p.m. B and C Companies, under Captain Temple, were sent out to trenches astride the Moulins—Vendresse Spur. By midnight the French had relieved the 2nd Brigade (the right Brigade of the 1st Division) but had suffered heavy casualties from hostile shell-fire, the enemy evidently suspecting that something unusual was taking place. However, by 3 a.m. on the 16th the Gloucesters were concentrated at Moulins and a few minutes later set out on the march to Bourg, where they crossed the river and moved via Dhuizel to Paars. Here the Battalion went into billets in two farms south of the village.

' Thus ', records an officer of the Gloucesters in his private record of the War, ' came to an end the first phase of the War, during which all ranks had been sorely tried in the most difficult and demoralizing opera-tion of war—a long retreat in the face of the enemy—and had not failed, but had added to the laurels the Battalion had gained in the past.'

At 4 a.m. the next morning the Gloucesters paraded and marched via Bazoches and Loupeignes to Fère-en-Tardenois, where they entrained for Flanders. They reached Cassel at 3.30 p.m. on the 18th and after detraining marched north-east to Longue Croix, a small village, where they billeted.

By this date the remainder of the Ist Corps had also begun to arrive about St. Omer and Hazebrouck, and by the 19th concentration was complete, the 1st Division in the area St. Omer—Cassel, the 2nd Division between Poperinghe and Steenvoorde.

CHAPTER VIII

THE MOBILIZATION OF THE RESERVE AND TERRITORIAL BATTALIONS OF THE REGIMENT

IN the meantime, whilst the 28th were fighting at Mons
wending their way back to the Marne, thence pursuing the
enemy back to the Aisne, and the 61st were on their way
home from North China, the Reserve and Territorial Battalions
of the Regiment had, after mobilization, proceeded to their war
stations and training centres.

The 3rd (Special Reserve) Battalion (Lieut.-Colonel G. H.
Burges, commanding) completed its annual training at Perham
Down and returned to Bristol where it was dismissed on the
27th June. No one in his wildest dreams expected to be called
up again in just over a month.

Orders to mobilize were received on the 4th of August, and
by the 8th 380 Special Reservists and 550 N.C.O.s and men of
Sections A, B and D Army Reserve had joined, or were attached
to the Battalion. At 10.15 p.m. that night the 3rd Gloucesters
left for Abbey Wood, near Woolwich, arriving at 3 a.m. on the 9th.
The camp taken over from a London Territorial battalion was
at first uncomfortable, but gradually they settled in. Besides
training, the work of the Reserve Battalion was the defence of
the Arsenal and to guard the huge supplies of explosives which
were distributed over the Abbey Wood Marshes. The War
Office had decided not to move Special Reserve battalions abroad,
but to keep them in England as ' feeding battalions ' for those
overseas. From September onwards, therefore, the 3rd
Gloucesters continually supplied drafts of officers and men to
the 1st Battalion and other corps, whilst there was always a
steadily increasing flow of drafts of new officers and men for
training.

For the Territorials mobilization had come at an awkward
period. Many battalions were either in camp undergoing their
annual training or were actually *en route* for their training areas.

The three Territorial battalions of the Regiment, i.e. 1/4th,
1/5th and 1/6th, were part of the South Midland Division

(subsequently the 48th Division), the 1/4th and 1/6th with the 7th and 8th Worcesters forming the Gloucester and Worcester Infantry Brigade (subsequently the 144th Brigade), and the 1/5th with the 4th Oxford and Bucks, the Bucks Battalion of the Oxford and Bucks Light Infantry, and the 4th Berkshires the South Midland Infantry Brigade (afterwards the 145th Brigade).

The 1/4th and 1/6th being brigaded together, their early history during the first few months of the War is very similar. They started for their annual training on the last Sunday in July, 1914, going down to Minehead but, owing to the grave outlook, returned to Bristol the following day. All ranks were dismissed to their homes to await mobilization, which was ordered on the 4th of August. After mobilization the Division began to concentrate at Swindon.

The 1/5th were only in camp at Marlow one night, but, as hostilities seemed certain, struck camp on the 3rd August and returned to Gloucester. On the declaration of war the Battalion mobilized and was sent off to its war station in the Isle of Wight until relieved by the 3rd Hants. The 1/5th then also moved to Swindon.

About the middle of August the Division moved to the eastern counties, the 1/5th Gloucesters to Chelmsford and the 1/4th and 1/6th to neighbouring villages. The 1/4th sent two Companies to guard petrol depots at Avonmouth; these Companies rejoined at the end of August. In these localities the Territorials remained throughout the autumn and winter, training hard and getting ready for service overseas. In March, 1915, the 48th Division was inspected by H.M. the King, and at the end of the month the Gloucesters with other units of their Brigades entrained for Folkestone and crossed over to France.

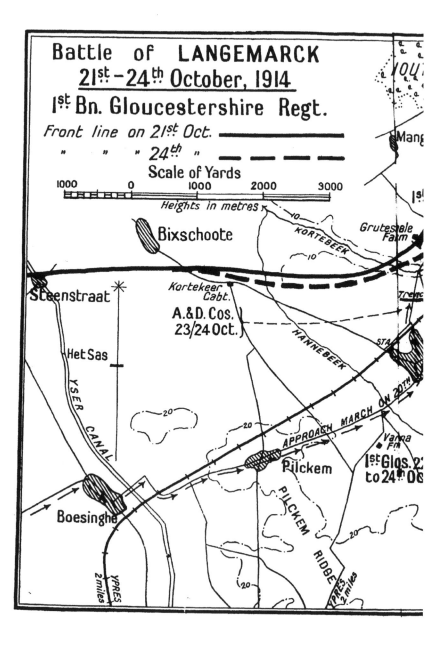

Battle of LANGEMARCK
21st – 24th October, 1914
1st Bn. Gloucestershire Regt.

Front line on 21st Oct. ——————
" " " 24th " – – – – –
Scale of Yards

1000   0   1000   2000   3000

Heights in metres

Bixschoote

KORTEBEEK

Grutesiele Farm

Steenstraat

Kortekeer Cabt.

A.&D. Cos.
23/24 Oct.

HANNEBEEK

Het Sas

YSER CANAL

20

APPROACH MARCH ON 20TH

20

Pilckem

Varna Fm.

1st Glos. 2?
to 24th Oc?

Boesinghe

PILCKEM RIDGE

20

YPRES 2 miles

YPRES 2 miles

20

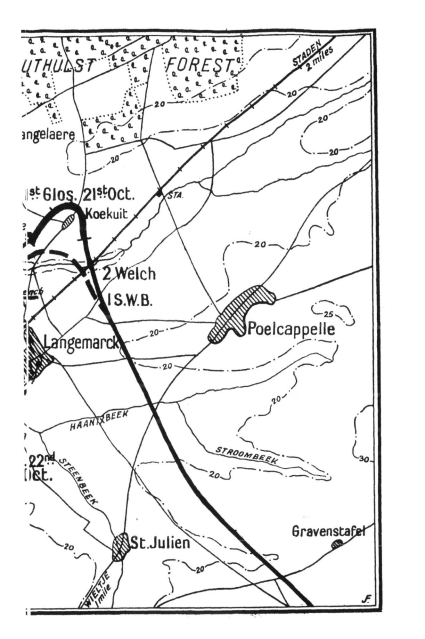

CHAPTER IX

THE BATTLES OF YPRES, 1914

THE BATTLE OF LANGEMARCK, 1914 : 21ST–24TH OCTOBER

THERE is no finer story in the annals of the British Army than the historic defence of Ypres in 1914, preceded as it was by a gallant, though fruitless, attempt to carry into effect the Allied plan of turning the right flank of the German Armies.

For a better understanding of the part played by the Gloucester Regiment in the Battles of Ypres, 1914, it is necessary to outline briefly not only the intentions of the Allied Commanders, but also the enemy's plan of attack, which closely resembled that formulated by General Sir John French, and General Foch who commanded the French troops in northern France.[1]

On the 19th October the Allied plan was for an advance eastwards from the line Ypres—Nieuport towards Roulers—Thourout and Ghistelles in order to break the enemy's front and separate the IIIrd German Reserve Corps (lately at Hamburg but now following up the Belgians) from the main German forces. The Belgians and left of the French Army were then to drive the IIIrd Corps against the coast, whilst the right flank of the French and the British Army were to wheel south-east from Menin and Ghent in the direction of the Lys, force the crossings of the river and attack the main German forces in flank and in reverse. Sir John French estimated that the Ist British Corps which, having

---

[1] The general situation of the Allied Armies at Ypres on the 19th October (as far south as Messines) was as follows : The left of the Belgian Army was on the coast at about Lombartzyde and right just north of Dixmude, where it joined up with French troops who carried the line south along the Yser Canal to just north of Boesinghe. French cavalry held the line from Bixschoote to Langemarck, in touch at the latter place with the left of the British 3rd Cavalry Division, whose right was at Zonnebeke : on the right of the 3rd Cavalry Division the 7th Division held from in front of Zonnebeke southwards east of the Polygon Wood, crossing the Menin Road east of Gheluvelt to Zand-voorde. From the latter place the 2nd Cavalry Division carried the line across the Ypres—Comines Canal to Messines.

on that date completed its concentration in the St. Omer—
Hazebrouck area, had received orders to move in a north-easterly
direction and attack the enemy north of Ypres, would not be
opposed by much more than the IIIrd Reserve Corps, which
had suffered in previous operations.

The German plan was similar, in that the enemy hoped to
break the line of the Belgian front, then wheel south-west and
outflank and roll up the Allied line, securing at the same time
the Channel ports.

Now the IIIrd German Reserve Corps, which Sir John French
had imagined were the only hostile troops in front of him, had
in reality acted as a screen behind which a new German Army
—the Fourth—consisting of four fresh corps, was being formed.
This powerful Army had, on the 17th October, reached the line
Oostcamp (south of Bruges)—Thielt (6 miles east of Courtrai),
the IIIrd Reserve Corps drawing away to the right wing, i.e. the
coast. The whole of the Fourth Army (with the IIIrd Reserve
Corps on its right) was to advance with its right between Ostend
and Lombartzyde, and its left through Menin.

But, all unconscious of the numerical strength of the enemy
on his front, Sir John French at 9 p.m. on the 19th ordered the
attack to begin on 20th. The Ist Corps was to move with its
right on Ypres—Passchendaele, using the roads north of the
Ypres—Zonnebeke—Moorslede road, allotted to the IVth Corps.[1]
The IInd and IIIrd Corps (from north of the La Bassée Canal
to Ploegsteert, north of Armentières) were also to continue their
operations against the enemy.

On the morning of the 20th October the Ist Corps moved
forward to take its place in the line. The 2nd Division, marching via Ypres, took up positions from Zonnebeke to St. Julien,
Pilkem and Steenstraat, 4th Brigade on the right, 5th Brigade
on the left, 6th Brigade in reserve. The 1st Division, however,
was only able to reach the line Poperinghe—Elverdinghe, the
1st Gloucesters, with other units of the 3rd Brigade, billeting
in Poperinghe.

Far different from the valleys and hills north of the Aisne
River, with their thickly-wooded slopes and re-entrants, was the
low-lying country about the ancient city of Ypres, to which the
Ist Corps had now come. The ramparts encircling the old city
of the Flemish cloth-workers looked out on all sides over a flat
country, intersected here and there by canals, roads and railways.
East lay the Menin Road which, passing first through the villages

---

[1] The 3rd Cavalry Division and the 7th Division formed the IVth
British Corps.

of Hooge, Gheluvelt and Gheluwe, reached the town of Menin,
some 12 miles distant from Ypres. Every foot of the road from
the cross-roads just east of Gheluvelt, thence westwards until it
passed through the Menin Gate into Ypres itself, was in time
to become terribly familiar to every British soldier who served
in the Salient. About Hooge both sides of the road were thickly
wooded : Zouave and Sanctuary Woods lay south ; north were
the Château Woods and a large stretch of water—Bellewaarde
Lake. Farther east and before Gheluvelt was reached were the
Herenthage Château and Wood and Inverness Copse.

South again of the Menin Road and between it and the Ypres
—Comines Canal (which flowed south-east from the city) lay
various other woods and châteaux, all to become in time terribly
famous. These were Shrewsbury Forest, Armagh Wood, Battle
Wood and Maple Copse. Stirling Castle and the villages of
Zwarteleen, Zillebeke, Klein Zillebeke and Verbrandenmolen
were other landmarks.

The Ypres—Roulers railway, which crossed the Menin Road
at a point which later bore the significant name of Hell-Fire
Corner, formed an angle with the line, within which many a hard
and bloody contest was to be fought, for it included the Polygon
Wood, Veldhoek, Polderhoek, Poezelhoek, Becelaere, Zonnebeke,
Broodseinde and Westhoek. The first three named lay close to
Gheluvelt, a name which will for ever live in the history of the
Gloucestershire Regiment.

North of the Ypres—Roulers railway were three roads which
were soon to become known to the Gloucester men. The first
was the Ypres—Zonnebeke road, which passed through Potijze
and Frezenberg : the next was the Ypres—Poelcapelle road,
which ran through the villages of St. Jean and St. Julien : the
third road was that which, running due north from Ypres as far
as Pilkem, turned abruptly north-east to Langemarck. Three
or four miles north of Langemarck was the great forest of Houthulst.

Geographically the principal feature east and south of Ypres
is the Wytschaete—Passchendaele Ridge, which runs from south-
west to north-east, and for the possession of which some of the
fiercest struggles of the War took place. Two other features,
the Yser Canal, running north-west from the city, and the Ypres
—Comines Canal south-east of it, were to become conspicuous.
Ypres, itself, lay in a depression and was under observation from
north, east and south, the highest ground in the neighbourhood
being the Kemmel Ridge, south of the city.

Much of the ground was cut up by ditches and dykes, and

of small lakes there were several : moated-farm houses were common in pre-war days. In such country the digging of trenches was a difficult matter, that is to say, if those who intended occupying them had any desire to keep dry, for water lay very near the surface.

But on the 20th October, when the Gloucesters reached Poperinghe, the country-side still held points of beauty and was pleasant to look upon, for the opposing guns had as yet done little damage.

On the night 20th/21st October the position of the Ist Corps was as follows : 2nd Division behind the 3rd Cavalry Division,[1] 1st Division to the left rear of the 2nd Division at Poperinghe and Elverdinghe.

G.H.Q. orders, issued on the night of the 20th, stated that the Commander-in-Chief intended acting vigorously with the Ist Corps which, on the 21st, was to advance in the direction of Thorout, using the road Ypres—Passchendaele—Roulers and the roads to the north.

' This Corps will attack the enemy wherever met.'

The 1st Division was ordered to march to Langemarck and attack from there, the 3rd Brigade being detailed as advanced guard : the 2nd Division was to attack Passchendaele.

At 1.45 a.m. the Gloucesters paraded and marched off at the head of the Brigade via Elverdinghe—Boesinghe and Pilkem to Langemarck. The early stages of the march were carried out in pitch darkness and the Battalion could therefore see little of the surrounding country. Just east of Boesinghe the Brigade crossed the Yser Canal, and a little farther on, after passing through Pilkem, which stands on what was known later as the Pilkem Ridge, took the road south of the Ypres—Staden railway, crossing *en route* the Hannebeck, a small stream running from northwest to south-east, south-west of Langemarck.

It was daylight, however, when the 3rd Brigade reached the village and orders were received to attack the Germans who were holding Poelcapelle village and station immediately. The Queen's and South Wales Borderers were to form the firing-line : the Gloucesters (who had acted as advanced guard) were placed in reserve.

The Queen's advanced in a north-easterly direction astride the Ypres—Staden railway on Poelcapelle Station : the South Wales Borderers were deployed on their right with the village as their objective. Heavy shell-fire met the advance and the attack

[1] Holding the line Zonnebeke—St. Julien—Langemarck, with the 7th Division on its right from Zonnebeke and Kruiseecke to Zandvoorde.

progressed slowly but steadily. German infantry were then advancing from the north, while on the left French cavalry were gradually being driven back, exposing the left of the 3rd Brigade. In order to counteract this thrust the Gloucesters, who had remained south of the Hannebeck stream, were ordered to send forward a company to act as flank guard. Accordingly, B Company (Captain Radice) moved forward and occupied Langemarck railway station, thus guarding the left flank of the 3rd Brigade. The village itself was then under violent shell-fire.

At about 10 a.m. the remainder of the Battalion was ordered to support the Queen's. C Company (Captain Temple) pushed through Langemarck and along the Koekuit—Staden road : D Company (Major R. M. S. Gardner), on the right of C, advanced between the road and the railway : A remained in Battalion Reserve south of Langemarck.

The advanced guard of C Company, under Lieutenant Wetherall, occupied Koekuit village after very little opposition, but considerable rifle-fire was coming from the direction of Mangalaere, farther to the west, causing several casualties. On the right difficult and enclosed country held up the advance of D Company, led by No. 13 platoon under Lieutenant Young. Gates and gardens on the outskirts of the village had to be nego- tiated, and by the time the leading platoon was able to deploy there were no signs of C Company. But Lieutenant Young, know- ing that he had to keep touch on his left with the latter Company and on his right with the Queen's, pushed on and eventually saw Lieutenant Wetherall's platoon on the rising ground to the left. Farther still to the left Captain Capel, with two platoons of C Company, had taken up a position on the right of Koekuit. Uncertain as to the exact disposition of Lieutenant Wetherall, Captain Temple went up to the village and as a result sent up his last platoon to reinforce the line.

About midday the enemy launched his first attack from Man- galaere. This was promptly brought to a standstill by Lieutenant Wetherall's men, who were lining a ditch facing north. About one hundred Germans attacked by short rushes, but could not get nearer than 600 yards : they then began to dig in but, losing more men, gave up the attempt and ran back to the hedges and cover about Mangalaere.

During this attack Captain W. A. M. Temple was shot through the right lung and shoulder,[1] and soon after Captain A. Capel

---

[1] Captain Temple died in the Casualty Clearing Station on the 23rd October. In him the Battalion lost a most gallant and efficient officer, beloved by all ranks and most sincerely mourned.

5

(second-in-command of the Company) received a bullet through the right eye.

At this period, and throughout the remainder of the day, heavy fire was maintained by the enemy from the direction of Poelcapelle railway station : it was directed on the Queen's and other troops attacking that locality. The Queen's were indeed having a very poor time of it, and as Lieutenant Young with his platoon topped a small rise, he could see their position some 400 yards off on the right of the railway. He halted his platoon for a while to open fire on the enemy who had just been beaten back by the Queen's, aided by the fire of C Company at Koekuit. Unfortunately, Lieutenant Young, in kneeling up to get a better view, was seriously wounded, but his platoon was led on by Sergt. Davis who, bearing down to the right, pushed on with the remainder of D Company which was just arriving in support. But the situation on this flank was becoming serious, and eventually the Queen's were forced to retire, D Company of the Gloucesters having to conform : a new position was then taken up in a ditch facing north-east.

On the left flank also (held by B Company) things had not been going well. The French had continued to fall back under heavy pressure and their cyclist scouts reported the woods in front full of Germans who could not be held up. B Company had been pushed farther forward to assist the left of C Company, and A advanced through Langemarck to 200 yards along the Koekuit road. The Machine-Gun Section, under Lieutenant Duncan, was also sent off to protect the exposed left flank.

Shortly after the first attack on Koekuit, Lieutenant Wetherall received further supports, i.e. a sergeant and 15 men of the Scots Guards of the 1st Brigade. They were placed on the right of C Company and protected that flank while the Queen's were falling back.

Another attack developed at about 2 p.m. against Koekuit, some two hundred Germans advancing along the main road from Staden. Again they were brought to a standstill by Lieutenant Wetherall's men, though the latter by this time were fast dwindling in numbers. The country through which both attacks were made was enclosed, giving a poor field of fire.

Matters now began rapidly to take a turn for the worse. Both flanks were threatened by the advancing enemy and casualties were becoming more frequent. Lieutenant Wetherall then sent back a message to Captain Temple, only to learn that the latter was lying wounded in a ditch some 300 yards away. He therefore went back to see him and to ask for reinforcements. The whole of C Company was, however, fully engaged, but Captain Temple was able to explain the position of Captain Radice with B Company, and suggested the latter might be able to assist. Captain Radice immediately gave Lieutenant Wetherall about 30 men, telling him to get back and re-occupy the position as it appeared to be the key to the defence. Whilst he was away the few surviving defenders had begun to evacuate that place, but Lieutenant Wetherall (with his reinforcements) succeeded in re-occupying the position, while B Company occupied Grutesaele Farm about 250 yards south-west.

The time was now about 4 p.m. Hostile fire on this flank began to slacken, but on the left of D Company heavy machine-gun fire opened. Shortly afterwards Lieutenant Caunter through his field-glasses saw columns of the enemy about to debouch from a road near the railway about 700 yards on the right front. In three intense bursts of rapid fire the Gloucesters broke up the threatened attack. The enemy, however, shelled the position and several wounded men lying in a ditch were killed.

For his stubborn defence and skill in handling his men Lieutenant Wetherall was subsequently awarded the Military Cross —one of the first in the War. C.S.M. Smith, Sergt. Stevens and Corpl. Birley all ably assisted in repulsing the enemy's attacks on Koekuit, whilst Sergt. Bray of B Company, having led his platoon forward to support C Company, maintained his position for several hours under heavy fire, until ordered to withdraw : his platoon suffered 14 casualties.

The line now held by the Gloucesters was a pronounced salient, but they clung to their position until midnight when, under orders, the Battalion withdrew to the farm south-west of Langemarck. Lack of stretcher-bearers somewhat delayed the withdrawal, otherwise it was carried out successfully and without loss.

As a result of the fighting on the 21st October the German advance had been stemmed, but the British attacks on Poelcapelle and Passchendaele had failed, though sufficient ground had been gained to enable the 3rd Brigade and 2nd Division to hold Lange-marck and Zonnebeke securely—no mean achievement in the face of the great superiority of the enemy in numbers and artillery, for the attacks of the new Fourth German Army had begun.

During the day the 1st Guards Brigade had come up on the left of the 3rd Brigade and had made good a line facing north from Langemarck as far west as Steenstraat : the 2nd Brigade was in reserve at Boesinghe.

Apart from the casualties to officers already mentioned, the total losses in other ranks suffered by the Battalion on the 21st October was 48.

For the 3rd Brigade the 22nd October was a day of comparative rest, the Gloucesters remaining in bivouacs round the farm, just south of the Hannebeck, where they improved the trenches dug during the night. At about 4 p.m. a large barn, in which A and C Companies were billeted, received a direct hit from the enemy's artillery and 5 men were killed and 12 wounded.

At 2.30 a.m. on the 23rd two platoons of A Company, under Captain Rising, were sent up to the northern outskirts of Langemarck in close support of the Welch. These two platoons, Nos. 4 and 3 (Lieutenants Hippisley and Baxter), were used to fill a small gap on the left of the Welch to link up with the right of the Coldstream Guards (1st Brigade). The two platoons dug themselves in, No. 4 to the right of the road, No. 3 across the road, in a narrow trench protected by a low barricade, and spread out to the left. From this position Koekuit was in full view for a considerable way. There was, however, a certain amount of dead ground about 500 yards long where the Kortebeek stream flowed across the front between steep banks some 5 feet high.

At 7.30 a.m. German columns were observed advancing from Koekuit. They came along the road, thence down along the banks of the Kortebeek where they collected in large numbers. During the advance they were covered by their guns, which opened heavy fire on Langemarck and on the trenches in front of the village. About 9 a.m., however, having fired a farm and hay-stacks on the southern banks, about 400 yards from the British line, they advanced under cover of the smoke. A party of the enemy also tried to advance down the road : they were led by a man carrying a flag. The latter was soon shot down and the party driven back. Covered by heavy machine-gun fire the enemy advanced to within 200 yards of the British trenches and then crawled through a root field to within 100 yards. Here they tried to build up a firing-line.

The German machine-gun was soon put out of action by the Gloucesters, but Captain Rising, seeing how serious the situation was becoming, went back for supports and succeeded in diverting No. 15 platoon, under Lieutenant Yalland, which was moving up with the rest of D Company to assist the Welch Regiment farther to the right. With these men he was able to strengthen the line on the left of the road.

Suddenly the situation became critical. In front of the Coldstream Guards there was a ditch leading up from the Kortebeek, undiscovered in the darkness by the relieving company. Along this covered approach the Germans had been creeping forward : there was a sudden rush and the Guards were taken in rear and flank. The Coldstreamers, however, managed to fall back some 200 yards to a fresh position in a turnip field. Here, greatly assisted by the three platoons of Gloucesters under Captain Rising, they held on.

The Gloucester platoons, exposed on one flank, were attacked again and again, but beat off every fresh attempt. Lieutenants Hippisley and Yalland fell dead, and Lieutenant Baxter was seriously wounded. The casualties among the other ranks of the platoons were severe.

Having tried in vain to overwhelm the Gloucesters, the enemy at about 1 p.m. gradually drew off, covered by his artillery, and by 3.30 p.m., but for hostile shell-fire, there was no further activity on this sector of the front.

In addition to the officers mentioned, the losses of the 1st Battalion in this attack and defence were : A Company—2 N.C.O.s and 7 men killed, and 2 N.C.O.s and 22 men wounded ; D Company—2 N.C.O.s and 4 men killed, and 3 N.C.O.s and 9 men wounded—a total of 3 officers and 51 other ranks out of three platoons already involved in previous fighting. B and C Companies had lost 4 men each.

But for the splendid resistance of the two platoons of A and one platoon of D Companies, the enemy might have broken through.

Captain R. E. Rising, who commanded the three platoons, was awarded the D.S.O., the official record stating that he ' went up with supports and conspicuously controlled the defence of the Battalion's trenches against a determined attack by the enemy. But for this stout defence the line must have been penetrated '. Lieutenant Baxter was awarded the Military Cross for his share in this gallant little action. No. 8015 Sergt. T. Eddy and No. 9360 Sergt. T. Knight and N. 6732 Pte. W. Crossman of A Company, and No. 5233 Sergt. J. Wilson of D Company, were each awarded the D.C.M. for their conspicuous conduct. The official citation is unique in that it mentions the work of each member of the two platoons of A Company :

' For gallantry in carrying out the defence of their trenches after all their officers had been shot and repulsing a very determined attack which reached within 50 yards of them, with great loss to the enemy. The two platoons concerned lost about 60 per cent. of their strength and they fired about 500 rounds of ammunition per man during the attack.'

No. 9566 Pte. F. Dutton, No. 7671 Pte. E. Robbins and No.

9669 Pte. O. Taylor and Drummer Moulder were also highly commended for their fine work in carrying messages under fire and in collecting and taking up ammunition. No. 6668 Pte. C. Parry, though wounded in the shoulder and sent back to Headquarters, returned to the front trenches to conduct an ammunition cart he had met.

The Brigadier, commanding 3rd Brigade (General Landon), thus described the above action in a letter :

'We had a great fight yesterday and were attacked all day : the Brigade did splendidly and inflicted great loss on the enemy. The Queen's made a most gallant charge and the Gloucesters (100 strong) fired over 500 rounds per man, lost all their officers and many N.C.O.s, had the Germans within 50 yards, and not a man retired. Some of their bayonets were shot off their rifles and they had over sixty casualties. A grand performance. The Welch also sat out an attack by numbers of Germans and " downed them " gallantly.'

The next day over 1,500 dead Germans were counted in front of Langemarck and, including 600 prisoners, the enemy's total loss in that sector for three days' fighting could not have been much less than 10,000 men.

The fighting of 23rd October witnessed the complete failure of the German attempt to outflank the left of the Allied line.

'For the time being, any further thought of a break-through,' states the German official account of Ypres, 'was out of the question. The troops up to now had met the enemy full of a keen fighting spirit and had stormed his positions singing " Deutschland, Deutschland über Alles " regardless of casualties and had been one and all ready to die for their country.'

Again that ' Little Mighty Force ' (the B.E.F.) had prevailed against overwhelming numbers.

The remainder of A Company, under Captain McLeod, were sent off at about 2 p.m. to the left to support the Coldstream Guards. By 7 p.m. they reported that they had succeeded in re-occupying the trenches previously lost by the Guards and were in touch with D Company on their right. During the evening of the 23rd the remnants of the two platoons of D Company, under Captain Burn, with the M.G. Section, took over the defence of the trenches on the left of the Koekuit road. Before relief was possible many men of D Company sheltered in the northernmost houses of Langemarck. One section was unfortunately knocked out by a direct hit on a cottage. The rest of the Battalion in the meantime was in reserve in its old position southwest of Langemarck.

At 6.30 a.m. on the 24th, General Landon addressed the men

of A Company, and congratulated them on their splendid work
in the trenches on the previous day.

On this day reinforcements from the IXth French Army Corps
began to arrive : the 1st Division was relieved on the night
24th/25th and withdrew to a point south of the Ypres—Menin
road near Zillebeke. The Gloucesters, the last Battalion of the
3rd Brigade to leave their positions, marched at daybreak on the
25th via Wieltje to the second kilo stone on the Ypres—Gheluvelt
road, where they went into bivouacs near Bellewaarde Farm.
On the 26th the Battalion moved to Hooge and halted in the
woods round the Château and began digging shelter trenches.
When darkness had fallen orders were received to take up and
entrench a position immediately north of the main Ypres—
Gheluvelt road, in support of the 1st and 4th Guards Brigades.
The Battalion Diary gives this position as ' on road running
north and south through O of Veldhoek from main Ypres—
Gheluvelt road to the bend of the road just south of the road
junction of the five roads '.

This position was held throughout the 27th and 28th. At 6
p.m. the following message was received by the Gloucesters from
1st Brigade Headquarters : ' 1st Division has given me authority
to call upon you as a reserve in case of necessity.'   In accordance
with the above order Lieutenant Wetherall with 60 men, and
Lieutenant Duncan and the Machine-Gun Section, were sent
forward to report to, and come under the orders of, the 1st Coldstream Guards at the cross-roads at the ninth kilo stone on the
Menin road, south-east of Gheluvelt.

The Battalion had by this time dug itself in north of Veldhoek
village and held support trenches facing east, running roughly
parallel with, and about 200 yards in front of, the road leading
from the village towards the south-west corner of Polygon Wood.

The remaining battalions of the 3rd Brigade were in rear of
the Gloucesters, at Hooge.   Gheluvelt village lay about half-way
between the Gloucesters and the detachment which had been
sent forward to the cross-roads to fill a gap between the right
of the 1st Division and left of the 7th Division.

On the left of the Gloucester detachment were the 1st Coldstream Guards and other troops of the 1st Guards Brigade who
carried the line north to just west of Reutel.   From this point
the 2nd Division front extended to about a mile east of Broodseinde.

On the right of the Gloucester detachment were the 1st
Grenadier Guards of the 20th Brigade (7th Division), who had
on *their* right the Gordon Highlanders.   The 7th Division held

the line as far as Zandvoorde, whence the British front to the Ypres—Comines Canal opposite Hollebeke was held by the 3rd Cavalry Brigade (3rd Cavalry Division).

THE BATTLE OF GHELUVELT : 29TH–31ST OCTOBER

Still unconscious, apparently, of the great and overwhelming numbers pitted against him, Sir John French at 8.15 p.m. on the 28th October issued orders for the attack to continue on the morning of the 29th. But at about midnight information was received of a probable German attack on Gheluvelt at 5.30 a.m. and troops were warned to be on the alert. For some reason unknown an impression became current that the enemy's attack would be made south of the Ypres—Menin Road, from the direction of Kruiseecke : there were also rumours that the German Kaiser had come up to urge his famous troops to break through the British front.

The German attack began punctually at 5.30 a.m. on the morning of the 29th. A thick mist, which prevented anyone seeing more than a few yards ahead, enabled the enemy to draw close to the British line unperceived. He broke through the line of junction between the 1st and 7th Divisions on the Gheluvelt road, about a mile east of the village, practically annihilating the troops of both divisions immediately north and south of the road, i.e. Coldstream Guards, Black Watch, Grenadier Guards and Gordons.

The detachment of Gloucesters had been split up into small parties to fill gaps in the line of the Coldstreamers and Black Watch north of the road, and the Grenadiers south of the road. They were spread over a front of about 500 yards. One of the machine-guns had been pushed about 200 yards north of the road and the other practically on the road, sited to fire down it.

The first definite news Lieut.-Colonel Lovett (commanding 1st Gloucesters) had of the break-through was from Lieutenant Duncan, who reached Battalion Headquarters at about 6.30 a.m. to report the loss of his guns : he also stated that the Germans had reached the trenches of the Black Watch, on the right of the Guards, and had got behind his position. Lieutenant Wetherall and several men had been wounded in this first attack.

An hour and a half after the storm had broken, that is to say at about 7 a.m., Lieut.-Colonel Lovett received a verbal message from Brigade Headquarters to advance his Battalion from north of Veldhoek village due east on Gheluvelt and counter-attack the enemy. The C.O. directed his companies to advance and act as the situation demanded.

But the fog and the (then) thickly wooded country through which the advance took place made the keeping of direction extremely difficult. Moreover, companies moved forward at slightly different times. The day's fighting, therefore, so far as it concerns the Gloucesters, is very disconnected and not easy to follow.

The first Companies to move forward were C and D.

C advanced on the left into Gheluvelt Château grounds. At the very outset of the advance several casualties occurred. Captain Radice was hit early, and the Company was seriously handicapped in the matter of officers. Lieutenant Wetherall (as already mentioned) had been hit in the knee, while Captain Chapman and Lieutenant Foster, the two other officers of the Company, had advanced with a small party to support the Scots Guards on the eastern outskirts of Gheluvelt and had become detached. From this stage C Company practically ceased to exist as a Company ; the few men who had not become casualties attached themselves to other Companies, and even to other regiments, so great was the confusion in the mist and stress of battle.

D Company, having begun its advance, eased off to the right, pushing along the Menin Road until within 300 yards of the Kruiseecke cross-roads, where they helped to rally the shattered remnants of the gallant 1st Brigade. Violent shell-fire swept the whole area and again and again the Gloucesters were attacked from the north-east. Using the main road as a breastwork, half of this Company faced north, whilst the remainder made what use they could of a ditch which faced east. The Germans continued to pour troops through the gap they had made in the British line : these, passing some 400 to 500 yards north of D Company, seriously threatened the line of retreat of the latter. No other British troops either to the north or to the south were in sight—only this one small party of gallant men striving to arrest and break the flow of that vast human tide. For the moment it is now necessary to turn to A and B Companies.

A Company, on the left, had advanced close behind C to the assistance of the Black Watch and Scots Guards. Of their movements during the early morning little is known. Lieutenant Greenslade was sent off with a section of his platoon to the left of the Scots Guards where, for the time being, all was quiet excepting for artillery fire. At about 10 a.m., however, they were suddenly attacked from flank and rear. The gallant fellows put up a stout resistance, but in the face of overwhelming numbers resistance was useless and all were either killed, wounded, or taken prisoner. Lieutenant Greenslade, together with an officer of the Scots Guards and some 120 men of all units (4 of the Gloucesters all slightly wounded were among them), were forced to surrender. Captain Chapman and Lieutenant H. K. Foster (both of C Company, which was near by) also became casualties, the former wounded and taken prisoner, the latter killed.

During this period B Company (Captain Blunt), which had advanced behind D, had skirted north of Gheluvelt Church and, leaving the Guards on their left still fighting hard in the Château grounds, crossed the Menin Road near the windmill at the eastern extremity of Gheluvelt, and pushed on towards Kruiseecke. This Company had to fight its way forward, but succeeded in reaching the rising ground to the south of the road, about 800 yards in front of Gheluvelt. Here, however, they were brought to a standstill, for gradually the pressure of the great mass of Germans, pitted against them, began to tell. Still fighting magnificently, the little Company of brave men fell back slowly to a point between the main road and a windmill some 200 yards to the south. During this retirement Lieutenant A. D. Harding was mortally wounded. Two men—one Pte. Ireland and the other a man from No. 7 Platoon—volunteered to bring in their platoon commander. They succeeded in dressing Lieutenant Harding's wound. But within a few minutes the Germans attacked again and Ireland was wounded in the leg and his comrade killed by a piece of shrapnel. The gallant private, nevertheless, stuck to his task and carried Lieutenant Harding back to safety, only to find that the wound was fatal. There were countless deeds such as this during that day of terrible fighting.

Turning again to D Company (under Major R. M. S. Gardner) : here also the same state of affairs existed, i.e. heavy pressure maintained by troops who greatly outnumbered the gallant Gloucesters. The latter stemmed the advance of the Germans as long as possible but were finally forced to withdraw. Fortunately a portion of A Company (Captain Rising) had been able to push forward to the right rear of Major Gardner's Company and covered the retirement of the latter to a second position some 300 yards farther back where another stand was made. Nevertheless, small groups had been cut off, a typical instance being a party of D Company, under Sergt. Warwick and Corpl. Birley.[1] They had taken up a position to the north of the Menin Road.

[1] Corporal Birley escaped from Germany, and in 1916 rejoined the 28th as an officer.

They numbered but seven all told, but still, after the Guards had retired, they clung with the utmost courage and tenacity to their precarious position and were eventually captured, fighting to the end.

Noon arrived and the 3rd Brigade was advanced forward to assist the shattered 1st Brigade. The South Wales Borderers, advancing on the left, reached the eastern edge of Gheluvelt Château grounds : the Welch pushed through the village itself and occupied the far edge and a portion of the cemetery to the south of the Menin Road : the Queen's, who were farther south, pushing ahead, eventually took up position to the right front of the Welch. The strain on the tired Gloucesters was considerably relieved by the advance of the three above Battalions, and they gradually withdrew (all that was left of them), all but a small party consisting of Captain Blunt, Lieutenants Morris and Bush and about some 50 or 60 men who were holding on to a spur with a windmill out in front of the line some 500 or 600 yards to their right front. Rumours had reached this small party of a counter-attack to be made by the 3rd Brigade and they gallantly determined to hang on to their advanced post in order to assist. Unfortunately the attack failed, chiefly owing to enfilade artillery fire from the direction of Becelaere, and the 3rd Brigade was forced to fall back to its original line about 200 yards from the village where, during the night of the 29th/30th, all battalions dug themselves in. Captain Blunt's party was relieved during the evening by the 2nd Queen's of the 7th Division, and withdrew to Veldhoek, where the remainder of the Gloucesters were concentrated.

Captain A. G. McBurn, East Surrey Regiment, who had been attached to D Company from the outbreak of war, was killed during the morning. Only Major Gardner and Lieutenant Caunter were now left to bring the Company back to a position just east of Gheluvelt Church, and later to Veldhoek. A Company had withdrawn much about the same time and was on the left of D Company.

As may be imagined, the day's fighting had caused much disorganization in the Battalion, but at Veldhoek the men were sorted out.

The casualties for the twelve hours' fighting totalled 7 officers and 160 other ranks, killed, wounded and missing.[1]

The night of the 29th/30th October was particularly quiet and,

---

[1] In detail : 3 officers, 14 N.C.O.s and 42 other ranks killed ; 2 officers, 14 N.C.O.s and 50 other ranks wounded ; 2 officers, 8 N.C.O.s and 26 other ranks prisoners of war.

indeed, so far as the Gloucesters were concerned, the 30th showed little more than normal conditions.   Certainly there were several alarms and the air seemed to be full of German aeroplanes, but most of the fighting took place farther south.   The 3rd Cavalry Division at Zandvoorde were being attacked, the enemy bombing their line : the 7th Division, on their left, were also driven back and another gap caused which had to be filled by two battalions from the 4th (Guards) Brigade (2nd Division) and two from the 2nd Brigade (1st Division).

Throughout the night of the 29th/30th October the continual rumbling of wheels behind the German lines announced the movement of troops, foreboding ill to the gallant defenders of Ypres.   German reinforcements (new corps) were arriving which were soon to be flung into the line to effect a complete break-through, which hitherto had been frustrated by the staunch defence put up by thin lines of tired khaki troops who formed a ring of steel around the ancient city of Flanders.

Throughout the 30th the Gloucesters remained in their support trenches about Veldhoek : they lost 7 men killed and 5 wounded during the day from shell-fire, but made no attack on the enemy. They had been ordered to hold themselves in readiness to assist the 7th Division if necessary, also to continue their line of entrenchments southwards across the Menin Road.   At night they received orders to be ready to support with the bayonet the Welch and the Queen's should those Battalions be attacked : the Gloucesters were to use every man—leaving none in support— if the enemy broke through.

When darkness fell on the 30th the line of the 3rd Brigade in front and in the neighbourhood of Gheluvelt was held as follows : The Welch held a frontage of about 250 yards, about a quarter of a mile east of the village and with their right resting on the Menin Road ; on the left of the Welch were the South Wales Borderers, who joined up with the Scots Guards (1st Guards Brigade, 1st Division) on their left ; on the right of the Welch were the 1st Queen's (less one Company), whose left rested on the Menin Road ; on the right of the Queen's were two Companies of the 2nd K.R.R. Corps (of the 2nd Brigade), then the remaining Company of the Queen's and two Companies of the Loyal North Lancashire Regiment.   In rear of this front line were the Gloucesters at Veldhoek and two Companies of the 2nd K.R.R. Corps and two of the Loyal North Lancs immediately south-west of Gheluvelt.   The whole front from the Ypres—Comines Canal, just east of Gheluvelt, to about a mile east of Broodseinde, was held by three weak and worn-out British divisions, i.e. 1st,

2nd and 7th, while against them were pitted almost double that number of practically fresh German troops.

The 31st was to be the supreme test of that thin line of khaki.

' The line that stood between the British Army and ruin was composed of tired, haggard and unshaven men, unwashed, plastered with mud, many in little more than rags.   But they had their guns, rifles and bayonets and, at any rate, plenty of rifle ammunition, whilst the artillery men always managed to have rounds available at the right place at critical moments.' [1]

For the 1st Division the night of the 30th/31st October was one of unrest.   With the German trenches only two to three hundred yards away, and a bright moon until 2 a.m. on the 31st, sniping and desultory shelling did not cease.

Very early on the morning of the 31st the British line was subjected to a very heavy bombardment.   The church at Gheluvelt, houses of the village and the windmill were reduced still further to a mass of ruins.   Just after 6 a.m.—it was by then daylight—the Germans attacked the whole line of the 1st Division. Only at one point, i.e. the corner of the salient—an orchard— held by the Queen's, did the enemy pierce the line : at all other points he was repulsed with very heavy losses.   Two counter-attacks to retake the portion of the line lost were unsuccessful. The German guns still continued to pour a merciless hail of shell upon the hard-pressed British infantry.   By 9.30 a.m. the Welch had suffered terribly.   Their right flank had been practically blown out of their trenches and fell back to the support line : the left flank remained in its position covering the right of the South Wales Borderers.

At about 5.30 a.m. the Gloucesters were ordered to move forward one Company to join the K.R.R. Corps, who by now had only one reserve Company out of the line, the other reserve Company having been absorbed as supports to the Queen's. Later, at about 10.30 a.m., the Battalion was ordered to take up a fresh line slightly farther east, to stretch south and cover the western edge of Gheluvelt village on either side of the Menin Road.   Urgent messages from units in the front line were sent back to Brigade Headquarters asking for reinforcements : many of these were never received, the gallant runners being shot down or blown to bits ere they reached their destination.   Similarly many messages from Brigade Headquarters to battalions in the line were never delivered, or else only after great difficulty.   An instance of this may be found in the story of Pte. Shipway of the Gloucesters.

[1] From the *Official History of the War, Military Operations.*

Shipway at this period was one of the Battalion signallers, attached to Brigade Headquarters near ' Clapham Junction ', some 2,000 yards west of Veldhoek. Early in the morning he was given a message to his Battalion by the Brigade-Major. At the same time another orderly, belonging to the South Wales Borderers, was handed a note to his commanding officer. Both men set out together on bicycles. A short distance along the Menin Road the South Wales Borderer orderly was knocked off his bicycle by a piece of shrapnel and killed. Shipway, therefore, took on both messages : he delivered the one to his own unit and obtained leave to take the other to the South Wales Borderers, who still held front-line trenches. Under very heavy shell-fire, from which there was little or no cover, Shipway made his way for 300 to 400 yards along the rear of the trenches, safely delivered his message and obtained a receipt for it. But owing to heavy shell-fire he had to wait for two hours before he was allowed to return to his own Battalion. On the way back he was wounded in the hand and wrist, but volunteered to return with an answer to the Brigade. His devotion to duty and resource in an emergency were rewarded by the D.C.M.

Through the gap which had been made in the line of the Queen's—the corner of the salient—the Germans had poured in great strength and were able to enfilade the flank of their opponents. About midday the Welch and Queen's were driven farther back and, even with the few supporting troops, were unable to stem the tide. Against the K.R.R. Corps, Queen's, Welch, South Wales Borderers and Scots Guards—five very weak battalions who all told numbered barely one thousand men —the enemy had flung thirteen battalions, of which six at least were quite fresh troops.

Gheluvelt was taken by the enemy and it was touch and go whether the line could possibly bend any more without completely breaking.

The C.O. of the Gloucesters was ordered to rally and collect the men who were streaming back, more dead than alive, from the awful shambles in front.

' Men from the 3rd Brigade, from the Guards and Black Watch, all mixed up and shaken, were gathered together by Lieut.-Colonel Lovett as they staggered back along the Menin Road, and by Major Ingram some yards farther back in the woods to the south of the road. Arms were picked up and as soon as the men had recovered they were sent forward again. Some Gordons, including an N.C.O. with ammunition mules, came up about this time and were also directed to their unit south of Gheluvelt. Counter-attacks were organized by the Commanding Officer and companies, acting on their own, were able, after

desperate fighting, to hold back the enemy.   B and D Companies had
the hardest of the fighting.   The former Company, with two platoons
on either side of the road, Lieutenant Morris on the north and Lieutenant Bush on the south, were ordered to advance and drive the enemy
from the houses on the western outskirts of Gheluvelt village.   This
they succeeded in doing and this portion of the line was held firm until
the Battalion was relieved.

     ' D Company, now only eighty strong, was ordered up at about mid-
day and told to recapture the trench which had been lost, immediately
to the north of the Menin Road.   The Company, under Major Gardner,
advanced under a terrific shell fire until they came in sight of the front-
line trenches.   Those immediately in front were safely in British hands,
and it was evident that the break had occurred more to the south.
Accordingly Major Gardner led the Company across a stretch of extremely open ground to a sunken road where the few remaining men
rallied.   There were only thirty left.   Knowing the urgency of the
situation, Major Gardner decided he could not wait for the possible
arrival of any more men and so ordered a further advance to the attack.
Within a few yards he and fifteen men fell and the remainder, under
Lieutenant J. Caunter, were forced to remain in a sunken lane where
they gallantly held out until the Germans swarmed over the position
and took prisoners the few who remained alive.   It seems highly probable that D Company had somehow pushed forward at a point where
there was a gap in the attacking line of enemy.[1]   The British front line
here had been almost wiped out and the enemy had pushed on.   This
would account for the fact that no British troops were visible and that
the Germans who were encountered later were advancing in small
columns and not as attackers in the first line.' [2]

During the critical events of the morning of the 31st Generals
French and Haig, who were at Hooge, awaited anxiously every
report from the front line.   At about 1.30 p.m. a shell fell on
and exploded in the Headquarters of the 1st and 2nd Divisions,
killing or wounding the two divisional commanders and several
other staff officers.   General Landon (commanding 3rd Brigade)
was then called upon to command the 1st Division and Lieut.-
Colonel Lovett to command the 3rd Brigade.   As the hours
passed the situation became gradually worse : at 2 p.m. another
powerful German attack wiped out the right flank of the South
Wales Borderers and the remnants of that Battalion fell back
through Gheluvelt Château grounds to the light railway.   From
this position they gallantly counter-attacked, drove the enemy
back and took up a position along the south-eastern edge of the
château woods.

Between 2 and 3 p.m., just when all seemed lost, news reached
G.H.Q. of a splendid counter-attack made by the 2nd Worcesters
of the 2nd Division under Major Hankey, whereby the enemy was

---

[1] Yes ! this was so.
[2] From Captain R. M. Grazebrook's *War Narratives*, 1914–1915.

cleared out of the woods north of Gheluvelt and the northern outskirts of the village occupied, the Worcesters linking up with the right of the South Wales Borderers. The effect was electrical : troops rallied and the line of the 1st Division was saved. Behind the Gloucesters, the Queen's and Welch were afforded an opportunity to rally and re-form. The moment of extreme danger had passed.

At one period during the afternoon the Germans rushed up a field-gun on to the Menin Road and prepared to fire down on to Veldhoek, where the Gloucesters were. But without a moment's delay Lieutenant Blewitt of the 54th Battery, R.F.A., man-handled one of his guns into position on the road and opened fire. The German gun fired one round and Blewitt's gunners two : the second shot of the latter blew the hostile gun and crew into the air.[1]

The Gloucesters then built a barricade across the road at Veldhoek cross-roads, and from this position shot down dozens of Germans who were still advancing along the road to Ypres. At about 6 p.m. those troops north of the Menin Road were ordered to take up a fresh line stretching from the left of the Gloucesters at Veldhoek past Polderhoek Château up to Polygon Wood. The movement was completed at about 9 p.m. without further trouble, the enemy apparently being too exhausted to continue his attack during the night.

Thus passed the 31st October, the most critical day in the Battle of Ypres, 1914, and one which will for all time live in the annals of the British Army as a splendid feat of arms. The 1st Division had made a most gallant stand and the part played by ' The Old Braggs '[2] did much to break the fighting spirit of the enemy at the psychological moment when one extra push by the latter might possibly have won through to Ypres and the Channel Ports.

The casualties suffered by the Gloucesters on the 31st were Major R. M. S. Gardner killed, Lieutenants Bush and Scott-Tucker wounded and Lieutenant Caunter missing.[3] The losses amongst other ranks were 66, nearly half of which were suffered by B Company. During the evening Major Ingram assumed

[1] One of the earliest instances of the use of high-explosive shell during the Great War, as the first round of this new explosive had been fired only a couple of hours earlier !

[2] The soubriquet of the 1st Gloucesters is ' The Old Braggs ', after a certain Colonel Bragg.

[3] Lieutenant Caunter was afterwards reported as a prisoner of war. He succeeded in escaping from Germany in July, 1917, and was later awarded the M.C. for his share of the fighting at Ypres, 1914.

command of the Battalion *vice* Lieut.-Colonel Lovett, who had
taken over command of the 3rd Brigade.

      *   *   *   *   *

On the 1st November the enemy's pressure was chiefly at
Messines and Wytschaete, though a portion of the 1st Brigade
was again temporarily driven from its trenches, the position being
restored by an immediate counter-attack.   The 3rd Brigade, now
complete again, with the Gloucesters in the line, came in for heavy
shell-fire and several infantry attacks.

During the day the barricade across the Menin Road at Veldhoek
and the houses on either side presented excellent cover for the
Battalion snipers.   Many Germans were picked off moving up
the road or among the ruins of Gheluvelt, and two N.C.O.s—
C.S.M. Long and C.Q.M.S. Mayell—accounted for many of the
enemy from one of the houses until driven downstairs by hostile
machine-gun fire.

In the evening the remnants of the 3rd Brigade were relieved
by the 2nd Brigade, and the Gloucesters, having handed over their
line to the K.R.R., marched back to Inverness Copse, about a
mile in rear.

Even on the 1st casualties had been heavy—76, of which
C Company lost the most.   The Battalion was now terribly weak
and could only muster between 200 and 300 all ranks.   A draft
of 50, which joined during the evening, only slightly increased its
strength.

At an early hour on the morning of the 2nd the Brigade,
numbering now about 800 all told, fell in and marched off in a
westerly direction along the Menin Road in the confident expecta-
tion of a real rest after the strenuous fighting of the past week.
But the situation was still too critical to allow troops to withdraw
out of the immediate neighbourhood of the front line, and before
the Gloucesters had passed through Hooge a halt was called.
Then, under orders, the whole column wheeled to the south into
Sanctuary Wood.

Considerable firing was heard during the morning from the
direction of Gheluvelt, and at about 1 p.m. the 3rd Brigade
received orders to advance and retake some trenches which had
been lost earlier in the morning.   The Brigade then moved off
to counter-attack towards Gheluvelt.   Shelled by ' coal-boxes ',
the Gloucesters pushed forward and crossed to the north of the
Menin Road, near ' Clapham Junction '.[1]   In the direction of
Veldhoek rifle fire was spluttering out accompanied by the ' rat-

---

[1] ' Clapham Junction ' was about 300 yards west of the western edge
of Inverness Copse.

tat-tat ' from a machine-gun mounted in a Belgian armoured car travelling up and down the Menin Road just short of the village. The situation was obscure, for no one knew where exactly the enemy had broken through : presumably it was south of the road as cavalry were seen galloping in that direction.   The Gloucesters next received orders to re-cross to the right (south) of the road, after reorganizing under cover of the Herenthage Wood, push north across the Bassevillebeck and up the further slope (known later as ' Tower Hamlets ').   A Company (Captain Rising) was left north of the road near the Veldhoek Château road, while B Company (Captain Blunt) advanced slowly through the woods, across the stream and up the hill to the eastern edge of the undergrowth fringing the Château of Herenthage.   C Company (Captain A. A. McLeod) followed B and, crossing up on the left of the latter, linked up with the remnants of the Bedfords and Yorkshires of the 7th Division.   On the left were a small number of French troops (part of Vidal's Force) and farther away, near the Menin Road, the Black Watch of the 1st Brigade.

Soon after the position was reached Captain McLeod was killed and Captain Blunt wounded in the shoulder—probably by a sniper. The Gloucesters then got into some trenches, which being very deep and narrow provided fair cover from shrapnel.

At about 6 p.m. D Company arrived behind the trenches held by A, B and C Companies.   Major Ingram was now up in the front line and in control.   He went forward to reconnoitre, for the situation in front was still far from clear.   Units at this period were much intermingled—Gloucesters, Welch, Bedfords, Yorks, Berkshires and a number of French troops, Turcos.   Nobody was actually in command until Brig.-General FitzClarence, from the 1st Brigade, took control of the front line.   An attack was then organized and a general advance ordered against the supposed German positions on either side of an isolated building which could be seen some 700 yards away.   The preliminary stages of this advance (it was now moonlight) were successful and a line of trenches on the farther side of the first field was rushed with much cheering : it was found occupied only by a few wounded Germans.   But the cheers had alarmed the enemy, for as the advance set out to cross the next field there was a sudden burst of rapid fire from the right front and a line of grey figures could be seen about a hundred yards off.   Firing then became general by the enemy in front, whilst behind the French troops who had refused to go forward without direct orders from one of their own officers, were busy shooting into the backs of the attacking troops.

The result was that the attack had to be abandoned and the

whole line fell back to the empty trenches previously mentioned.
The defence of this line was then reorganized by General Fitz-
Clarence, the 2nd Welch taking over the sector held by the
Gloucesters, who withdrew to Sanctuary Wood.

The total casualties suffered by the Battalion on the 2nd
November were 2 officers, 11 other ranks killed, Captain Blunt,
Lieutenant R. M. Grazebrook and 45 other ranks wounded, and
2 missing.

The night of the 2nd/3rd and the whole of the latter date passed
quietly, though several more casualties were suffered—2 killed
and 9 wounded—from shell-fire. In the evening a further (and
greatly welcome) reinforcement of 200 men, under Captain Pritchett, arrived.

An early-morning move up to a support position along the
near edge of Herenthage Wood, where a number of ' all-round
redoubts ' had been constructed, was the sole move of the
Gloucesters throughout the daylight hours of the 4th. They were
not, however, required and were soon moved back to Sanctuary
Wood. Late that night, however, they relieved the South Wales
Borderers in the front line, east of Herenthage Wood, with orders
to hold on for twenty-four hours *at ' all costs '*, after which they
would be relieved. No infantry attack took place on the 5th,
but hostile shell-fire was very heavy and at nightfall the
Gloucesters had lost 41 other ranks (13 killed and 28 wounded).
The 3rd Brigade was relieved by the 6th Cavalry Brigade that
night and moved back to Railway Wood, near Bellewaarde Farm.

The morning of the 6th was spent in reorganizing, but that was
carried out only just in time, for the Germans having resumed their
attacks on the southern end of the Salient, French troops, defending the line south of the Zillebeke—Zandvoorde road, had been
forced back, uncovering the right flank of the Irish Guards
(4th Brigade) who, with other troops, had been sent down to that
part of the line under Lord Cavan. The Guards had put up a
stout resistance, but they were driven in and a dangerous gap had
been formed. The three regiments of Household Cavalry arrived
at a gallop, flung themselves into the gap and restored the situation
after driving back the enemy several hundred yards. But again
the French were forced back, creating another gap on the right
which the Germans immediately exploited. The Blues were put
into the gap, but a certain amount of ground had to be abandoned :
Zwarteleen and ' Hill 60 ' were reoccupied.

The Gloucesters, as well as other troops, were ordered down to
this part of the line. The Battalion left Bellewaarde Farm at
4 p.m. and, arriving in the dark, were immediately told to relieve

the cavalry north of Zwarteleen. The situation in this part of the line, through the constant moving of units, was most confused, but eventually the Gloucesters, having relieved the Horse Guards, consolidated the eastern end of Zwarteleen and the woods further to the north. Touch with the Munsters in the woods on the left was obtained and snipers posted in the houses. The actual frontage occupied by the Battalion was considerable and could only be divided roughly into sectors held by batches of men with here and there one of the few surviving officers.

The morning of the 7th was misty and little reconnaissance (of any value) was possible. At about 6 a.m. orders were received for the Gloucesters to assist in an attack to be made by the 22nd Brigade (7th Division) on the right, by firing into the wood on the left and left front. On account of fog, through which it was impossible to see for more than a few yards, this order had to be cancelled. Later, however, word was received that the 22nd Brigade had captured their objective and that the enemy's trenches opposite the Gloucesters were empty. The latter accordingly pushed forward in two lines, the first led by Captain Rising and the second by Major Ingram, 50 yards in rear. Other troops of the 3rd Brigade were to support this advance. But in issuing from Zwarteleen the Battalion was met by intense rifle and machine-gun fire : the enemy was holding some detached houses at the eastern end of the village.

The ' Old Braggs ' were sorely tried that day. Their advance had been hurried, without definite orders. Officers and men alike were exhausted and could do no more than clear a few of the houses. Many men had to lie down all day in the open and only a few could get back to the trenches they had dug the night before. Almost superhuman efforts were made by the few surviving officers to keep control of the poor fellows who were worn out after many days and nights of the severest trials. Major Ingram and Lieutenant Halford tried their utmost to check a tendency to retire to the cover of the houses, but there were not enough officers to lead the men forward. Lieutenant M. Kershaw, with his platoon of A Company on the right, had been cut off and nothing more was ever heard of him.[1] Major Ingram, in crossing the road in full view of the enemy for the fifth time, was shot in the knee whilst attempting to point out the line to be held. But he managed to crawl to Captain Rising and discuss the situation with him before he was carried back to the dressing-station. A few minutes later Captain Rising himself was brought into the dressing-station mortally wounded. This very gallant officer,

[1] He was killed on that day (7th November 1914).

who had so splendidly carried out his duty in many a desperate
situation and was beloved by all in the Regiment, died the same
day of his wounds.   Just a little later and Lieutenant Halford was
wounded.   The only surviving officers were now Captain Pritchett (who had taken over command of the Battalion), Lieutenant
Duncan (acting Adjutant), Lieutenant Morris (B Company) and
the Quartermaster.

At roll-call that evening only 213 men answered their names,
the strength by Companies being A—61, B—44, C—49 and D—59.
No accurate casualty list for the 6th or 7th November is in
existence, but the estimated losses in other ranks were 43 killed,
47 wounded and 8 missing.   There were no sergeants left, so
deserving men amongst the ' other ranks ' were promoted direct.

Amongst those who specially distinguished themselves during
the desperate fighting at Zillebeke was L/Corpl. G. Royal.   He
was a bandsman and, with other members of the band, had
become a stretcher-bearer—very gallant fellows they were too.
On the 7th November, Royal organized a first-aid post in a cottage
behind Zwarteleen and throughout the day he carried out his
work under very heavy shell-fire.   The roof of his cottage was
blown in by shells, but with the utmost coolness and courage he
supervised the removal of the wounded to a place of greater
safety.   During the day the stretcher-bearers of the Gloucesters
collected the wounded not only of their own Battalion but of the
Welch and a French regiment.   From all these men L/Corpl.
Royal was selected for his gallantry and awarded the D.C.M.

Major Ingram, who was largely responsible for the manner in
which the Gloucesters had held their own in defence and whose
gallant conduct had set so fine an example to his men, was
subsequently awarded the D.S.O.

During the night of the 7th Captain Bosanquet with 20 men
joined the Battalion, bringing the total of officers up to 4.   He
assumed the duties of adjutant.[1]

On the 8th the remnants of the 1st Gloucesters were relieved
and marched back to Herenthage Wood, where they remained for
two days in close support of the 1st Brigade.   Captain Blunt
rejoined, but no fresh men arrived to fill the gaps in the ranks.

On the afternoon of the 10th a move was made to north of the
Menin Road.   The Gloucesters again bivouacked near Bellewaarde Farm and dug trenches along the road east of the Lake.

---

[1] He held the post of Adjutant until wounded in December.   In
November the Battalion War Diary was looted from his valise and much
valuable information was thus lost.

THE BATTLE OF NONNE BOSSCHEN : 11TH NOVEMBER
THE PRUSSIAN GUARD ATTACK

None of the survivors who were present at Ypres on the 11th November 1914 will ever forget the final and violent effort of the Germans on that day to break through the British line which barred the way to Ypres and the Channel Ports. Twelve battalions of the famous Prussian Guard, with other German troops,[1] were brought up to do what their comrades had failed to accomplish. In all the panoply of war, four of the most renowned regiments of the German Army, each consisting of three battalions of fresh troops, advanced as if on parade against the thin line of khaki-clad troops, who for three weeks had been engaged in incessant fighting and were almost worn out from fatigue.

The attack was spread over a wide front, but only with that about the centre of Shrewsbury Forest, then across the Menin Road to the south-western corner of the Polygon Wood (the front attacked by the German 2nd Guard Division) is this story concerned.

The morning of the 11th was grey and foggy, but as soon as there was any light (shortly after 6 a.m.) the enemy's artillery opened a terrific fire on the British line. There was no doubt that it presaged another violent attack. Worn out as they were, our gallant infantry in the front line crouched behind whatever scanty cover they had in their shallow trenches and awaited the advance of the hostile infantry.

It was, however, about 9 a.m. when the Prussian troops moved forward on either side of the Menin Road. They came on in great numbers in many lines with their rifles at the secure, i.e. under their arms. They were caught by the British artillery, which tore gaps in their ranks with shrapnel, and by the infantry, who shot down hundreds in bursts of rapid fire which seemed to daze the enemy. They swarmed into the woods east of Hooge, facing to the south of the Polygon Wood, from which they were headed off by troops of the 2nd Division, which took heavy toll of them as they passed. They penetrated as far as the Nonne Bosschen, almost up to the guns of the 61st Brigade, R.F.A., but here they were repulsed and a fine counter-attack by the Oxford and Bucks Light Infantry, with details of every descrip-

---

[1] *The Official History (Military Operations) of the War* gives the number of hostile troops which attacked on either side of the Menin Road on the 25th as at least 17,500 infantry, the British troops opposed to them as about 7,850.

tion, drove them back out of the wood and all the gain they had
to show was a narrow strip of trench south of the Polygon Wood.

At 8.15 a.m. the Gloucesters and Grenadier Guards, who then
formed the Corps Reserve, had been ordered to be ready at short
notice to support the 1st Brigade, which was holding the line
from the Menin Road northwards to the Polygon Wood. At
10 a.m. they received definite and urgent orders to move to the
road just south-east of Hooge Château, the Grenadiers on the
right next to the Menin Road and the Gloucesters on the left.
At 11 a.m. the Gloucesters were again advanced, i.e. to the cross-
roads 600 yards south of Westhoek, in order to co-operate with
troops of the 2nd Division advancing from the north, who had
orders to clear the enemy out of Nonne Bosschen.

Only a small portion of the Gloucesters actually took part in
the counter-attack, but in the afternoon the whole Battalion was
ordered to take up a new position stretching from Inverness Copse
towards Verbeck Farm, near the south-western corner of the
Polygon Wood. Here front-line trenches were dug on a frontage
of some 400 yards and were held for four days. By that time
the enemy's attack was over and the enemy's finest troops had
received such a repulse as to compel the German General Staff
to admit that a break-through was impossible.

Into all the details of the prodigious valour of the British soldier
during those days of great trial it is impossible to go. For all
time the Battles of Ypres, 1914, will remain an epic in the annals
of the Army and those regiments who bear upon their colours
the names of Langemarck, Gheluvelt and Nonne Bosschen may
be proud indeed, for they bear witness to the glory won by those
gallant soldiers who, outnumbered both in men and guns, held the
line and threw back the enemy and frustrated his efforts to
' break through '.

Between the 12th and the 15th November, except for a continuance of shell-fire and a few minor attacks, the line was quiet.
It was during these days that the Gloucesters first encountered
' Minnies ', or German trench-mortar bombs. These projectiles
could be seen twisting and twirling in the air before they reached
our trenches and gave the men time to take cover before the
bombs burst with a terrifying roar.

Shortly after midnight on the 15th the Battalion was relieved
and in the early hours of the 16th the Gloucesters marched away
west, leaving behind them what, at the cessation of the German
attacks, had become the Ypres Salient. An impenetrable ring
of steel had formed round the ancient city of the plains of
Flanders : a ring, which often bent but never gave way entirely :

a troubled area where, night and day, there was no peace from the boom of guns or the ' rat-tat-tat ' of rifle and machine-gun fire.

But for the moment the Gloucesters had left it, without any regrets it may be imagined. On the 16th the Battalion, without other units of the 3rd Brigade, was in Corps Reserve just west of Ypres, but at 4 p.m. the march was continued via Vlamertinghe and Ouderdom to Locre, a village some 7 or 8 miles south of Ypres. The march was continued on the 17th when, after covering another 7 miles via Bailleul, the Gloucesters reached Outtersteene—destined to be the resting-place of the Battalion until the 20th of December.

There was, however, one short interruption in this period of much-needed rest. On the 21st November the Battalion was called upon to do a tour in the front-line trenches near Kemmel. The Gloucesters were relieved on the 24th and returned to rest billets in Outtersteene, having lost 4 men killed and 10 wounded.

Before the Battalion went into the line at Kemmel 400 men joined and on the 23rd November the strength was 9 officers and 752 other ranks. On the 19th October, when the Gloucesters marched out from Poperinghe to take part in the Battle of Langemarck, their strength had been 25 officers and about 970 other ranks, but now of that number only 2 officers and not more than 100 men remained.[1]

On the 1st December the Gloucesters were inspected by Sir John French and congratulated on their gallant fighting, and on the 3rd H.M. the King passed through Outtersteene and inspected the whole of the 3rd Brigade.

On the 14th, when an attack was made on the enemy's trenches at Wytschaete, the 1st Division was ordered to be prepared to move at two hours' notice : but nothing transpired to make the move necessary.

Training and bomb-throwing practice occupied the Gloucesters during this period, as well as route-marching and entrenching by night. On the 20th, however, the ' rest ' out of the front line came to an abrupt end !

[1] In detail the 1st Gloucesters had lost between 19th October and 23rd November : Officers—10 killed or died of wounds, 11 wounded, 3 prisoners of war, 1 sick—total 25 ; other ranks—189 killed or died of wounds, 413 wounded, 62 prisoners of war, 285 sick—total 945.

The Battle of GHELUVELT, 29th

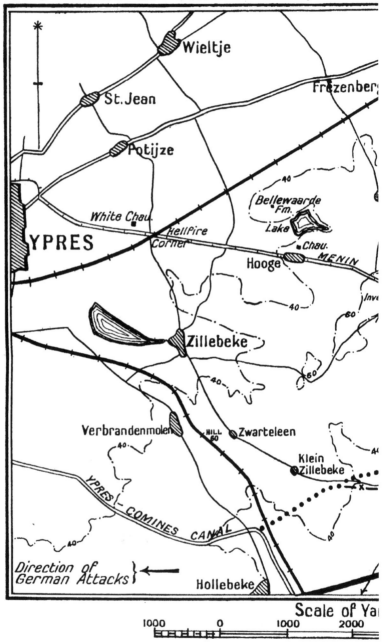

Wieltje

Frezenberg

St. Jean

Potijze

White Chau.

Bellewaarde Fm.

YPRES

HellFire Corner

Lake

Chau.

Hooge

MENIN

Inve

Zillebeke

Verbrandenmolen

HILL 60

Zwarteleen

Klein Zillebeke

X

YPRES—COMINES CANAL

Direction of German Attacks ←

Hollebeke

Scale of Ya

1000   0   1000   2000

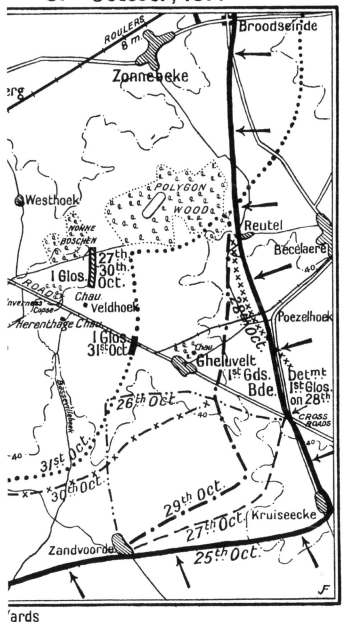

ROULERS 8 m.

Zonnebeke

erg

POLYGON WOOD

Westhoek

NONNE BOSCHEN

I Glos. 27ᵗʰ 30ᵗʰ Oct.

ROAD

Inverness Copse

Chau. Veldhoek

Herenthage Chau.

I Glos. 31ˢᵗ Oct.

Bassevillebeek

Broodseinde

Reutel

Becelaere

40

Poezelhoek

Chau. Gheluvelt

1ˢᵗ Gds. Bde.

Detᵐᵗ 1ˢᵗ Glos. on 28ᵗʰ

CROSS ROADS

26ᵗʰ Oct.

40

31ˢᵗ Oct.

40

30ᵗʰ Oct.

29ᵗʰ Oct.

27ᵗʰ Oct. Kruiseecke

Zandvoorde

25ᵗʰ Oct.

40

JF

'ards

3000   4.000   5000

CHAPTER X

THE DEFENCE OF GIVENCHY, 1914

A T daylight on the 20th December the whole front of the Indian Corps from Cuinchy, just south of the La Bassée Canal, to the cross-roads south of Neuve Chapelle was severely bombarded by the enemy's artillery and trench mortars, and at 9 a.m. ten mines were exploded beneath the British trenches in front of Givenchy. Following the mine explosions the enemy's infantry, using bombs freely, attacked Givenchy and the front as far north as La Quinque Rue. North and south of Givenchy trenches were lost and the village itself was in danger as the enemy had entered the eastern half of it, while on the front east of Festubert a breech 300 yards deep had been made by the enemy.

G.H.Q. ordered a brigade of the 1st Division to be sent to the assistance of the Indian Corps, and at 4.30 p.m. the 3rd Brigade, then at Outtersteene, was instructed to be prepared to march to Merville. At 5.40 p.m. definite orders were received by the 3rd Brigade, together with the Field Ambulance, to march at 6.30 p.m.

On reaching La Brianne, on the outskirts of Merville, the Brigade was ordered to billet in the latter place for the night. This was done, though the last units did not get in until nearly 1 a.m. on the 21st.

Just after midnight orders came to hand from 1st Divisional Headquarters to resume the march on Bethune, via Hinges, at 4 a.m.

In wet weather, the Gloucesters leading as advanced guard, the 3rd Brigade set out at that hour, and on the arrival of the head of the column on the western edge of Bethune at about 8 a.m., a halt was called. The Brigade was warned that the halt would be for an hour and breakfasts were to be cooked and issued during that period. Meanwhile the Brigadier reported at Divisional Headquarters and was then driven to the Headquarters of the Lahore Division and then on to the Headquarters of the Sirhind Brigade at Borre. In the latter village at 11 a.m. verbal orders were issued by the G.O.C., 1st Division, to attack the trenches which had been taken from the Lahore Division on the 19th and 20th December. The first objective of the attack was the trenches on the general line Givenchy—second *T* of Festuber*t*—cross-roads ¼ mile eastwards along the Rue de Cailloux : the second objective was the enemy's former fire-trenches extending northwards from Givenchy through the north-western corner of Rue d'Ouvert. The 1st (Guards) Brigade was to attack on the right and the 3rd Brigade on the left.   The attack, supported by the artillery of the Lahore Division, was to begin at 2 p.m., preceded by a five minutes' bombardment.

The Brigadier then went back to the level-crossing on the Vendin—Bethune railway and there issued verbal orders for the attack.

The 3rd Brigade marched at once in the following order : 1st Gloucesters (Lieut.-Colonel Lovett), 1st South Wales Borderers, 2nd Welch, 4th R.W. Fusiliers, 2nd Royal Munster Fusiliers.

The route taken was by Bethune—Le Quesnoy—Pont Levis —Gorre, a distance of about 5 miles.   Be it remembered that the leading battalions of the column had already marched 14 miles, and the rear battalions 17 miles since 6 p.m. on the previous evening, with only a halt varying from three to four hours at Merville, and a wayside halt with a hasty meal outside Bethune. But the move was urgent and the march was ordered to be continued without further halts *and at a rapid pace.*

By 1.45 p.m. the head of the column (the Gloucesters) had arrived at Gorre and there received orders from the 1st Division that the attack had been postponed until 2.45 p.m.   But before that hour arrived another, and more urgent, order came to hand : the French and British were falling back from Givenchy in face of a heavy German attack, that the 1st Brigade was to recover the village at once, and that the main attack was to begin forthwith.

The Gloucesters and the South Wales Borderers were therefore pushed on without a halt and marched in column of route until they reached the road-junction, 1½ mile west of Festubert.   Here the Gloucesters turned to the right along the Le Plantin road, while the South Wales Borderers extended and advanced eastwards through Festubert.   The 2nd Welch, in support, were brought up to the eastern end of the Tuning Fork roads (½ mile west of Festubert) and the 4th Welsh Fusiliers and 2nd Munsters were retained in reserve at Gorre.

It was 3.5 p.m. when the Gloucesters and South Wales Borderers debouched from Festubert.   Immediately they came under artillery and heavy rifle-fire, the latter principally from the south-east.   As soon as they left the village both Battalions lost touch with each other.   Progress was very difficult, for the attack had to move over very heavy water-logged country, intersected by deep ditches.   Splashed from head to foot with mud, which also clogged their rifles, the Battalion found it difficult even to cover their own advance with rifle-fire.

The Gloucesters, advancing on a three-company front, reported that there was a gap on the right and that they were not in touch with the 1st Guards Brigade.

At 3.15 p.m. both Battalions were ' ordered to throw in their whole strength and to push the attack home '.[1]   The 2nd Welch were ordered to fill the gap between the Gloucesters and South Wales Borderers with two companies and send a platoon to gain touch with the Guards Brigade.

On the left the South Wales Borderers had, by 5.25 p.m., reached the original support trenches of the Sirhind Brigade, a small portion of them being held by a party of Highland Light Infantry : the remainder were, apparently, unoccupied by British or Germans.   The Borderers, weakened by casualties and suffering from the effects of the hard march, found the enemy 150 yards to their front.   They were still not in touch with the Gloucesters.

The latter Battalion on the right had encountered very heavy rifle-fire, mostly from the high ground north-east of Givenchy, and could not approach within 250 yards of the enemy's trenches. They were in the terrible position of not being able to reply effectively to the enemy's fire owing to the state of their rifles, which were clogged with mud and in such a state that it was impossible even to fix bayonets.

On discovering a gap on his right Colonel Lovett sent off his support Company, under Captain W. P. Pritchett, to obtain touch with the Guards. The Company failed to do this, and the Company Commander reached the enemy's trenches without sufficient men to force an entry. Captain Pritchett was here wounded.[2]

When darkness had fallen the Gloucesters had advanced 500 yards, but their losses were heavy. In A Company Captain N. W. F. Baynes had been wounded, also 2nd Lieutenant R. W. Dancwerts [3] : 2nd Lieutenant Templer was a prisoner ; in B Company 2nd Lieutenant D. H. Wiggins was wounded and died of his wounds ; in C Company, besides Captain Pritchett, Lieutenant Seldon had been wounded. Captain G. B. Bosanquet was also wounded.

In other ranks the losses were 45 killed, 109 wounded and 4 taken prisoner.

At 2 a.m. on the 22nd the disposition of the 3rd Brigade (from right to left) was roughly as follows : 2nd Munsters, about the

[1] Narrative in 3rd Brigade Headquarters Diary.
[2] Died of wounds 26th December 1914.
[3] Died of wounds 21st December 1914.

road junction on the Givenchy—Festubert road, 500 yards west of Givenchy, with two companies entrenched about two hundred yards to the east, covering the road junction : 1st Gloucesters, entrenching and reorganizing on the trench running from Le Plantin to La Quinque Rue, in touch on the left with the right of the Welch Regiment, who were in the old support trenches of the Lahore Division.   On the left, but not in touch with the Welch Regiment, were two platoons of the same Regiment, on the right of the South Wales Borderers, who also occupied the old support trenches, their left resting on the Festubert—La Quinque Rue road.

At this period it was not possible to discover the width of the gap existing in the centre of the Brigade front, but later the breach was found to be from 600 to 700 yards in extent and was occupied by the Germans.

Orders had been received to attack the enemy again at dawn on the 22nd, but later they were cancelled and the Gloucesters dug in where they were, on ground saturated and muddy and pockmarked with shell-holes.   The Welch came up on their left to connect up with the South Wales Borderers.   During the day Lieutenant M. C. N. Herbert was badly wounded.[1]

On the 23rd the Battalion set to work to extend and improve their trenches as far as possible.   But on such ground, the water and mud could not be overcome.   To put a spade into the earth meant drawing water.   The cold was intense, which, combined with wet weather, resulted in appalling sickness from frost-bite and rheumatism.   The stretcher-bearers were continually at work, casualties occurring faster than they could be carried away. During the last week in December there must have been nearly two hundred cases.   In those early days elaborate precautions and preventatives were not thought about.   Fur coats were issued on the 2nd December and a gift of body-belts from H.M. the Queen added greatly to the comfort of the men.

Until the end of December A and B, and C and D Companies took turn and turn about in the front-line trenches, tours lasting forty-eight hours.

Two D.C.M.s were awarded to N.C.O.s for gallantry on the 21st December.   One was to Sergt. W. Duddridge

' for conspicuous gallantry and ability.   After his officers were wounded he took over the command of the platoon which was acting as a covering party and remained in position until he was wounded and most of the platoon killed or wounded.'

---

[1] Died of wounds 2nd January 1915.

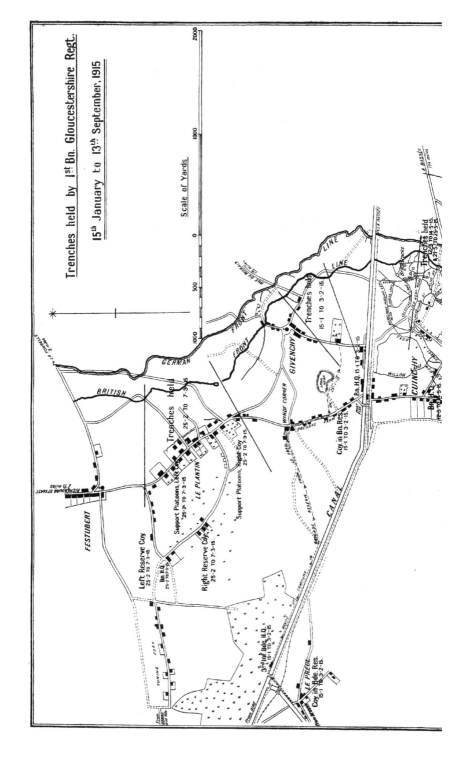

Trenches held by 1st Bn. Gloucestershire Regt.

15th January to 13th September, 1915

Scale of Yards

2000   1000   500   0

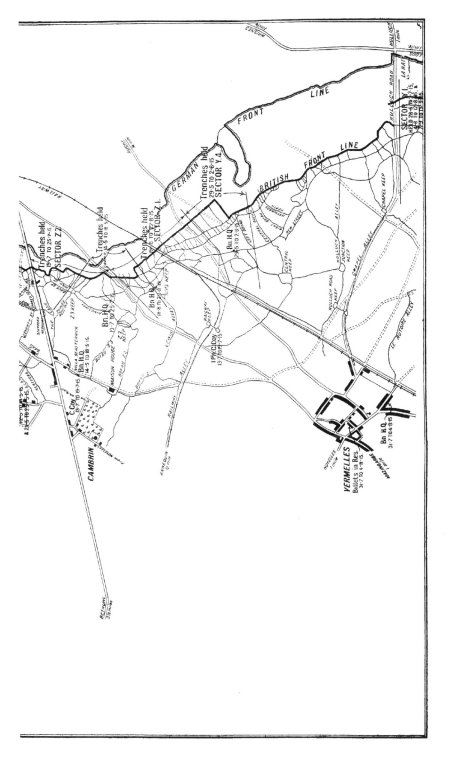

The other was to Sergt. T. Harding who ' being the only N.C.O. surviving in his platoon, he remained for two days under a heavy fire within 50 yards of the German trenches '.

Thus ended the operations of 1914. The 1st Battalion, Gloucestershire Regiment, had seen hard fighting and had fought most gallantly, as their records show. Their losses had been very heavy, in fact by the end of the year the Battalion had been practically re-formed.

CHAPTER XI

THE FIRST ACTION OF GIVENCHY, 1915

25TH JANUARY

WITH the exception of the appalling conditions in the front-line trenches, there is little to record during the first three weeks of January 1915. Heavy rain, alternating with frost and snow, turned the trenches into muddy waterways, in which men were forced to stand for hours on end suffering all the agonies of rheumatism, frost-bite and ague. The Battalion Diaries at this period make tragic reading: often the elements were more bitter in their fight against humanity than the enemy in the opposing trenches. The story of these terrible days and nights in the trenches is told in terse sentences, as if to suffer and say nothing about it was preferable to a long description of seemingly never-ending agonies.

On the 12th January the 1st Gloucesters relieved the Cameron Highlanders at Givenchy, three companies going into the front line and one remaining just south of Pont Fixe in reserve. Companies relieved one another at intervals of forty-eight hours.

There was only one line of trenches, no support or communication trenches, no dug-outs nor any shelters.

The conditions of the line may be gathered from the following phrases selected from the records: 'Snowed all day, condition of trenches getting bad', that was on the 18th January. The next day it is stated that 'a severe thaw set in, condition of trenches very bad, water causing parapet to collapse'. On the 20th: 'Weather conditions still extremely bad for trenches, men undergoing great hardships during their forty-eight hours on duty owing to wet and sharp frost at night. *In spite of this all ranks most cheerful.*' The inherent cheerfulness under all circumstances, combined with his indomitable pluck, were the things which kept the British soldier's soul alive. Again on the 21st the conditions in the trenches were appalling:

'A Company relieved B in trenches. No change in the situation. Great difficulty experienced in keeping the trench fit to occupy on account of continual collapse of parapet owing to water. On the right of trench it has been found necessary to sap forward in twelve different places with a view to joining up and forming a trench a few yards in front.'

On the 24th the enemy's guns were specially active. They shelled the Lock on the La Bassée Canal, east of Pont Fixe, very heavily all day, firing no less than 125 9-centimetre shells on that point alone. That meant about 11 tons of metal. Fortunately little damage was done and no casualties were suffered from the severe gruelling. Indeed, in this instance it was a case of an ' ill wind ', etc., for the enemy's shell-fire killed many fish in the Lock, which, during the intervals of the shelling, the men caught in nets.

At daybreak on the following morning (25th January) the enemy's artillery again became very active, his guns heavily bombarding the British lines. Many bombs were thrown into the trenches held by the Gloucesters, but with the exception of one portion of the trench, which was completely destroyed, little damage was done.

A deserter, who had given himself up early that morning, gave warning of an attack on a large scale against the French and British lines south of the La Bassée Canal,[1] and against Givenchy, held by the 3rd Brigade.

At 7.30 a.m. a rifle rocket soared up into the air from the German lines. Immediately the enemy launched his attack. At this period the 3rd Brigade had all four battalions in the line, two companies of each holding the front-line trenches, one in local reserve and one in brigade reserve. A and D Companies of the Gloucesters were in the front line.

The Germans attacked down the road and along the hedge running by The Orchard. Numbers of them were shot down by the Gloucesters, and many of them ran back to their own line. Others, however, still came on, but were eventually brought to a standstill some 45 or 50 yards from the trenches. With the exception of a few who took refuge in a communication trench south-east of the road, all were killed.

At about 7.35 a.m. Captain H. C. Richmond and Captain W. K. George, both belonging to D Company, were killed, and one of the Battalion machine-guns was put out of action. Five minutes later a verbal message reached 2nd Lieutenant Hodges (who had taken command of D Company) that the enemy had broken through on the left clear of the Gloucesters' front. He at once sent reinforcements to the left trench in order to prevent

[1] The 1st Brigade held the Cuinchy sector with the French on their right.

any incursion by the enemy from that quarter. By this time about sixty Germans had penetrated the village behind the Gloucesters, and in order to deal with attacks from the rear as well as from the front, Pte. W. Hotchkins, who was in command of the left section of the trench, placed his men so that they lined both the front and rear face of the trench. In this incident history repeated itself, for at Alexandria in 1801 the old 28th Foot, attacked by the French from front and from rear, fought back to back with such good effect that they were granted the privilege of wearing their regimental badge in the front and back of their headdress.

The fighting was reaching a critical stage when two platoons of the Black Watch, then in local reserve, made a brilliant counter-attack, killing or taking prisoner all the Germans who had got into Givenchy. B Company of the Gloucesters, under Captain Blunt, from local reserve just north of Pont Fixe, then reinforced A and D, and C moved up to Pont Fixe. The latter Company lost 1 officer (2nd Lieutenant W. R. N. Leslie) and 4 other ranks killed, and 1 officer and 3 other ranks wounded, all from shell-fire, in moving up.

North of the Canal at Givenchy, the enemy's attack failed completely, for, although his troops had penetrated as far back as the strong points behind the support line, all were either killed or captured and not one yard of ground was lost. Though at one time in a most desperate position, the Gloucesters held their own completely.

By nightfall the situation once more became normal and remained so until the Battalion was relieved on the 3rd February and moved back to Marles les Mines.

All battalions of the 3rd Brigade received congratulations from the Commander-in-Chief and the Corps Commander on their fine tenacity and courage in holding to their positions.

In addition to the three officers mentioned as being killed on the 25th January, the Battalion Diary records the losses on that date as 9 other ranks killed and Captain W. P. S. Foord and 27 other ranks wounded.

Two Military Crosses and three D.C.M.s were awarded to the Regiment for gallantry during the fighting on 25th January.

CHAPTER XII

THE 2ND BATTALION ARRIVES IN FRANCE

WHILE the 1st Battalion (the 28th Foot) was enduring the rigours of that first terrible winter in the trenches in France and Flanders, the 2nd Battalion (the 61st Foot) had reached England from Tientsin.

When war was declared, the 2nd Battalion was stationed in North China. The Battalion had 2 companies at Tientsin, 1 company at Peking, and 1 company, with married families, at Shan-Hai-Kwan.

On the declaration of war, rumours at once began to circulate as to the movements of the Battalion. At first the Battalion was to proceed overland to attack Tsingtao, later it was to proceed by sea and take part with the Japanese in the siege of that port. The Battalion actually prepared for the latter operation and all kits, etc., were stacked ready for embarkation. At the last moment the move was cancelled and eventually in September, with twenty-four hours' notice, the Battalion, complete with wives and children, except transport, was ordered to embark in the P. & O. *Arcadia* at Ching-Wang-Tao for Sialkot, India.

Only one horse accompanied the Regiment, Lieutenant A. C. Vicary, the Adjutant, obtaining special permission to take his whaler mare, ' The Sikh '. The experiences of this mare and her war record must be unique. She was bred in Australia and sold to India. The 36th Sikhs brought her to North China. During the eight weeks' voyage home to England from China this mare lived in a makeshift open box on the after-deck ; when sea conditions allowed she was exercised on the deck and went ashore at Hong Kong, Singapore, Colombo, Port Said and Gibraltar. She accompanied her master throughout the whole War, regularly coming up to the trenches at reliefs, and led the 61st in the victorious march through Serbia and Bulgaria. Finally, she proceeded with the Regiment to South Russia and, following the Regiment home through Turkey, Greece, Italy and France, she died in peace at Lieut.-Colonel Vicary's home in Devonshire.

Many men in the Battalion looked on this mare as an omen of good luck.

Although the eight weeks' voyage home was for the most part very tedious, it was relieved by a few interesting incidents. The *Arcadia* was escorted by a Russian light cruiser, the *Ascold* (known by the troops as ' the packet of fags ' owing to her having five very high funnels), which had been sunk in the Russo-Japanese War and afterwards salved, and a Canadian Pacific liner, the *Empress of India*, manned by the Royal Navy. Further transports of troops were picked up at Hong Kong, Singapore and Colombo, this being the foundation of the 27th Division which formed at Winchester in November 1914.

At sea off Shanghai, much to every one's joy, orders were received to proceed direct to England for France.

On coming through the Straits of Malacca, it was reported that the German cruiser, the *Emden*, was lying in wait for the convoy. This ship had become famous, and had caused very considerable damage by her raids. She was eventually run to ground and sunk by H.M.A.S. *Sydney*.

The convoy therefore changed course south and fortunately avoided the *Emden*. A few days after this it was discovered that the freezing apparatus of the ship had broken and the liquid had got into the baggage. Accordingly all baggage in the hold had to be hauled out on deck and examined. It was found that the acid had ruined practically all the baggage, which had to be thrown overboard. Winter clothes for the children to land in were made out of G.S. blankets. The Government eventually paid compensation for losses to all those concerned. The compensation was shamefully inadequate, but it had a humorous side because, in some cases, the Government in error paid twice. No one in the Regiment accepted the responsibility of informing the Government of their error.

The Regiment landed at Southampton on the 8th November and proceeded to camp near Winchester. The 27th Division was formed round the 61st, and until the Divisional and Brigade Staffs were appointed an immense amount of extra work was thrown on the Battalion H.Q. Staff. When formed, the Division must undoubtedly have been one of the finest divisions ever formed. It consisted almost entirely of regular troops on foreign service at full war strength. Every soldier had at least eighteen months' service, the average being five years or more. The N.C.O.s were all old soldiers, most of the senior ones having served in the Boer War. The only non-regular unit was the Divisional R.E. Company. Just before leaving for France the Division was inspected by His Majesty King George V and Lord Kitchener.

It was while the Battalion was at Winchester that ' Buller ' joined. Where he came from or how he was come by no one knows, but suffice it to say that he appeared one morning in the transport lines. He was a clean-bred, magnificent specimen of a bull terrier. His massive jaw and shoulders rendered him un-defeatable throughout the whole of his active service. No dog in France, Belgium, Greece, Bulgaria, or South Russia ever dared to come near the 61st Transport Lines.

' Buller ' never missed a day's service with the 61st during the whole War. Night after night he came up to the trenches with the rations. During the 2nd Battle of Ypres, when the regimental transport was forced to gallop through Ypres and up the Menin Road to reduce the chances of casualties from shell-fire, and for one period to avoid the flames of burning Ypres, he always appeared with the ration limbers behind the front line. ' Buller ' came back with the Battalion cadre from South Russia in July 1919, but was stopped at Boulogne. A special dispensation, how-ever, was granted by the Ministry of Agriculture from quarantine and he was allowed to go to Lieut.-Colonel Vicary's home in Devonshire. He ended his days on duty at the Regimental Depot, Horfield Barracks.

After five or six weeks at home, first at Hursley Park and then at Magdalen Hill Camp, spent in refitting and training, the Battalion at a few hours' notice embarked at Southampton on the *City of Chester* on the 18th December and crossed the Channel to Le Havre. On disembarking at the latter port the Battalion moved by train to Aire and occupied French barracks in the town.

The 2nd Gloucesters were commanded by Lieut.-Colonel G. S. Tulloh, and formed part of the 81st Brigade (Brig.-General MacFarlane) of the 27th Division (Major-General T. D'O. Snow) —a division made up of battalions from outlying garrisons of Asia and the Mediterranean. The Gloucesters were brigaded with the 1st Royal Scots, 2nd Cameron Highlanders and 1st Argyll and Sutherland Highlanders.

The remainder of December was spent at Aire, though on the 20th the Second-in-Command and several other officers were sent off to the 1st Battalion in order to get an insight into trench warfare.

On the morning of the 7th January the 81st Brigade set out to march to Dickebusch, where it was to be in support of the 80th Brigade, then holding front-line trenches. That march was the first real experience the Battalion had of the *pavée* roads, and many men suffered from sore feet. The 8th and 9th were spent in work, but on the 10th the Brigade began the relief of the 80th Brigade in the front line.

The Gloucesters set out from Dickebusch between 5.40 and 6.30 p.m. to relieve the K.S.L.I. in the line near St. Eloi. They were new to the discomforts and difficulties of night reliefs and, as may be imagined, the mud, the pools of water, the gaping shell-holes, the communication trenches were not easily negotiated. Each man carried 220 rounds of S.A.A., in addition to full pack and trench equipment. Splashing and squelching through the mud and water, the relief was eventually carried out and the Battalion at last found itself in the front line. It is of historical interest to give the happenings of the 11th January as written down in the Battalion Diary, even though they were merely the normal proceedings which took place every day :

' Artillery fire carried on all day, particularly heavy between the hours of 2 p.m. and 4 p.m. From observation our artillery fire seemed good. Artillery fire ceased at nightfall. At 6.30 p.m. there was very heavy rifle-fire which lasted about twenty minutes : after that there was continual sniping all night. Snipers between our fire trench and Battalion Headquarters were very annoying. Great difficulty about water and rations which had to be fetched from Kruisstraathoek, a mile in rear of Headquarters. Rations were eventually man-handled to Headquarters and issued there, this took from 9 p.m. to 3 a.m. Platoons sent men direct to Kruisstraathoek for water.'

At 9 a.m. on the 12th January the relief of the Battalion began, the 2nd D.C.L.I. taking over the trenches held by the 2nd Gloucesters. The latter marched back to Dickebusch. That first tour in the line had resulted in the loss of 12 men wounded and 5 missing. The next day the Battalion marched to Mount Kokerelle,[1] a distance of only 6 miles, but 54 men had to be carried in carts owing to bad feet caused through having to stand in wet and muddy trenches for hours on end. There were also many stragglers—poor fellows who could hardly drag themselves along the bad roads : they were not yet used to the terrible condition of the trenches.

After this first experience of trench warfare the Battalion gradually became hardened : all battalions had to go through this ' hardening ' process. It was terrible while it lasted, for in those early days the trenches were not the highly scientific constructions of later years, things were primitive in the front line and, whereas the enemy was plentifully supplied with all the paraphernalia wherewith to carry on static warfare, i.e. bombs, rifle grenades, mortars, howitzers, etc., we had practically to improvise whatever we had until they could be made in England.

[1] The strength of the Battalion on marching out was 23 officers and 757 other ranks.

For the first few months of 1915 the records of the 2nd Battalion are concerned only with trench warfare, but such details are not of outstanding interest : it was too early for raids and all the excitements of encounters in No-Man's Land which took place later.

The first officer casualty was recorded on the 17th January, 2nd Lieutenant F. C. Basdell being wounded : on the 3rd February Lieutenant L. A. W. B. Lackland and 2nd Lieutenant A. J. Blake were wounded. On the 14th of that month, when the enemy attacked St. Eloi, the 2nd Gloucesters were out of the line in billets at Westoutre, and although they ' stood by ' were not called upon. Lieutenant J. B. Smalley was wounded on the 20th February.

On the 14th March, when the Germans mined and blew up the Mound at St. Eloi,[1] the Gloucesters were holding Trenches 12 to 8 in the New Farm sector. During the counter-attack to regain the Mound and Trenches 15 to 21, the Battalion remained in the front line, but did not take part in the action. On the 20th Lieutenant H. M. Harrison was killed and 2nd Lieutenant R. J. Croft was killed on the 21st.

The 2nd Gloucesters were relieved on the night of the 23rd/24th and marched to Rosen Hill huts near Reninghelst, where the accommodation was so bad that two companies were forced to bivouac all night in the open in heavy rain. During the period the Battalion occupied the trenches in the neighbourhood of Dickebusch the casualties were two officers and 32 other ranks killed, 4 officers and 131 other ranks wounded. By the end of February reinforcements had brought the strength up to 23 officers and 833 other ranks.

Early in April the 27th Division moved north to a new sector east of Ypres. On the 8th the 2nd Gloucesters relieved the Argyll and Sutherland Highlanders in Trenches 55—51.

It was during this tour in the front line that the Battalion obtained complete mastery over the enemy's snipers. The Gloucesters' snipers, working in pairs in trees and old houses close up behind the firing-line, not only silenced the German snipers but shot several of them.

During an attack by the 5th Division on Hill 60 on the 17th April, the troops of the 27th Division, holding the front line, took part in a fire demonstration. The next morning the German trench mortars were very active and 100 mortar bombs were placed on the Gloucesters' trenches in rapid succession. In the bombardment 2nd Lieutenant B. E. Brown and 1 man were killed

---

[1] Action of St. Eloi, 14th–15th March 1915.

and 8 other ranks wounded.   The parapet of the trench was badly damaged and in several places blown away completely.

The 18th to 21st April was a very noisy and nerve-racking period : the enemy, smarting no doubt over the loss inflicted on him at Hill 60, kept all that area and the neighbourhood under very heavy artillery and trench-mortar fire : the Gloucesters' losses in killed and wounded were 35 other ranks.

CHAPTER XIII

THE BATTLES OF YPRES, 1915

(1) THE BATTLE OF GRAVENSTAFEL RIDGE : 22ND/23RD APRIL

ALTHOUGH the 2nd Gloucesters (as part of the 27th Division) were within the official area [1] of all four of the actions which form the Battles of Ypres, 1915, in only one—the Battle of Frezenberg Ridge, 8th–13th May—was the Battalion engaged with the enemy's infantry in attack and counter-attack.

Of the first dastardly gas attack, launched by the Germans on the evening of the 22nd April, the Battalion Diary has the following note :

'At 12 midnight received wire from Brigade saying French line about Square C5 was broken and fell back about 1,000 yards. Canadian left brigade fell back on account of this. French counter-attack ordered from direction of Boesinghe.'

The 22nd of April was an ideal spring day with a soft breeze blowing gently from the north-east. At about 5 p.m. observers were mystified at the sudden appearance of a greenish fog cloud floating from the German lines between Poelcapelle and Bixschoote, over towards the trenches of French Territorial troops and Algerians. Simultaneously a furious bombardment of Ypres was opened by the enemy's heavy howitzers.

At this period the British front (Vth Corps) from Zwarteleen to south-west of Poelcapelle was held as follows : 27th Division from 400 yards north of Hill 60 to a point at the centre of Polygon Wood where it joined up with the right of the 28th Division, which carried the line via Broodseinde to Berlin Wood, just east of the village of Gravenstafel. From Berlin Wood the Canadian Division held the line to the right of a French Algerian division, south-west of Poelcapelle, and from the latter point the French line bent back in a westerly direction to Steenstraat.

The greenish-grey cloud seen by the observers was asphyxiating

---

[1] The Comines—Ypres canal as far as Voormezeele : thence the road to Vlamertinghe Château—Elverdinghe Château—Boesinghe—Langemarck.

gas, of the treacherous use of which the Allies had received warning, but refused to believe the Germans would use it. In the face of this new deadly weapon, which threw all who breathed it into a comatose condition and excruciating agonies, the French had fallen back, and during the night of the 22nd/23rd April German covering parties had occupied roughly a line from the left flank of the Canadian Division (which was in an extremely dangerous situation) in a south-westerly direction to Oblong Farm, thence Welch Farm, north of Turco and Fusilier Farms, in a north-westerly direction to Het Sas, the French from the Ypres—Staden railway to Steenstraat having fallen back west of the Ypres Canal.

Such was the position when dawn broke on the 23rd, but, barring mention of very heavy rifle-fire to their front and to the north-east throughout the day, the Gloucesters took no actual part in the battle.

(2) THE BATTLE OF ST. JULIEN : 24TH APRIL–4TH MAY

At about 4 a.m. on the 24th very heavy rifle-fire again broke out in front of the Battalion and on the left. From Stirling Castle to Sanctuary Wood, and the Menin Road from Clapham Junction to the west end of Hooge, the enemy plastered the ground with shrapnel and ' Jack Johnson ' shells. After about an hour this fire died down in front of the Battalion. At 10 a.m. Colonel Tulloh received orders to place two companies at the disposal of the 82nd Brigade. These orders were followed by others at 2 p.m. for the whole Battalion to march at once to Potijze.

In column of route, by platoons at intervals of seventy paces, the 2nd Gloucesters set out for Potijze. In full daylight, on the move, they naturally attracted the enemy's gun-fire and all the way they were heavily shelled, but not once was there a check. On the way up the Battalion passed close to a battery whose alternate guns were facing and firing north and south, due to the pronounced salient in which the troops were fighting, and a most disquieting sight for incoming troops to see. At about 3 p.m. they arrived at Potijze and dug themselves in in the wood in front of Potijze Château. To their immediate front very heavy fighting was evidently going on, but the Battalion was not called upon and, after remaining in the wood for several hours, they returned to Sanctuary Wood where they passed a quiet night.

The Gloucesters remained in Sanctuary Wood throughout the 25th and it was not until the afternoon of the 26th that they again marched off to reserve positions at Potijze. There orders were received at 3.30 p.m. and at once the Battalion set out, shelled practically all the way as on the 24th. By 4.30 p.m. the

Gloucesters had reached the G.H.Q. line, east of the Ypres—Potijze road, where they sheltered from the terrific shell-fire which swept the whole battle area. In front of them a hard struggle was evidently going on : ' Terrific fighting to our front ', records the Battalion Diary. At 8.15 p.m., however, the Battalion was ordered to return to Sanctuary Wood.

On the night of the 28th April a portion of the Battalion relieved the Argyll and Sutherland Highlanders and Royal Scots in Trenches C9 and C10, but little happened until the night of the 3rd May when the British line was withdrawn to conform more closely to the French line on the left, the French having failed to regain their original position held before the gas attack on the 22nd April.

The depth of the retirement south of the Menin Road was small, but was an extremely difficult affair : north of the road the new line ran along the eastern edge of the wood, east of Bellewaarde Lake, thence to Frezenberg, bending back in a north-westerly direction to just north of Mouse-trap Farm, thence to Turco Farm where the British and French lines met. The 27th Division had now all three brigades in line, 82nd, 81st, 80th (in that order from right to left). The 2nd Gloucesters were along the eastern edge of Sanctuary Wood, just south of the Menin Road : the 9th Royal Scots were on their right and 2nd Cameron Highlanders on their left. This was the situation on the 4th May at 2 a.m.

At about 6 a.m. patrols reported that the enemy were advancing in small parties of two or three.

They reached Stirling Castle Wood, collecting in groups of from fifteen to twenty men. The Gloucesters at once opened fire on the Germans with machine-guns and rifles : the enemy then dispersed and began to dig in. Other parties of hostile troops attempted to double across from Bodmin Copse to Stirling Castle, but those who were not shot down were forced to retire. It was, however, hardly possible to prevent the enemy occupying the ground we had evacuated, though we made his advance costly. At nightfall on the 4th of May, therefore, his main line, on which he was partially entrenched, ran from north-west of Clonmell Copse—Green Jacket Ride—Stirling Castle and Clapham Junction : parties of Germans were also seen near Westhoek.

The next four days were exceedingly uncomfortable : shell-fire was heavy, though intermittent. In consequence both sides found it difficult to do any digging, though the new lines needed strengthening badly.[1]

[1] Lieutenant C. S. W. Greenland was wounded during this period and killed later by a shell in the dressing station on the 8th May.

(3) The Battle of Frezenberg Ridge : 8th–13th May

On the 8th of May the enemy again attacked our line north of the Ypres—Menin Road, directing their efforts chiefly against the village of Frezenberg and the ridge of that name. At 7 a.m. a terrific bombardment broke out all along the front from Menin Road to Mouse-trap Farm, and at 8.30 a.m. the Germans advanced to the attack, expecting, no doubt, that the gallant troops of the 80th, 83rd and 84th Brigades would be too weak or demoralized to resist him : he was quickly undeceived, for both his first and second attempts failed.

South of the Menin Road the trenches of the 81st and 82nd Brigades were similarly subjected to a furious bombardment. Shells began to fall on the trenches of the 2nd Gloucesters along the eastern edge of Sanctuary Wood at about 6.45 a.m., and from that hour until 11 a.m. there was no cessation of that holocaust of fire. At noon again the enemy's guns opened fire and soon the forward Companies (A and C) of the Gloucesters were suffering heavy casualties, but no hostile infantry attack developed south of the Menin Road.

At 6.30 a.m. on the 9th the enemy opened a terrific bombardment on the front trenches of the Battalion. Two guns—' whizz-bangs '—firing from the right in enfilade were particularly dangerous. In reply to this bombardment our guns were almost powerless, for they had little ammunition, most of which with many guns had to be sent farther south to take part in the Battle of Aubers Ridge. A Belgian battery, behind the Gloucesters, firing salvoes, gave confidence to the latter, while a couple of 4·7's did all they could to assist the Battalion.

The dispositions of the Battalion when the bombardment opened were as follows : D Company (Lieutenant R. M. Grazebrook) held the right half of the trenches, and B Company (Major F. C. Nisbet) the left half : A Company was in close support of B : C Company was in reserve at Battalion Headquarters.

The first bombardment lasted ten minutes and was directed on the left half of the Battalion front where three platoons of B Company were holding the line. After ten minutes, hostile shell-fire ceased and the German infantry opened very heavy rifle-fire which lasted fifteen minutes. Another ten minutes' violent shell-fire was followed by further heavy rifle-fire and machine-gun fire. Great damage had by now been done in the front line and it was found that at least one platoon of B (under Lieutenant E. D'O. Aplin) was completely cut off. Major Nisbet therefore ordered all but ten men per platoon to try to get back

to the main line in rear. The situation in the front line was by
now desperate. ' It was hell,' said one officer. The ten-minute
bombardment, followed by the fifteen-minute rifle-fire, had made
all movement practically impossible. Yet it was imperative to thin
out the line and save as many officers and men as possible.
Lieutenant Aplin, though seriously wounded, succeeded in getting
back with three men—the sole survivors of his platoon—to the
main line, but on his right Sergt. Coopey, with a few men of a
machine-gun post, was quite cut off after the third bombardment.

At 7.15 a.m. the enemy attacked from the direction of Stirling
Castle and from the right front. A platoon, under Sergt. Ball,
and a machine-gun tore gaps in the advancing Germans, but the
latter were in great force and succeeded in penetrating the trenches
and the communication trenches of the forward positions. A
number of men of B Company managed to get back from the
forward trenches, but very many were either knocked out or buried
in the debris by shell-bursts. Major Nisbet, with Captain
W. V. Churchill-Longman and some twenty-nine men with two
machine-guns, were at the time near the telephone dug-out on
the right of the forward line. By now the Germans were pouring
into the left portion and were digging-in and bringing up machine-
guns. Their losses were, however, great, for the Gloucesters shot
hard and at least 350 of the enemy were killed—the trenches and
ground being littered with dead and wounded. With great
gallantry Major Nisbet's party manned the shattered and broken
parapets and opened fire to the south and east, but the enemy
succeeded in getting behind them and astride the communication
trench. There was, however, a circular bit of trench round a
bump in the ground in the centre of the line. This proved to
be defensible, for the slight rise prevented the men being shot in
the back. But casualties were mounting up and one of the
machine-guns was put out of action by a German officer with a
revolver. He was, with many others, shot down, but still the
enemy kept pouring in from the corner of the wood.

The first word of the attack had reached Battalion Headquarters
at 7.30 a.m., by runner, for all telephonic communication had been
destroyed in the terrific bombardment. The support Company
—A—(under Major R. Conner) was rushed up into the main
trench to meet the attack. Simultaneously, C Company moved
up from reserve and with Battalion Headquarters occupied the
partially-formed second line, some 250 yards in rear of the main
trench. Two companies of Leinsters were also sent up in support.

Major Conner apparently pushed ahead of the support Company
and endeavoured to advance along the communication trench

leading to the left of the advanced position, which was by this time in the hands of the enemy. He therefore rushed straight into the enemy and he and the few men behind him were either killed or taken prisoner. The Major was wounded and taken.[1]

So far as could be observed from Battalion Headquarters the situation at 9.10 a.m. appeared to be normal. But there was still no real communication with B and D Companies, for the ground in rear of their line was almost impassable after the bombardments of the past few days. Besides being churned up with shells, full of gaping craters and holes, there was an appalling entanglement of shattered trees and undergrowth, and masses of barbed wire. The communication trenches had practically disappeared, having been filled with debris and, in places, blown out of existence.

But at 9.45 a.m. Sergt. Smith, the Signalling Sergeant, who had been sent forward to mend the telephone wire, returned with the information that the Germans were in the trenches on the left. Colonel Tulloh, therefore, immediately ordered up the reserve Company (C) to just behind the right main trench held by B, and gave instructions for bombing parties, under Major Nisbet, to turn the enemy out. Major Nisbet was to advance down the trench to his left, while A Company (under Captain A. C. Vicary) was to move up the left-hand communication trench and push back the right flank of the enemy. It was a brave but forlorn attempt. Our grenades—of the primitive ' jam-tin ' type—were no match for the German grenades, and although both bombing parties gallantly worked up to within 20 yards of the enemy they were driven back by the superior bombs of the Germans. By now also the enemy had got his machine-guns into position and one, concealed in the open on the right, continually swept the parapet of D Company's trench on the right of the main line and prevented them assisting the attack with covering fire.

Many brave actions were performed during that heavy fighting : two will suffice to show the spirit of the Gloucesters even under the desperate situation they were in. A number of wounded men were attempting to creep back to the dressing-station. One, a sergeant, badly wounded, was seen running back towards D Company when he was again wounded and fell. Immediately, without hesitation, Pte. Gigg, followed by Pte. Maidmont (both of D Company), jumped over the parapet and brought him in. For this the two men received the Russian Order of St. George (Third Class). The other instance concerned Lieutenant E. D'O. Aplin, who, it will be remembered, had been wounded

[1] He was repatriated on account of ill health later in the year, but died on the 7th September 1915.

but had got back to the main line.   The track was too narrow
for a stretcher and he could not be moved.   On seeing this,
Lieutenant Sherlock, the Battalion Medical Officer, ordered the
men near by to open rapid fire, under cover of which in full view
of the enemy he, with a couple of stretcher-bearers, worked his
way back, carrying the wounded officer, and succeeded in getting
away safely.[1]

The bombing attack having failed, a counter-attack was then
organized by Brigade Headquarters.   It was to be covered by
artillery.   Two platoons of A Company, under Captain H. B.
Spear, were to form up in the main-line trench on the left,
and two platoons of C, under Lieutenant G. B. Rayner, on the
right.   Both parties were to go ' over the top ' and advance
straight on to the enemy's position over the open.   The advanced
party of B Company was to send out men against the enemy's left.
Two platoons were to remain in reserve on the main line, while
two companies of 9th Royal Scots were brought up to the second
line.   The attack was to begin at 3.30 p.m., the signal for the
advance being a burst of rapid fire from Captain Spear's party
on the left.   The guns were to shell the enemy in front of Stirling
Castle from 3.15 p.m. to 4 p.m., while the 2nd Camerons, on the
left of the Gloucesters, were simultaneously to open rapid fire
on the enemy.

By 3 p.m. the attacking parties were in position.   The signal
to advance was actually given at 3.45 p.m. and the three parties
' went over '.   On the left there was a slight hitch, but soon the
whole line was struggling through the tangle of trees and wire.
They were met by a terrific fire, especially from a machine-gun
at the apex of the wood, and from two more guns near Stirling
Castle.   But, pushing on gallantly, they got to within 15 to 20
yards of the enemy and began to establish a firing-line there.   If
supports could have been rushed up, there is but little doubt that
the enemy would have been pushed back, but the condition of the
ground made the bringing up of more men a very slow proceeding,
and before they could arrive the brave fellows who had pushed
forward so close to the enemy's wire were practically wiped out.
Three small parties, under Captain A. C. Vicary, Lieutenant
Rayner and Sergt. Barber, held on for a while, throwing bombs,
but in the end were forced to retire.   The counter-attack also
was a failure.

Worse still, the Gloucesters had lost in this attack their C.O.,
Lieut.-Colonel Tulloh, who, while ammunition was being passed
up the communication trench, exposed himself too much : he was

[1] Lieutenant E. D'O. Aplin died of his wounds on the 13th May.

hit in three places and killed.   Captains D. Burges and H. B. Spear were also wounded.

No news had been received from the advanced trenches where Major Nisbet's party had originally been, and signallers were sent forward to try to find out if there were any survivors.   After a while these men returned with the information that no one could be found and that the whole line appeared to have been blotted out. On this report Captain A. C. Vicary assumed command of the Battalion and reported to Brigade Headquarters.   The Brigadier, realizing that it was impossible with the small number of men at his disposal to retake the lost trenches, ordered no further attack to be made, but the old main line was to be cleared up and improved.   At this period there were left one and a half companies in the main trench and one company in reserve.   Besides Captain A. C. Vicary and Lieutenant R. M. Grazebrook, there were only three very junior attached subalterns known to be alive and still with the Battalion.   But presently things became quieter, the enemy no doubt being busy consolidating his gains, though after the struggle and the losses inflicted upon him he could have been in no position to extend his success.

It must have been about 5.30 p.m. that Captain Vicary went out to find out definitely what had become of the little force which had been holding out under Major Nisbet.   He succeeded eventually in creeping up to the position and found Major Nisbet, with Captain Halford, Captain W. V. Churchill-Longman and Lieutenant Steele and a few men, still alive and safe near the old telephone dug-out.   Major Nisbet then crawled back down the remains of the communication trench—over the living and the dead—a terrible journey and, as he said, he had ' never been so far on all fours in his life '.   Reporting at Brigade Headquarters, he was ordered to withdraw the survivors from the advanced line and hold on in the main trench until relieved in the evening. The withdrawal to the main trench was very difficult : in the darkness men lost the gap in the wire and several were hung up for some time.   The enemy also, probably hearing the movement, sent up showers of flares and then opened a rapid fire all along his front.   In the middle of this firing, at about 1 a.m. on the 10th, the 1st Royal Scots arrived to relieve the Gloucesters and eventually the line was handed over.   With all their wounded the survivors of the Battalion marched back to the G.H.Q. line of reserve trenches about a mile east of Ypres, just south of the Menin Road, near to where it was crossed by the Roulers railway : this spot was known later as ' Hell Fire Corner '.

The losses of the 2nd Gloucestershire Regiment on the 9th

of May were very heavy for one day's fighting, i.e. 5 officers
and 140 men, and but for the continuous gallantry of Lieutenant Sherlock and his band of stretcher-bearers, the number
of men lost would have been far greater. The signallers also
did magnificent work—Sergt. Smith, L/Corpl. Cullimore and
Pte. Fortune being conspicuous for their devoted efforts in
keeping up communication.

The Gloucesters had arrived in the G.H.Q. line at about 3.45
a.m. and were allotted some 300 yards of trench which, during
the day, they were ordered to improve and put out wire. But
whenever the men showed themselves they were greeted by
bursts of shrapnel. In the afternoon heavy firing was heard
from the direction of Hooge, and news reached the Battalion
that the 9th Argylls and Sutherlands had been practically wiped
out in their dug-outs in Zouave Wood, while the Camerons in
Sanctuary Wood had been forced back to the second line.

At about 6.15 p.m. on the 11th the Gloucesters received word
that the Brigade was really going back for a proper rest : guides
were sent off to reconnoitre the road and the Battalion was to
move at 9 p.m. But just before 8 p.m. orders were received
from 27th Divisional Headquarters to report to 81st Brigade
Headquarters in Sanctuary Wood at once. Immediately the
Battalion hurried off and reached Brigade Headquarters at 9.15
p.m., where it was learned that the Camerons, holding the left
of the Brigade frontage, had been forced to evacuate part of the
front line, which had been almost obliterated by shell-fire. The
enemy had then pushed forward large numbers of men and had
seized the position, and also a slight mound to the south from
which they could enfilade the trenches of the Royal Scots on
the right.

In order to clear up the situation a reconnaissance was made
at midnight. The story of that reconnaissance is worth recording :

' On arrival at 81st Brigade Headquarters in Sanctuary Wood,' said
Captain A. C. Vicary, who made the reconnaissance, ' Major Nisbet
and myself (Adjutant) at once reported to General Croker for orders.
It appeared that the Camerons had evacuated a little hill overlooking
Cameron Gully and that it must be retaken at all costs, but it seemed
impossible to get information whether the Germans were holding the
hill or not.'

The telephone bell rang while Major Nisbet and Captain
Vicary were at Brigade Headquarters and the Divisional Commander spoke to General Croker and said the hill must be taken
at once.

' I therefore volunteered,' said Captain Vicary, ' to find out what had happened. The General jumped at this, but Major Nisbet refused to let me go on the grounds that, owing to casualties, I was too valuable to throw away on someone else's job. Eventually he very reluctantly consented.

' I at once set off to see what I could find out about this hill. I took Pte. Long, 61st, with me. I found the Royal Scots and Leinsters holding a line astride a road which ran straight up over the hill. There was a good deal of rifle-fire going on but no artillery fire, as neither side knew what was happening. I asked the C.O. of the Royal Scots to stop all firing whilst I went forward. I left Pte. Long about 100 yards from the top of the hill on the road and went forward alone to the hill. I knew the hill very well, having been on it for four days when the Battalion was on it in close support only ten days before. It was very dark but I walked right over the hill to the cutting beyond when I heard the enemy talking and moving and also found myself within a few inches of a German. I returned to the top of the hill when I was astonished to see a line of the enemy running along between me and our trenches. They were silhouetted against the sky and were only a few yards from me : they then faced their front and started digging.

' After a considerable amount of crawling I managed to get right up to these Germans. I then got up and made a dart for it. I had gone about 50 yards when I tripped up. I found I had tripped over a wounded German officer (hit through the thigh). I managed to drag him back to the Royal Scots lines. I considered he would be valuable from the information and identification of units point of view.

' I then reported to General Croker, who ordered the Leinsters to attack. This attack never materialized, and Major Nisbet was ordered to send a company to take the hill, guided by myself. I took B Company (Captain J. Fane). It was just getting light and we could plainly see the top of the hill from our front line. We deployed as we passed over our front line and went straight at the hill with fixed bayonets. The Company was into the Bosche before they had time to retire. L/Corpl. Keegan bayoneted no less than six of the enemy himself.'

Under very heavy artillery and machine-gun fire B Company held the little hill until about 4.45 p.m. (12th May) and then Captain J. Fane decided to withdraw.[1] An hour later the enemy was seen to be massing once more behind the rise. B Company again took the hill with the bayonet and dispersed the Germans, but under the terrific shell-fire to which they were exposed, it was impossible for Captain Fane's men to stay there. C Company (Lieutenant Baxter) and a machine-gun were then sent up to hold the line and to allow B Company, which had lost about thirty men and was very exhausted, to withdraw. But early on the 13th a withdrawal was made to the second line : the losses sustained in holding the hill were not justifiable. During the withdrawal 2nd Lieutenant C. B. Rayner was killed.

[1] Brig.-General F. C. Nisbet adds the following note : ' Captain Fane reported in his own forcible way : " I can go on taking the damned hill as often as you want, but I cannot hold it." '

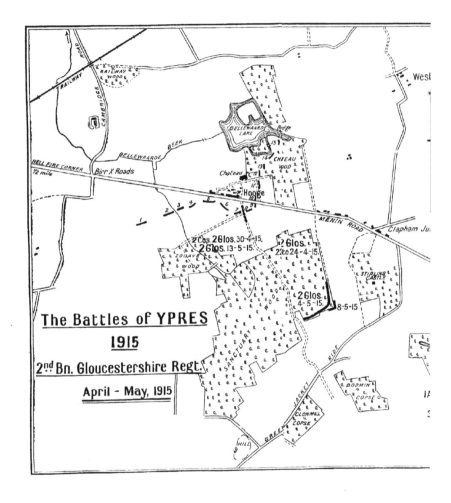

The Battles of YPRES
1915
2nd Bn. Gloucestershire Regt.
April - May, 1915

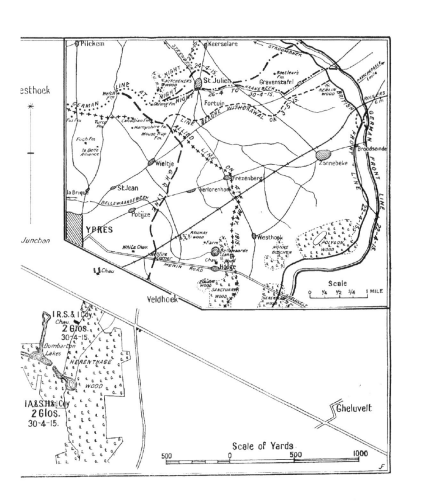

On this day the Germans made another attack north of the Menin Road, about Bellewaarde Farm, and the Gloucesters were ordered to ' stand by ', but were not engaged.

During the day the following wire was received :

' To units, 81st Brigade. The Corps Commander has just visited the Divisional Headquarters and says he is lost in admiration at the way the Brigade sticks out the pounding it has been taking. The Divisional General hopes to be able to arrange some relief shortly.'

General Joffre, the French Commander-in-Chief, also wired his congratulations.

The close of the 13th May saw the end of the Battle of Frez-enberg Ridge, and when the 81st Brigade had been relieved and the Gloucesters were out of the line in bivouacs south of Poperinghe, Sir John French, who inspected the Brigade on the 20th May, said : ' Your Colours have many famous names emblazoned on them, but none will be more famous or more well deserved than that of the Second Battle of Ypres. I want you one and all to understand how thoroughly I realize and appreciate what you have done. I wish to thank you, each officer, non-commissioned officer and man, for the services you have rendered by doing your duty so magnificently, and I am sure your country will thank you too.'

The 2nd Gloucesters entered no more into the Battles of Ypres, 1915. During the Battle of Bellewaarde Ridge (24th/25th May), the Battalion being then resting near Busseboom (the 81st Brigade in reserve), an order was received at 5.30 a.m. on the 25th to ' stand to ' but, barring a move to Vlamertinghe where with the Camerons they were held in reserve, they took no part in the operations. At the end of the month the 27th Division moved by march route to Armentières, the 2nd Gloucesters marching out at a strength of about 550 all ranks.

CHAPTER XIV

THE BATTLE OF AUBERS RIDGE: 9TH MAY, 1915

ON the very day (9th May) that the 2nd Gloucesters—61st—were undergoing their terrible ordeal in Zouave and Sanctuary Woods, the 1st Battalion—28th—were facing terrific machine-gun and rifle-fire from the enemy's trenches opposite Richebourg L'Avoué, in the Battle of Aubers Ridge.

From the 3rd of February, when the 1st Gloucesters were relieved from the Givenchy trenches and moved back to Marles-lez-Mines to the end of the above Battle, the Battalion passed through a comparatively quiet existence. They were out of the line until the 24th of February, but on the 25th went into the front line of the Festubert defences. During this tour, which lasted a week, nothing unusual happened.[1] There were no trenches, for the front line consisted of breastworks which were solid and good but were not continuous. The ground behind the breastworks was extremely muddy and there were few shelters. About the village there were numerous graves of the men of the Regiment who had been killed in the fighting during the previous December, including that of Sergt. H. James, who scored the try by which the 61st won the Army Rugby Cup at Twickenham in 1910. Also the graves of two privates—Hayward and Trenfield—who had lived next door to one another in Gloucester, had enlisted together and were killed together. On the 7th of March the Battalion moved back to Gorre until the 14th, and after a short period of rest in Hinges, spent 16 days in the line at Neuve Chapelle and Port Arthur. A further period of rest was passed

---

[1] On the 24th February Lieut.-Colonel A. C. Lovett became ill and proceeded to hospital, Major G. F. Gardiner assuming command of the Battalion. Colonel Lovett never returned to the Battalion as his health would not allow it. He had commanded the Battalion during the arduous days of the Retreat from Mons in 1914, throughout the Battle of the Aisne and the First Battles of Ypres, and his work and example were never forgotten by those who served under him. At this period Lieutenant D. Duncan was acting as Adjutant and companies were commanded as follows : A—Captain R. D. Scott, B—Captain A. St. J. Blunt, C—Captain A. W. Pagan, and D—Captain F. C. Finch.

in Locon and was followed by a spell in the line in front of Richebourg L'Avoué. Trench warfare of a normal character when
in the line, and training and resting when in billets, sums up the
life of the Battalion for those few weeks.

On the 3rd of May they were again billeted in Hinges, in the
midst of lovely country and perfect spring weather, when another
move took place to fresh billets—dirty and bad they are described
—about the main Bethune—Locon road, south of Locon. Here
the Battalion remained until the 7th of May.

The first intimation of the impending Battle was on the 5th
of May, when Major Gardiner, Captain Pagan and Captain
Bosanquet (Adjutant) were summoned to 3rd Brigade Headquarters, where the plan of operations was explained. The next
day the C.O. and Company Commanders went to Richebourg
L'Avoué to reconnoitre the ground over which the attack was
to be carried out.

The Battle of Aubers Ridge was part of one of three offensives
which the Allied Commanders-in-Chief had planned for 1915,
with the intention of breaking the enemy's front. The Tenth
French Army, on the right of the British, was to attack from
west of Loos (south of the La Bassée Canal) to as far south as
the Vimy Ridge : the First British Army (Ist, IVth and Indian
Corps), on the left of the Tenth French Army, was to attack
from just south of Neuve Chapelle and from west of Fromelles.

The first objective of the First British Army was the line Rue
de Marais—Lorgies—La Cliqueterie Farm—Fromelles, and the
second objective the line Bauvin—Don.

The attack was first ordered to take place on the 8th of May,
and at 7 p.m. on the 7th the 1st Gloucesters paraded to march
off to assembly positions, when orders were received to proceed
to billets round Lannoy, west of Hinges : the attack had been
postponed for twenty-four hours. At 6.30 p.m. the next evening
the Battalion again paraded and marched via Hinges, Locon and
Lacouture to the assembly trenches in the fourth line, immediately
in front of Richebourg L'Avoue. They arrived at about 11.30
p.m. and the night was spent in drawing bombs, respirators,
rations and other stores.

The 3rd Brigade was to attack with its right on the Cinder
Track running from Richebourg L'Avoué to the Festubert—
La Tourelle road : the first objective was on the road from
Festubert to La Tourelle, and the second objective Rue de Marais
and Lorgies.

The 2nd Royal Munster Fusiliers on the right and 2nd Welch
on the left (the first-line assaulting battalions of the 3rd Brigade)

were to move into No-Man's Land. The barrage, which was to become intense at 5.30 a.m., was to lift and both Battalions were then to advance and capture the enemy's front-line trenches, move to the first objective and consolidate. The 4th Royal Welch Fusiliers were to follow in rear of the two forward battalions and 'mop up' the hostile trenches. Simultaneously the two reserve battalions, 1st Gloucesters on the right, and 1st South Wales Borderers on the left, were to leave the fourth-line trenches and move above ground to the first line: there they were to await orders from Brigade Headquarters to advance, pass through the assaulting battalions and capture the second objective, i.e. Gloucesters to Rue de Marais, South Wales Borderers to Lorgies.

At 5.30 a.m. on the 9th, when the artillery fire became intense, the leading waves of the two front-line battalions of the 3rd Brigade 'went over the top', but no sooner had they left their trenches than they were met by a terrific rifle and machine-gun fire: many fell dead on the ladders and on the parapets, but the survivors gallantly rushed forward and formed a general line not far short of the intended one. Ten minutes later, when the guns lifted (5.40 a.m.) the attacking troops rose and rushed towards the German trenches, but they were met by a deadly and accurate fire which tore gaps in their ranks, and only a few reached the enemy's wire. Some lay down seeking whatever cover shell-holes offered, others tried to get back to their own lines. Thus the attack had failed to capture the German first line.

Meanwhile the 4th Royal Welsh Fusiliers, who were to 'mop up' the captured trenches, moved up to the front-line trenches, but as there was nothing to 'mop up' they did not leave the 3rd Brigade line.

Behind the Fusiliers, the Gloucesters and South Wales Borderers, moving over the open, crossed the 150 yards between the assembly trenches and the front-line trenches, having a fair number of casualties in so doing. When these two Battalions reached the front line it was found to be full of men of other units, principally Royal Welsh Fusiliers.

The Gloucesters (Captain A. W. Pagan, commanding [1]) were disposed as follows: C on the right, B on the left, D in support: A had been detailed to carry for the Royal Engineers.

A further bombardment of the enemy's trenches was then ordered, to be followed by another attack by the Gloucesters and South Wales Borderers in the hope that they would penetrate and capture the German front line.

[1] Major Gardiner had been evacuated sick.

The attack took place at 7 a.m.

It was with extreme difficulty that orders for the attack (owing to the packed nature of the front line) had been passed along. As a result of the confusion which existed only a portion of the leading companies started off across No-Man's Land, the remainder following when they saw their comrades were advancing.

Again the attack was met by overwhelming machine-gun and rifle-fire. For some 40 or 50 yards the men gallantly struggled on but could make no further headway. The survivors then laid down, forming a line, until they received orders to return to their trenches. Some succeeded in doing so by crawling back, others waited until darkness had fallen before they risked that perilous journey.

In this attack C Company had lost 2 officers and about 60 other ranks : B Company suffered less casualties.

The Gloucesters were then ordered back to the third-line trench.

At 11 a.m. orders were received to repeat the attack at 2.40 p.m., but the hour was subsequently altered to 4 p.m. By this time the front-line trench was less congested, and the two attacking companies—D on the right and A on the left—were able to form up with comparative ease.

At 4 p.m. the assault was delivered, but our artillery support was far inferior in volume to that given by the German artillery to the enemy's front-line troops. Indeed, the hostile troops facing the Gloucesters did not even take shelter, but lined the parapet and greeted the new attack with intense small-arm and machine-gun fire, many German machine-guns being actually on the parapet.

Gallantly led by Captain F. J. Brodigan, D Company got about 120 yards forward, some men being actually killed on the enemy's wire. Very heavy losses were suffered by the Company, which lost all its officers, most of its N.C.O.s and about 90 men. A Company did not get as far.

Seeing the failure of this fresh attempt Divisional Headquarters ordered a retirement, and such men as could do so got back to their trenches. As soon as it was dark search parties went out to look for wounded and many were brought in.

The 1st Gloucesters were relieved by the 1st Royal Berkshires, and by midnight had assembled in the Ruedes Berceaux, just north of Richebourg L'Avoué, whence they marched to farms near Locon. Dead tired the Battalion reached billets at about 6.15 a.m. on the 10th of May.

The losses of the Battalion in this disastrous battle were 11 officers and 253 other ranks. Of the former Captain Brodigan, Lieutenants R. de Trafford, W. P. Heffernan and 2nd Lieutenant P. H. Lawrence were killed ; and Captains F. C. Finch and G. B. Bosanquet, Lieutenants F. K. Griffiths and G. C. Firbank and 2nd Lieutenants J. H. Jevons, F. H. Bowles and W. H. Hodges wounded.

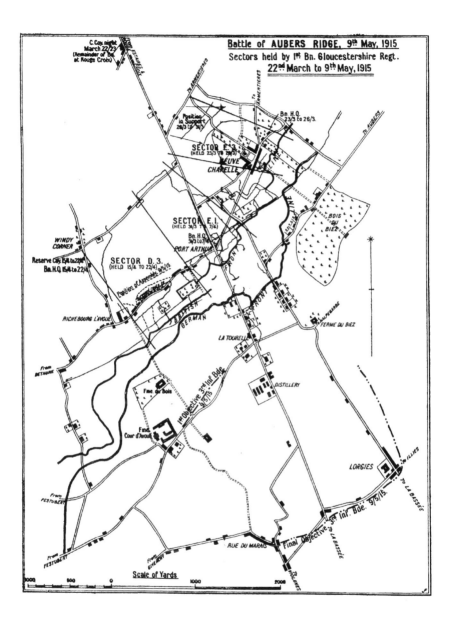

Battle of AUBERS RIDGE, 9ᵗʰ May, 1915
Sectors held by 1ˢᵗ Bn. Gloucestershire Regt.
22ⁿᵈ March to 9ᵗʰ May, 1915

C.Coy.night March 22/23 (Remainder of Bn. at Rouge Croix)

TO ESTAIRES

TO ARMENTIÈRES

Bn.H.Q. 23/3 to 26/3.

TO ARMENTIÈRES

TO AUBERS

Position in Support 26/3 to 4/4.

SECTOR E.3. (HELD 23/3 TO 26/3)

NEUVE CHAPELLE

SMITH-DORRIEN LINE

BOIS DU BIEZ

SECTOR E.I. (HELD 3/3 TO 7/4)

Bn.H.Q. 3/3 to 7/4

WINDY CORNER

PORT ARTHUR

SECTOR D.3. (HELD 15/4 TO 22/4)

Reserve City 15/4 to 22/4
Bn.H.Q. 15/4 to 22/4

Position of Assembly 8/5/15

RICHEBOURG L'AVOUÉ

BRITISH FRONT

GERMAN FRONT

LA TOURELLE

SALPÉGARRE

FERME DU BIEZ

From BÉTHUNE

Fme. du Bois

DISTILLERY

1ˢᵗ Objective 3ʳᵈ Inf.Bde. 9/5/15

Fme. Cour d'Avoué

LORGIES

TO ILLIES

TO LA BASSÉE

From FESTUBERT

Final Objective 3ʳᵈ Inf.Bde. 9/5/15

TO LA BASSÉE

From GIVENCHY

RUE DU MARAIS

TO BÉTHUNE

From FESTUBERT

Scale of Yards

1000   500   0   1000   2000

CHAPTER XV

THE BATTLE OF LOOS: 25TH SEPTEMBER— 8TH OCTOBER

IN the Battle of Festubert, the Second Action of Givenchy, the First Attack on Bellewaarde and the Actions of Hooge, which intervened between the Battle of Aubers Ridge and the Battle of Loos, the Gloucestershire Regiment took no part.

The Battle of Loos, however, saw the 1st Battalion once more in the thick of the fight. The great battle which opened on the 25th September was the culminating Allied offensive of 1915 in which the Allies sought (i) to break the enemy's front, (ii) prevent him re-establishing his line, and (iii) to defeat decisively his divided forces. To carry this into effect there were to be two offensives, one by the French in Champagne and the other by the French and British in Artois. The latter offensive was to be carried out by the Tenth French Army from south-west of Lens southwards to the Vimy Ridge, and by the First British Army from the left of the Tenth French Army (from about Grenay, south-west of Loos) to Givenchy, north of the La Bassée Canal. The Second British Army, on the left of the First, was to make subsidiary attacks from opposite Pietre, Fromelles and Bellewaarde.

The attack of the First Army was to be carried out by the IVth, Ist, Indian and IIIrd Corps (from right to left), from south-west of Loos to south-east of Armentières. The XIth Corps (Guards, 21st and 24th Divisions) was in reserve to the IVth Corps. The latter consisted of the 1st, 15th and 47th Divisions, in that order from left to right.

The doings of the Gloucesters between the 9th of May at Aubers Ridge and Loos may be summarized briefly.

Three days after the former battle they took over the Sector, termed A.1. of the Brickstacks immediately north of the Bethune —La Bassée road. Two days later they migrated and relieved French troops in Z2 Sector, which was that next but one south of the same road.

Their next sojourn in the line was again in the Brickstacks, and after that in Sector Y4, the third sector southwards from the road.

Following a period in Divisional Reserve with the remainder of the 3rd Brigade in Bethune they returned after a 20-mile march to the line in front of Vermelles, occupying Sector Y1. This tour was followed by one in Z2 Sector, immediately south of the Bethune—La Bassée road, a most unpleasant place popularly known as Bomb Alley.

Followed a further spell in Y1 and then another in Z1. The final sector occupied shortly before the Loos Battle was again Y1.

These tours in the line were interspersed with periods in Brigade Reserve in such places as Cambrin, Bethune, La Bourse, La Beuvrière, Verquin and Philosophe—all pleasant places. The summer was remarkably fine and casualties were remarkably few.

The principal drawbacks to this existence were the lack of bathing facilities and of new clothing for the men, and the enormous amount of digging and carrying that had to be done.

On one occasion, for seven nights in succession, the whole Battalion was employed in two relays during the hours of darkness in making a line 200 yards in front of their front line south of the La Bassée road, preparatory to the Loos Battle.

Captain A. W. Pagan had been confirmed in command of the Battalion with the rank of Lieut.-Colonel [1] : many new officers had also joined and drafts of reinforcements had arrived to replace the large numbers of N.C.O.s and men lost during the heavy fighting in May.

When Operation Orders for the Battle of Loos were issued it was found that the attack was first of all to be carried out by the 1st and 2nd Brigades of the 1st Division, the 3rd Brigade being in Divisional Reserve.

The 1st Division was to attack on the front Northern Sap (inclusive)—Hulluch Road (exclusive). The first objective included Puits No. 14 Bis—Bois Hugo—Chalk Pit—southern portion of Hulluch village ; second objective the German second line with Puits No. 13 Bis.

The 2nd Brigade, on the right, was to attack on the front Northern Sap—south of 81 both inclusive : the 1st Brigade, on the left, was to attack on the front ' The Haie '—and a point 600 yards south of it. A detached force known as Green's Force (consisting of two Territorial battalions commanded by Lieut.-Colonel Green, Royal Sussex Regiment) was to advance, watch for, and move forward to meet, any counter-attack which the enemy might attempt to push in between the 2nd and 1st Infantry

---

[1] Major G. F. Gardiner had reassumed command of the Battalion on the 29th May but had fallen ill during leave in England and Captain Pagan took over command on the 28th July.

Brigades. The 3rd Brigade (the Divisional Reserve) was to move forward to a position of readiness south of Le Rutoire on the night 24th/25th, the 1st Gloucesters leading, at 1 a.m.

The Battalion had arrived at Philosophe on the 13th of September from a tour in the trenches, and the following day was hard at work digging out some old French trenches south of Le Rutoire which were to be occupied the night before the battle, as a ' position of readiness '. This work was continued until the night of the 17th. On the 18th, work of an entirely different nature was carried out by the Battalion—the carrying up of gas cylinders to the front line.

In retaliation for the use of gas at Ypres, a few months earlier, the Allies had also decided to use poison gas : the first time it was to be tried on the British front was on the morning of the 25th September, immediately preceding the infantry attack. Months had been spent in experimenting with different kinds of gas and that first adopted was a mixture of chlorine. It was anticipated that the gas would be so deadly that the following instructions were issued to the troops :

' There is no danger in following up the gas in the open, but no one should enter a German trench, dug-out or cellar without having his smoke helmet properly fastened, as the gas sinks into these and remains there until dispersed by the Vermorel Sprayer. No food or water found in German trenches should be used as it will be poisoned by the gas.'

Each battalion was to be issued with two sprayers and eight tins of solution.

The Gloucesters had finished their carrying duties on the 20th and then marched to bivouacs near Sailly le Bourse, but on the 22nd moved to bivouacs in Vaudricourt Woods. On the 24th packs and blankets were handed in and the Battalion marched from the Woods to the assembly trenches, arriving there at 4 a.m. on the 25th.[1] En route tea and rum were issued in the streets of Philosophe.

[1] Captain G. B. Bosanquet was Adjutant. A Company was commanded by Captain R. D. Scott, B by Lieutenant R. A. Angier, C by Captain N. Durant and D by Captain H. N. Vinen. At this period Captain Blunt had handed over command of B Company on appointment as a Brigade Major in the 20th Division. This officer, who belonged to the York and Lancaster Regiment, was on the outbreak of war on leave from India, and came to France with the Gloucesters. He fought with them during the whole of the Battles of Ypres, 1914, and was never away from them till his final departure. His gallantry and good leadership were outstanding at all times ; during the whole War the 28th never had a better officer nor a better Company Commander than he : he will never be forgotten by his adopted Regiment

The Battalion at this stage numbered 22 officers and 787 other ranks.   Each man, in addition to his rations for the 25th and iron ration, carried a filled water-bottle, two sandbags, two smoke helmets, waterproof sheet and 220 rounds of ammunition, excepting the Battalion bombers who, besides the five ' cricket ball ' bombs allotted to each, carried 120 rounds of S.A.A.

At 6.30 a.m. the attack began, the gas having been discharged some forty minutes earlier.   But the wind was unsuitable and the fumes, blowing back into the British trenches, seriously affected many officers and men.   The 2nd Brigade, attacking on the right of the 1st Division front, was at first held up but later advanced, assisted by the 15th Division on its right.   The 1st Brigade was, however, more successful, and although the attacking battalions [1] lost heavily, they overran Bois Carré and carried the German front line where they were held up by heavy rifle fire from the enemy's support line.

It will be remembered that the attacks of the 2nd and 1st Brigades were to be divergent and that as they advanced Green's Force was to fill the gap between them.   The 3rd Brigade, waiting in reserve, was to support the attack against the German second system of trenches, a thousand yards beyond their first line between Bois Hugo and Hulluch.

At 7.15 a.m. the 1st Gloucesters received orders from 3rd Brigade Headquarters to move up to the support and front-line trenches directly Green's Force was clear of the British trenches. But it was an hour later before a message came to hand that Green's Force was moving forward and 9.5 a.m. before the Gloucesters were ordered to follow the former up to the front line.

But in spite of their endeavours to get forward the Battalion found the old support and firing-line trenches still blocked by Green's Force, and it was 11.30 a.m. before the Gloucesters were able to get even into the third and fourth line trenches.

These positions were held until 2.15 p.m., when a message was received from 1st Divisional Headquarters, via 2nd Brigade Headquarters, placing the Gloucesters at the disposal of the latter.

At the same time another order came to hand from the 2nd Brigade to move southward and to attack, in flank, the Germans who were holding up the advance.   The left Battalion of the 15th Division was also held up.   South of this our troops had gone straight through to their objectives.

The Battalion moved off at once southwards, with a view to

[1] One of these battalions was the 10th Gloucesters, who were practically destroyed, there being only some 60 survivors.

getting on to the Loos—Haisnes Road and thus outflank the enemy. Before it deployed to attack, however, the Germans, numbering about 400, surrendered.

At about 4 p.m. verbal orders were received from the Brigadier to cease the flank movement and advance direct on Bois Hugo and make good the Wood.

Opening out into extended order, the Battalion advanced in three lines to the northern side of Chalk Pit Wood. Owing to casualties sustained by rifle-fire from Hill 70 a short halt took place while a reconnaissance was made. On resuming the advance in order to avoid the German fire the Battalion crossed the Hulluch—Loos road about 300 yards north of the Chalk Pit, then, wheeling south, advanced on Bois Hugo. On reaching the Wood the Battalion entrenched, B, D and half of C Company along the railway line south of Bois Hugo and facing south. The trench dug by the half of C Company ran back towards the Wood at right angles to the railway, facing east to cover the left flank. A Company and the remaining half of C entrenched north of Bois Hugo with the left flank thrown back towards the Lens—Hulluch road.

All night long the men continued digging, but with only their entrenching tools (very inadequate for such a task) and the soil mainly chalk, little progress could be made and when dawn broke on the 26th the trenches were only of an average depth of 3 feet.

Orders during the night stated that the Gloucesters would be relieved by the 8th Lincolns of the 21st Division ; the 28th returning to the 3rd Brigade. On the arrival of the Lincolns they were taken into the trenches, which were handed over to them. This took a very long time and it was getting light before the Gloucesters commenced to withdraw. Before the last men were out it was broad daylight and numerous casualties were incurred by B and D Companies while they were getting from their trench to the Wood. The last to leave had to crawl over the open ground and many of these were hit. It was impossible to extricate the machine-gunners and Lieutenant G. E. Clairmonte, commanding the Section, was ordered to remain where he was until it was possible for him to rejoin the Battalion. Neither Lieutenant Clairmonte nor any of his men were seen again and there is little doubt that they were all killed when the Lincolns were driven out by the Germans. The bodies of Lieutenant Clairmonte and of some of the men were found years later.

The Battalion proceeded to Le Rutoire Farm where they had an excellent breakfast, the first hot meal since early on Saturday morning at Philosophe.

Little rest, however, was allowed the Battalion, for at 8.30 a.m. orders from Brigade Headquarters directed the Gloucesters to move into the old German front-line trench at Bois Carré.

All ranks were still very tired when between 9 and 10 a.m. the 3rd Brigade received orders to move forward and attack Hulluch, the Gloucesters to be in support ; the Brigadier, considering that the Battalion had already done sufficient, cancelled this order and they remained in the old German front-line trench with posts holding the German support trench. The Gloucesters held this position until the evening of the 29th, when they were relieved by the Irish Guards (Guards Division). Companies moved off independently to billets in Nœux-les-Mines, B Company being the last to arrive, not getting in before 3 a.m. on the 30th.

So far the 1st Battalion had not actually attacked the enemy, neither had they been attacked, but their turn was coming soon : they were to engage the enemy and hold him in an attack which will for ever remain one of the proudest memories of the Regiment.

Until the 5th October the Battalion remained billeted in Nœux-les-Mines, but at 5.30 p.m. on that date marched via Mazingarbe to Loos, relieving the 5th Royal Berks and a company of Essex, in the Chalk Pit sector, which included Chalk Pit Wood. The relief was completed by 12 midnight. In this part of the line the British trenches formed a re-entrant opposite the Bois Hugo, the Gloucesters holding the northern angle. They were, therefore, open to enfilade fire and soon after dawn on the 6th shells began to pitch along the line of the Chalk Pit Wood. As the shelling continued two platoons of D Company were sent back to support trenches in rear of the Loos—Hulluch road, for the trenches were overcrowded and, even with a thinned-out garrison, were shallow and offered insufficient protection from the enemy's fire. By incessant work, however, the line was rendered tenable by the evening of the 7th. Hostile shell-fire was just as heavy and a platoon of B and one of D from the support trenches took over one hundred yards of trench running north along the Hulluch road from the Chalk Pit. Seventeen other ranks were wounded during the day.

On the 8th the expected German counter-attack was launched from the Double Crassier to Hill 70, thence to, and including Chalk Pit Wood. The intention of the enemy was to re-occupy Loos Village and the neighbouring trenches as a preliminary to regaining his original line.

The enemy's artillery opened at about noon on the whole front from the La Bassée Canal to opposite Loos, the hostile guns gradually increasing their fire, which reached its greatest intensity between 3 and 4 p.m.

At 4 p.m. the enemy's guns ceased firing on the front to be attacked and his infantry advanced. Twelve battalions were flung against the French line from east of Loos to the Double Crassier, but all they gained was a small strip of trench about 400 yards in length. On the British front the attack was launched against the 1st Division, holding the line from the Loos—Puits 14 Bis track to the northern end of the Chalk Pit. Here the 2nd Royal Munster Fusiliers were on the right, the 1st Gloucesters (Lieut.-Colonel A. W. Pagan) in the centre, and the 1/9th King's on the left.

Already the enemy's intense shell-fire had caused terrible casualties among all three battalions, and when the Germans advanced there were few men to oppose them.

In massed formation, as if determined at all costs to break through, the enemy's infantry advanced not only from the direction of the Bois Hugo, but endeavoured to cross the Hulluch road north of the Gloucesters : they also attacked from a trench which ran parallel with, and about 250 to 300 yards from the Hulluch road.

Although vastly outnumbered by the oncoming lines of Germans, every rifle and machine-gun in the trenches of the Gloucesters opened fire, and soon the ground in front of the Battalion's trenches was littered with dead and wounded Germans. A few got within about 60 yards of our trenches east of the Chalk Pit, where they were shot down, but one unarmed German actually got over our parapet and surrendered, having miraculously escaped being shot. He complained that he was a sailor by trade and didn't like land fighting. Within fifteen minutes of the beginning of the attack the Germans were hurrying back to their trenches, leaving on the ground behind them some four or five hundred killed and wounded. Numbers of the enemy flung themselves on the ground in an endeavour to escape the withering fire poured on them by the Gloucesters and the flanking battalions : when it was getting dark they tried to return to their lines, but the majority were shot down and only a few succeeded in reaching their trenches.

The estimated strength of the enemy attacking in the neighbourhood of the Chalk Pit was two regiments, i.e. six battalions—each German regiment consisted of three battalions.

The 1st Gloucesters had 20 other ranks killed, 96 wounded and 5 missing throughout that terrible day, but they had splendidly upheld the reputation of the Regiment, i.e. that they had never lost a trench. It was a glorious fight and later drew from Army,

Corps, Divisional and Brigade Commanders the highest praise. In a Special Order of the Day, issued on the 10th of October 1915, the G.O.C., 1st Division said :

' The Corps Commander has desired the General Officer Commanding to convey to the General Officer Commanding, 3rd Infantry Brigade, and all ranks under his command, his appreciation of the gallant defence made by the Brigade against the German attack on the 8th inst., and especially of the good work done by the 1st Battalion Gloucestershire Regiment and the 1/9th Battalion Liverpool Regiment.'

The Corps Commander's own words were :

' I particularly admire the splendid tenacity displayed by our infantry in holding on to their trenches during so many long hours of heavy shell-fire, and the skill with which they so gloriously repulsed, with bomb and rifle, the enemy's most determined onslaught.'

The Gloucesters and King's had, indeed, broken up an attack the success of which might have had the gravest results on the whole line.

The work of the Signalling Sergeant, Sergt. Biddle, was outstanding, both during the bombardment and during the infantry attack. This very gallant man started the war as the Signalling Storeman and finished up as a Company Sergt.-Major with a Military Cross, a D.C.M. and Bar, and a Military Medal and Bar. He was a great leader of men and was entirely fearless. He was in the thick of everything that the Battalion did from the beginning of the War until he was wounded, well on in 1918.

At about 11 p.m. that night the 1st Gloucesters were relieved by the South Wales Borderers and moved back to the support trenches east of the Loos—La Bassée road. But they were not beyond the enemy's fire, for on the 9th many howitzer shells fell all along the line of the road. At night the Battalion sent up working parties to construct four advanced saps running south from the fire-trench immediately south of the Chalk Pit Wood. The 10th and 11th were similarly spent : Lieutenant L. C. Brown was killed on the latter date.

On the 12th the Battalion again went into the front line, the Gloucesters relieving the South Wales Borderers in the old trenches south of the Chalk Pit Wood.

The 13th saw the final British attack on the enemy's positions at the Hohenzollern Redoubt.

The 1st Brigade attacked Hulluch with its right on a point 200 yards north of the junction of the Loos—Hulluch and Lens—Hulluch roads, and the left 800 yards north of this point.

The Gloucesters were ordered to hold the Germans on their

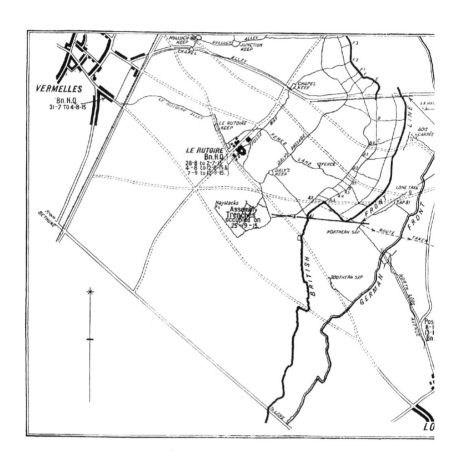

The Battle of LOOS
25th Sept. to 8th Oct. 1915
Trenches held by 1st Bn. Gloucestershire Regt.

Scale of Yards

From HAISNES

HULLUCH ROAD

From LA BASSEE

LA HAIE

DIS ARRÉE

10th Bn. Captured this line on 25th Sept.

Trenches held
28-6 TO 2-7-15.
4-8 TO 12-8-15, &
7-9 TO 13-9-15.
SECTOR Y.I.

AFTERNOON 25th SEPTEMBER 1915

TO

Position in Support
8-10 to 12-10-15, &
13-10 to 14-10-15.
Bn.H.Q. in trench

Trenches held
5-10 TO 8-10-15 &
12-10 TO 13-10-15.

CHALK PIT
Bn.H.Q.

GERMAN COMMUNICATION

OLD BARRACKS

8-10-15

BOIS HUGO

To ANNAY

Line occupied & trenches dug from 4p.m. 25-9 to 5 a.m. 26-9-15.

PUITS 14 BIS

To VENDIN

From LOOS

LOOS

front by throwing smoke-bombs for an hour previous to the assault, and by rifle and machine-gun fire on the enemy's trenches at the moment of assault.   The Germans retaliated with intense shell-fire (H.E.) and during the day the Battalion lost 5 officers [1] and 50 men killed or wounded.

At 10 p.m. the Battalion was relieved by the South Wales Borderers and returned to the support line, and on the following day moved to billets in Mazingarbe.   On the 15th the Battalion marched to Nœux-les-Mines and on the 19th to Cauchy à la Tour, where the Gloucesters occupied their old billets and remained at rest until the 14th of November.

The rest did not come a moment too soon.   For six weeks previous to the Battle of Loos the Gloucesters had been incessantly at work preparing for the operations and there were few nights, when not in the line, when every man was not employed on difficult and dangerous work, often out in No-Man's Land. During the Battle they had had hard fighting and when they were not fighting they were digging.

The total casualties of the Battalion during the Battle of Loos were 5 officers and 63 other ranks killed, 5 officers and 251 other ranks wounded.

[1] Captain R. D. Scott and 2nd Lieutenant R. A. M. Chambers were wounded and died of their wounds : Lieutenant R. A. Angier (second time) and 2nd Lieutenants R. Hewitt and C. C. C. Case were wounded. Officers killed between the 25th and 30th September were Captain R. Montgomery, R.A.M.C. (the Battalion Medical Officer), a very gallant doctor who had been with the Battalion since early in March, and who did excellent work, particularly on the 9th May, and whatever the Regiment was doing was always on the spot, having a complete disregard for his own safety ; 2nd Lieutenant G. E. Clairmonte.

CHAPTER XVI

THE TERRITORIAL BATTALIONS ARRIVE IN FRANCE

IN the meantime, at the end of March, the 48th (South Midland) Division T.F. had landed in France. Of the three infantry brigades the 144th contained the 1/4th and 1/6th Gloucesters and the 145th Brigade the 1/5th Battalion of the Regiment.

The 1/5th (strength 28 officers and 916 other ranks, Lieut.-Colonel J. H. Collett commanding) was the first to arrive, landing at Boulogne at 11 p.m. on the 29th. The following morning the Battalion entrained for St. Omer and Cassel, and on arrival at the latter place marched off to Steenvoorde. The 1/4th (strength 29 officers and 997 other ranks, Lieut.-Colonel S. Davenport commanding) landed at Boulogne on the 30th, and the 1/6th (strength 29 officers and 975 other ranks, Lieut.-Colonel Anderson commanding) disembarked the following day. The 1/4th, after reaching Cassel, moved to the Winnezeele area, and the 1/6th to Oudezeele.

On the 3rd April the Division was reviewed by General Smith-Dorrien and the next day the 145th Brigade marched to billets in the Oultersteen area, the 144th moving on the 5th to Bailleul. On the 7th the former Brigade marched to the Le Bizet area held by the 4th Division, immediately north of Armentières, for attachment during instruction in trench warfare. The 144th Brigade left Bailleul on the 10th for Armentières, where units of the Brigade were to go into trenches held by the 6th Division.

Of the three Territorial Battalions the 1/5th was the first to go into the front-line trenches, and the first also to suffer casualties. The Battalion was attached to the 11th Infantry Brigade (4th Division) and reached Ploegsteert during the evening of the 7th. The following evening Nos. 9 and 10 platoons went into the trenches of the London Rifle Brigade in Ploegsteert Wood, and A Company joined the 1st Somersets in the trenches at St. Yves. The German trenches in this part of the line varied from 70 to 200 yards from the British trenches, and those in close proximity to one another were comparatively free from shell-fire, though sniping was very active, also bomb-throwing and trench-mortaring. The first casualty was reported at 10 a.m. on the 9th—Sergt. Lloyd wounded by a sniper. An hour later Pte. Lee was shot in the left eye. On the 12th the 145th Brigade marched, from being attached to the 4th Division, to billets between Bailleul and Steenwerck.

Meanwhile the 1/4th and 1/6th had also been serving their novitiate in the trenches of the 6th Division. The former Battalion, on arrival on the 10th at Armentières, billeted in a convent in the Rue de Rutours, and that night A Company and two platoons of B Company went into the trenches of the K.S.L.I., York and Lancaster and Buffs for instruction. On the 11th three men were wounded by the explosion of a trench-mortar bomb. There is little to record concerning the 1/6th Gloucesters during those first few days in the trenches, for their Diary has the following brief entry : ' 10/4/15. Armentières. Battalion arrived to be attached to 17th Infantry Brigade for instruction. 17/4/15. Ploegsteert. Battalion in Brigade Reserve.'

About the middle of April the 48th Division assumed responsibility for sectors of the line in Ploegsteert Wood, the 145th Brigade on the 15th taking over from a point 400 yards north of the River Warnave by Le Gheer, and from St. Yves to Prowse Point (600 yards north-west of St. Yves).

The 1/5th Gloucesters went into the north-western section. The 144th Brigade took over the section allotted to it on the eastern edges of Ploegsteert Wood on the 17th, the 1/4th Gloucesters and 1/7th Worcesters going into the front line, with the 1/6th Gloucesters in support at Ploegsteert.

The Gloucestershire Territorials had come to a part of the line which in 1914 had witnessed very severe fighting. Their tour in this new sector was therefore strenuous and far from comfortable.

Although trench warfare was never the dull business which so many people imagined (for there was plenty of excitement) there are, nevertheless, no incidents of outstanding importance during the period the three Battalions were at ' Plugstreet ', to give it its popular name, and the following notes by officers of the separate Battalions give an excellent résumé of the next few months in and out of the line.

' About April the 16th the (1/4th) Battalion marched to Ploegsteert and took over its own line of trenches, embracing the south-eastern corner of Ploegsteert Wood and the village of Le Gheer. This was just inside the Belgian border. These trenches formed part of those held by the 4th Division throughout the winter of 1914, and which they

9

now handed over " intact "—as a notice in the Wood informed the
world—to the 48th Division.

' Throughout the Battle of Hill 60 and the Second Battles of Ypres
these trenches were held by the Battalion : also during the action at
Fromelles in May by the 8th Division when the Battalion, with others,
co-operated by vigorous demonstrations.'

' At the end of May mining activities were commenced by the Germans blowing a mine opposite the 1/6th Battalion front. Mines, in
those days, were a novelty and this occurrence drew crowds of red-
hatted spectators to view the crater. The mine and subsequent shelling
did very little damage however.'

The mine crater extended from the edge of our wire into
No-Man's Land. At dusk two parties, each under a subaltern,
were ordered to seize and consolidate the crater. They were
provided with Mills bombs which had just been received for
the first time. Simultaneously the Germans set out to consolidate their side of the crater—they were driven off by our
consolidating parties, who then carried on their work successfully.

' Shortly afterwards the British retaliated by exploding a successful
mine opposite the " Birdcage ", a strongly-fortified German work just
north of the Ploegsteert—Warneton road. This was followed by a
second German mine going up, again unsuccessfully.

' In the middle of June 1915 the Divisional line was re-arranged and
the Battalion took over trenches opposite Messines. At the end of
June the Division, after handing over the line to the Canadians, was
withdrawn and marched south via Bailleul, Merville and Lillers to be
billeted in an area south-east of the latter and including the fringes of
the mining area around Loos. The 1/4th Battalion was billeted in
the village of Hurionville, 3 miles south of Lillers, where it remained
training until the end of July. Just before the end of the month the
Brigade (144th) moved up to the line opposite Loos (then in the hands
of the Germans) to continue support trenches. After four days there
they were suddenly withdrawn and returned to Hurionville. Two
days later the Division entrained at Lillers and proceeded south via
Doullens to Mondicourt. Detraining here, the Battalion was billeted
in the village of Louvencourt and afterwards in the Bois du Warnimont.
From the latter place the Battalion marched into the trenches opposite
Serre. This had been the scene of an attack by the French on the
previous 8th of June and the captured trenches were handed over by
them to the 48th Division. After a fortnight in these trenches a re-
arrangement took place. The 4th Division, which had followed the
48th, took over the trenches opposite Serre and Pusieux and the 48th
extended its line north to Fonquevillers. The 1/4th Battalion was
allotted trenches east of Hébuterne, extending from the Hébuterne—
Pusieux road to a point 100 yards north of the Hébuterne—Bucquoy
road.'

On the 5th September the 1/4th Battalion went into the
trenches at Hébuterne which they were to occupy alternately
with the 8th Worcesters till the following June. During this

1915]   TERRITORIAL BATTALIONS IN FRANCE   131

time the Battalion snipers probably achieved their highest standard of efficiency. Various types of telescopic sights, largely
obtained through private sources, were used most effectively.
Appropriately enough the leader of this band of assassins was
Sergt. Bisley. On the 2nd October the Germans attempted a
raid on the B Company trenches which was successfully
repulsed. Lieutenant A. L. W. Newth, commanding No. 8
Platoon, Sergt. Walford and Pte. Gould exhibited conspicuous
ability and bravery. The former was awarded the M.C. and
the latter each obtained the D.C.M. These were the first
decorations to be won by any members of the Battalion and
among the first awarded in the 48th Division.

The doings of the 1/5th and 1/6th resemble closely those of
the 1/4th Battalion. Of the former an officer wrote :

' The three months spent here (Ploegsteert) were more or less uneventful, except for the fact that by the time we left we had conquered the
German snipers, thanks to our system of double loophole plates. We buried
about eighteen men in our cemetery in the famous Wood, in addition
to Lieutenants Barnett and Guise (accidentally killed by a bomb explosion)—two very fine officers. At the end of June to Nœux-les-Mines
and about to take over the line. However, the 47th did so instead and
off we rushed to Doullens, taking over from the French at Hébuterne
on July 23rd, the gift of a cow from the French commander being much
prized.' [1]

On the 3rd August a brilliant little patrol engagement took
place between the 1/5th and the enemy. Lance-Corporals
Knight and Harvey with a small patrol met a German patrol in
No-Man's Land. Knight instantly gave the word to charge.
Three Germans were killed and the remainder fled.

An officer of the 1/6th Gloucesters said they

went to Armentières for instruction in trench warfare and, about eight
days from the time of landing, took over the line of trenches in front
'of Ploegsteert Wood, where they remained for six weeks. Here Colonel
Anderson went sick and the Battalion was taken over by the Adjutant
—Captain J. Micklem (Rifle Brigade). This officer had been all through
the Retreat and had been wounded at Ploegsteert in 1914. In June the
Battalion moved to the trenches opposite Messines and from there to
Les Brebis, near Loos. In July, having entrained at Lillers, they were
sent to the line south of Arras which had been taken over from the
French : they detrained at Mondicourt and marched to Louvencourt.
They were the first British troops to arrive in this area. After holding
various parts of the line in this locality they were sent to Hébuterne,

---

[1] The 1/5th first went into the Hébuterne trenches on the 20th July,
according to the Battalion Diary.

which was afterwards the left flank of the Somme Offensive and where
they settled down for the winter of 1915–16.'[1]

---

[1] Casualties amongst officers of the three battalions from April to
about the middle of October, inclusive, were : 1/4th Battalion—Lieutenant Mansell wounded 5th June 1915, Lieutenant H. G. Phippen
wounded 10th June 1915, 2nd Lieutenant H. Merrick wounded 11th
June 1915, 2nd Lieutenant G. K. Savile killed 20th June 1915. 1/5th
Battalion—2nd Lieutenant C. E. R. Barnett killed 19th April 1915,
2nd Lieutenant H. G. C. Guise accidentally killed 6th May 1915, 2nd
Lieutenant G. Hawkins wounded 17th August 1915, Lieutenant T. H.
Moore killed 26th September 1915, Lieutenant C. W. Winterbotham
wounded 17th October 1915. 1/6th Battalion—the Battalion Diary
mentions no names, but 1 officer (2nd Lieutenant W. H. Young, 30th
May 1915) was killed and 2 wounded during the period April to the
middle of October.

CHAPTER XVII

THE WINTER OF 1915–16

THE Diaries of the 1st Battalion from the close of the operations at Loos in October to the end of 1915 contain little but the records of training and resting when out of the line, and brief references to trench warfare—shell-fire, machine-gunning, trench-mortaring, etc., when in the front-line trenches. Throughout that period, and indeed for a considerable time after, the situation on the Loos front remained as it is constantly described in the diaries—' unchanged '. The attempt to break through had failed, though we had pushed our line forward a considerable distance. As was the case with every advance, considerable work was necessary, entailing the digging of new trenches and repairs to old ones : there was, therefore, plenty of manual labour to keep the troops busy, in addition to the ceaseless watch kept upon the enemy, and all the duties of maintaining the line.

The Battalion returned to the Loos sector in the middle of November, relieving the Cameron Highlanders in the trenches on the 19th.

The portion of the line occupied during this period was the Chalk Pit sector, where the Battalion had fought on the 8th October. This portion was again taken over on the 30th November. Next, trenches facing Hulluch and St. Elie were occupied twice in succession. The final spell was once more in the Chalk Pit sector.

These periods in the line were interspersed with spells in close support trenches and with sojourns in Philosophe, Mazingarbe and Nœux-les-Mines, in reserve.

Despite the heavy shell-fire to which this salient in the line was always subjected, casualties were few, the most notable being No. 7177 Corpl. B. Rogers, who was killed on the 23rd November whilst laying a telephone line. This N.C.O. had served with the 28th since the beginning of the War as a signaller, and had frequently distinguished himself.

The Gloucesters were fortunate in that on Christmas Day they were out of the front line and held their festivities at Nœux-

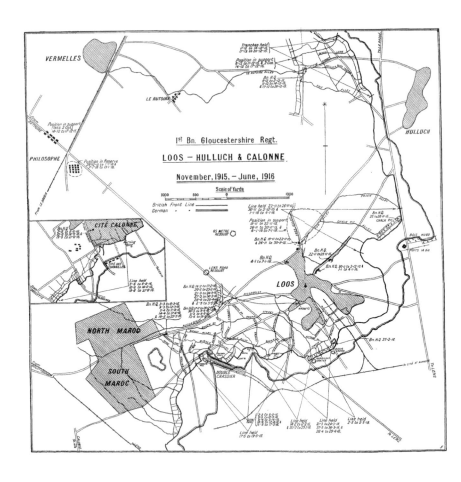

les-Mines, where they had dinner by half-battalion in the School. On the last day of the year they were in Brigade Reserve at Philosophe.

As will be seen, the 2nd Gloucesters were not destined to spend the whole of the winter of 1915–16 in France. The Battalion on the 29th May marched from Locre to Bailleul, thence on the 30th to a field west of Armentières, and at night relieved a battalion of the 16th Infantry Brigade (6th Division) in the Chapelle Armentières sector.

The 2nd Battalion had now come to a quiet part of the line, the enemy was not very active, the trenches were good and casualties small. On the 19th June, Lieut.-Colonel K. M. Davie arrived and assumed command of the Battalion, which at that date had a strength of 23 officers and 921 other ranks. June, and almost the whole of July, were uneventful.

August was uneventful as a whole and the Battalion on the 31st was billeted in La Rolanderie Farm, in Brigade Reserve. Here the 2nd Gloucesters stayed until the middle of September, when the 27th Division moved south to the Somme area, the Battalion arriving in billets at Morcourt on the 22nd. On the 1st October, officers and N.C.O.s proceeded to Fontaine les Cappy to view the trenches held by the 2nd Royal Irish Fusiliers, to be taken over on the 4th.

At 5.55 a.m. on the 4th the 2nd Gloucesters marched out of billets in Morcourt and arrived at Fontaine les Cappy at about 9 a.m., where they breakfasted. At 10 a.m. they began to relieve the Royal Irish Fusiliers.

The sector of the line to which the 2nd Battalion had come was comparatively quiet so far as the opposing artillery and infantry were concerned, mining and counter-mining being the chief means of warring between the opposing forces. No-Man's Land, in front of the Gloucester's trenches, was a mass of mine craters, some of which were held on one side by the Battalion and on the other by the enemy. The fire trenches were generally poor and much work was needed. On this day Lieutenant R. M. Grazebrook was wounded. The next morning at 7.30 a.m. the enemy exploded a mine under the right of Payan Trench : no damage was done and no casualties were suffered by the Gloucesters. About an hour later the Germans exploded another mine with similar results ; the only outcome was to add two more craters to those already existing. Again on the 6th the Germans exploded two mines and we replied by exploding one mine. Their howitzers and ' whizz-bangs ' also shelled our trenches, but our guns eventually silenced them. On the 8th

the Battalion was relieved by the Argyll and Sutherland Highlanders and moved back to Chuignolles in Brigade Reserve.

On the 11th of the month the Gloucesters received orders to
take over the same sector of trenches on the 12th, and here, for
the interest of those who served in what was altogether an extraordinary part of the line, the full description is given just as it
is contained in the Diary of the 2nd Battalion :

' Following is a description of these trenches.   In contrast to the flat
monotony of the north-west corner of France (the Armentières district)
this country is undulating and wooded comparatively thickly.   The
soil is chalk with a few rifts of clay and green sand, the two last being
bad from a mud-producing point of view, in wet weather.   The left
(Trench G2) and extreme right (F1) lie in low ground, but the two
centre trenches stand high.   These trenches had been occupied by the
French before the 27th Division took them over, and, as usual, they
had made very little effort to increase the strength or the comfort of
the lines, the fire trenches being particularly dilapidated, though the
communication trenches came nearly up to the Rue du Bois standard.
G2 is about 400–600 yards from the enemy and consists of two continuous lines and a broken line of " T " heads in front.   This is the
safest and most comfortable trench in our lines.   The right portion
runs up to Bois Commun, an oval wood, round the front of which runs
the front line.   At this point G1 begins with a remarkable specimen
of trench.   In most places there are two lines, in some three, none of
them properly traversed or with strong enough parapets.   In this trench
the distance from the enemy steadily decreases until opposite the right
centre by the Payan crater only 30 yards separates us from the Germans.
At this point is the first crater Payan and from here to the right the
centre trench is simply a line of craters, some on our side and some in
the enemy's trenches.   The first crater Payan, which is the highest, is
about 60 feet high and the hole sinks to about 70 feet.   The whole is
one mass of chalk, looks at night like the top of a snow mountain.   F2
crater Rayon is not so remarkable for the size of the craters, but more
for the number of the craters and shafts which our sappers have sunk,
seven in number, and for the fact that part of the Trench Jeanny is
mined by the Germans.   This fact has an unnerving effect on the
occupants especially as the R.E. consider the mine complete and may
go off at any moment.   Our right trench F1 Filippi is really the most
interesting of all.   The line runs in a very sharp salient the front of
which is wooded and runs close up to the enemy on the sides of the
large crater Filippi.   From this point again run out two listening posts
situated on the lip of the crater 15 yards from the Germans.   The last
platoon lies on the receding side of a hill and the right of the Battalion
line is right down in a small ravine about 400 yards from the enemy.
Total length of line held by Battalion 2,000 yards, with every conceivable
kind of trench and trench warfare, i.e. shelling, mining, bombing,
patrolling, trench-mortaring, sniping.'

One seldom finds such a complete description of the trenches
as that given above.

The 2nd Gloucesters duly relieved the Argyll and Sutherland Highlanders in the line on the 12th. On the 13th the enemy took it into his head to become specially aggressive. Before it was light he began with bombs and rifle grenades on the sap-heads on the Filippi crater. Immediately the Battalion replied and soon the enemy ceased and ' after having the last word we also stopped '. In a little while, however, a green light went up from the enemy's trenches and the latter again began to fling bombs and fire rifle grenades into the trenches of the Gloucesters. So once again the Battalion replied, adding 33-pdr. bombs from the trench mortars. At the expiration of ten minutes the Germans had had enough and stopped, and ' after giving them *ten minutes more of the best* we also stopped '. For the remainder of the day the Germans were quiet, contenting themselves with the ordinary sniping. On the 16th the Gloucesters were again relieved by the 1st Argyll and Sutherland Highlanders and marched back to billets in Chuignolles.

On the 23rd October French officers visited the line (the Battalion being then back in the front line) with a view to taking over on the 24th. The relief was completed by 3.45 p.m. and the Gloucesters returned to Morcourt : on the 26th they moved to Boues and on the 27th to Seux, where they remained until the 14th of November.

The Battalion had received information on the 1st of the month that the 27th Division was destined for Salonika, and from that date until the 14th preparations were made for moving to that theatre of the war. At 2.30 p.m. on the latter date the Battalion marched to Clary.

Movement orders to entrain at Longeau at 7 a.m. were received during the evening of the 21st November, and before dawn the next morning the Gloucesters were on the way to the station. By 7.30 a.m. the whole Battalion had entrained. On arrival at Marseilles on the 24th, Companies went into a rest camp about two and a half miles from the station. Embarkation began on the 25th and by the 26th all were aboard. The strength of the Battalion was then 26 officers and 882 other ranks : Lieut.-Colonel F. C. Nisbet was in command.

On the 28th the transport put out to sea and at midday on the 6th December passed up the Gulf of Salonika. Dense fog, however, compelled the boat to anchor and it was the 7th before the vessel finally reached Salonika Harbour.

Several days were spent aboard, for it was the 12th of December before the ship was berthed alongside the quay. Disembarkation began at 2.45 p.m. and at 3.30 p.m. the 2nd Gloucesters set out

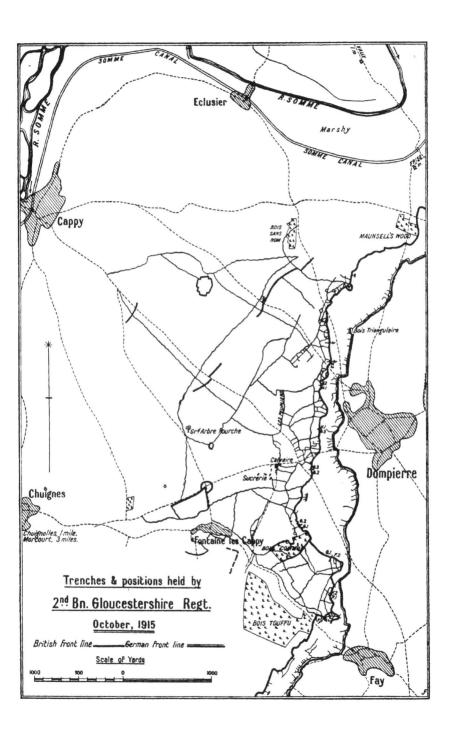

SOMME CANAL

VAUX m

Eclusier

R. SOMME

R. SOMME

Marshy

SOMME CANAL

FRISE Bn.

BOIS SANS NOM

MAUNSELL'S WOOD

Cappy

Bois Triangulaire

Dompierre

Grd Arbre Fourche

Calvaire

Sucrèrie

Chuignes

Chuignolles, 1 mile.
Marcourt, 3 miles.

Fontaine les Cappy

BOIS CORNU

BL.F2

BOIS TOUFFU

Fay

Trenches & positions held by

2ⁿᵈ Bn. Gloucestershire Regt.

October, 1915

British front line ———— German front line ════

Scale of Yards

1000   500   0   1000

on a four-mile march to Lembet Camp where, for the time being, the Battalion must be left.

In the meantime the three Territorial battalions of the Regiment (1/4th, 1/5th and 1/6th) were by the end of October busily engaged in preparing for the winter, which indeed had already set in. In some of the diaries the trenches are described as beginning to fall in. There was, therefore, a good deal of work before the Battalions. The enemy does not appear from the records to have been more than normally active : no incidents of outstanding importance are mentioned, excepting a raid by the 1/6th Gloucesters in November.

The condition of the trenches is well illustrated in an entry in the diary of the 1/4th Gloucesters on the 7th December, the Battalion on that date holding the front line immediately east of Hébuterne.

' Battalion in the trenches. Night 6th/7th December rather finer and very quiet. Men hard at work baling and pumping and removing fallen side of trenches, pumping out sumps and repairing same. The shelters for officers and men are untenable as most have fallen in owing to the wet and are half full of mud and water. The communication trenches are especially bad. " Biron " [1] for the last hundred yards towards the firing line is practically impassable and " Montrallier " in same condition from " Haddon " to firing line. " Napier " could not be used, also " Surcouf ". The right company's post in " Hoche " could only be relieved at dusk and had to remain for twenty-four hours at a time, and the listening post for thirteen hours : and the left company's post in " Bataille " could only be relieved by night along the parapet. Continuous baling and pumping is being kept up and sumping. " Haddon " trench was kept free but very bad by barricade and " Remaud " is impassable too.'

A very bad state of affairs but, if it was any consolation to them, the Gloucesters knew that the enemy's trenches seemed to be in an even worse condition !

The 1/5th also comment on the bad state of the trenches as the winter advanced.

Before the bombing raid described below, the diaries of the 1/6th Gloucesters from October to the end of the year contain nothing worth recording, for each ' diary ' consisted of one sheet of paper only—one for each month—with barely sufficient writing on it to constitute a short letter : moves up to and from the trenches at Gommecourt and Hébuterne, and billets in Couin. But both the diaries of 144th Brigade Headquarters and the Battalion contain as appendices a full account of the raid, though

[1] The trenches all had French names, having been recently held by French troops.

for some reason unknown the former deletes the name of every officer.

The Battalion Diary calls it an ' Enterprise by C Company, 6th Battalion, Gloucestershire Regiment on the night of the 25th/26th November, 1915 '.

The intention was to raid the German trenches and shelters at the south-eastern corner of Gommecourt Wood, for the purpose of obtaining prisoners and information as to the trenches, garrisons, etc. Strong works were known to exist at this point.

The ' scheme ' of the attack, because it was the first of its kind made by the 1/6th Battalion, is given in full :

' Strength of party 5 officers, 100 other ranks ; of these two parties of 25 each under an officer told off to enter trenches at X and Y on attached plan.[1] Remaining three officers and fifty other ranks to be in support in Z hedge at W on plan.[2] As soon as the two parties are in position 70 yards from German trenches, " ready " to be signalled back to artillery who commence first barrage as shown on plan.[3] The object of this barrage is to make the German sentries take cover, drown the noise of our party approaching and cutting the wire, and subsequently to prevent German reinforcements coming up from second line. The first gun to be the signal for the assaulting parties to rush. Bombing parties to be left at each communication trench, and the remainder of the two assaulting parties to work to the central part and then retire on to the support. The whole party then to retire to our trenches and second barrage to open to cover retirement.'

A preliminary bombardment was to take place during the afternoon of the 25th in order to cut the enemy's wire, damage his trenches and attract a working party from whom prisoners might possibly be captured when the raid took place.

The raid had been carefully rehearsed both by day and by night over model trenches. The composition, formation and equipment of the storming parties are interesting details, given because the next generation may wonder in what way the raiders were armed. Each assaulting column (there were two, the right and the left), led by an officer, consisted of four men with rifles and fixed bayonets, four men each carrying twelve bombs, bludgeon and bayonet as dagger, four men each with bludgeon and bayonet as dagger, four men with revolvers and bayonets

[1] X and Y were two points at the south-eastern corner of the Wood.

[2] Between our lines and the enemy's trenches was a hedge known as Z Hedge. At point W the hedge formed a semicircle, the right resting on the Hébuterne—Gommecourt road, which crossed No-Man's Land in a north-east to south-west direction.

[3] The first barrage was to fall round the German trenches on the south-eastern corner of the Wood (not on the front line) so as to prevent reinforcements from arriving, or hostile troops in the front line retiring.

as daggers (for escort to prisoners), four men with rifles and fixed bayonets, four men with twelve bombs each, bludgeon and bayonet (these last two sections of fours were detailed to block and hold communication trench and point of entry) : finally, the sections of fours were to be followed by two telephone men with instrument, to remain at point of entry.

The support party at Z hedge was to consist of three officers, six grenadiers with rifle grenades, fifty men in fighting order with rifles, bayonets and reserve of bombs, one officer, R.F.A., with telephone and operator, three telephone operators for infantry with their instruments.

The above raid was under Captain V. L. Young ; 2nd Lieutenant T. T. Pryce and 2nd Lieutenant J. M. C. Badgeley commanded the right and left parties respectively.

At 2.40 p.m. on the 25th the Divisional Artillery opened fire in order to cut the wire and damage the enemy's trenches. When darkness had fallen Lieutenant H. P. Nott and twenty other ranks crept out to the Z hedge in order to prevent German patrols occupying it. At 11.25 p.m. ninety men of C Company, including the two raiding parties under Captain Young, left the trenches and joined the party already at Z hedge. In bright moonlight, but moving very slowly for fear of attracting the Germans, the two parties under 2nd Lieutenants Pryce and Badgeley left the hedge and crossed to positions of readiness 70 yards from the German trenches. They were in position by 12.45 a.m. and at 12.58 a.m. Captain Young received a report from them by telephone that they were ready to assault. He waited two or three minutes until a cloud obscured the moon, and then asked the artillery officer with him to signal back for the barrage. The word ' ready ' was 'phoned to the Divisional gunners at 1.3 a.m. and with a crash the barrage fell all round the sector of the trenches to be raided.

The raiders dashed forward.

The right party (under 2nd Lieutenant Pryce), whose point of entry was Y, found only low wire confronting them and they were able to enter the hostile trenches without alarming the enemy. The first shelter met with was a telephone office : a German coming up the steps met Lieutenant Pryce. The latter called on him to surrender. He refused and was shot. Three bombs were then thrown into the shelter. A block was then formed and an N.C.O. in charge of the blocking party pulled up a sump cover which effectively prevented the German supports from reaching the raiders. Led by their officers the latter then ran down the trench, bombing six more shelters in succession. Three unarmed Germans were taken during this rush down the trench. As they were being passed down for evacuation they suddenly darted into a shelter, re-appearing almost immediately armed, and attacked the raiders in rear. The three were then killed. Lieutenant Pryce had now lost touch with the left party and began to retrace his steps up the trench, but found it full of hostile troops who had apparently come up from their underground passages. The raiders then bombed this crowd of Germans most successfully, climbed out of the trench and retired with all their wounded. The enemy tried to pursue them but were again driven back with bombs. Lieutenant Pryce had been slightly wounded by a pistol fired by a German officer, but he killed the latter with his revolver.

With the exception of one man who had been sent back with a message to the signallers and was never seen again, the right party reached Z hedge safely, bringing back one wounded German with them.

The left party, however, under 2nd Lieutenant Badgeley, were not quite as lucky. When they reached the German wire they found it had not been cut by the artillery. They had to cut their way through two belts of wire, the second being very new, thick and strong wire 5 yards deep—no easy task. The unavoidable noise caused by the wire-cutters gave the German sentries the alarm. Nevertheless, Lieutenant Badgeley and ten men managed to get into the trench, where they bombed the first dugout, the officer having shot down two Germans. The enemy then retired along the trench to the left. From the parallel trench in rear bombs were thrown at the raiders : they were replied to with interest ! Touch was gained with the right party, but Lieutenant Badgeley was wounded by a bomb which fell and exploded at his feet. The party then retired to Z hedge, bringing back all their wounded. One of the latter was unfortunately killed by a chance bullet on the way back.

Having now concentrated the raiders at Z hedge, Captain Young telephoned to the artillery to stop the first barrage. He then sent the men, in small parties, back to the trenches. Lieutenant D. H. Hartog, with the rifle-grenade party, moved off to the left, where he was able to enfilade the enemy's trench, which by now was presumably crowded. He fired twelve grenades into the trench and then withdrew.

The whole party returned without further casualties.

The raid was most successful and many Germans must have been killed, for they were caught crowded together in big, deep shelters which were heavily bombed. The prisoners stated that the trench garrison was a company numbering 180 men.   Eight Germans had been killed in the trench outside these shelters.

The raiders' casualties were 1 man killed, 1 man missing and 2nd Lieutenants Badgeley and Pryce and 18 other ranks wounded —all slight wounds.

Both the Corps and Divisional Commanders and G.H.Q. heartily congratulated the Battalion on this successful enterprise.[1]

Two officers of the 1/6th lost their lives in November : Lieutenant C. E. Schwalm was killed on the 22nd and Captain P. G. Irvine on the 26th.

December may be written down as without special interest.

*   *   *   *   *

January the 1st, 1916, found the 1st Gloucesters holding the extreme right of the British line in the Loos sector, with French troops immediately south of them.   With the exception of spasmodic heavy shell-fire the first month of the year was passed in comparative quietude, for on the 16th the Battalion moved back to billets in Cauchy, where the remainder of January was spent in training.

Previously the line had always been occupied north of Loos, but from now until the 1st Division proceeded to the Somme Battle early in July, the Gloucesters were destined to hold alternately the Maroc and Loos sectors, both situated south of Loos, and were never, except for one short period, to get farther from the line than the model village of Les Brebis, the distance from which to the foremost trenches was little over 2 miles.

It was not until the 14th of February that front-line trenches were again taken over in the Loos sector, one notable feature of which was a huge crater—Harrison's Crater—the result of a recent great mine explosion.   This crater was, with another— Hart's Crater—the scene of many a bitter struggle.   On the 19th February the Gloucesters received verbal orders from the Brigadier to take part in a bombing attack on both craters.   B Company in South Street, with the bombers of A Company, was detailed to help the South Wales Borderers and also provide a party to dig a sap up to Harrison's Crater : C Company moved

---

[1] For this affair Lieutenants Pryce and Badgeley were awarded the M.C.

Lieutenant Pryce joined the 1/6th Gloucesters from the H.A.C. : he was invalided to England as the result of his wound in the raid and later proceeded to France with the 2/6th Gloucesters.   He was awarded a Bar to his M.C. on 19th July 1916, for an act of exceptional gallantry. Later he transferred to the Grenadier Guards and was killed near Vieux Berquin, while commanding No. 2 Company of the 4th Grenadier Guards, being awarded a posthumous V.C. for a magnificent fight against overwhelming odds.

up to Regent Street to support the South Wales Borderers and to come under the orders of that Battalion.

The attack took place at 7.10 p.m. but the Battalion Diary of the Gloucesters records that ' Bombing attack instead of being carried out quietly was made into a shouting charge and we suffered casualties—2 killed, 12 wounded and 5 missing '.

Nevertheless by 4.35 a.m. on the 20th the South Wales Borderers were able to report that ' we had established posts on our side of Harrison's Crater (to remain during the day) : our side of Hart's Crater is not occupied by either side as both we and the enemy command it with machine guns '.

On the 25th of February the C.O. having been ordered to secure Hart's Crater, after two mines had been exploded under it at 7 p.m. took a party of 7 officers and 180 other ranks to the left sector of the line.

The party assembled in Regent Street, on the left of the sunken road which ran along the western side of the Loos Crassier from the front line to Loos Church. The intention was to establish two bombing posts (the right under 2nd Lieutenant W. R. K. Heath and the left under Lieutenant R. M. Hart) on the crater with a communication trench to each and eventually join them up. Special digging parties (under 2nd Lieutenant J. K. George and 2nd Lieutenant W. W. Morgan) were ready behind the two bombing parties. Each man of these two parties carried a sand-bag filled with chalk, the sand-bags to be dumped along the line marked out as a communication trench, to provide cover for the men while they were digging.

At 7 p.m. the mines ' went up ' [1] and immediately the enemy opened fire with trench mortars and rifle grenades on the crater and sunken road, but without hesitation both parties rushed forward. The right party dashed over the front line and reached the lip of the crater from which a view of both the new craters (formed by the explosion) could be obtained. Although heavily fired on by the enemy trench mortars and worried by the Divisional 4·5-inch howitzers which were ' firing short ', the work of holding the lip while digging went on was carried out. The left party, however, encountered such heavy machine-gun fire in the sunken road and left slopes of the crater that it was held up and could not get on : this fire was continued throughout the night.

[1] They were made and ' blown ' by the 173rd Tunnelling Company R.E. When the Gloucesters took over the Germans had the upper hand in mining, but owing to the activities of this Company of R.E. the reverse was very soon the case.

At about 11 p.m., after sending up a lot of flares, the enemy opened machine-gun fire from their right front, but by this time the working party was more or less under cover. Just after midnight a party of Germans appeared on their side of the crater but were dispersed by rifle fire. By 5.15 a.m. on the 26th the communication trench from our front line to the post on the lip of the crater was finished—a dug-out had also been made in the post. The party then retired to billets in Les Brebis.

This brilliant little affair carried out by the Gloucesters in extraordinarily severe weather consisting mostly of blizzards of snow, cost the Battalion 1 officer (2nd Lieutenant W. R. K. Heath) killed, who was shot down during the rush with the right party to the lip of the new crater, 1 other rank killed and 2 injured.

The Battalion remained in billets in Les Brebis, finding large working parties daily until the 9th March, when it relieved the 6th Welch in the Double Crassier sector. A Company held the Crassier with B on the left, D in support in Dugout Row and the old German front line, and C in reserve in cellars round Battalion Headquarters.

The enemy shelled the line very heavily on the 10th and 11th of March with all sorts of projectiles and early on the 12th he began an intense bombardment of the Crassier and the neighbourhood with 8-inch and 5·9-inch shells and aerial torpedoes : it was continued with intervals all that day and until early the next morning.

A Company had one platoon on the northern arm of the Crassier with another in a disused mine-shaft, supporting the one on the Crassier. During the bombardment these two platoons were entirely cut off and no information could be got from them. About 2 p.m. the shelling slackened and it was then found that the entrances to the mine-shaft were entirely blocked, in fact the ground had been so flattened by the bombardment that the position of the entrances could not be detected.

The platoon on the northern arm of the Crassier was next visited and found to be all right as they had moved to the forward end of their sap, which was close to the enemy and therefore unshelled. The rearward part of their position and the trench leading to it was obliterated. Working parties were then moved to the site of the mine-shaft, and with the technical assistance of an officer of the 173rd Tunnelling Company, two places were selected at which to start digging with a view to releasing the buried platoon.

The work was arduous and dangerous as the shelling was severe, and the working-parties had frequently to cease work and lie flat. A certain amount of head cover was arranged with trench boards but casualties occurred frequently. The difficulties of the situation were added to by the fact that at night the Battalion was relieved by the 6th Welch and proceeded to South Maroc in Brigade support.

The digging was continued all night and at 6.30 a.m., after being buried for twenty-two hours, Sergt. Drake and his men emerged at a place about midway between those at which the parties were digging. Only six of the twenty-five men were dead, though others died later, and eight of them were actually able to walk down to Maroc.

The fact that the whole were not dead was due entirely to the leadership of No. 14162 Sergt. W. Drake. This N.C.O. organized his men into working parties which he kept at work for very short periods and then relieved them. He encouraged the faint-hearted, and by the courageous way in which he faced the situation and organized the work, saved the lives of the greater portion of his men. He was recommended for the Victoria Cross but was awarded the D.C.M. The reason given for withholding the V.C. was that he was saving his own life as well as those of his comrades.

The total casualties of the working parties were 15. Lieutenant N. Durant [1] was killed at dusk while superintending the work.

Mining and counter-mining, with heavy bombardments by the guns of both sides, characterized the remainder of March, and April was hardly less active. Indeed, with the advent of spring, trench warfare became ever more vigorous. On the 9th April, 2nd Lieutenant H. M. Goulding was wounded (the Battalion being then in the line at Maroc), and on the 15th, during very heavy shell-fire, 2nd Lieutenant C. A. Olds and 1 other rank were killed and 6 other ranks wounded. The explosions of camouflets and mines became more frequent as the ground dried up and gave better facilities for digging underground. In May nothing of outstanding importance occurred, but on the 8th of this month, Captain G. B. Bosanquet left the Battalion on appointment as a Brigade Major in the 21st Division. This officer was a Territorial Adjutant when the War began and joined the 28th during the darkest days of Ypres 1914, and took over the duties of Adjutant. He was wounded at Festubert in December 1914, returned in March 1915, and was again wounded on 9th May 1915. He was back again in August and fought in the Loos battle with his usual gallantry. He was killed on 1st July 1916 on the Fricourt-

---

[1] This officer had been with the Battalion since May 1915 and had commanded C Company well during the Loos fighting and afterwards.

Contalmaison road while leading the advance of the 64th Brigade on the first day of the Somme Battles. The Regiment suffered no greater loss during the War than it did by his death.

On the 2nd of June, the Gloucesters being then at Les Brebis in reserve, moved to new trenches in the Calonne sector, south-west of Loos. But here again the normal activities of the enemy were not broken by any incidents worthy of record, and on the 21st the Battalion marched back to Les Brebis, where they were still billeted on the 30th of the month.

The 1st of January 1916 still found the three Territorial Battalions of the Regiment in the Hébuterne Sector. Of the 144th Brigade the 1/4th Gloucesters were in billets in Authie, the 1/6th in the front line in ' K ' Sector ; the 1/5th Battalion of the 145th Brigade was also in the front line. Possibly by the time another war happens the regulations concerning the keeping of war diaries will have been made more stringent and historians of the future will be able to depict the lives of battalions on active service with some degree of accuracy not only during operations but in those periods of *comparative* inactivity which, during the Great War, were often as interesting as a big battle.

January proved to be an exceptionally mild month and trench life was almost bearable. On the 18th February, owing to a re-arrangement of the line, the 1/4th Battalion took over trenches in the Hannescamps Sector, north of Fonquevillers, relieving a Battalion of the 37th Division. The same night the 1/8th Worcesters (on the right) were raided by the enemy, the 1/4th Gloucesters also suffering casualties through a feint bombardment on their front. After two tours in the trenches, during which the weather was extraordinarily bad, snow, rain and wind vieing with each other in intensity and frequency, the original occupants returned to them and the 144th Brigade took over the Serre Sector on the right of the 48th Divisional front. On the night of the 18th/19th of March the 1/6th Battalion was attacked by a strong party of Germans but, notwithstanding the intense bom-bardment to which the Gloucestershire Territorials were sub-jected by shells from guns of all calibres (including gas and tear) and the difficulties of defending their isolated posts and positions, they put up an excellent fight and repulsed the enemy. The 1/4th Battalion, then in reserve at Colincamps, received orders to move up to reinforce, but their services were not needed. During the next tour in the front line the 1/4th was ordered to retaliate on the enemy for their raid, but at the last moment orders were cancelled.

Early in April units of the 31st Division were put into the
10

trenches of the 1/4th Gloucesters in order that the latter might
give them preliminary instruction in trench warfare : later the
31st Division took over that part of the line, the 1/4th Gloucesters
returning to their old sector at Hébuterne. The Divisional
front line was during April considerably lessened and in consequence only one brigade held the line. This enabled the 144th
Brigade on the 4th of May to move back to rest billets in Beauval,
11 miles from the front line : it was the first occasion that units
of that Brigade had been out of the immediate neighbourhood
of the trenches for eight and a half months, and the short respite
was greatly appreciated. On the 15th, however, the 1/4th
Gloucesters again got on the march and moved into local reserve
at Couin, whence on the 20th they moved once more into the
Hébuterne trenches.

During this period the Battalion took an active part in the
preparations then in hand for the coming great offensive. Cable
burying, the construction and wiring of assault trenches in front
of the village, occupied much of their time, training being carried
out when opportunities occurred. The month of June was thus
spent and final training took place in the neighbourhood of
Oneux and St. Riquier, some 18 miles behind the front line.[1]
On the last day of the month the 1/4th Gloucesters were in
Corps Reserve in the Sailly Bivouacs : the Battalion strength
was 35 officers and 1,002 other ranks.

With the exception of certain incidents, the story of the 1/6th
Gloucesters for the first six months of 1916 closely resembles
that of the two other Territorial Battalions, i.e. 1/4th and 1/5th.

In the affair mentioned above, i.e. the German raid on the
1/6th Battalion on the 18th/19th of March, the Battalion lost
12 other ranks killed, 29 wounded or gassed and 3 missing. The
line held by the Battalion at that period consisted of a series of
isolated posts which could only be relieved after dark. Practically
all the casualties were caused by the enemy's shell-fire.

From the diaries of the 1/5th Gloucesters (145th Brigade) for
January to June, inclusive, there is similarly little to record.
They also took their part in the strenuous preparations for the
Somme Battles, and on the last day of June the strength of the
Battalion was 35 officers and 913 other ranks.

---

[1] Officer casualties from January to June were as follows : 2nd Lieutenant R. A. Chattock, 1/4th Battalion, killed 14th March 1916 ; Captain V. L. Young and 2nd Lieutenant G. Brindal, 1/6th Battalion,
wounded 18th March 1916 ; 2nd Lieutenant J. G. Holman, 1/6th
Battalion, gassed 19th March 1916 ; Lieutenant H. P. Nott, 1/6th
Battalion, killed 27th April 1916.

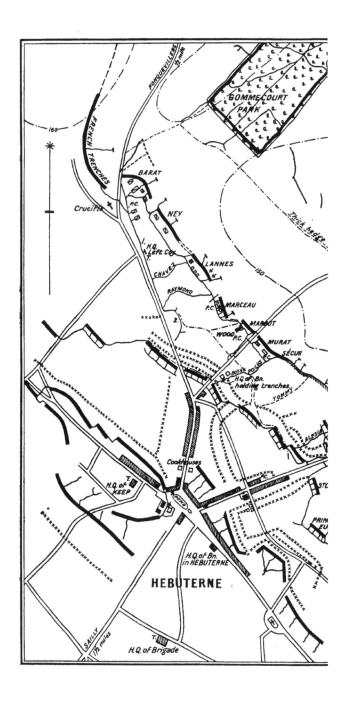

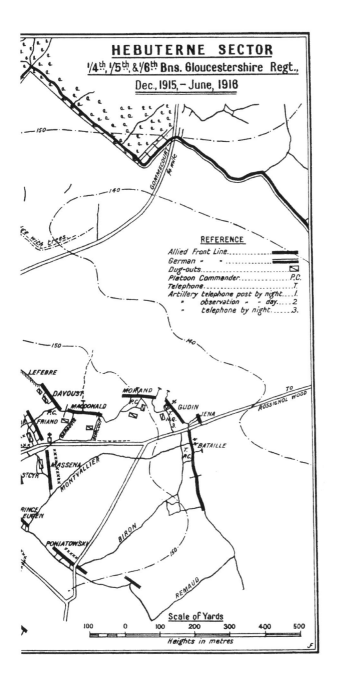

HEBUTERNE SECTOR

1/4th, 1/5th, & 1/6th Bns. Gloucestershire Regt.,

Dec., 1915, – June, 1916

REFERENCE

Allied Front Line.................
German   "   "   ....
Dug-outs.................................
Platoon Commander..................P.C.
Telephone..................................T.
Artillery telephone post by night....1.
    "   observation "   - day.....2
    "   telephone by night.......3.

LEFEBRE
DAVOUST
MORLAND
P.C.
MACDONALD
GUDIN
FRIAND
JENA
BATAILLE
MASSENA
MONTVALLIER
ST CYR
PRINCE
EUGEN
PONIATOWSKY
BIRON
REMAUD

GOMMECOURT PARC

TO ROSSIGNOL WOOD

Scale of Yards

100   0   100   200   300   400   500

Heights in metres

CHAPTER XVIII

THE SOMME BATTLES OF 1916

THERE is not a regiment of the British Army that does not number ' Somme, 1916 ' amongst its battle honours : and the majority can claim service in every battle which comes under the heading of those important operations grouped together under the one great title of the Somme Battles.

Sanguinary as were the battles of 1914–15, and in several ways of equal importance, the terrible struggle which took place on the Somme from the 1st of July to the third week in November 1916, had no equal before that period in ferocity or in the enormous losses sustained by both sides : nor were previous operations of such strategical importance.

At the close of 1915 representatives of all the Allied Powers had met at French G.H.Q. at Chantilly, where the principle of our offensive campaign during the summer of 1916 was discussed and finally decided. In France, Italy and Russia the enemy was to be attacked.

In France the British and French were to make a combined attack, as neither was deemed strong enough to undertake unaided an offensive on a really large scale: the terrain selected as the scene of operations being the country south and north of the Somme River.

It is, however, necessary to point out that as first planned the French were to launch the main attack south of the Somme, while the British made a subsidiary attack north of the river. Subsequent events reversed this plan, i.e. the British attack north of the river became the main attack with the French attacking astride the Somme as a subsidiary operation. The reason was as follows : In February, while yet the French were concentrating their forces south of the Somme for the attack the Germans, in great strength, attacked at Verdun, and gradually the French divisions were withdrawn from the Somme and thrown in there to stem the tide. But the struggle was so intense that practically all the French reserves were absorbed and it became impossible for our Allies to make the principal attack on the Somme. In May the Austrians attacked in the Trentino and forced the

Italians back to Asiero and Asiago. But still the relentless pressure on Verdun continued. Then in June the Russians attacked in Galicia and their successes forced the Germans to transfer troops from the west to that front.

All this while Sir Douglas Haig was preparing for his great offensive on the Somme, and although desirous of postponing his attack as long as possible in view of the large numbers of officers and men of the ' New Armies ' who had to complete their training, and the great extent of the preparations to be made, it was evident that the strain on Verdun and in Italy might become too great to be borne unless timely action were taken to relieve it. Arrangements were then made to attack at the end of June, though subsequently the date had to be altered to the 1st July.

In view of the fact that there are many who still affirm that the objectives of the Somme Battles of 1916 were to break through the enemy's front, roll up his flanks and defeat his divided forces, and that we ' lost the Battle ' (whatever that may mean) because we did not do so, the three objectives as given by Sir Douglas Haig are here set forth :

' (i) To relieve the pressure on Verdun.
(ii) To assist our Allies in the other theatres of war by stopping any further transfer of German troops from the Western front.
(iii) To wear down the strength of the forces opposed to us.'

The front selected for the British attack ran from just north of the Somme at Maricourt

' round the salient at Fricourt to the Ancre in front of St. Pierre Divion. To assist this main attack by holding the enemy's reserves and occupying his artillery, the enemy's trenches north of the Ancre as far as Serre, inclusive, were to be assaulted simultaneously : while further north a subsidiary attack was to be made on both sides of the salient at Gommecourt.' [1]

The enemy's defences on the Somme were extraordinarily powerful. Starting from the Somme River near Curlu the German front line ran at first northwards for 3,000 yards, then westwards for 7,000 yards to near Fricourt : here it turned nearly due north, forming a great salient in the enemy's line. Some 10,000 yards north of Fricourt the trenches crossed the Ancre and ran northwards, east of Hébuterne to Gommecourt, thence in a northerly direction towards Arras.

Between the Somme and the Ancre the enemy held a strong

[1] From the official despatches of Sir Douglas Haig, dated 20th December 1916.

second line at an average distance of from 3,000 to 5,000 yards behind his first system of trenches.

'During nearly two years' preparation he had spared no pains to render these defences impregnable. The first and second systems each consisted of several lines of deep trenches, well provided with bomb-proof shelters and with numerous communication trenches connecting them. The front of the trenches in each system was protected by wire entanglements, many of them in two belts 40 yards broad, built of iron stakes interlaced with barbed wire, often almost as thick as a man's finger.'

'The numerous woods and villages in and between these systems of defence had been turned into veritable fortresses. The deep cellars, usually to be found in the villages, and the numerous pits and quarries common to a chalk country were used to provide cover for machine guns and trench mortars. The existing cellars were supplemented by elaborate dug-outs, sometimes in two storeys, and these were con-nected up by passages as much as 30 feet below the surface of the ground. The salients in the enemy's front line, from which he could bring enfilade fire across his front, were made into self-contained forts and often protected by mine fields, while strong redoubts and concrete machine-gun emplacements had been constructed in positions from which he could sweep his own trenches should they be taken. The ground lent itself to good artillery observation on the enemy's part and he had skilfully arranged for cross fire by his guns.

'These various systems of defence, with the fortified localities and other supporting points between them, were cunningly sited to afford each other material assistance and to admit of the utmost possible development of enfilade and flanking fire by machine guns and artillery. They formed, in short, not merely a series of successive lines but one composite system of enormous depth and strength. Behind his second system of trenches, in addition to woods, villages and other strong points prepared for defence, the enemy had several other lines already com-pleted : and we had learnt from aeroplane reconnaissance that he was hard at work improving and strengthening them and digging fresh ones behind them and still further back.

'In the area above described (between the Somme and the Ancre) our front-line trenches ran parallel and close to those of the enemy, but below them. We had good direct observation over his front system of trenches and on the various defences sited on the slopes above us between his front and second systems : but the second system itself in many places could not be observed from the ground in our possession, while except from the air nothing could be seen of his more distant defences.

'North of the Ancre, where the opposing trenches ran transversely across the main ridge, the enemy's defences were equally elaborate and formidable.'

No easy task lay before the attacking troops.

On the 24th June the preliminary bombardment began and continued with increasing violence until zero hour on the 1st July, when at 7.30 a.m., after a final hour of exceptionally heavy shell fire from some 1,500 guns, the attack was launched.

In the first of the battles, which grouped together formed the Battles of the Somme 1916, neither the 1st, 1/4th, 1/5th, nor 1/6th Gloucesters were engaged : they made no attack on the enemy until the Battle of Bazentin Ridge, which opened on the 14th July.[1]

The 1st Battalion remained in Les Brebis until the 4th July, upon which date the 40th Division relieved the 1st Division, the latter moving back out of the line for a well-deserved rest, the Gloucesters to Bruay, where comfortable billets were obtained. From the 14th February to the 4th July the Battalion had never been farther from the line than Les Brebis, except for six days at Petit Sains. During that period they had been continuously in and out of a rather unpleasant bit of line, against which the enemy directed a surprising variety of projectiles.[2]

On the 5th, training areas were reconnoitred, but later in the day the 1st Division[3] was ordered to proceed to the Somme. The next day the Gloucesters marched to Chocques and entrained for Doullens. On reaching the latter place at 11 p.m. the C.O. was given a map and was told to march to Vignacourt, but was given no route. After passing through Beauval the Battalion bivouacked in a field at 3 a.m. It was raining hard and in such comfortless conditions the Battalion had to breakfast and march off again at 10 a.m. However, at about 4 p.m. the Battalion marched into Vignacourt.

There is little need to detail the remainder of that march to the battle area, sufficient to say that on the 10th the Gloucesters reached Albert and went into billets, the 3rd Brigade relieving a reserve brigade of the 23rd Division. Albert was at that time under shell-fire and several casualties were suffered while the Battalion was billeted in the town. The whole of the ground between the Albert—Bécourt and main Albert—Bapaume roads (and south of the former) was one vast camp.

---

[1] For full details of the Battle of Albert, 1st to 13th July, the official despatches (preferably Boraston's edition with maps) should be studied.

[2] From 14th February to 4th July the Battalion's casualties were 41 killed and 96 wounded.

[3] Shortly before the 1st Division proceeded to the Somme, Major-General E. P. Strickland took over command, which command he retained until the end of the War. The 28th therefore served under this fearless leader until the Armistice and afterwards during its march into Germany. They were also destined to be under his command after the War, in Ireland, at Aldershot and in Egypt. General Strickland frequently ' bit ' the 28th and ' bit ' them hard, and when he did so, they usually deserved it ; it was equally characteristic of him that units and individuals who did their jobs properly were assured of his effectual support and approval.

On the 14th the 1st Gloucesters moved up into the line. The way up led across the old front-line trenches of British and German. Many of the dead had not been buried and the whole area showed signs of the recent heavy fighting. The Battalion moved up via Bécourt across country to the Fricourt-Contalmaison road, thence along that road to the front line which ran north and east of Contalmaison village.

So confused was the front line that headquarters of the battalion the Gloucesters were relieving were not sure of the positions of their companies and it was daylight on the 15th before the latter were correctly placed. Dispositions were then as follows : D Company on the right on the Contalmaison—Longueval road, B Company on the left in the cutting just north-east of Contalmaison, and A and C Companies with Battalion Headquarters in support in the village. Throughout the night of the 14th/15th the enemy's shell-fire was heavy, but very few casualties were suffered. On the following day also he continued to bombard the village. Patrols pushed out discovered that his infantry was some way off and the line facing north-east was advanced from 200 to 300 yards, Contalmaison Villa being occupied without opposition.

The 1/4th and 1/6th Gloucesters (144th Brigade) were in bivouacs south of Sailly and the 1/5th Battalion (145th Brigade) at Couin when the offensive was launched on the 1st of July. The 48th Division was in VIIIth Corps reserve : the three other divisions—29th, 4th and 31st—(in that order from right to left) were holding the front line from the northern bank of the Ancre to west of Serre. The Division was, however, early on the move and both the 144th and 145th Brigades reached Mailly Maillet during the day and went into bivouacs in the neighbourhood of the village.

On the 2nd orders were received for the 48th Division, in conjunction with the 29th Division, to attack the German front line from the Ancre to Y Ravine, but after moving up to assembly positions the operation was cancelled and the 144th and 145th Brigades returned to bivouacs.

On the night of the 4th/5th the 144th Brigade (right) and 145th Brigade (left) took over front-line trenches west of Serre and south-east of Hébuterne. Of the former, the 1/6th Gloucesters relieved troops of the 94th Brigade, the relief being completed by 12.30 a.m. on the 5th. On the 6th B Company attempted a raid on the enemy's trenches but it was not successful.

On the night of the 8th/9th the 1/4th Gloucesters took over the line from the 1/6th Battalion. The forward trenches were still very bad—full of mud—and the front line contained numerous dead still awaiting burial.   Three shells fell on a working party on the 9th, killing 2nd Lieutenant H. P. Fisher (K.S.L.I. attached) and 5 other ranks and wounding another man.   The Battalion made no raid on the enemy but nightly patrolled No-Man's Land.

The 1/4th Gloucesters were relieved by the 1/6th on the 12th and hardly had the latter been in the line when on the 13th D Company raided the enemy, but this also was unsuccessful.   The next day (14th) the 1/6th Battalion was relieved and marched back to bivouacs on the southern side of the Couin—St. Leger road, the 1/4th Gloucesters bivouacking at Bouzincourt.

Of the 145th Brigade the 1/5th Gloucesters also attempted a raid on the German trenches on the 13th of July, but the enemy was too alert and the raiders were driven back, 2nd Lieutenant Houghton and 5 other ranks being wounded.   The 1/5th Battalion was not relieved until the 16th when they also marched back to bivouacs at Couin.

In the meantime the Battle of Bazentin Ridge had opened on the 14th July.

CHAPTER XIX

THE BATTLE OF BAZENTIN RIDGE: 14TH— 17TH JULY 1916

BY the 13th of July we were in a position to undertake an assault upon the second system of the enemy's trenches. Accordingly, orders were issued to deliver an attack at daybreak on the morning of the 14th against a front extending from Longueval to Bazentin-le-Petit Wood, both to be included in the attack. Contalmaison Villa, on a spur some thousand yards west of Bazentin-le-Petit Wood, had already been taken, the left flank of the attack would therefore be secure.

Late on the night of the 13th white tapes were laid out on the ground to assist the attacking troops in forming up on their proper positions. In the early hours of the 14th the assaulting battalions of the several divisions [1] taking part in the operations moved out over the open for a distance of from 1,000 to 1,400 yards and in the darkness lined up just below the crest some 300 to 500 yards from the enemy's trenches.

Dawn had begun to break and there was just sufficient light to enable the attackers to distinguish friend from foe when, at 3.25 a.m. on the 14th, the attack was delivered. The extreme left of the line (south of Pozières and the Albert—Bapaume road) was held by the 34th Division, the 1st Division being on the immediate right of the 34th. But the 3rd Brigade was in reserve and did not take over the line until midnight 14th/15th, the 1st Gloucesters (as already mentioned) relieving the Berkshires in the right sub-sector.

On the 14th the 1st Division had gained ground to the west of Bazentin-le-Petit Wood and the 34th Division had established posts immediately south of Pozières.

On the 15th the Gloucesters were not actually engaged in the fighting, but their patrols, pushing forward, discovered that the enemy was some distance off, and the line facing north-east was accordingly advanced some 200 or 300 yards, Contalmaison Villa being occupied.

---

[1] The divisions which made the initial attack were, from right to left, the 18th, 9th, 3rd, 7th, 21st, 1st and 34th.

153

At noon on the 16th the Battalion was ordered to attack and capture the enemy's positions in front, which appeared to be more or less parallel with a line drawn from Contalmaison Villa to Pearl Wood, south-south-east of the Villa. This position was reconnoitred during the afternoon, but even though the map co-ordinates were given it was difficult to recognize them on the ground. The enemy being very much on the alert it was impossible to move troops before dark and the following plan was therefore adopted—a signalling lamp was placed in Pearl Wood so that it could be seen from the Villa. At 10.20 p.m. B and D Companies moved out along the Contalmaison—Martinpuich road as far as the Villa and then, wheeling to the right, marched on the signalling lamp until the rear of the column was clear of the road : they then turned left and deployed into line, B and D Companies in front, A 100 yards in rear of the two forward companies and C 100 yards in rear of A. A proportion of the rear-rank men of A, B and D Companies carried tools, each man of C Company carried one tool and ten bombs.

As soon as companies had deployed they advanced 150 yards and halted. It was calculated that they were now about 100 yards from the line upon which the barrage would fall. The time was about 11.40 p.m. At 11.50 p.m. the barrage came down, which was replied to at once by the enemy putting down a protective barrage on the line of the Contalmaison—Longueval road, of which the Gloucesters were by that time clear.

At midnight the barrage lifted and the Gloucesters, with the 2nd Welch and Munster Fusiliers (on the right and left respectively), advanced to the attack.

As B and D Companies reached the German front line a number of the enemy ran from it : the two companies did not wait but pushed on to the second line, A Company halting in the enemy's front line where they cleared dug-outs and began consolidation. On crossing the German support line the two leading companies ran into our standing barrage and had to fall back. Meanwhile C, following in the wake of B and D, had begun to consolidate the support line. The Germans had evacuated their trenches hurriedly, leaving all their kit behind them. The weather was wet and nearly every man equipped himself with a German great coat as a protection against the rain. In the trenches over 150 dead Germans were found and as more than one unit was identified among them it is possible a relief was in progress when our barrage fell on their trenches.

The enemy was undoubtedly ' on the run ' and, but for the standing barrage, the Gloucesters might have occupied Martinpuich. Later, when patrols were pushed forward, the enemy's opposition had hardened.

At the close of this very successful attack C Company held the old German support line (which then became our front line). D and A Companies were in the old German front line and B was withdrawn to Contalmaison.

The total casualties suffered by the Gloucesters were 3 killed and 25 wounded, including one officer (2nd Lieutenant G. Cryer). More casualties occurred on the 18th when 3 other ranks were killed, 6 wounded and 20 gassed from the enemy's shell-fire. At 10 p.m. that night the Battalion was relieved and moved back, first to Scott's Redoubt and later to Bécourt Wood.

OVILLERS CAPTURED

In the meantime the Territorial Battalions had taken part in the capture of Ovillers. The official despatches state that

' On the 16th July a large body of the garrison of Ovillers surrendered and that night and during the following day by a direct advance from the west across No-Man's Land, our troops (48th Division) carried the remainder of the village and pushed out along the spur to the north and eastwards towards Pozières.'

What had happened that Ovillers should have for so long been left uncaptured ? There was a reason other than the stout defence put up by the gallant German garrison.

After the first day of the Somme Battles, when the attack from the Albert—Bapaume road northwards had resulted in no gain of ground, Sir Douglas Haig said :

' I decided that the best course was to press forward on a front extending from our junction with the French to a point half-way between La Boisselle and Contalmaison, and to limit the offensive on our left for the present to a slow, methodical advance.'

So until the possession of the ruined village was absolutely essential, as it was interfering with our progress in the direction of Pozières and beyond, Ovillers had merely been subjected to what was termed ' relentless pressure '.

But now that Bazentin Ridge was necessary, Ovillers also had to be taken.

The 144th Brigade of the 48th Division on the night of the 15th of July took over a portion of the line in front (west) of Ovillers from half of the 97th Infantry Brigade and the whole of the 14th Infantry Brigade, coming under the orders of the 32nd Division. Only the 1/4th Gloucesters and the 7th Worcesters, however, went into the front line, the 1/6th Gloucesters and 8th Worcesters remaining in reserve in bivouacs near Senlis.

The 1/4th Gloucesters (Lieut.-Colonel H. T. Dobbin, commanding) took over trenches facing the northern half of Ovillers. On the right were the 7th Worcesters, whose position extended across No-Man's Land to the old German front line, thence along the south-eastern edge of Ovillers. On the left of the Gloucesters were troops of the 49th Division.

The Battalion had B Company in the front line and in Coniston, A Company in support in the Quarries, C and D in reserve in Quarries just north of Aveluy. The relief was completed by 9.15 p.m.

At 4 p.m. on the 16th orders were received at Brigade Headquarters to assault and capture the German front-line trench facing the Gloucesters. Owing to the formation of the ground the line was not visible from anywhere in the Gloucesters' trenches. The artillery were therefore ignorant of the state of the enemy's wire entanglements, which were generally reported in good condition. It was, therefore, decided to reconnoitre the wire before the assault and decide the actual formation of the attack on receiving the patrol report. Zero was also left unfixed until the former point was cleared up. D and B Companies were detailed to make the attack, the former to be in readiness in the assembly trench, 150 yards in front of the front line, at 10 p.m. after darkness had fallen. B Company was to assemble in the communication trench leading to the assembly trench. Both of these companies were to stand fast in their positions until the reconnaissance report had been received. The right of the attack was to gain touch with the left of the 7th Worcesters.

At 10 p.m. D Company moved into the position assigned to it and at the same time 2nd Lieutenant C. F. Holland, with six N.C.O.s and men from the attacking companies, crossed No-Man's Land to reconnoitre the wire. B Company then moved up into the communication trench.

Each man carried four No. 5 grenades and four sand-bags : in addition, one man in each platoon carried twelve No. 5 grenades : one hundred shovels and a similar number of picks were to be carried : Lewis guns accompanied companies.

At about 11.30 p.m. 2nd Lieutenant Holland returned. He had made a close reconnaissance of the German front line, and, as he was fired at on several occasions, came to the conclusion that it was strongly held. But the wire in front of it was very much cut about and did not form a serious obstacle.

On this information the following plan was drawn up : the attack was to take the form of a surprise after ten minutes' bombardment to cover the advance of the two companies.   The latter were to attack in line, B on the right, D on the left.   Zero was fixed at 2 a.m.

At 1.50 a.m. the artillery barrage fell on the German trenches and the Machine-Gun Company covered the left of the attack, which began precisely at 2 a.m.

The first news from the front line was received at 2.30 a.m. when a wounded man of D Company reported that his company had occupied the German trench.   Fifteen minutes later a written message from Captain Castle, commanding D Company, was brought in by a runner, stating that all was well, but that owing to a misunderstanding a verbal message from B Company reported touch gained with the 7th Worcesters on the right—this was not so.   Following this message several wounded men came in and reported things going well.

At 5.25 a.m. Captain Castle sent back another message by a runner who had to pick his way carefully across No-Man's Land, which by this time was under very heavy shell-fire, stating that the two companies were not yet in touch with the Worcesters and that he was being heavily bombed by the enemy on both flanks.   C Company, which was in touch with the Worcesters, was then ordered to work up by bombing attacks along the German front-line trench until touch was gained with B Company.   Major Slade and Lieutenant Fisher (commanding C Company) personally supervised the bombing attacks, which were eventually successful, and at about 12 noon on the 17th communication was opened with the right flank of the attack.   Stokes mortars had played an important part in this successful operation.

By this time each Company had suffered about 80 casualties. They were, however, not short of bombs, for German bombs had been found and they were used against the enemy.   At about 3 p.m. C Company took over the line from B, the latter withdrawing to Crucifix Corner.   At 7 p.m. A Company relieved D, which withdrew to Coniston.

A Company then held the left of the Battalion front.

The successful attack by the 1/4th Gloucesters on the 17th had cleared the enemy from his front line west and north-west of Ovillers, though there was still a small pocket of Germans who held out in between the Gloucesters and 7th Worcesters.   These were, however, cleared out later.

At about 1 p.m. on the 18th the Battalion was ordered to push forward its line north of the village, the Worcesters moving forward parallel with the Gloucesters.   A Company began the advance at about 5 p.m., pushing forward up the old German front line : C Company advanced parallel with A up the old German second line.   The objective, a line facing north about 250 yards north of Ovillers, was gained at about 8 p.m. with only few casualties.   A further advance was ordered to take place at 1.30 a.m. on the 19th : each company was to bomb up its own trench. But the left party was met by a devastating machine-gun fire and the dug-outs had been set alight, which impeded the advance. On the right the 7th Worcesters were held up by machine-gun fire.

The remainder of the 19th was spent in consolidating the positions won and on the 20th the 1/6th Gloucesters relieved the 1/4th, the latter marching back to Donnet Post and Ribble Street, where they were in support.[1]

Thus Ovillers had fallen, but it would be more correct to say that it fell to the 48th *and* 25th Divisions, as the latter was on the right and certainly cleared part of the village.

[1] Casualties suffered by the 1/4th Gloucesters from the 16th to the 20th of July were as follows : Killed 37, wounded 211, and missing 27.

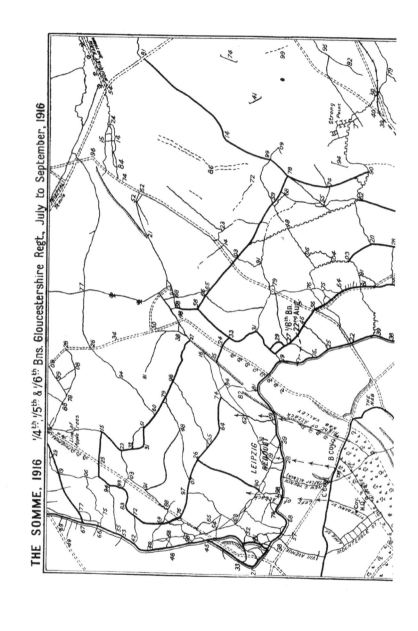

THE SOMME, 1916   1/4th 1/5th & 1/6th Bns. Gloucestershire Regt., July to September, 1916

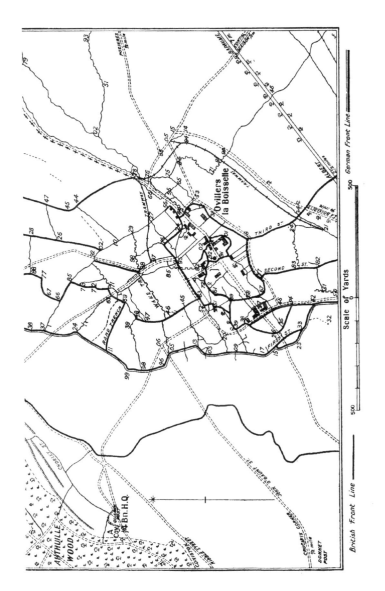

Ovillers
la Boisselle

AUTHUILLE
WOOD.

Bn. H.Q.

British Front Line

German Front Line

Scale of Yards
500   0   500

CHAPTER XX

THE BATTLE OF POZIÈRES RIDGE: 23RD JULY— 3RD SEPTEMBER 1916

THE long-drawn-out struggle for the possession of the Pozières Ridge began (approximately) on the 23rd of July, but between that date and the final capture of Ovillers on the 17th of July local attacks were made by the 1/4th, 1/5th and 1/6th Gloucesters in an endeavour to push forward the line of the 48th Division.

At 6 p.m. on the 19th July the 1/5th Battalion relieved the Royal Warwicks in the front line north-east of Ovillers, B and D Companies in the front line, one Company in support and the fourth in reserve.

At 11 p.m. B Company was ordered to capture Point 79 by bombing. But the Point was too strongly held and could not be captured, though the Gloucesters advanced their barricade. On the 20th A Company relieved B, and C Company, D. Another attack on Point 79, as well as on Point 40, took place at 11.30 p.m. on the 20th, but again failed to capture the objective. In both these attacks the 1/5th lost heavily: Lieutenant W. Fream and 2nd Lieutenant C. V. N. Puckridge and about 50 other ranks were killed, and Captain H. C. B. Sessions, 2nd Lieutenant P. Baldham and nearly 60 other ranks wounded: 2nd Lieutenant J. Farrimond was missing.

On this date also the 1/6th returned to the front line, relieving the 1/4th Battalion in Points 37–66–0·2–26 and 47 (i.e. north of Ovillers). In the very early hours of the 21st, while it was yet dark, the Battalion attacked the enemy on the line 39–88–28–20–62.

A Company attacked a barricade at Point 39 and by 3 a.m. had gained possession of it. But shortly after the enemy made a powerful bombing attack and, assisted by a shower of small bombs, succeeded in rushing and regaining the Point. The Gloucesters, not to be robbed of their gains, returned to the attack and the barricade was taken once more. Ten minutes later the enemy again rushed the barricade and obtained possession of it. For the time being he was allowed to retain it.

The attack on Point 88 was successful and by 3.45 a.m. it had been taken and held. Fifteen minutes later the enemy counter-attacked, but he was driven off and suffered heavily in the attempt. On Points 20–62 the attack was a failure.

The losses of the 1/6th were rather heavy in this attack : Captain G. E. Elliott, commanding B Company, and 9 other ranks were killed, 2nd Lieutenants A. R. Smith [1] and H. E. H. Sutton and 83 other ranks were wounded and 9 were missing.

The 1/5th (B Company) also at 11 p.m. on the 21st again attacked Point 79, while D Company tried to capture Point 40, but without success. B Company reached the objective but, finding no cover, had to fall back. D Company was held up by machine-gun fire, the gun being mounted on a barricade and firing straight down the trench, along which the Company tried to force its way. Three officers (2nd Lieutenants R. E. Knight,[2] K. G. Durrant and F. R. Bell) were wounded in these attacks.

The 1/4th relieved the 1/6th on the 22nd, as the latter had orders to attack Points 90 and 40 at 12.30 a.m. on the 23rd. The former Battalion took over the line Points 37–67–88–28–47, two companies in the front line, C on the right and B on the left, with D Company supporting B and A supporting C. The 1/4th were to assist the 1/6th by bombing forward from Points 47 and 28, i.e. on the left of the 1/6th.

The full narrative of the attack by the 1/6th, by the C.O.—Lieut.-Colonel Micklem—is given here because, although it was a failure, it was a very gallant failure :

' Party of R.E., under Lieutenant Briggs, with a covering party, moved off ahead of the Battalion to place a tape on a due east line from Point 47 to the railway. Lieutenant Briggs worked rapidly and well and the tape was fixed just before the head of the Battalion reached the railway end of the tape.'

Three companies were attacking with one in reserve.

' The Battalion moved through Ovillers along the road and emerged at Point 78. They proceeded in single file along the left of the railway and formed up on the tape behind the covering party. The area over which they had to move was being steadily shelled with 5·9s, but the men behaved well and the companies moved into their assembly positions without a hitch.
' At about 12.15 a.m. they started moving forward, and though the shelling continued there were few casualties. Shortly before zero the leading waves were roughly 70 yards from their objective and still moving steadily. At this period machine-gun fire was opened from the front and fell about 39 and 40 on the right. The fire was very accurate and

---

[1] Died of wounds 22nd July 1916.
[2] Died of wounds the same day.

the leading waves were cut down.   The subsequent waves moved on but very few got through the zone of the machine-guns.

' As far as I can gather from statements of the few N.C.O.s and men who returned, a party of about six men entered the enemy trench just north-west of Point 40 and engaged the enemy with bombs.   One of this party has returned.   He states that he was captured and his equipment and bomb bag taken from him.   However, in the excitement he managed to get a bomb out of his pocket, which he threw among his guard, and in the confusion escaped.   All the officers but one who started are casualties and information is difficult to obtain, but it seems that the last waves of the consolidating company did not get into the zone of machine-gun fire They state that they saw the whole of the unit on their right retire and retired after them.   The following numbers have been reported un-wounded up to the present : A Company (left assault) 42 ;   C Company (right assault) 29 ; D Company (consolidating company) 71.

' Casualties were difficult to collect as gas shells were fired on roads 78–39 and gas helmets had to be worn, but at 6.15 a.m. bearers and volunteers were working in the open quite unmolested up to a line about east and west through 47.

' One of C Company's Lewis guns, with three of the team, is reported to be dug in about 40 yards west of Point 40.

' Casualties among officers were very heavy, C and D Companies losing all theirs and only one coming in from A Company.   As far as I can gather they are as follows : 3 killed, 2 probably killed, 4 wounded and brought in, 1 suffering from gas.   The R.E. officer whose section went forward is also missing.

' The cause of the failure was, in my opinion, the lack of artillery preparation.   None of the machine-guns previously reported had been knocked out and the enemy line had hardly been shelled at all.   The barrage which I understood was to keep the enemy's heads down while the assaulting troops advanced was quite useless as there were long inter-vals when not a single shell burst on the front to be attacked.   The result of this was that the enemy's machine-guns, having nothing to worry them, were able to fire on the assaulting troops as they pleased.

' From all accounts the men behaved very well and moved steadily through a heavy shell-fire, but the zone of the machine-gun fire seems to have been quite impassable.   The commanders of the leading com-panies were killed and the men who have returned state that their behaviour was magnificent, particularly Lieutenant Parramore, O.C. A Company, who they say behaved as if he was on the barrack square though he was hit and . . . [word indecipherable] a very heavy fire from machine-guns.   Even after being hit in the stomach he continued to lead the men till he fell dead.   Reliable information is difficult to obtain now the officers and nearly all the N.C.O.s of the leading companies are casualties.'

A subsequent account of the action from men who came in during the night of the 23rd/24th July follows :

' The men all state that the attacking party started off all right in its proper waves.   When they approached the German parapet they found *good wire* and were held up by very heavy machine-gun fire.   Second-Lieutenant (H.) Corbett and most of the leading wave were killed.   The

11

second and third waves came up under 2nd Lieutenant (H. I.) Balderson, who was killed. Major (C. E.) Coates, commanding the assaulting troops, then came up with the next waves. Three other officers just behind were wounded and this accounted for all the officers.'

The 1/4th did their best to help their comrades of the 1/6th by bombing forward from Points 47 and 28. 'Our companies worked hard to gain ground,' records the Battalion Diary, ' but it was useless, the enemy was too strongly posted and his infernal machine-guns were practically able to do as they pleased and shoot down the gallant attackers, unmolested by artillery fire.' The 1/4th stopped their attack at about 5 a.m. on the 23rd when news of the failure of the attack by the 1/6th reached them. But a little later, at 7.30 a.m., when the 145th Brigade attacked between Points 37 and 79 (on the right) the 1/4th resumed their bombing attacks and on the success of the Brigade attack ceased their own bombing. During these attacks by the 1/4th 2nd Lieutenants Maclean and Fraser were severely wounded : the former could not be got in as he lay just in front of the German barricade.

There is a strange discrepancy between the above report of the 1/4th Gloucesters (that the attack of the 145th Brigade was successful) and the narrative of operations by the 1/5th Gloucesters who, with the 1/4th Oxford and Bucks, made the attack, for according to the 1/5th Battalion the attack was not a success but a failure.

The Battalion was ordered to capture Points 0·2 to 79 on the right and railway on the left ; 79 was to be captured from the west and 40 from the east. The Oxford and Bucks were to attack Point 81.

The 1/5th attacked with A Company on the right, C on the left, B in support and D in reserve. But no sooner had the attacking troops begun their advance than they were spotted by the enemy, who met them with a murderous machine-gun and rifle fire. B then reinforced the first line, but in spite of the extra weight and a heavy artillery barrage and machine-gun fire, the objectives could not be reached. A fresh attack, after another bombardment of the enemy's trenches, also failed.

Again casualties were heavy : 2nd Lieutenant W. B. Lycett was severely wounded and died later. Captains R. J. C. Little, F. W. Cole, L. R. C. Sumner and R. N. F. Cooke ; Lieutenant H. S. King and 2nd Lieutenants L. J. Clayton and W. J. Pearce were wounded : in other ranks the losses were 12 killed, 113 wounded and 23 missing.

It was later that the Oxford and Bucks, the 1/5th Gloucesters having been withdrawn at 3.30 a.m. on the 23rd, attacked and captured Points 28, 11, 79, together with 120 prisoners and two machine-guns.

The 1/5th Gloucesters then moved back to bivouacs east of Albert, where they spent the 24th July. The remnants of the 1/6th had already moved back to Donnet Post at 10 a.m. on the 23rd, and the 1/4th went to Ribble Street and Crucifix Corner on the 24th.

Before the latter Battalion was relieved the enemy on the night of the 23rd/24th made a determined attack on the barricades at Points 88 and 28. He first put a double barrage, including gas and lachrymatory shell, on the centre of the 144th Brigade front and his bombers then advanced to the attack. But he had a warm reception from the artillery, Stokes mortars and Lewis guns and his attack melted away.

The whole intent of these bombing attacks was to gain ground towards Pozières Ridge and to provide good jumping-off positions when the Ridge itself was attacked. The gallant efforts of the Gloucestershire Territorials deserve to be related in full, for their brave efforts in the face of very strong positions and a resolute enemy will live long in the history of the three Battalions.

In the meantime the 1st Battalion had withdrawn on the 18th July to trenches in and around Scott's Redoubt, a strong point about 400 yards west-north-west of the northern end of Round Wood, on the Fricourt—Contalmaison road, and the same distance behind the old German front line. Battalion Headquarters were in a large underground German dressing-station in the Redoubt. The following day they moved still further back and bivouacked in Bécourt Wood. Before this move took place, however, a gallant N.C.O.—No. 6016 Sergt. F. Murray—was killed. He was cooking his breakfast when the heat of his fire exploded a buried bomb and Sergt. Murray was killed by the explosion. He had started the War as a private and was with the 28th from the very beginning. His fifteen years' service had been spent with the Battalion and he was very well known to all as ' Ginger Murray '; he had played for years as ' stand off ' half in the 28th XV.[1]

On the 20th the Gloucesters went into billets in Albert until the 22nd. They had, however, to find fatigue parties for various duties and between the 19th and 20th suffered a number of casualties.

During the evening of the 22nd the Battalion moved forward

[1] His scrum-half, Pte. Stephenson, was equally well known and did the whole war with the 28th, afterwards proceeding with the 61st to India.

again to the old German front line east of Bécourt Wood.   The
1st and 2nd Brigades were attacking the German Switch Trench,
north-west of the position captured by the 3rd Brigade on the
16th July.   Had the attack been successful the 3rd Brigade was
to occupy the captured position, but it failed and on the 23rd the
Gloucesters moved back to a position north of the position
occupied on the previous night.

At 5.30 a.m. on the 24th the Battalion relieved the 2nd Royal
Sussex in front-line trenches rather north of those captured by the
28th on the 16th July.   This position was held until the evening
of the 25th.   On the left of the Battalion the Australians had just
captured Pozières and during the 25th they were heavily counter-
attacked by the Germans.   During these attacks several barrages
were put down on the line held by the Gloucesters, but did not
prevent the latter taking a great share in repelling the enemy.
The Lewis guns of the 28th were holding a sap running out from
near the left of the line, and as the Germans advanced they were
able to catch the latter in flank and inflict great losses on them.
Till later in the day the German shell-fire was heavy and the
Gloucesters suffered considerable casualties before getting out of
the line to their quarters for the night in Scott's Redoubt.   Among
those killed was another gallant N.C.O.—No. 7612 Sergt.
R. Minahan.[1]

On the 24th the 1st Gloucesters were relieved and marched
back via Albert to Millencourt.   On the 1st August the Corps
Commander inspected the 3rd Brigade and congratulated all
battalions on their fine fighting on the 16th July.   In this connection it is interesting to quote a memorandum issued by IIIrd
Corps Headquarters to its divisions :

'The Corps Commander wishes again to draw attention to the immense
importance of getting the troops to realize the great advantages which
result from pushing boldly up under cover of the barrage and risking
casualties from our own artillery rather than from the enemy's machine
guns.'
'Some 1,200 yards of two lines of trenches, both of which were wired,
were captured and held by a night attack with a loss of 70 casualties.
'The success of this operation is to be attributed mainly to two fac-
tors.   Firstly, that our most dangerous enemies, the machine guns
(hidden not in emplacements but in grass, hedges, shell-holes, etc., where
it is difficult to locate them) were robbed of their power owing to dark-

[1] This N.C.O. played wing three-quarter for the 61st when they won
the Army Rugby Cup at Twickenham in 1910.   He was the first Reservist to rejoin at the Depot on mobilization, was badly wounded on
the 9th May 1915 with the 28th, and when he was killed was on the
point of getting a commission.

ness. Secondly, by a short, but very intensive bombardment by field
guns, followed immediately by the assault.

'The infantry moved close to the enemy's trenches under cover of
the barrage and risked and incurred casualties from our guns in order
that no interval should elapse between the lifting of the barrage and
their entry into the trenches.

'The assaulting battalions got to within 150 yards of the enemy's
trenches by the time the bombardment began and rushed forward at
midnight. The trenches were strongly held and the resistance was
overcome at once with only slight casualties. About fifty Germans were
killed and a few made prisoner, but most of the garrison retired hastily
before the attackers got in, leaving rifles, greatcoats, field-glasses, etc.,
and a good many dead killed by our artillery.'

To return to the Territorial Battalions : The 1/5th (145th
Brigade) had been relieved by the 1/4th Gloucesters on the
25th July, the former marching back to Bouzincourt. The
48th Division was due for relief and gradually all units were being
withdrawn from the line. By the end of July the 145th Brigade
had reached Cramont, where training began.

Meanwhile the 1/4th, having relieved the 1/5th on the 25th July,
remained in the line a few more days. On this date the Transport
Officer—Lieutenant Master—was killed. An attempt by D Company to push forward during the morning of the 26th met with
strong resistance and the attack was broken off. The next day
a brigade of the 37th Division relieved the 144th Brigade, the
1/4th Gloucesters marching back first to Hedauville, thence by
stages to Franqueville, where they were on the 31st July. The
1/6th,[1] after relief on the 26th, proceeded by march route to
Fransu, where they were billeted until the last day of the month.

The 1st Gloucesters remained out of the line at Millencourt
until the 15th August. On that date, however, they paraded at
6.30 a.m. and, marching via south of Albert and Bécourt Wood,
reached Railway Copse, relieving a battalion of the 34th Division.

[1] The 1/6th Battalion give their full casualties during the month of
July as follows : Officers killed—Captain G. E. Elliott (21st July 1916),
Major C. E. Coates (23rd July 1916), Lieutenant R. E. Parramore (23rd
July 1916), 2nd Lieutenants H. Corbett and G. C. Dillon (23rd July
1916) ; missing, believed killed, Lieutenant H. L. P. Balderson (killed
23rd July 1916) ; died of wounds—2nd Lieutenant A. R. Smith (22nd
July 1916) and Captain E. W. Bird (27th July 1916) ; wounded—Lieutenants H. E. Tucker (7th July 1916) and W. H. Anderson (23rd July
1916), 2nd Lieutenants J. A. Fletcher (7th July 1916), G. A. B. Montague
(7th July 1916), A. Fowler (7th July 1916), C. H. Carruthers (23rd July
1916), M. Durant (23rd July 1916), L. A. H. Stovell (23rd July 1916),
H. E. Hicks-Sutton (21st July 1916), L. Scull (24th July 1916) ; gassed
—2nd Lieutenant V. Coombes. Other ranks, killed 15, missing 62,
wounded 296, died of wounds 5.

This Copse was a collection of old German trenches in the valley north-east of Fricourt, about half-way between that village and Mametz Wood. But only one night was spent here, for next day the 28th retraced their steps and bivouacked in a dirty orchard named Black Wood, just east of the Albert—Bécourt Wood road. Here the Battalion remained until the 20th. The previous day orders had been received to relieve the Northants of the 2nd Brigade in the line roughly north-west of Bazentin-le-Petit. The Gloucesters set out to carry out the relief at 1 p.m. on the 20th, but *en route* were stopped and assembled in Mametz Wood and given fresh orders to relieve the 2/60th Rifles (who had suffered seriously) on the right of the line immediately west of High Wood. The Welch *should* have relieved the Rifles, but the Gloucesters, being ahead of the former, were switched from left · to right of the line.

The trenches taken over by the Gloucesters were, to say the least of it, extremely awkward : they had not been reconnoitred and the relief was difficult. The line began on the right with a small redoubt, about 200 yards from the west side of High Wood, running thence for 100 yards just south of the Flers—Bazentin-le-Petit road where it crossed the road and ran north-west. Towards the left of this line a long sap ran forward towards the enemy : this sap was held by a platoon.

The Germans held High Wood to a depth of about 200 yards from the northern end, on the western side. Their forward trench ran diagonally across the Wood so that on its eastern side they held its whole depth. The ground between the right of the Gloucesters' front line and the Wood was unoccupied by either side.

Three hundred yards in rear of the Gloucesters' front line a trench ran from the Wood roughly parallel with the front-line trench : this was occupied by C Company. On the right, the trench entered the Wood and there became our foremost line and was held by troops of a neighbouring division, on its left it faded away to nothing.

Battalion Headquarters were in a sunken road, called Mill Street, running northward past a ruined windmill : D Company were also in this road. B Company occupied various small shelters and trenches between Mill Street and the front line.

The dispositions of companies are given in full because the Gloucesters, remaining here until the early morning of the 28th August, were subjected to concentrated shell-fire such as the 28th had not experienced during the whole period of the War to that date.

Those seven days in the line alongside High Wood were a veritable nightmare. After about three days the front line was practically obliterated and shell-holes in front of it were occupied. Battalion Headquarters, in a tin-roofed shelter, got a direct hit one afternoon and the journey from Mill Street to the front line was an object lesson in the art of shell-dodging. Oddly enough, despite the fact that there were Germans in High Wood on the right flank to a depth of 200 yards in rear of the Gloucesters' front-line trench, it was possible to walk over ground from the front to the support line in perfect safety, i.e. in so far as bullets were concerned.

During this period in the line working parties from the reserve companies dug a trench (intended as a jumping-off place for a future attack on that portion of High Wood held by the enemy) parallel with the western side of High Wood and about 100 yards from it. It began at the redoubt on the right of the front line, ran to the support trench and thence to a trench further in rear, named Leith Walk.

At 5 p.m. on the 27th August the relief of the Gloucesters began, but it was 5 a.m. the next morning before the last party of men of C Company got into their shelters at Bécourt. Thus ended as hard a seven days' tour in the line as any that the 28th did during the War. Employed simply in holding the line, though neither attacking nor attacked, the total casualties incurred were 46 killed and 141 wounded. The shell-fire suffered by the Battalion was unexampled in the history of the Regiment.[1]

For two days in heavy rain the 28th remained bivouacked in Bécourt Wood, then moved to Albert on the 30th, where they remained until the 2nd September. On the latter date the Battalion moved forward again to the Quadrangle, a conglomeration of old German trenches 400 yards west of Mametz Wood. In this position the Gloucesters remained until the 5th.

In the meantime the Territorial Battalions had again returned to the trenches in the neighbourhood of Ovillers. The 1/6th went first into the front line, taking over a front from 37 through 66, 67, 77, 88, 28, 26, 47 to 90 on the 13th August. During the night patrols were sent out towards Points 74 and 79. On the right of the Battalion the Germans attacked and re-captured Skyline. At 10 p.m. on the 14th B Company attacked Point 62 unsuccess-

---

[1] Among those killed was No. 9767 Ptc. Mitchell. He had acted as H.Q. Orderly from the first day of the War until 25th August 1916 and had till then borne a charmed life. A good, cheerful and gallant soldier under all difficulties, he was a great loss to the Gloucesters.

fully, 2nd Lieutenant Barrington being wounded. At about midnight this Company again attacked the enemy and before dawn A Company attacked twice. But owing to the brilliant moonlight, which threw the attackers into prominence, no progress was made. At 3 p.m. on the 15th the 1/4th Gloucesters took over the trenches of the 1/6th, the latter moving back to reserve trenches at Ribble Street.

Previously to relieving the 1/6th in the line the 1/4th had sent up A Company to support the former Battalion during the night attacks of the 13th/14th.

The 1/4th were hardly settled in the line when they were ordered to attack a line of Points X.2.b 2·0—62—90 with two companies. A and D were detailed to attack, the former on the right from 90 exclusive to 62 inclusive, and the latter from 62 exclusive to 20 inclusive. Two platoons of each Company were to attack, two of D and one of A being in reserve, the remaining platoon of A receiving orders to make a simultaneous bombing attack from 90 towards 62.

The artillery barrage fell at 2 a.m. on the 16th, the attacking troops creeping forward ready to assault when the barrage lifted. It was a very dark night, though the platoons were met by some rifle fire as they moved forward from the trenches. When the barrage lifted and the attackers rushed forward they were met by violent rifle and machine-gun fire as well as bombs. No advance could be made in face of such a resistance and the attacking troops fell back to their trenches. A Company lost 2nd Lieutenant R. H. Down (died of wounds 17th August) and 2nd Lieutenants R. Bird and H. G. Baker who, first reported missing, were afterwards found to have been killed : Lieutenant Crump was badly wounded in the arm. In other ranks the losses were about 70 killed, wounded and missing. The 1/4th were relieved later in the day by the 6th Worcesters and marched back to Bouzincourt.

On the left of the 1/4th the 1/5th had also attacked the enemy early on the 16th. A and D Companies had attacked Points 78–74. Their attack also failed, 2nd Lieutenant D. G. Durrant and three other ranks being killed and 2nd Lieutenants J. H. A. Wood, R. L. Harmsworth, N. Vears, F. Chapman and 99 other ranks being wounded and 21 other ranks missing, most of whom were probably killed. The 1/5th were also relieved later and moved back to the Gun Pits.

The next attack, which began on the 21st August, was more successful. The 1/5th were not, however, engaged in this operation. The Battalion had moved up to support the 4th

Warwicks during an attack following a successful attack by the 143rd Brigade on the 18th August. They took over the line from the Warwicks early on the 19th, but were themselves relieved at 7 p.m. that night and marched back again to Bouzincourt. They moved forward to support trenches on the 23rd in rear of Donnet's Post, but were not called upon until they again took over the front line at 6 a.m. on the 25th.

On the 20th the 1/6th Gloucesters relieved the 5th Royal Warwicks on the line 16–25–46–56–65–76, these points being directly north of Ovillers and east of The Nab, the latter a salient in the old British line south of the Leipzig Redoubt and of Thiepval.

The 1/6th had a strenuous three days in the line, i.e. 21st–23rd. They had relieved the Warwicks at 4 p.m. and by 8 p.m. Captain Hartog, O.C. A Company, had pushed his line forward to the line Points 19–29–27 and held forward barricades 50 yards north-west of 19, and 70 yards south-west of 31. Early the next morning at 5.30 a.m. (21st) the Germans made a weak attack against the barricade near 31 which was easily repulsed. Between that hour and 12 noon the Gloucesters made three attempts to occupy Point 31 and on each occasion were bombed out. At 12 noon B Company received orders to take the line 31–51, but these orders were late in arriving and with little time to organize the attack the Company failed.

At about 6 p.m. C Company took over the front line from A, D moved up into support and A and B were withdrawn. The night of the 21st/22nd was quiet, but at 5 a.m., under cover of a thick mist—one of those early autumn mists which shroud the plains of Picardy—the Germans attacked, collected under the bank immediately north of 31–19 and broke in east and west of the latter point. The platoon holding the trench north-east of 19 was cut off and scattered. The remainder of the Company was forced back on to their original line taken over from the 5th Warwicks, i.e. 16–25–46, with a small party holding on to the barricade 100 yards south of 19. The O.C. D Company (Major Nott) then pushed out bombing parties, one in the direction of 19, the other towards 27 via 25 and 46. Two machine guns were mounted on the parapet between 16 and 19 to cover the left front. While they were being mounted No. 2019 Pte. Kerr spotted a German machine gun coming into action in the open just north of 19. He got up and knelt on the parapet where he was exposed to the full view of the enemy and succeeded in shooting down three of the German machine-gun team and prevented the gun opening fire. A Lewis gun belonging to the Royal Sussex Regiment, which at the time of the attack was just leaving the front line, was borrowed and mounted on 46.

In organizing a counter-attack against 29 Captain J. K. Gilmore was killed. At 6.15 a.m. on the 22nd the situation was as follows : the enemy held 19–29–27 and the 1/6th Gloucesters barricades between 16 and 19, 16 and 27, 46 and 27.

In the meantime the 1/4th had also attacked the enemy on the previous evening, on the left of the 1/6th Battalion.

The 1/4th Gloucesters moved from Bouzincourt to Ribble Street on the 19th and it was there that on the following day orders were received to attack the southern face of the Leipzig Redoubt on the 22nd, which date was subsequently altered to the 21st. Officers and N.C.O.s began at once to reconnoitre the trenches of the 11th Cheshires who were then holding the front line and whose position the 1/4th Gloucesters had to take over before the attack.

The following narrative is given from notes prepared by Major (then Captain, O.C. B Company) E. E. Wookey of the 1/4th Gloucesters :

' At 6 a.m. enemy are shelling trenches we wish to reconnoitre. We wait till 7 a.m., then start. . . . I go up 8th Avenue to the captured portion of the Leipzig Redoubt and interview the 1st Wilts who are holding the line there. . . . I gather from them that they are to attack simultaneously and capture the remaining portion of the Leipzig Redoubt, gaining touch with our left at the same time. A large bomb store is to be established just inside their line. They are boring underneath every barricade and will then explode an elongated Bangalore torpedo which will have the effect of destroying barricade and constructing a trench at the same time. Having obtained all information possible from Wilts we return to Headquarters at 10.30 a.m. and then hear the cheerful news that we shall probably attack this afternoon. At 12.30 p.m. we meet C.O. and Brigade orders arrived. We are to attack this evening, zero being fixed for 6 p.m. The Wilts will attack on left from the north and gain touch with us at 98 and 90. The 6th Gloucesters will push on and gain touch with us at 81 on the right. . . . There will be an intense artillery barrage on enemy front line from 6 p.m. till 6.5 p.m. At 6.5 p.m. it will lift on to enemy second line. At 6.10 p.m. it will lift on to enemy third line. I will arrange to get my company well out before barrage starts. When it lifts we should be in enemy wire. . . . Men's dinners are served at once. From 1 p.m. to 2 p.m. enemy bombard trenches we are to assemble in this afternoon. We watch them from left of our dug-out. I will admit that I had a sort of sinking feeling when I saw it going on : if they were bombarding in a similar way at 6 p.m. it was doubtful whether we should be able to leave trenches. At 1.45 p.m. gave final instructions to platoon sergeants. . . . At 2.15 p.m. Company assemble and draw stores, etc. Each man is to carry four Mills grenades and two sand-bags. There are also thirty spades per company. Personally I think far too few spades are being carried. We have two pairs of wire cutters left and take these with us. No one else seems to have any. At 2.30 p.m. we shall move off via Coniston to Authueille (Blighty)

Wood and up railway to Cheshires' trenches. Here there is very great congestion. . . . The Cheshires have received instructions to remain in the line (contrary to what we had been told to expect) and occupy all the dug-outs. Aintree Street has been knocked in in several places by the heavy shelling at midnight and is impassable, from 3 p.m. till 5 p.m. The trenches are shelled intermittently with heavy and light shells (including 8-inch). Sergt. Blackmore is wounded going up. He only returned four days ago. Trapnell gets No. 7 Platoon in position to the right of Aintree, under great difficulties : later No. 7 are in position on the left. At 4 p.m. Nos. 5 and 6 are in Mounteagle Street. Two platoons of C are in Tithebarn Street. The congestion is frightful, time passes slowly.[1]

' Trestrail gives us a cup of tea at Company Headquarters (which is packed with people) and does everything he can for us. At 5.15 p.m. move remaining platoons into front line, a matter of great difficulty. They are still shelling and trenches are very bad. At 5.30 p.m. we are in position and we make an issue of rum to the company, bid farewell to Trestrail and depart for the front line.

' At 5.50 p.m. Trapnell and Phippen lead first two platoons, 7 and 8, over the parapet. A German machine gun opens to our right, but as far as I can see causes no casualties. At 5.55 p.m. remaining two platoons with myself swarm over parapet and form the second line of the advance some 50 yards in rear of the first. One or two casualties occur here.

' At 6 p.m. (we are half-way across the open) the bombardment opens. Under its cover we advance right up to the enemy's wire, C Company, who had the shorter distance to cover, also swarm over the parapet and get rapidly into line with us on the left. Both my lines become merged into one owing to the keenness of the troops behind. The barrage put on the enemy's trenches is extraordinarily accurate. We have halted in the enemy wire, the shells are bursting 30 yards away, and yet we are in comparatively little danger.

' At 6.5 p.m. the barrage lifts on to the second line and we go into the enemy first line. . . . Dead and wounded enemy are lying about but there is little resistance—most of them are still in dug-outs. A number of Germans assemble in the second line and open fire, but under the barrage and our advance soon turn tail. At 6.10 p.m., as the barrage lifts to the third line, we push forward and occupy the second trench. Barricades are erected across communication trenches from 90 to 62.

' On investigation I find from the map that we have reached all our objectives. Had we sufficient men I am sure we could push on and occupy third line. We are, however, short of men, especially on the right where it is important to gain touch with the 6th Gloucesters at 81. I collect various men therefore and take them down to right where we establish a barricade at 59 and push on beyond. Corpl. Knight does good work here and reports having obtained touch with the 6th. Shellard established temporary headquarters in a bomb store in old German front line, afterwards moving into excellent ruined dug-outs just off our new second line where the C Company servants, who have risen to the occasion, have meal ready at 8.30 p.m. I dine with them. It is arranged that I take command of the new front line and I establish headquarters

---

[1] It is rare to find a narrative of events written like this just when things were happening.

at Point 19 in a dug-out Trapnell has located. Some time since I had sent to A Company asking for reinforcements and about fifty of A Company have arrived and are distributed along the line. Unfortunately they have brought no bombs or stores of any kind—a mistake here by someone. . . . The situation now is as follows : A and B Companies in the first line and one section of C : at Point 59 there are details of A, B and C. Main portion of C is in second line near Shellard's (Major Shellard, O.C. C Company) Headquarters. All available men work on consolidation of positions, but find themselves very short of sand-bags, picks and shovels. The enemy has made no attempt to molest us thus far.'

The 1/4th in this attack captured 150 Germans.

The night of the 21st/22nd was comparatively quiet and consolidation went on without interruption in spite of the non-arrival of R.E. parties. The 7th Worcesters began work on a communication-trench across No-Man's Land : they dug some distance but were unable to complete it before dawn. During the night the Germans made a bombing attack down a communication trench, running in a westerly direction, and drove out a working party : for the time being touch was lost with the 1/6th Battalion.

To return now to the 1/6th Gloucesters and the morning of the 22nd. A constant supply of bombs having been arranged, Point 27 was re-occupied by 8 a.m. The enemy, holding barricades at 29 and 19, was making full use of the Gloucesters' bomb store which he had captured and after a time began to out-throw the Battalion bombers. But the O.C. D Company sent up a few selected bombers who so altered the situation that a move up, one barricade nearer to 29, was made. Corpl. Gunston, in particular, distinguished himself by fine bomb-throwing from 27.

About 10.30 a.m. a Stokes gun was moved into the trench between 25 and 46 and, after the enemy's trenches had been subjected to ' intense fire ', two platoons of D Company rushed the barricade north-west of 29, finding all of the enemy knocked out : those Germans who had remained at 19—11 in number —were all bayoneted. The survivors of C Company were then withdrawn and D Company took over all the front line. A relieved D at about 5 p.m.

The night of the 22nd/23rd of August witnessed further fierce fighting. Using large quantities of high-explosives and smoke bombs the enemy attacked the barricade north-west of 29 at about 8.30 p.m. With the exception of Lieutenant Titley the whole of the garrison of the barricade was wounded, and the post almost fell to the enemy. Lieutenant Titley, with the assistance of No. 2897 Sergt. Pearce (who had been knocked out by a bomb but had recovered), hung on and beat off all attempts. Two platoons of D were moved up into close support, but the Germans had had enough and for the time being fell back.

Two hours later, after shelling our front line fiercely, during which a Stokes gun was buried with 200 rounds of ammunition, the enemy launched another attack on the barricade north-west of 29. It was repulsed. Two further attacks were made but shared the same fate. The enemy then appears to have ' thrown up the sponge ', for when at 2 a.m. a patrol reconnoitred the ground north-west of trench 19–31 all trenches within 100 yards north of 19 had been abandoned, and A Company moved up to the old barricade south-west of 31 without opposition. The trenches between 19 and the barricade, and the ground in the neighbourhood of it, were a horrible sight—dead Germans in all the horrors of *mutilated death* lying about in large numbers.

After dawn on the 23rd the enemy made no further attack and the line from 70 yards south-west of 31 to 81 (exclusive) was handed over to the Bucks Battalion at about 11 a.m. and the 1/6th Gloucesters withdrew to Bouzincourt. On the 29th they moved to Forceville and later in the day back to front-line trenches east of Auchonvillers.

With the exception of three counter-attacks launched against the 1/4th Gloucesters on the night of the 22nd/23rd, all of which were repulsed (the enemy leaving 15 prisoners of the 15th Guards Reserve Division in our hands) that Battalion had a comparatively quiet forty-eight hours after the exciting events of the 21st. They were relieved on the 23rd and moved back to Bouzincourt, where on the 27th they also took over trenches east of Auchon-villers on the right of the 1/6th Battalion.

The 1/5th Battalion made no new attack before they also were relieved.

It will be remembered that the 1/5th Gloucesters had come back again into the line on the 25th. On the 27th they were ordered to attack trench, Points 50–33 The attack was made by C Company on the right and B on the left, in two lines across the open : two platoons of A Company advanced up a com-munication trench running into Points 50–33.

A three-minutes ' intense barrage ' was first put down on the enemy's positions, and so eager were the men to attack that C Company, on the right, entered the hostile trench ' in their own barrage ', B Company getting into the enemy's lines at the very moment the barrage lifted. Only the bombing platoon of A Company, working their way up the communication trench, met with serious opposition, where a large party of Germans held out between 31 and 51 until ultimately they were forced to retire across the open : few got away, for our Lewis guns shot down all but three. Several dug-outs were bombed and the trench consolidated and held. About 50 prisoners were taken in this successful attack and the enemy's losses in killed and wounded were estimated at 200 at least. One machine gun was also taken.

The 1/5th Gloucesters lost in this affair Lieutenants L. W. Moore and C. W. Winterbotham and 2nd Lieutenants A. L. Apperly and C. Brien and 14 other ranks killed, 2nd Lieutenants L. N. Graves-Smith and W. F. Rigger and 84 other ranks wounded, and 10 other ranks missing.

During the night of the 27th/28th the trench captured by the Gloucesters was heavily shelled by the enemy and on the 28th the Battalion was relieved and marched back to bivouacs north-west of Bouzincourt.

Both the 1/4th and 1/6th, in the trenches east of Auchon-villers, held the line during an attack by the Division on their right on the 3rd of September. The attack was from the Mary Redoubt to the Ancre and from south of that river. The Gloucesters were heavily shelled and their trenches barraged, considerable damage being done, but casualties were slight. Neither Battalion took any actual part in the attack. The 1/5th were in billets in Bus les Artois.

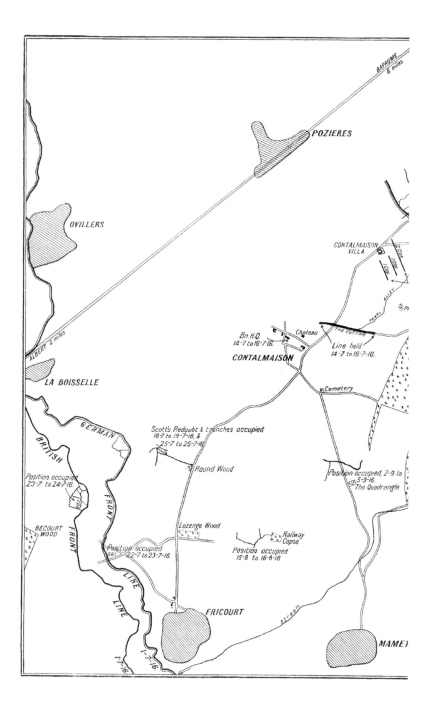

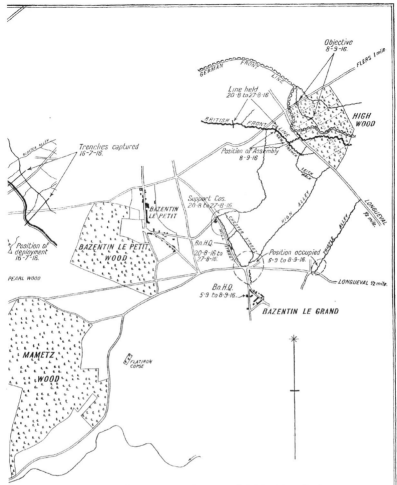

Objective
8-9-16.

FLERS 1 mile

GERMAN FRONT LINE

Line held
20-8 to 27-8-16.

HIGH
WOOD

BRITISH FRONT LINE

Position of Assembly
8-9-16

GLOSTER ALLEY

Trenches captured
16-7-16.

Support Cos.
20-8 to 27-8-16.

BAZENTIN
LE PETIT

LONGUEVAL
½ mile.

HIGH ALLEY

LEITH WALK

WOOD STREET

LONGUEVAL STREET

Bn.H.Q.
20-8-16 to
27-8-16.

THISTLE ALLEY

Position of
deployment
16-7-16.

BAZENTIN LE PETIT
WOOD

Position occupied
5-9 to 8-9-16.

PEARL WOOD

Bn.H.Q.
5-9 to 8-9-16.

LONGUEVAL ½ mile.

BAZENTIN LE GRAND

MAMETZ
WOOD

FLATIRON
COPSE

Battles of the SOMME, 1916

Positions occupied & trenches held by 1st Bn. Gloucestershire Regt.

14th July to 8th Sept., 1916

Scale of Yards

1000   500   0   1000   2000

TZ

F

CHAPTER XXI

THE ATTACK ON HIGH WOOD

DURING the period the 1st Gloucesters were in the Quadrangle, i.e. from the 2nd to the 5th September, the C.O. was warned that his Battalion would be required to take part in another attack on High Wood on the 8th of the month. Already the 28th had been involved in attempts to take that formidable position and, in so doing, had lost heavily.

For weeks High Wood, like Guillemont and Delville Wood, had defied final capture. Again and again our troops had entered all three places and had for a time held their positions, finally having to fall back. The guns of the opposing sides had so heavily shelled the two woods and the village that when at last we did capture them they existed as place names only—a ghastly testimony to the enormous destructive power of modern artillery fire.

On the 4th, Colonel Pagan went up to make a preliminary reconnaissance of the ground. The next day (the 3rd Brigade having received orders to relieve the 1st Brigade) the Gloucesters moved forward and took over various trenches and dug-outs north of Bazentin-le-Grand. The next two days were spent in getting ready for the attack which had been planned on the following lines :

The 2nd Welch, on the right, were to attack northwards from that portion of our front line which ran through the Wood. The Gloucesters, on the left, were to attack eastwards from the trench running parallel with the western side of the Wood, which trench had been dug by them when last in the line. The objective laid down for the 28th was the second ride east of the western edge of the Wood. The South Wales Borderers were to support the Gloucesters and troops of the 15th Division on the left were to attack a small trench which the 28th were to take over when captured.

The attack was to be launched at 6 p.m., assisted by *flammenwerfer*. The guns were to shell the Wood from 12 noon until 5.30 p.m., then, after half an hour's bombardment by 2-inch trench mortars, the attacking troops were to advance.

The Gloucesters were to attack in two waves, i.e. B Company on the right, A Company on the left, D Company behind B, and C in rear of A.

The assembly (or 'jumping-off') trench, however, could only accommodate the two front-line companies and, although it was strongly represented that the attack would have a far better chance of success if the second-line companies were placed lying in the open in rear of the 'jumping-off' trench, 'higher authority' decided that they were to be placed in a trench called Leith Walk, a continuation of the 'jumping-off' trench, southwards. This necessitated their filing into the 'jumping-off' trench after the front-line companies had started the attack.

At 12 noon the 28th moved forward to assembly positions. This early move was occasioned by the fact that the enemy's barrage usually fell between Bazentin-le-Grand and the Wood, the area which had to be crossed in moving forward. When the bombardment of the Wood opened there was short shooting on the right of the line and B Company suffered several casualties before a message could be got back to the guns to lengthen their range. The Company Commander—Lieutenant J. Peate—and C.S.M. Hird were both, unfortunately, killed by this short shooting. The C.S.M. had served throughout the War with the Battalion.[1]

It was a gorgeous autumn day when the Gloucesters 'went over the top': A Company, on the left, though their left platoon had been practically wiped out by machine-gun fire, went straight on to the objective and began consolidation. On the right, B Company had a stiff fight on the edge of the Wood where the enemy, in an unidentified trench, put up a stubborn resistance. But they also eventually reached their objective alongside A Company, though very weak in numbers.

From the high ground north-west of the Wood came the ceaseless 'rat-tat-tat' of a merciless enfilade machine-gun fire as C and D Companies filed into the 'jumping-off' trench.

---

[1] When the 28th first went into the Somme Battles of 1916, on the 14th July, Lieut.-Colonel Pagan was in command, Lieutenant M. A. Green, who had taken over from Captain Scott-Tucker in June, being Adjutant. The companies were commanded as follows : A Company —Captain D. Baxter, B—Captain H. E. de R. Wetherall, C—Captain K. A. R. Smith, D—Captain A. M. Jones. Captain Wetherall was wounded on the 21st August while acting as second-in-command. For the attack of the 8th September Lieut.-Colonel Pagan commanded, Lieutenant Green was Adjutant and, with the exception of B Company, companies were under the same commanders. B Company was commanded by Lieutenant J. Peate.

When the two companies began to advance they were sw
a storm of bullets : only a few men got across unhurt an_
joined up with A and B Companies on the objective. Touch
was obtained on the left with troops of the 44th Brigade, but it
was impossible to spare men to take over the trench these troops
had captured.

Meanwhile casualties among the brave fellows who had reached
and were consolidating the objective were occurring continually.
Moreover, appeals for reinforcements brought no response and
when darkness had fallen the remnants of the 28th were ordered
back to the trenches from which they had so gallantly started :
by 10 p.m. they were in position there.

During the attack the enemy had put down, and maintained
until 10.30 p.m., a very heavy barrage between High Wood and
Bazentin-le-Grand, and a number of Gloucester men going back
to the dressing-station were killed by it. One, No. 8015 Sergt.
Gray, the Sergeant of the Scout Section, after being wounded
in the arm, was told to go back : he was not seen again until
his body was recovered after the War. He had done exceptional
work as Scout Sergeant for over a year and had been recommended for a commission. His father was Regimental Sergeant-
Major of the 28th and his uncle and grandfather were both
Quartermasters of that Battalion.

Another case was that of Captain A. M. Jones who, desperately
wounded during the attack, was being carried down when his
stretcher-bearers were both killed. Captain Jones remained out
all night on his stretcher until he was found still alive at daylight
next morning.

At 3 a.m. on the 9th September the enemy counter-attacked
the left of the line held by the 28th, but the only outcome (for
him) was a bloody repulse and the loss of 2 officers and 16 other
ranks left as prisoners in the hands of the Gloucesters. At
11 a.m. the Battalion was relieved and marched back to the
Quadrangle and remained there until the 11th.

When they ' went over the top ' on the 8th September the
Gloucesters were already weak owing to casualties received since
the beginning of the Somme Battles. Of the officers who took
part in the attack, Lieutenants J. A. P. Parnell and J. Peate and
2nd Lieutenants A. F. D. Brown were killed, and 2nd Lieutenants
J. E. S. Wakeley and E. A. Cockett died of wounds. Lieut.-
Colonel A. W. Pagan, Captains K. A. R. Smith, A. M. Jones,
S. T. Cross and 2nd Lieutenants A. Birley, A. C. Sly, C. H.
Steele and E. Duff were wounded. In other ranks the losses
were 84 killed and 122 wounded. Only Captain D. Baxter and

Lieutenants M. A. Green, C. E. W. Lavender and F. C. Davis and 96 other ranks were unwounded.

The 1st Division on the 11th September, having been relieved by the 47th Division, moved back out of the line, the Gloucesters marching via Bécourt, Albert and Millencourt to a camp for the night in Henencourt Wood. On the 12th they moved to Franvillers, remaining there until the 15th. On the latter date began a series of moves to Henencourt Wood, Black Wood, the neighbourhood of Bazentin-le-Grand, the eastern side of Mametz Wood, Black Wood again, Millencourt and, finally, a return to Henencourt Wood on the 29th,[1] where they remained until the 3rd October, on which date the 1st Division, having been transferred to the IVth Corps, moved to an area round Abbeville, the 28th being billeted in Feuquières.

Thus the Gloucesters, for the time being, left the Somme Battlefields, where they had fought since the 14th July, having lost in all 546 officers and men.

While he was lying in the casualty clearing-station at Heilly, after the attack of the 8th September, Colonel Pagan received the following letter from the G.O.C., 1st Division (Major-General Strickland) :

' Your Battalion did *splendidly* yesterday and got their objectives. I sent the Corps Commander's congratulations to your Battalion this morning and am writing to convey them to you with my own, not only for this occasion but for all others when you've been engaged.'

The 1st Gloucesters remained in Feuquières until the 31st October, when once again the Battalion (in Brigade and Division) began to move back to the Somme, though spending several days in villages *en route*, where training was carried on. By the 10th November they had reached a camp at Mametz Wood within 300 yards of the Quadrangle where they were before the attack of the 8th September, where also for the time being they must be left.

---

[1] About this time Captain E. A. D. C. Chamier, at the age of 20 years, commanded the Battalion for a short period. Later Capt. H. N. Vinen rejoined and assumed command of the 28th.

CHAPTER XXII

THE THIRD WINTER IN THE TRENCHES : 1916–17

IT is said that Time dims the memory of all things, but few of those living who went through that first winter on the Somme after the battles of 1916 will ever forget the awful conditions under which men lived and fought. Nothing can ever take away the vision of the ghastly dreariness of great stretches of mud and morass, of a country pock-marked with shell-holes full of noisome water, of those long stretches of duck-boarded tracks along which weary and worn-out men trudged either to the front line or back to billets, of trenches ankle-deep, knee-deep and even waist-deep in water which, made muddy with earth, had taken on the consistency of soup. Of the pitiless rain, followed by frost and then snow : of the gales and blizzards which swept the trenches in the midst of which reliefs, and even attacks on the enemy had to take place : the while, with greedy, ever-outstretched hands Death clutched and snatched the lives of brave and gallant men, of whom, indeed, some minded not the going —since it meant release from the manifold miseries of a terrible existence.

It fell to the unhappy lot of the 1st Gloucesters and the three Territorial battalions of the Regiment—1/4th, 1/5th and 1/6th —to spend part of the winter of 1916–17 at least in the Somme trenches.

The day following the arrival of the 28th in camp at Mametz Wood, i.e. on the 11th November, Lieut.-Colonel Pagan rejoined the Battalion, having recovered from his wound.[1]

The whole area round and in Mametz Wood was a pestilential spot. The camp into which the Gloucesters had moved in bitterly cold weather was soon knee-deep in mud. In this place they remained until the 21st. With the exception of one day off (Sunday, the 19th) they paraded daily at 5.30 a.m. and from 6.30

[1] At this period Lieut.-Colonel Pagan commanded, Major H. N. Vinen was second-in-command, Lieutenant M. A. Green was Adjutant and companies were commanded as follows : A—Captain E. A. D. C. Chamier, B—Captain W. Wynter-Morgan, C—Captain F. C. Davis and D—Captain C. E. W. Lavender.

a.m. until 11 a.m. and again from 12 noon until 3 p.m. they were engaged in road-making. The weather was vile and often after the day's work all ranks returned to camp with their clothes sodden with rain. In this condition they marched back to their only habitation—cold and clammy tents—pitched amid seas of mud. Even a plentiful supply of wood, used for the purpose of keeping huge fires burning outside the tents by which to dry clothing and webbing equipment, failed to dissipate the hard lot of these unfortunate men. Only the inherent grit and pluck and good humour of the British soldier kept soul and body alive, and probably as he sat or crouched drying his socks by the fire he would sing to himself, shivering the while :

'Oh my Gawd, what a life !'

Many new hands—reinforcements—had joined the 1st Battalion since they were in the line and these experienced for the first time the rigours of winter campaigning.

On the 21st the Gloucesters moved forward to support positions and occupied huts in the most westerly of two camps between High Wood and Bazentin-le-Petit. Conditions here were an improvement on the Mametz tents, but still the Battalion was engaged in road-making until, on the 27th, front-line trenches on the right of the Albert—Bapaume road, north-east of Le Sars and facing the Butte de Warlencourt (held by the Germans) were taken over.[1]

These trenches were described by the C.O. as 'a particularly bad sample of the Somme trenches of the winter of 1916'. They were reached only after a long trek overground, by communication trenches full of deep, sticky mud, which were merely man-traps. The front line consisted of broken-down trenches not continuous.

By an unfortunate error of judgment—an error never repeated—the Battalion had been ordered to parade in gum boots and, despite orders to the contrary, one or two platoons attempted to use communication trenches to the front line. These, to a

---

[1] On the 19th November 1916 Brig.-General H. R. Davies gave up the command of the 3rd Brigade. This very gallant soldier had commanded the 3rd Brigade since February 1915 and his worth was appreciated by those who had served under him long enough to know him. He commanded the Brigade wisely and sympathetically not only during the battles of 9th May 1915, of Loos and of the Somme, but also when it was in the line and during its periods of rest. A day in the front line without a visit from him was so infrequent as to cause inquiries to be made as to what had happened to him. General Davies, who belonged to the Oxfordshire Light Infantry, finished the War in command of the 11th Division. His Irish terrier, Freddy, which he acquired soon after getting the 3rd Brigade, continued with him till the War ended.

man, became stuck in the mud and were only extricated by being pulled out by men outside the trenches, leaving their gum boots behind them. A large number of men who reached the front line overground soon suffered in the same way, with the result that many had to remain until the following morning (when supplies of boots and socks were brought up) *in their bare feet.*

A and B Companies took over the front line while C and D Companies were in support in Eaucourt-l'Abbaye, a vast entrenched ruined building, very difficult to find in the dark : in consequence it was late before they also were in position. The relief, therefore, was not completed until 4.30 a.m. on the 28th. The ' new hands ', both officers and men, who formed a large proportion of the Battalion, hardly appreciated their first introduction to trench life.

Barraged three times on the 28th, trench-mortared and shelled again on the 29th, shelled intermittently and ' pip-squeaked ' on the 30th, the Battalion remained in this iniquitous spot until the 1st December when, a friendly mist covering the trenches, a quick daylight relief by the Cameron Highlanders enabled the Gloucesters to move back unmolested to High Wood Camp East. On the last day of November the Battalion Medical Officer— Captain P. Smith, R.A.M.C.—was wounded by shell-fire.

From the huts at High Wood the 28th moved forward on the 5th December to support trenches for three days, thence back again on the 8th to the tented camp at Mametz Wood. This camp had become even worse than when the Gloucesters were there before : mud, 6 inches deep, was everywhere. Pelting rain, snow and sleet fell alternately. On the 14th the Battalion relieved the Munsters in the front line east of the Eaucourt-l'Abbaye—Le Barque road. The morning after the relief, however, it was discovered that the line taken over was considerably in rear of the position which should have been held according to the map. The remainder of the time in the line was, therefore, occupied by the 28th in re-establishing the proper position, fog and mist aiding the work.

There is little to record for the remainder of December. Front-line and support trenches and reserve positions were occupied in turn. On the 31st the Battalion was in an excellent hutted camp [1] east of Bécourt Wood.

The discomforts and hard conditions which beset the 1st Gloucesters were shared, though of course in different localities and sectors of the line, by the 1/4th, 1/5th and 1/6th Battalions. From the 3rd September until the end of the year the Territorials

---

[1] The town major of this camp was Albert Coates, the famous tenor.

were not engaged in any attack upon the enemy, neither were they attacked. Trench warfare did not differ materially in any part of the line, and there is little use in reiterating all that has been said of the 1st Battalion.

From the line north-west of Beaumont Hamel the three Battalions after a period out of the line took over trenches in the Hébuterne sector. Then followed a further tour in rest and training areas until a move down south brought them to east of their old sector (Ovillers) in the trenches about Martinpuich and Eaucourt-l'Abbaye, the Butte de Warlencourt and Le Sars. They also knew the miseries of Mametz Camp, for they were there towards the end of December when the place was *at its worst*.

When the year closed the 1/4th and 1/6th Battalions were billeted in Contay and the 1/5th at Brésle.[1]

On New Year's Day, 1917, therefore, the 1st Battalion and the three Territorial Battalions were out of the line.

The 1st Gloucesters held their Christmas festivities on the 4th January—a splendid feast being again provided by friends of the Regiment in England.

Apart from continuous work mostly on the roads in very bad weather, life in Bécourt Camp was comfortable, but seldom was a unit allowed to live in comfort and on the 23rd January the Battalion moved back to Contay. Billets were good in the latter village, but the cold was intense and nobody could keep warm in large and airy barns. Trees were bought, cut down and used as firewood, but still everyone found the cold extremely uncomfortable. For ten days the Gloucesters trained hard, the training ground being excellent.

Towards the end of the month the Gloucesters were informed that the 1st Division would shortly relieve the 48th French Division in the line opposite Barleux, a village south of the Somme River and about 3 miles south-west of Péronne. The line was

[1] Casualties among the officers of all three Battalions between the 3rd of September and the 31st of December were as follows : 1/4th Gloucesters—Lieutenant E. M. Matthews (killed 8th November 1916), Captain E. E. Wookey (wounded 8th November 1916), Lieutenant H. G. Phippen (wounded 8th November 1916, died of wounds 9th November 1916), Lieutenant B. Clark (killed 9th November 1916), Lieutenant Langland (wounded 9th November 1916), 2nd Lieutenant Taylor (wounded 24th November 1916). 1/5th Gloucesters—2nd Lieutenants Howard and McI. Miller (wounded 18th November 1916), Lieutenant Nason (wounded 29th November 1916). 1/6th Battalion—2nd Lieutenant Kinneir (wounded 18th October 1916), Lieutenant Score (wounded 6th November 1916).

reconnoitred and on the 2nd February the Battalion marched via Basieux, Ribemont, Sailly-Laurette and Cérisy to Morcourt on the Somme. The river was frozen, for a hard frost still covered the countryside.

The Gloucesters remained at Morcourt until the 5th, when they marched to a camp south of Cappy and the following day relieved French troops in the front line opposite Barleux.

Owing to the hard frost the front-line trenches were in excellent condition : the communication trenches and dug-out accommodation were also good. The front line faced almost due south and was about 500 yards north of Barleux. A and B Companies took over the front line, with C and Headquarters in Crousaz Trench about 800 yards behind the front line : D Company was in reserve in Meudon Quarry.

The line was quiet and the first tour uneventful. The Battalion was relieved on the 10th February and moved back into support, Headquarters to an excellent dug-out close to Flaucourt at the head of a long communication trench—Boyau de Boulogne—and Companies in the Bois de Bretons, adjoining Flaucourt, Meudon Quarry, the Sugar Factory in Flaucourt and in Flaucourt Quarry.

The next tour in the line began on the 14th February when the Gloucesters took over trenches farther to the south (the 1st Division having side-stepped to the right), the front line facing east and a little closer to Barleux. Battalion Headquarters were in Boulogne Quarry, about a mile south of Meudon Quarry. The first tour in the line had been comparatively peaceful, but the second tour was marked by increased hostile shell-fire. On the 17th the great frost, which had lasted for five weeks, showed signs of breaking. On the 18th the Battalion was relieved and moved back to Telegraph Camp, west of Dompierre. This camp was filthy. The thaw had produced mud knee-deep and dug-outs and shelters were falling in so that everyone was glad to move back to the front line on the 21st. But when the relief was over the trenches also were found in an indescribable mess. The Battalion had been ordered to raid the enemy and on the 22nd 2nd Lieutenant Grainger went out to reconnoitre the ground. In broad daylight he walked into the enemy's front line and found it evacuated, but the state of No-Man's Land and the hostile trenches were even worse than those held by the Gloucesters and, on reporting this fact to higher authority, the raid was cancelled.

On relief on the 23rd the Battalion marched to Chuignes for a short period of training, returning to the line on the 7th March, when trenches farther south and clear of Barleux, on the southern side, were taken over.

One more tour was spent in reserve, from the 11th to the 15th March, before great changes took place on the Somme. On the latter date the 1st Gloucesters again took over the front line south and clear of Barleux, the relief being completed [1] at 3 a.m. on the 16th, but the dramatic events which followed must form the subject of a separate chapter.

Meanwhile the three Territorial Battalions had also arrived south of the Somme, for the 48th Division at this period formed part of the same Corps (IIIrd) to which the 1st Division belonged, and while the 1st Gloucesters were living in more or less discomfort in the Barleux sector, the 1/4th, 1/5th and 1/6th Battalions were going through similar discomforts on the left flank of the senior Battalion of the Regiment west of Biaches and La Maisonette immediately south of Péronne.

The 48th Division spent the whole of January out of the line in training, and it was not until the 2nd February that, the Division having in the meantime moved down south of the Somme, the 1/4th and 1/6th Battalions relieved French troops in the front line north of Barleux and east of Flaucourt, the 1/5th with other units of the 145th Brigade being then in reserve at Marly and Froissy.

For all three Battalions the remainder of February passed without incident of special importance. The 1/6th had two officers wounded during the month—2nd Lieutenants Stephens and Dibble—whilst on patrol. The first fortnight of March also was uneventful, though there was a marked improvement in the weather and the ground had begun to dry, for which everyone was devoutly thankful.

The Battalion Diary of the 1/5th Gloucesters, however, is the only record of those kept by the Territorials which gives any clue to things which were about to happen. On the 12th March their Diary has the following entry : ' Weather very good and dry. In the evening many fires could be observed in front, *but still no signs of an enemy retreat : can't be long delayed now !* '

---

[1] One officer (2nd Lieutenant R. A. Beale) and 1 other rank were killed during the relief.

CHAPTER XXIII

THE GERMAN RETREAT TO THE HINDEN-
BURG LINE

IF any justification for the Somme Battles of 1916 were needed surely the most cogent may be found in the German Retreat to the Hindenburg Line in 1917, for *one* of the objects of that first terrific struggle on the Somme, as given by Sir Douglas Haig, was the wearing down of the enemy's forces, and that this was achieved is evident : the Germans had lost so heavily that they were forced to shorten their line.

'The decision to retreat', said the Chief of the German Imperial Staff, 'was not reached without a painful struggle. It implied a confession of weakness bound to raise the *morale* of the enemy and lower our own. But as it was necessary for military reasons we had no choice—it had to be carried out.'

On the 9th February the Germans began their work of demolition over a wide area extending from the northern bank of the Aisne River to the Scarpe, east of Arras :

' Our first object was to avoid a battle, our second to effect the salvage of all our raw material of war and technical and other equipment that was not actually built into the positions, and finally the destruction of all high roads, villages, towns and wells, so as to prevent him establishing himself in force in the near future in front of our new position.' [1]

The ' new position ' was the Hindenburg (or Siegfried) Line —a powerful system of defences which ran generally in a north-westerly direction from just north of the Aisne and east of Crouy —La Fère—St. Quentin, thence to the Scarpe east of Arras.

The first day of the enemy's retirement to the Hindenburg Line was to be the 16th March, though he anticipated that, under pressure, it might begin earlier : it did begin earlier, notably on the Ancre in February, where he was forced to abandon his positions and fall back upon his new line. But, so far as the Gloucesters were concerned, the actual date of the enemy's retreat coincided closely with his declared intention.

At 12 noon on the 16th the C.O. of the 1st Gloucesters was summoned to a conference at 3rd Brigade Headquarters at which

[1] General Ludendorff in *My War Memories*, 1914–18.

orders were issued for strong patrols from all battalions in the line
to endeavour to penetrate the enemy's lines.   If these patrols were
successful the German trenches were to be occupied at once.

The 28th, it will be remembered, had only taken over front-line
trenches on the night of the 15th/16th, the relief not being completed until 3 a.m. on the 16th, so that they had been in the line
only nine hours when they received the above orders.   The line
lay south and clear of Barleux.

There was little time to prepare for the operation.   The place
selected, on the Gloucesters' front, was at the northern end of their
line where the remains of an old trench ran out to the enemy's
line : this old trench had been reconnoitred frequently and would
give good cover to the patrol.   The latter was supplied by
C Company under 2nd Lieutenant F. C. Grainger.

Having successfully crossed No-Man's Land, the patrol reached
the enemy's wire but were unable to cut a way through.   However, a gap was found through which they crawled to the enemy's
parapet, only to be greeted by a hail of bullets and bombs.[1]   The
officer and three men were wounded and it was only after some
difficulty that the patrol returned, bringing in all the wounded.
For the moment the operations ceased.

Meanwhile the 48th Division, on the immediate left of the
1st Division, had also been engaged in testing the strength of the
enemy's lines.   The Diary of the 1/6th Gloucesters has the
following entry on the 15th March :

' Information received from Brigade at 9 p.m. that a deserter had come
in on our left stating that the enemy were withdrawing on our front and
had only left twenty men per company in trenches.   Orders were issued
to C Company ordering a fighting patrol to be sent out.'

When these orders were received the support and reserve
companies of the 1/6th were engaged in relieving the front line
and the relief was not completed until 1 a.m. on the 16th.

The fighting patrol consisted of a platoon, twenty strong, under
Lieutenant Byard.   On reaching the enemy's wire a gap had to
be cut through which the patrol entered the German trenches.
No sign of the enemy could be seen in the hostile trenches, and
dug-outs were empty : new stick grenades were lying about and
several sniper plates were in position.   As it was after 5 a.m. and
getting light the patrol returned and reported that the only sign
of the enemy was a sniper who fired from the reserve line, though

---

[1] The Germans left behind in their front-line trenches rearguards,
plentifully armed with machine guns, with orders to hold us up as long
as possible : these rearguards fought well.

right and left of the point at which the patrol entered the German trenches Véry lights were ' going up '.

Another patrol from the left company reached the enemy's wire, but were fired on. On receiving reports on the results of these patrols the G.O.C., 48th Division, ordered a raid on La Maisonette to take place at 2.30 a.m. on the 17th. The 1/5th Gloucesters were to make the raid.

Two companies of the 1/5th—A and C—moved up to the sector opposite La Maisonette on the night of the 16th/17th. under the command of Captain Conden, who was O.C. raid.

As soon as the Divisional Artillery opened fire to cover the raiders, the enemy's guns also came into action, but their fire did not delay the Gloucesters and they went forward to time. They entered the German trenches, A Company leading, and killed several Germans, also bombing dug-outs. C Company followed A and, passing through the latter, occupied the enemy's support line. Patrols were then pushed forward through La Maisonette buildings and they took possession of the German third line and began the work of consolidation. A message was then sent back to Battalion Headquarters giving the situation in the front line. As soon as this information was received and circulated the Warwick Brigade pushed on to Biaches. By the evening of the 17th the patrols from the 1/5th Gloucesters had reached the Péronne—Eterpigny road, finding everywhere that the enemy had flown.

Their Battalion Diary records : ' We were the first Battalion in Brigade and all the divisions in IIIrd Corps to discover the enemy retreat and follow it up.'

The 1/4th and 1/6th also sent out a patrol which reached the banks of the Somme opposite La Chapelette without meeting the enemy.

Meanwhile, between 8 a.m. and 9 a.m., the 1st Gloucesters had sent out further patrols. Their first attempt on the 16th had been unlucky, for either the enemy had not begun to evacuate his trenches or the patrol had struck a party detailed to cover his retirement.

The second attempt, however, was eminently successful. The patrols penetrated the German front and second lines, those on the right meeting with a certain amount of opposition : on the left the advance was unopposed.

As rapidly as possible the whole Battalion then got on the move and by 1 p.m. the leading platoon was east of Villers-Carbonnel, touch being established with the 2nd Welch on the right and 10th Gloucesters (1st Brigade, 1st Division) on the left. Patrols

were then pushed down to the Somme at Brie Bridge, but the
Germans were holding trenches on the eastern bank of the river
and any considerable movement by the Gloucesters immediately
drew machine-gun, rifle and shell fire.

An outpost position was, however, established in the old
German trenches 600 yards west of the river and the remainder
of the Battalion bivouacked in old German trenches on the western
side of the Villers-Carbonnel—Péronne road and north of the
former village.   A large dug-out, full of rooms and stairways and
three storeys deep, was used as Battalion Headquarters, but only
after it had been cleared of several ingenious ‘ booby traps ’.

In this position the 1st Gloucesters remained until the evening
of the 18th March, when they were relieved and withdrawn to
dug-outs round Boulogne Wood.   During the day a patrol, under
2nd Lieutenant S. F. M. Forbes, crossed the Somme, and advancing about a mile on the other side, gained useful information
regarding the enemy’s dispositions.   The Battalion withdrew
from Boulogne Wood on the evening of the 19th to the neighbourhood of Chuignes.

On the morning of the 18th the 1/4th Gloucesters, who had
relieved the 1/5th on the previous evening, sent forward A Company, who established posts east of Biaches.   Three picquets
were also found which placed sentry groups to watch the Somme
crossings.   Patrols were then sent out to reconnoitre the Faubourg
de Paris, Flamicourt and Péronne.   The latter was found to be
held by the 8th Warwicks.   All bridges had been destroyed, but
there were no signs of the enemy.   On the 20th the Battalion
crossed the Somme and established Headquarters in Little Flamicourt, B Company taking over the outpost line from D Company.
Cartigny, Brusle and Buire were then reconnoitred but no signs
of the enemy were seen.   The Battalion was relieved on the 21st
and moved back to Sophie.

The 1/5th Gloucesters moved to Peronne on the 20th March
and were billeted in the hospital opposite the barracks : ‘ Town
very much damaged,’ their Diary records.   ‘ Hardly a house left
standing.’   In the hospital there was no glass in the windows.
Many houses were still burning.

The next day the Battalion supplied working-parties to
extinguish fires and clear the streets of bricks and rubbish : the
Bosche had been pretty thorough in his demolition.   The railway
station had been badly knocked about and the barracks partially
destroyed.   The Palais de Justice was quite unrecognizable as
such.   On the 22nd the Battalion marched via Doingt and
Courcelles to Cartigny and Catelet, two companies in each village.

The following day working-parties began filling up crater-holes at cross-roads and clearing trees which had been placed across the main road from Doignt to Tertry.

The 24th saw the 1/5th marching to Bouvincourt, where the C.O. was presented with a wreath and a tricolour by the civilian inhabitants (about four hundred) in honour of the arrival of British troops. B Company moved to Beaumetz. On the 25th C and D Companies marched to Vraignes and Hancourt respectively, with outposts at Pœuilly, Fléchin and Bernes. Very little of the enemy was seen—'Only a little shelling indulged in by our playful friends the enemy'.[1]

Vraignes was very little damaged : about 1,400 civilians remained who were taken back west and south of the Somme to Bray and the surrounding villages as soon as possible. On the 27th the Battalion moved back to Cartigny, where by this time the 1/4th had also arrived. The 1/6th were in billets in Péronne.

The 1/4th moved from Cartigny on the 29th to Villers-Fauçon, and on the following day attacked and captured the village of St. Emilie. The attack was carried out by two companies, D Company starting from the north-western end of Villers-Fauçon with the object of working round the left flank and attacking St. Emilie from the north-west, whilst A Company was directed against the western face of the village. A battery of Field Artillery was to co-operate, but unfortunately the orders failed to reach the gunners and at 4 p.m. the attack commenced without artillery support.

The left company got on well but encountered a good deal of opposition at the entrance of the village where the enemy made a spirited counter-attack. This, however, was met by Lewis-gun and rifle fire and repulsed. Second-Lieutenant C. F. Hall, M.C., was able to establish a Lewis-gun post in the corner of the Sugar Refinery which enfiladed German machine-gunners who were firing on the right company. These gunners had, for the moment, held up A Company, but the progress made on the left enabled them again to move forward and the enemy was driven from the village. Although from one to two hundred Germans retired in the direction of Epéhy, the enemy machine-gunners held on to the last and when the village was finally captured the story of their gallant stand was revealed by their dead bodies which lay about the gun positions. In this action 2nd Lieutenant A. McClelland was killed, both company commanders—Captain F. L. Hall and Lieutenant A. J. Gardiner—as well as 2nd Lieutenants C. F. Holland and L. E. Wakefield wounded, whilst 6 other ranks were killed in action and 47 wounded.

[1] Battalion Diary, 1/5th Gloucesters.

The 1/5th ended the month at Tincourt and the 1/6th holding an outpost line near Villers-Fauçon.

On the 1st April the 144th Brigade attacked Epéhy, the 1/6th Gloucesters with the 7th Worcesters taking part in the operations, while the 1/4th 'stood to' at Longavesnes, and the 1/5th in Tincourt.

The 1/6th attacked with A, C and D Companies in the firing line at 5 a.m. and, although met by brisk rifle fire from the outskirts of Epéhy, the attackers pushed on, getting through a belt of very weak wire in which were numerous gaps. The village was entered at about 5.50 a.m., the enemy making no serious resistance until the objective, the railway bank east of Epéhy, was reached. Here rapid fire was exchanged and bombs were also thrown. It was by this time close upon 6.30 a.m., at which hour our guns were to place a barrage along the bank. As soon as the barrage ceased A and C Companies again moved forward and consolidated the position along the railway bank.

The western side of the village, the village itself and the railway bank were shelled by the enemy's artillery, but his infantry made no counter-attack.

The 1/6th lost in this attack 1 other rank killed and 9 wounded.

On the 5th April the 145th Brigade attacked Lempire with Ronssoy and Basse Boulogne. In this attack the 1/4th Royal Berks were on the right (south and south-east of Ronssoy and Basse Boulogne), 1/4th Oxford and Bucks in the centre (south-western end of Ronssoy) and 1/5th Gloucesters on the left (La Paurelle and Basse Boulogne) with a detachment directed on Maye Copse.

The Gloucesters formed up west of the railway, south-east of Epéhy, and companies were ordered to move on their objectives in the following order : C, and D (less two platoons directed on Maye Copse), A Company (less one platoon holding Malassise Farm) : B Company was in reserve.

Zero hour was 4.55 a.m.

The enemy appears to have expected this attack as he opened a heavy artillery barrage at 5 a.m., but it fell well behind the attacking troops, who assaulted the position in fine style. By 6 a.m. the Gloucesters were through Lempire and had taken up position on the north-eastern and eastern sides of the village. Nine prisoners were captured by the Battalion, also two machine guns, and a few Germans were killed. The attacks of the Berks and Oxfords were equally successful. Severe opposition was put up by the enemy and a lot of hand-to-hand fighting took place. A line east of the village was then consolidated and held.

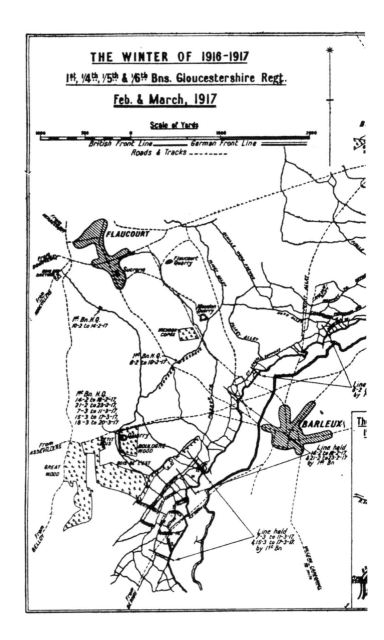

THE WINTER OF 1916-1917

1ˢᵗ, 1/4ᵗʰ, 1/5ᵗʰ & 1/6ᵗʰ Bns. Gloucestershire Regt.

Feb. & March, 1917

Scale of Yards

British Front Line _____ German Front Line _____
Roads & Tracks ----------

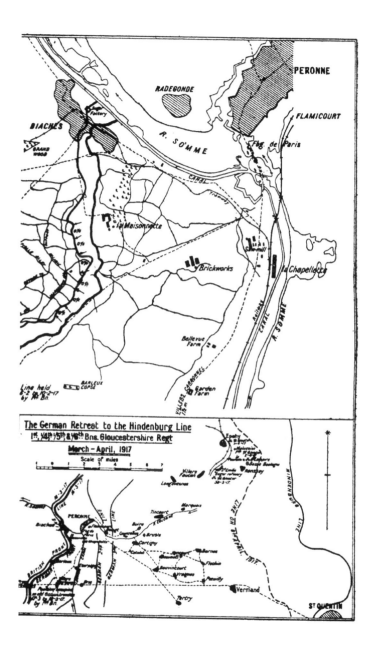

The German Retreat to the Hindenburg Line
1st, 1/4th, 1/5th & 1/6th Bns. Gloucestershire Regt
March – April, 1917
Scale of miles

The 1/5th Gloucesters lost in this attack 15 other ranks killed and Captain Conder and 40 men wounded. In the evening the Battalion was relieved and marched back to Villers-Fauçon.

The German Retreat to the Hindenburg Line officially ends on the 5th April, and on that date the two other Territorial Battalions were in Cartigny (1/4th Gloucesters) and Marquaix (1/6th Gloucesters).

CHAPTER XXIV

SALONIKA

LEMBET CAMP, to which the 2nd Gloucesters [1] marched on the 12th December 1915 on arrival at Salonika, was about 4 miles from the quay where they had disembarked. 'Camp' was but a name for a rocky, sandy plain, relieved by occasional hillocks, which rose gradually to stony hills above, intersected here and there by nullahs, though boasting only one clump of trees.

The Battalion reached camp at about 4.30 p.m. and then had to pitch tents : as tentage was none too plentiful both officers and men were very much overcrowded.

The general situation when the Gloucesters arrived in Macedonia was that the Allied forces (British, French and Greeks) held a circle round Salonika, and not a very wide one at that. The 10th Division, on the right, held two narrow necks of land, the first between the Gulf of Orfano and Beshik Lake and the second from Beshik and Langaza Lakes : the Division's second line ran from the south-western corner of Langaza Lake to Akukli. On the left of the 10th, the 26th Division held the line Tumba—Kavalar—Ajvatli where the 28th Division carried the line to just north-west of Balja : the 22nd Division was on the left of the 28th, with its left flank at about Pirnar, French troops carrying the line westwards to the Vardar River. The 27th Division on arrival was placed in Army Reserve in, and in the neighbourhood of, Lembet Camp.

But a few weeks previously Servia had been overrun by Bulgarian and German troops and the unfortunate Serbs practically turned out of their own country. Allied assistance had arrived too late, the 10th Irish Division and a French division, sent to Macedonia from the Dardanelles, being unable to do more than land at Salonika and secure a precarious footing.

In December 1915 things were still somewhat chaotic. The first need was military roads, for no advance could take place over the existing highways, which were little more than tracks—

---

[1] The Battalion strength on arrival in Macedonia was approximately 26 officers and 882 other ranks, Lieut.-Colonel F. C. Nisbet commanding.

frequently bad at that. Then the Allied circle around Salonika had to be made secure, which meant that miles of trenches had to be dug and wired. Something had also to be done for the comfort of the troops, who early perceived that they were likely to fare badly and would have to put up with much harder conditions than those which obtained along the Western Front. In a barren and inhospitable country they had been (as it were) ' planked down ' there to fight not only the enemy but disease and discomforts of the worst type. Such was the hard lot of the Salonika Force.

The day following their arrival at Lembet the Gloucesters set about improving their camp, turning their attention specially to the digging of drains and preparing generally against the ravages of wet weather. The next day the Battalion began company training, but thereafter until the 28th December they were set to work at road-making and, for the time being, became navvies, for that was what their task amounted to. On Christmas Day they were given a half-holiday, each man receiving a quart of beer and half a pound of plum pudding (made by the regimental cooks). There were sports in the afternoon, fine weather doing its best to make the day enjoyable. The King's Christmas Message was also read out to the troops.

On the 27th, however, the Gloucesters received orders to move to a camp on the Monastir road. The Battalion marched out of Lembet Camp at 10.30 a.m. and arrived at their destination at about 11.45 a.m., where they took over from the 2nd Cameron Highlanders.

The Gloucesters' Diary for the 29th December records that they ' got five side drums, one bass drum, eight flutes from Ordnance. Started forming " drums " '. Only a soldier knows the heartening sound of the ' drums and fifes '.

Next came a turn at guard duties which lasted two days, the Gloucesters finding 10 officers and 550 other ranks for guards and picquets, presumably in Salonika. On the 30th the Battalion records that the Town Guard arrested German, Austrian, Bulgarian and Turkish civilians, in all a total of 65 persons, and handed them over to the French. At about 12 noon on the same day two German aeroplanes appeared over Lembet Camp and dropped ten bombs : they were driven off by guns from ships in the harbour and French aeroplanes.

The Argyll and Sutherland Highlanders took over guard duties from the Gloucesters on the 31st December, but the latter resumed the following day.

On the 2nd January an amusing (and what at one time was likely

13

to prove an awkward) incident took place. Second-Lieutenant G. H. Oxley, in charge of the guard over the German consulate, found a German flag on the roof. French sentries were also on guard there and the difficulty was how to get the flag away without being seen and thus arousing the jealousy of our Allies. An N.C.O. (No. 21417 Corpl. Young), Corporal of the Guard, solved the difficulty by tying the flag round his portly frame and marching away without being seen. Lieutenant Oxley also found the Bulgarian flag at the Bulgarian consulate and brought it away.[1]

The Gloucesters paraded on the 4th January and marched round Salonika, the ' Drums ' being on parade for the first time since the Battalion went on active service in December 1914.

On the 12th the Battalion again changed camp. The 3rd King's Royal Rifles relieved the Gloucesters from all guard duties and the latter marched up to a new camp near Kapujilar (south-west and about 4 miles from Salonika), where once again road-making and making drains occupied the attention of the Battalion.

Our relations with the Greeks were none too cordial at this time and on the 17th January there happened a small incident which reflected the attitude of the Greek soldiery towards the Allies. The Gloucesters were out road-making near Kapujilar Camp when a troop of Greek cavalry galloped across the road under construction, knocking down a man of the Battalion. The case was reported immediately to Army Headquarters and the Colonel of the Greek cavalry regiment apologized in person to Lieut.-Colonel Nisbet, the Greek officer in charge of the troop being given two months' imprisonment.

During the third week in January the 81st Brigade began to relieve troops of the 10th Irish Division between the Beshik and Langaza lakes. The Gloucesters set out on what was a long, tiring march on the 19th, over hills and mostly along stony tracks, to Hortiack, where an uncomfortable night was spent in a wet camp. The following day the march was continued to a bivouac camp at Gomonic where the Battalion arrived at about 5 p.m., very tired. A 16-mile march over stony and hilly ground, carrying a heavy load, is no light task. The Battalion Transport, especially, had considerable trouble in getting down the very steep hill into Ajvasil, through which the Gloucesters marched *en route* to

[1] The Battalion Diary states that both flags ' were sent to Mrs. Vicary (mother of Captain A. C. Vicary, Adjutant of the 2nd Gloucesters at that period), " Dyrons ", Newton Abbott, Devon, to be kept until asked for by the Officer Commanding, 2nd Battalion, Gloucestershire Regiment (61st) '. They now hang in the Regimental Museum at the Depot, Bristol.

Gomonic. Moreover, all ranks were not in the best of health : during the previous week no less than 4 officers and 45 other ranks had been sent to hospital sick, while between the 12th December and the 20th January 4 officers and 121 other ranks had been evacuated, mostly suffering from influenza, and others were sickening.

On the 21st the Gloucesters relieved the 7th Dublin Fusiliers in the front line, from a nullah ¼ mile east of Gomonic, to Beshik Lake. On this date Captain D. K. Garnier was accidentally wounded.

The Battalion promptly named the nullah ' Gloucester Gully '. Battalion Headquarters were established in another nullah about a mile east of Gomonic, immediately behind the front-line trenches.

In this place the Gloucesters remained until early June. Work on defensive positions, training, field exercises and route marches practically sums up the life of the Battalion during those months. Through the snows and frosts of winter, the heavy rains which followed and the beginning of a hot, sweltering summer, all ranks lived in dug-outs and bivouacs for the simple reason that there were no billets such as in France and Flanders.

Several changes took place in the Battalion : Captain A. C. Vicary, the Adjutant, was appointed G.S.O.III, XVIth Corps, and left on the 15th February. On the 17th March Lieut.-Colonel K. M. Davie arrived from England and assumed command of the Battalion, Lieut.-Colonel Nisbet taking over the duties of second-in-command : on the 19th April the latter officer left to command the 8th D.C.L.I., while two days later Major J. L. F. Tweedie, having been appointed to command the 11th Welch Regiment, joined that Battalion.

Throughout this period nothing had been seen of the Bulgarians, they were away somewhere ' in the blue ', but on the 8th June the Battalion Diary records that ' the Battalion marched out 4 miles east of Arnold's Gully and proceeded to attack a party of Comitadjis on the hills '. The comitadjis were Bulgarian bandits who occasionally made incursions into the plains, but whether the Gloucesters killed, wounded or captured any of these roving robbers it is impossible to say. The affair cannot have been of much importance for no mention is made of it in the Brigade or Divisional Headquarters Diaries.

Towards the end of June the Gloucesters began to move east, and on the 21st arrived at Stavros on the Gulf of Orfano. But they returned westwards again on the 27th July, on which date they marched to Pazarkia, continuing the march on the 28th to

Gomonic. In this (now) familiar spot they remained bivouacked throughout the remainder of the day, leaving at 4 a.m. on the 29th for Jerakaru. The same evening they resumed the march to Hortiack,[1] bivouacking about a mile outside the village.

On the 22nd the Battalion marched out of Hortiack for Guvezne and, after halting at Lajna from 8.25 a.m. to 5.30 p.m., resumed the march, arriving at their destination at 9.50 p.m., going into bivouacs near the 26th kilo stone on the Salonika—Seres road, where the 23rd was spent in bivouacs. The march was resumed on the 24th and each day until the 28th when, having reached the 62nd kilo stone, the Gloucesters went into bivouacs and remained there until the 30th. On the latter date (they were now within 5 or 6 miles of the Struma) they reached a point about half a mile west of Mahmudli and pitched camp. The 81st Brigade was now in XVIth Corps Reserve.

On the 31st the G.O.C. Brigade reconnoitred a position astride the Salonika—Seres road near the 65th kilo stone and gave orders that the 2nd Gloucesters were to begin digging third-line defences on the 1st September. At 11.30 a.m. on that date the Battalion began work and for eight days dug hard. For the first time the guns are mentioned as being in action (on the 3rd), the Battalion Diary recording : ' Increased artillery activity during the morning.'

On the 10th September the 10th and 28th Divisions attacked the villages of Karajakoi, Jenikoj and Nevoljen, the 27th Division also attacking the enemy along the Divisional front. The 81st Brigade was, however, not engaged but remained in Corps Reserve, the 2nd Gloucesters continuing their work on the defences. On the 15th the 10th Division and 7th Mounted Brigade again attacked the villages of Dzamimah and Komarjan (10th Division), Kato Gudeli and Ano Gudeli (7th Mounted Brigade), but the 81st Brigade still remained in Corps Reserve. It was not until the end of the month that the Gloucesters took part in operations against the Bulgarians.

In order to assist the progress of the Allies towards Monastir by maintaining such a continuous offensive as would ensure no transference of Bulgarian troops from the Struma front to the west, instructions had been issued by General Milne (G.O.C. British Salonika Army) for operations on a more extensive scale.

[1] Colonel A. C. Vicary adds the following note : ' The Regiment moved to Hortiack with a view to proceeding to the Vardar front where the main attack was to take place. The attack did not progress as hoped and in order to divert the enemy reserves the 27th Division was at a moment's notice ordered to the Struma.'

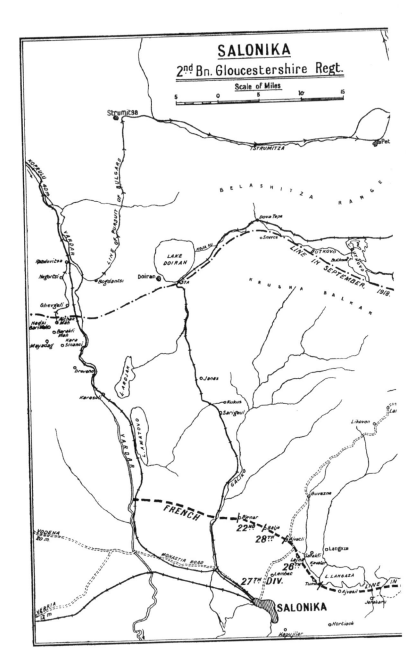

SALONIKA
2nd Bn. Gloucestershire Regt.

Scale of Miles

5   0   5   10   15

Strumitsa

Pet

"STRUMITZA"

BELASHITZA   RANGE

KOPRULU 400

VARDAR

LINE OF PURSUIT OF BULGARS

Dova Tepe

Snevce

KOJA SU

BUTKOVO

Budkovo

LAKE DOIRAN

Rabdovitsa

Negortsi

Bogdantsi

Doiran

STA

KRUSHA   BALKAN

LINE IN SEPTEMBER, 1918.

Ghevgeli

Hadzi Barimalo

Ach Mah

Barakli Mah

Kara

Mayadag

Sinanci

Dreveno

K. ARDJAN

Karasuli

Janes

Kukus

Sarigeul

Likovan

Lai

L. AMATOVO

VARDAR

Guvezne

GALIKO

FRENCH

Pirnar

Aselia

22nd

28th

Ajvasli

Sarakli

Langaza

VODENA
20 m.

MONASTIR ROAD

26th

Laina

Kavalar

27th DIV.

Lembet

Tumba

L. LANGAZA

LINE IN

Ajvasil

Jenekarli

VERRIA
12 m.

SALONIKA

Hortiack

Kapujilar

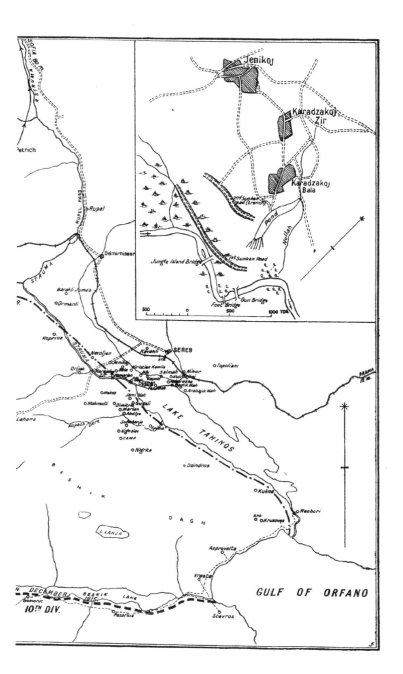

R.SOFIA OR VLOS

Petrich

RUPEL PASS

b.Rupel

STRUMA

Demirhissar

Barakli Juma'a

Ormanli

Kopriva

Neroljan

Orljak

Mahtos

Jami Mah

Mahmelli

Lahana

Kopach pert

Nigoslav

CAMP

Nigrika

BESNIK

L.LANJA

DAGH

Jeniko

Kavakli

SERES

Niriciae Kamila

Adli

Salmah

Minor

Topoliani

Ada

Topmah

Nazerua

Orula Mah.

English Mah

Arabajik Mah

Dimu

Boukali

Marian

Abdiye

Suhohanje

Nplas

Dzindros

Kukos

Necbori

Ano

Krusovas

PRAMA
15.m.

LAKE   TAHINOS

Aspravalta

Vrasta

GULF OF ORFANO

IN DECEMBER 1915.   BESNIK   LAKE

Somanic

10TH DIV.

Pazarkia

Scavros

Jenikoj

Karadzakoj Zir

Karadzakoj Bala

Pond

Sunken Road (trench)

Pond

Neilah

1st Sunken Road

Jungle Island Bridge

Foot Bridge

Gun Bridge

500   0   500   1000 YDS

These operations were to begin by seizing and holding certain villages on the left bank of the river with a view to enlarging the bridge-head opposite Orljak, where the troops taking part would be in a position to threaten a further movement either on Seres or Demirhisar. In these operations the 61st were to take part.

At 5 p.m. on the 29th the Gloucesters paraded and marched via Mahmudli to the Two Mounds, near Mekes, where they rested until 1 a.m. on the 30th. At the latter hour they paraded in battle kit and marched to the Gun Bridge, which spanned the Struma, arriving at 4.30 a.m. They then crossed to the left bank of the river and took up their assembly positions for the attack.

ACTION OF THE KARAJAKOI'S [1] : 30TH SEPTEMBER— 4TH OCTOBER 1916

The Karajakoi's consisted of two villages—Karajakoi Bala and Karajakoi Zir—the latter north of the former, the two being connected by a south to north road. North-west of Zir was Jenikoj. Between the Struma and Bala there was a large pond, oblong in shape, and following a south-westerly to north-easterly direction. A sunken road crossed the ground between the south-western extremity of the pond and Gun Bridge, while there was another sunken road running in a north-westerly direction west of the pond.

Both villages were to be attacked by the 81st Brigade. The 2nd Gloucesters, with their right on the pond (directing the attack), and the 2nd Camerons on their left, were to attack Bala : the 1st Argyll and Sutherland Highlanders were to be in support and the 1st Royal Scots (less one company) were to follow the Highlanders. The remaining company of Royal Scots with a section of machine-guns was to move east of the pond and demonstrate towards Bala. After taking Bala the 2nd Gloucesters and 2nd Camerons were to establish themselves east and north of the village, while the 1st Argyll and Sutherland Highlanders, supported by the 1st Royal Scots, attacked Zir.

Such, briefly, were operation orders for the attack.

So far as the Battalion Diary of the 2nd Gloucesters is concerned the narrative of the operations is all too brief and gives no details of the attack : it was as follows :

' Advance to the attack of Karajakois-Bala 05.30 hours with Camerons on left of line. The Battalion captured Bala 09.00 and consolidated. All ground held. The Battalion repulsed counter-attacks from 20.00 hours 30/9/16–08.00 hours 1/10/16. Total casualties other ranks 55.'

---

[1] The spelling adopted by the Battles Nomenclature Committee. The official accounts give it as Karadzakoj.

From the 81st Brigade Headquarters Diary, however, it is possible to supplement the above meagre report by further details :

At about 3.45 a.m. on the 30th the detached company of Royal Scots, with one section of the 81st Machine-Gun Company, crossed the river by Gun Bridge and then, turning east, deployed north of a road about three-quarters of a mile east of the Bridge. Their orders were to get into position south of the pond and bring an enfilade fire to bear on Bala. A section of the Argyll Mountain Battery accompanied this detached party and took up position midway between the nullah and the pond, about 2,000 yards south of Bala Church.

The 2nd Camerons and 2nd Gloucesters, on crossing Gun Bridge, moved north-west until the latter were 400 yards clear of the bridge : they then turned and faced north-east, i.e. the village of Bala, and deployed for the attack. The formation for the attack was A Company on the right, C on the left, B supporting A and D supporting C, each company on a two-platoon frontage. The Camerons were similarly deployed, each Battalion occupying a front of about 1,000 yards. Deployment was completed by 5.15 a.m. A composite battalion of the 29th Brigade (10th Division) was to patrol the right flank of the 81st Brigade by working up the nullah towards Bala, while another battalion of the same brigade was to cross Jungle Island Bridge and, working up towards Zir, patrol the left flank of the Brigade.

The 1st Argyll and Sutherland Highlanders and 1st Royal Scots, who were to attack Zir, crossed the Struma by the foot-bridge just west of Gun Bridge and deployed just clear of a clump of trees on the left bank, i.e. the Highlanders were to follow in support of the Gloucesters and Camerons and Royal Scots in rear of the Highlanders.

At 5.30 a.m. the Gloucesters and Camerons moved forward to the first sunken road and laid down. Fifteen minutes later the barrage fell on Bala and the Bulgar trenches in the neighbourhood of the village. At 6.30 a.m. the artillery lifted to the second sunken road and the advance of the infantry began. The Camerons, on the left, were subjected to enfilade fire from Trench 26, but this they rushed and captured. On the right, however, the Gloucesters came under heavy enfilade fire from their right and halted until the guns began to shell the hostile trenches whence the fire came. At 6.45 a.m. the line was again advancing, the artillery dealing with the enemy's trenches on the Gloucesters' right. An hour later the Camerons were advancing on Bala while the Gloucesters were already halted a hundred yards from, and

on the south-western edge of, the village.   Having reached a point
north-west of Bala the Camerons then began to press into the
village, and by 8.10 a.m. had captured the northern end of Trench
25, taking 25 prisoners.   The Gloucesters were, however, still
held up by fire from their immediate right and right flank : they
had, nevertheless, taken 20 prisoners.

By 8.30 a.m. the Camerons had cleared the northern end of Bala
and were working south towards the Gloucesters who were pushing through the southern portion of the village.

The whole of Bala had been captured by 9.10 a.m. with 87
prisoners, the Gloucesters being in touch on their right with the
battalion of the 29th Brigade.

Both attacking battalions then began to consolidate their positions.   Wiring parties from the Wessex R.E. and carrying parties
for R.E. material and S.A.A., who were ' standing by ' at Gun
Bridge, were sent up and the whole of the front of Bala from the
north-eastern corner to the pond was wired by 4 p.m.

By 10 a.m. the enemy's artillery had the whole area under shell-
fire.   Bala village and neighbourhood, the track from Gun Bridge
to Bala and all bridges over the Struma were shelled heavily at
intervals throughout the day.

The attack on Zir had been timed for 11.30 a.m. and at 11 a.m.
the Argyll and Sutherland Highlanders and Royal Scots were
forming up in Bala, the 2nd Royal Irish Fusiliers taking over the
duty of supporting the Gloucesters and Camerons.   At 11.30 a.m.
the Highlanders advanced, but were met by very heavy machine-
gun and rifle fire, particularly from a trench hidden from view by
standing crops.   Very gallantly the attack went forward, but the
first attempt failed.   At 3.30 p.m. the Camerons were ordered to
attack Zir, but it was impossible to get the Battalion out of their
positions in time and the Royal Scots, with the Camerons following
in support, were ordered to make the attack.

At 4.45 p.m. the Royal Scots, moving out from the Bala—Zir
sunken road in four waves, advanced to the attack.   The records
state that the 2nd Camerons, following in support close in rear,
were led by their Pipers who played throughout the attack—a
most inspiring sight.   Heavy but inaccurate fire met the advance
of the Royal Scots, but they pressed on, and as they neared
Trench 25 a Bulgar officer and 82 other ranks left the trench and
surrendered.

At 5.30 p.m., closely followed by the Camerons, the Royal
Scots entered Zir from the south-western side of the village and
consolidation began shortly afterwards.   An attempt by the
enemy to counter-attack from the south-western side of the village

was easily repulsed. A more serious attack against the eastern side of Zir was also beaten off, the guns rendering valuable assistance.

Thus both Bala and Zir had fallen into our hands.

At 6.15 the Royal Scots and Camerons began entrenching and wiring. The line at that period ran from the pond to east of Bala Church (2nd Gloucesters), thence to the fork roads half a mile north of Bala (1st Argyll and Sutherland Highlanders), thence to Trench 34 (2nd Cameron Highlanders), thence through Trenches 34–35 along the north-western side of Zir, Trench 33 and south-west to join up with a battalion of the 29th Brigade (1st Royal Scots).

The whole front was wired by 11 p.m. and all troops dug in. The number of prisoners taken during the day was two officers and 250 other ranks and three machine guns.[1]

The night of the 30th September/1st October was broken by strong attacks on the Gloucesters and very heavy rifle and artillery fire. But the enemy was everywhere driven back and work on the Bala defences continued. The wind and dust at this period were very bad and the conditions in the front line were anything but comfortable : indeed, it was not until the 5th that the Battalion Diary records wiring nearly completed and trenches habitable. On that date a party consisting of 2nd Lieutenant Swan and 6 other ranks, patrolling eastwards for 1,200 yards, found no enemy west of Hristian-Kamila.

On the 5th October also General Milne (Commander-in-Chief, Salonika Force) visited the Gloucesters in their trenches and congratulated them on their work both during the attack and after. The G.O.C. 27th Division (General Ravenshaw) visited the Battalion on the 6th and also congratulated all ranks on their conduct.

There now followed a good deal of work on the newly-captured positions and it was the 15th before the Gloucesters were relieved, after which they marched back to the right bank of the Struma and bivouacked close to Gun Bridge. They had, however, but two days' rest, for on the 18th the Battalion marched to Hristian-Kamila, taking over the village from the 1st Royal Scots. B Company acted as outpost company and went forward to Homondos.

Work on the Hristian-Kamila defences, such as wiring and the digging of new trenches, kept the Gloucesters busy for some days.

---

[1] The narrative in the 81st Brigade Headquarters Diary was written by Lieut.-Colonel A. C. Vicary, Gloucestershire Regiment (then Major), who at that period was Brigade Major.

There was little Royal Engineer material available, and as new dug-outs had to be constructed the village was practically demolished to provide the wherewithal for shelters for the troops.

THE AFFAIR OF BARAKLI JUMA'A : 31ST OCTOBER 1916

On the 31st October the 28th Division attacked Barakli Juma'a and, although the 2nd Gloucesters of the 27th Division were not among the assaulting troops, they nevertheless lent valuable aid in that, under instructions from 81st Brigade Headquarters, they demonstrated against the enemy.

On the night of the 30th the Battalion was relieved in trenches at Hristian-Kamila by the Camerons and withdrew to some old Bulgar trenches behind the village. Heavy rain fell throughout the night and all ranks were drenched.

At 8.30 a.m. on the 31st the Battalion advanced from the sunken road north-west of Hristian-Kamila in a north-easterly direction until the road running north-west from Homondos to the Jenikoj —Kavakli Track was reached. In this road the Battalion, under cover from the enemy, massed for the attack. A Company was on the right, C on the left, D behind A and B in rear of C.

Just after 10 a.m. the Gloucesters advanced against the railway south-west of Seres, the line being reached at 11.40 a.m. The Battalion had advanced over 2,000 yards from Homondos across difficult ground, which, sodden by rain, made the ' going ' heavy. Touch also had to be maintained with the 29th Brigade on the left and Camerons on the right (left and right flank guards respectively). Each wave as it advanced was shelled by the enemy on the left of the sunken road, but owing to the troops being extended and the sticky, sodden nature of the ground, the effect of high-explosive and shrapnel was very local. At 12.20 p.m. patrols were sent out to Kavakli Wood where some sniping followed, with one casualty to the Gloucesters. Corpl. Gardiner and Pte. Ashmead volunteered to carry the wounded man back, which they did under sniping and shrapnel fire.

From the time of leaving the sunken road till 5 p.m. the Battalion was continually under enfilade fire, which at times caused casualties.

At 6 p.m. the G.O.C. 81st Brigade ordered the Gloucesters to withdraw to bivouacs. The withdrawal was made in good order and the sunken road was reached at 7.30 p.m.

The casualties suffered by the Battalion in this affair were 4 other ranks killed and 31 wounded.

The 31st October found the Battalion resting in bivouacs on the left bank of the Struma, near Gun Bridge.

At the beginning of November certain changes took place in the organization of the brigades of the Division which gave rise to much heart-burning. The 2nd Gloucesters who, for two years, had formed part of the 81st Brigade and had been close friends with other battalions of the Brigade, were transferred to the 82nd Brigade. They were informed of the re-organization on the 2nd November, on which date all company commanders rode over to Dimitric to reconnoitre the new trenches to be taken over in the 82nd Brigade area. On this date also the Brigadier of the 81st Brigade addressed the Battalion, expressing his keen regret at losing the Gloucesters. The following day the latter marched into the area of the new Brigade, the pipes of the 1st Argyll and Sutherland Highlanders playing the Battalion away.[1] The Gloucesters then relieved the 1st Royal Irish Regiment in trenches between Komarjan Bridge and Zouave Ford.

There is little to report of the early part of November until on the 13th the Gloucesters were relieved and marched to Osman-Kamila, which they reached at 3 p.m. The weather was abominable—rain was falling heavily and marching conditions were bad when at 8 p.m. the Battalion continued the march to Kispeki, arriving at midnight. Battalion Headquarters with D Company then went into Big Barn while C Company took up a defensive position at Kispeki and dug in round the village, putting out an outpost at Ada : B Company marched to Salmah.[2] A Company, marching on past Salmah, reached a point where the track was cut by the Meander Stream and dug in. For four days the Battalion continued work on the Ada—Kispeki—Salmah—Ford line.

On the 16th November, in continuation of the policy of harassing the enemy, operation orders were issued by 82nd Brigade Headquarters for an attack on Tumbitza, in which the 2nd Gloucesters were to take part by making a demonstration against Tumbitza Farm.

The Battalion paraded at Ford at 2 a.m. on the 19th and were in position in Pheasant Wood by 6.30 a.m., B Company on the right, D on the left, C in reserve and half a company of A protecting the left flank, the other half remaining with Battalion Headquarters. Tumbitza Farm was being attacked by the 2nd D.C.L.I.

At about 8 a.m. the enemy fired several searching shells and

[1] The 2nd Gloucesters were now brigaded with the 2nd D.C.L.I., 10th Hants and the 10th Camerons. The latter were formed out of Lovat's Scouts in 1916 and are often referred to as such in diaries dealing with Salonika.
[2] Shown as Sal Mahale on some maps.

continued spasmodic and desultory artillery fire throughout the
day. Patrols from the Gloucesters approached to within 250 yards
of the Farm but were forced to retire by machine-gun fire. At
11 a.m. the Divisional Artillery opened on Tumbitza Farm and
the Bulgar guns immediately ceased firing. At 12 noon our guns
ceased fire, the enemy's opening fire again. The Gloucesters
withdrew to their original defences in the Salmah—Kispeki—Ada
line, though they occupied the defences from Salmah to Ford.[1]

The Battalion lost 1 other rank killed and 6 wounded in this
affair.

The 2nd D.C.L.I. failed to capture the Farm, the attack
evidently being expected by the enemy.

On the 22nd the 2nd Gloucesters marched from Kispeki to
billets in Jenimah, though on the 25th the Battalion took over a
certain proportion of the defences. On the 30th the strength of
the Battalion was 20 officers and 690 other ranks.

At the beginning of December another attack on Tumbitza
Farm was ordered, and on this occasion the 2nd Gloucesters were
to be in the actual attack, having received orders to support the
10th Camerons, who were to assault the Farm. The attack was
to take place on the 6th. Two days previously the Gloucesters
had marched from Jenimah to Kakaraska, where A Company
occupied trenches from that village towards Begilk Mah and half
of B Company between Salmah and Kakaraska ; the remainder of
the Battalion billeted in Kakaraska. The same night the 10th
Camerons occupied Pheasant Wood.

At 5.30 p.m. on the 5th the Gloucesters paraded at the wooden
bridge over the Meander Stream, north-east of Kakaraska, and
marched off along the track which ran in a north-easterly direction
to Pheasant Wood, where they rested from 10 p.m. till 4 a.m. on
the 6th. At the latter hour they again paraded for the purpose
of marching to Rabbit Wood.

Rabbit Wood was about 500 yards west of Tumbitza Lake,
in the centre of which was a small island. About 200 yards south
of the Lake were the Farm buildings, while south of the latter
again, and also about 200 yards distant, was a bridge which
spanned a stream running in a north-westerly direction and along
the eastern edges of Rabbit Wood. Some 500 yards east of the
Farm was a large mound. Entrenchments, protected by barbed-
wire entanglements, protected the Farm from attack from the
south and west, while the Mound was included in a line of

---

[1] ' Ford ' appears to have been Trent Ford, east of Salmah : there
were two other fords—Corner Ford and Scot Ford—north of Trent
Ford.

trenches. West and north-west of the Lake the ground was of
a marshy character, the eastern side being covered by another line
of trenches, also wired.

Having paraded at 4 a.m. on the 6th (as already stated) the
2nd Gloucesters were ready to march to Rabbit Wood, but at that
hour violent rifle fire broke out in the wood and the Battalion
waited until the fire had died down. It was then pitch dark.
The story of the attack which followed is related in the Battalion
Diary in the following words :

'At 04.30 (4.30 a.m.) the rifle fire had ceased and the Battalion marched
off. It arrived at Rabbit Wood and dug in, in a nullah running south
of the Wood. At 06.45 (6.45 a.m.) the 10th Camerons, followed by the
2nd Gloucesters in support, attempted to cross the Tumbitza Stream
and assault the trenches on the left bank. The attacking troops were
beaten back by rifle and machine-gun fire. Any movement in Rabbit
Wood immediately drew shell fire and casualties were becoming fairly
heavy. The Gloucester Regiment in this attack was unable even to
leave the Wood. Matters being thus, the 10th Camerons retired to the
Wood and again manned the trenches. Machine-gun fire was heavy
and accurate all day. With the intention of knocking out these, the
O.C., left attack, asked for an intense bombardment by every gun available. At 16.00 (4 p.m.) this bombardment started and seemingly silenced
the machine-guns, but as soon as movement occurred in the Wood the
machine-guns opened again, apparently untouched. Any movement in
the Wood drew intense fire both from artillery and machine-guns. At
18.45 (6.45 p.m.), when dark, the 10th Camerons were relieved in Rabbit
Wood by the 2nd D.C.L.I. The 2nd Gloucestershire Regiment then
held the Wood, the D.C.L.I. being in immediate support. O.C., left
attack, resolved on a night attack but, fearing that this might lead to
confusion over unknown ground, it was postponed until 06.45 (6.45
a.m.) when, immediately following up barrage given by our artillery,
the 2nd Gloucestershire Regiment, followed by the D.C.L.I., would
attack the Tumbitza position. From 18.00 (6 p.m.) till 24.00 hours
(midnight) machine-gun fire was heavy and almost continuous.

'After bombardment of the trenches around Tumbitza Farm at 06.40
(6.40 a.m.) on the 7th October, the 2nd Gloucestershire Regiment,
followed in support by the 2nd D.C.L.I., advanced. C Company and
half of D Company of the 2nd Gloucestershire Regiment succeeded in
crossing the stream, but rifle, machine-gun and artillery fire was as
intense as on the previous day, and none of the remainder of the attacking troops were able to cross. The D.C.L.I. were unable to move out
from the Wood. The two companies of the Gloucestershire Regiment
which had succeeded in crossing the stream found cover under a high
bank. At 08.00 hours (8 a.m.), still being unable to advance, Lieut.-
Colonel Kirk, commanding D.C.L.I., ordered the two companies which
had succeeded in crossing the stream to fall back again into the Wood.
The troops in the Wood remained there, being unable to do anything
as the slightest movement immediately drew artillery fire from the direction of Nihur and Topoliani. At 18.30 (6.30 p.m.) the 2nd Gloucestershire Regiment withdrew to Pheasant Wood, and thence to Kakaraska, in
which village it billeted.'

The 2nd Gloucesters lost in this affair 1 officer (Captain D. K. Garnier) and 33 other ranks killed, many of the latter being reported missing, 4 officers and 76 other ranks wounded.

From the 8th to the 10th December inclusive the Battalion rested in Kakaraska, but on the 11th (less two platoons of B Company left as observation posts at Salmah) withdrew from the outpost line and marched to Jenimah.

For the remainder of the year the Gloucesters were located in Jenimah, chiefly at work on the defences. On the last day of the year 1 officer and 35 other ranks cleared Beglik Mah of the Bulgars after wounding 3 of them.

CHAPTER XXV

TRENCH WARFARE FROM THE 5TH OF APRIL TO THE 10TH OF JULY, 1917

IN their pleasant billets in Chuignes the 1st Gloucesters remained until the 7th April, and although the weather was mainly bad—heavy rains and snow falling—much good training was done, fatigues being remarkable by their absence. The form of trench attack then in vogue was continually practised and battalion and brigade operations carried out. In sport also the 28th upheld their fine reputation, beating the South Wales Borderers soundly at Rugby and winning an officers' Rugby match against the Munsters : two matches in the Brigades Association Cup were also won.

On the 7th April, however, the Gloucesters marched via Dompiere—Assevillers—Barleux and La Chapellette to Péronne and were billeted in ruined houses. The fine old picturesque town had been badly handled by the enemy, who had destroyed a great many houses and had cut down or sawn half through most of the trees.

In Péronne the 28th were employed daily in repairing the railway which had been destroyed by the Germans. On the 16th they moved to camp at Beilevue Farm (on the Péronne—Villers Carbonnell road), where they remained until the 7th May, still engaged in repairing the railway. A few tactical exercises for the officers was the only training done, excepting a daily parade for the whole Battalion at 7 a.m. lasting only ten minutes, during which the handling of arms was practised.

May had opened with glorious summerlike weather and the country round Péronne, which consisted of rolling downland over which were scattered small coverts and villages, took on a cloak of green very pleasant to the eye : the fields had evidently been cultivated up to the beginning of the Somme Battles of 1916, for the unreaped crops of the harvest for that year were still standing.

The gun positions of the German ' heavies ', on the high ground east of Le Mesnil—Brentel, about 4 miles south-east of Péronne, were of considerable interest. The observation-posts for these guns were platforms, reached by long ladders, in the tall trees of the Bois des Cerisiers : beneath were magnificent dug-outs for the observers. These observation-posts gave a wonderful view of the British lines for miles.

In the Péronne neighbourhood the Gloucesters again played ' rugger ' matches with unvarying success. Their drums also, which at this period had attained a very high standard of efficiency, performed on two or three nights a week, to the delight of the troops of other divisions in the neighbourhood.

About this time also Captain H. E. de R. Wetherall left the Battalion to command the 2/4th Oxford and Bucks Light Infantry. He had landed in France in August, 1914, with the 28th as a platoon commander in C Company and did extraordinarily good work in the first Battles of Ypres until badly wounded in the knee. On returning to duty he served continuously with the Battalion until wounded again on the Somme, and from his recovery until May, 1917. He was an officer of the finest type, full of knowledge and ability in applying it, cool and fearless under all conditions and thoughtful always of his men.

On the 7th May the Gloucesters moved to Eclusier, a delightful village on the river about 7 miles west of Péronne. The village lay on either side of the main stream of the Somme, which here flowed through a wide ravine, and was a bower of spring greenery. The men were accommodated in large French huts and the officers in small shelters and tents. In this pleasant spot and in glorious weather, the 28th remained until the 19th. But it was a strenuous period : Battalion drill was carried out before breakfast and Battalion training from 9 a.m. to 2 p.m., on good ground situated on the southern side of the river. When drill was over the afternoons and evenings were equally strenuous, for the Brigadier believed in games and gave cups for Rugby and Association football, also for swimming and boxing. At the latter the Gloucesters did little good, but in the final for the Rugby Cup they beat the 2nd Welch by 2 tries to nil, and they got into the final for the Association Cup, winning that also (later) at Warfusée. They also carried off every open event in the swimming sports, 50, 100 and 500 yards, relay race, diving and water polo : they were only beaten in the veterans' race.

Thus, when on the 19th the Gloucesters marched to Warfusée —Abancourt, just east of Villers—Bretonneux, all ranks were very fit, and although the day was exceedingly hot and the marching trying, the Battalion got along very well.

Warfusée was a pleasant spot and the billets again good. A week of excellent training was carried out there, the Battalion marching out daily to ground in the neighbourhood of Morcourt and Cérisy on the Somme. But it was the close of those quiet and happy weeks out of the front line which had begun in the third week of March, for the 1st Division had been ordered to move to the Ypres Salient.

The Gloucesters paraded at 11.35 p.m. on the 26th May and marched first to Guillaucourt, where tea was taken : they then entrained and began their journey northwards at 2.30 a.m. on the 27th. They reached Caestre and detrained at 4.30 p.m., resting for two and a half hours, during which the men had their first meal since midnight, the fault of a succession of inefficient Railway Transport Officers. The Battalion then had a march of 4½ miles to a camp about 1½ miles north of the Flêtre—Meteren road and half-way between these two places. The 1st Division was now in the Second Army and formed part of the XIVth Corps, which Corps was in reserve for the Messines Battle.

Another short period of training kept the Gloucesters busy until the 31st, when sudden orders were received to move forward to Reninghelst. The 28th marched at 7.45 p.m. and at about 12.30 a.m. on the 1st June arrived at a field, about 2 miles due east of the village, where they bivouacked.

Preparations for the Battle of Messines, 1917, were in progress and the Gloucesters were attached to the 41st Division to carry stores, principally trench mortars and bombs, up to the front line about St. Eloi. Day and night (principally the latter) the whole Battalion worked and, though hostile shell-fire was considerable, there were no casualties. On the day of the Battle, the 7th June, the Battalion marched back to the camp between Flêtre and Meteren, remaining there until the 9th, when at short notice a move was made to a camp pitched in a field close to, and at the north-eastern corner of, Dickebusch Lake. Roadmaking and the laying of water-pipes on the ground captured during the Messines Battle now kept the Gloucesters busy until the 15th June. The weather was excellent and the work, though arduous, was interesting. Again there was considerable shell-fire but only one casualty—2nd Lieutenant W. L. Underhay wounded on the 11th—was suffered.

At 7 a.m. on the 15th the Gloucesters left Dickebusch to rejoin the 3rd Brigade. A halt was made at Berthen for dinners, but when the march was continued the weather was tropical. Already the men, carrying heavy packs and equipment, had marched a good distance and many were affected by the heat. A halt was therefore made just west of Flêtre, the cookers which had gone on ahead were recalled and the Battalion had tea. In the cool of the evening the march was resumed and that night the Battalion billeted in Hondeghem, about 4½ miles south-east of Cassel : the march was continued the next day at 5 p.m., and after a short and pleasant march the 28th reached Staple, where companies were billeted over a wide area in farms with friendly inhabitants. During the next four days a certain amount of training was done though the closely cultivated ground curtailed movement.

At this period Sir Douglas Haig had agreed to relieve French troops which were holding the sector extending from the sea, where the canalized Yser River entered it, to the junction of the Belgian and French lines south of Nieuport. The 1st Division was one of the British divisions detailed to relieve the French and on the 21st June the 3rd Brigade began its march to the coast.

The heat was still almost tropical and the march began early in the morning, the Gloucesters having to pass the Brigade starting-point at 4.30 a.m. The first stage was to Wormhoudt, which was reached at 9 a.m. : the Brigade then billeted for the day. At 3.15 a.m. the following morning the Brigade again took the road and the Gloucesters reached billets at Malo-les-Bains at 9.40 a.m., having marched the last two hours in heavy rain.

Malo-les-Bains was a seaside resort adjoining Dunkirk. The Gloucesters were billeted in villas on the sea front—a novel experience for a hard-bitten Battalion which had been through all the hardest fighting in France and Flanders since 1914. But their joy was short, for on the 25th the 28th marched to Leffring Houcke Bridge on the Dunkirk—Furnes Canal where again a strange experience awaited them, for they embarked on five barges and travelled in this novel manner to Furnes and, after disembarking there, moved by route march to St. Iddesbalde, another seaside resort on the sand-dunes about 10 miles east of Dunkirk. The majority of the men were accommodated in tents, the remainder in villas on the sea front : the officers billeted in two hotels, one of which was still open, several English being among the visitors, despite the fact that the place was periodically shelled. On the 1st July the Brigade race meeting was held on the sands, at which the Prince of Wales was present.

The Battalion was still commanded by Lieut.-Colonel A. W. Pagan, with Captain K. A. R. Smith as second-in-command and Lieutenant Green as Adjutant. Companies were commanded as follows : A—Captain D. Baxter, B—Captain P. Mallet, C—Captain C. L. Priestley, D—Captain C. E. W. Lavender.

After a ' Brigade Scheme ' which took place on the 3rd the

14

Gloucesters marched to a camp at Coxyde Bains, another water-ing-place immediately eastwards of St. Iddesbalde. On the 4th the march was continued to a hutted camp named Juriac, among the sand-dunes about 2 miles east of Coxyde and north of the Coxyde—Oost Dunquerque road. One incident, which took place at Coxyde, is worthy of mention. The Gloucesters played a Rugby match on the sands against an Australian heavy artillery brigade who claimed to have been unbeaten since their formation. Many of the Australians played stripped to the waist, so low collaring was essential. The Gloucesters beat them by 11 points to 3 and while at Juriac overwhelmed the 10th Battalion of their own Regiment at the same game.

The 1st Division had by now taken over the sector of the line adjoining the sea. The trenches held were on the east side of the Yser Canal and were reached by two or three bridges across the Canal. Dug in the sand, the defences were very susceptible to shell-fire.

Meanwhile the three Territorial Battalions down on the Somme had been having anything but a restful period. They were last mentioned on the 5th April, that being the date upon which the German Retreat to the Hindenburg Line was supposed to have ended. In some parts of the line it may have been so, but not in those sectors where the 1/4th, 1/5th and 1/6th were located, for repeated attacks took place as the narrative shows.

The 1/5th Gloucesters, it will be remembered, having captured Lempire on the 5th April, marched back to Villers Fauçon : the 1/4th were at Cartigny and the 1/6th at Marquaix.

On the 13th April the 1/4th Gloucesters again attacked the enemy. The Battalion had relieved the 1/6th in the line (Lempire sector) on the 11th. Orders from 144th Brigade Headquarters stated that on the night of the 12th/13th the 7th Worcesters, on the right, and 1/4th Gloucesters, on the left, would advance the Brigade outpost line. The Worcesters were to attack from a line south of Queuchettes Wood and the Gloucesters from a line north of the Wood. B and C Companies of the latter were detailed for the attack. There is, however, no narrative of the attack, and only the following brief account is contained in the Diary of the Gloucesters :

' B and C Companies attacked enemy line and had taken all objectives by 4 a.m. (13th). B Company was immediately counter-attacked but drove the enemy back. During the day our line was heavily shelled. Our casualties were fairly light. At night Battalion was relieved by the 1/5th Gloucesters and moved to billets at Hamel.'

The 1/5th Gloucesters were next involved with the enemy. The Battalion, having relieved the 1/4th (as stated), had come out of the line again on the 15th. The next night, however, they moved to the neighbourhood of Esclainvillers Wood in order to support an attack by the 1/4th Berkshires on Gillemont Farm, and by the 1/1st Bucks on Tombois Farm and The Knoll. The weather on the night of the 16th/17th was abominable : heavy rain, alternating with snow, drenched the Gloucesters as they waited in support all night in an open field. The attack on Gillemont did not progress : at Tombois Farm the Bucks got in on the left, but the right was hung up by wire. The O.C. 1/1st Bucks then ordered B Company (that Company having moved direct to Lempire from camp) to move down the road and attack the right of the Farm. The movement was well carried out and Captain Holling then led his Company through the wire and up a sunken road where several Germans were killed, No. 6 Platoon, under 2nd Lieutenant Grubb, doing particularly good work. At 1 a.m. A Company was ordered up to Lempire and later three platoons of the Company were moved to Tombois Farm. At 5 a.m. Battalion Headquarters, with C and D Companies, returned to camp, soaked through.

At about 6 a.m. (17th) Major Baker, 1/1st Bucks, ordered a fighting patrol to be sent out by B Company, 1/5th Gloucesters, to Petit Priel Farm for the purpose of finding out if that position was held by us or by the enemy. The patrol, consisting of Corporal Butt and eight men, were unable to get near the Farm as it was being heavily shelled by our guns. When the shelling stopped they pushed forward and occupied the Farm all day until relieved by a patrol from the 143rd Brigade, on the left of the 144th Brigade. Corporal Butt received the Military Medal for his fine work on this occasion, while Sergt. Coopey was also awarded the same honour for good leadership and gallantry in the attack on Tombois Farm.

The 1/5th relieved the Bucks in the newly-captured positions on the 18th, but were themselves relieved by the 1/6th Gloucesters on the 19th.

The 1/6th, on the morning of the 18th, had suffered a severe loss. Battalion Headquarters were in a cellar at Villers Fauçon. Suddenly, at about 3.55 a.m., there was a tremendous roar—the cellar had been mined by the enemy with a delay action fuze. The C.O. (Lieut.-Colonel T. W. Nott), Major R. F. Gerrard, Captain and Adjutant L. C. Nott, Captain E. Harrison, R.A.M.C. (the Battalion Medical Officer), Captain M. F. Burdess and Lieutenant L. King were all killed. Captain J. N. Crosskey,

1/5th Warwicks, attached, took over temporary command of the 1/6th.

On the 23rd the 1/6th Gloucesters were ordered to attack the enemy. The 8th Worcesters, on the right, and the 1/6th Gloucesters, on the left, were to attack the line Gillemont Spur—The Knoll in conjunction with the brigades on either flank. The 1/6th were allotted The Knoll as their objective.

A and B Companies were detailed to attack this position, with C in support and D in reserve to hold the original outpost line.

The two attacking Companies formed up, A on the right, B on the left, the right of A Company being just north-east of Tombois Farm.

At zero hour—3.45 a.m. 24th April—the two Companies advanced against The Knoll with two platoons each in support. The attack had advanced some 200 yards when the enemy opened fire with rifles and put down a machine-gun barrage. The first line reached the objective but the second line lost its objective and got broken up, thereby failing to support the first line. The troops actually on the objective found themselves outnumbered and after considerable hand-to-hand fighting both companies fell back to their original assembly positions where they re-formed. The O.C. C Company was then ordered to throw out two fighting patrols from the right of Tombois Farm. But as soon as they showed themselves on the sky-line they were subjected to very heavy rifle-fire and retired again to their original position. The attacking companies were then ordered to withdraw to Lempire, D Company remaining in the original outpost line with C in support.

The 1/6th lost in this attack 2nd Lieutenant J. F. Brown and A. Pears and 2 other ranks killed : Lieutenant R. H. Ball, 2nd Lieutenants J. G. Shuttleton, W. H. S. Rose, A. R. Coombs, A. H. Watts and 72 other ranks wounded, 12 other ranks missing and 2 other ranks died of wounds.

At 6.30 p.m. that night orders were issued for a continuation of the operations begun at 3.45 a.m. Three Battalions were to be employed, 4th Berkshires on the right, 7th Worcesters in the centre and 1/4th Gloucesters on the left : the latter were to attack The Knoll from the south and south-west, while the 126th Brigade was to attack it from the west and north-west.

Zero for the attack was 11 p.m.

At dusk the 1/4th moved up to their assembly positions, C Company on the right, A' in the centre, D on the left : B Company was in support.

Just before zero hour the 126th Brigade, on the left of the

144th Brigade, was attacked by the enemy and was unable to co-operate [1] in the attack on The Knoll. Major L. G. Parkinson, commanding 1/4th Gloucesters, was killed in the railway cutting at St. Emilie, while receiving his orders for the attack over the telephone. The consequence was that at zero, when the 1/4th Gloucesters advanced to the attack, C Company reached its objective, but A and D Companies had pushed too far forward in their efforts to gain touch with the 126th Brigade.

Gillemont Farm had been captured by the 7th Worcesters.

The 25th was uneventful so far as the 1/4th Gloucesters were concerned until just before dusk when A and D Companies were forced to retire in order to avoid being surrounded. C Company, however, extended its line farther up the south-eastern slope of The Knoll.

The 1/5th Gloucesters relieved the 1/4th during the night, the latter moving back to Villers Fauçon.

On the 27th, Major H. St. G. Schomberg, East Surrey Regiment, joined the 1/6th Battalion and assumed command.

No further attacks on or by the enemy took place during the remainder of April and on the last day of the month the 1/4th Battalion was in Lempire and St. Emilie, the 1/6th holding the outpost line in front, and to the right of, Tombois Farm and the 1/5th at Tincourt.

Comparatively, May was an uneventful month until the second week, when the 48th Division, moving first back to Péronne, took over about the middle of May a new sector north of the Somme. On the 14th the 1/4th were at Lebucquière, the 1/6th at Fremicourt and the 1/5th at Beaumetz. The front-line trenches were in the neighbourhood of Bemicourt and Boursies and Hermies, but with the exception of patrol encounters and two or three raids on hostile positions the month passed quietly. The 1/5th Battalion had 1 officer—2nd Lieutenant Bamberger —wounded on the 31st.

June was characterized by considerable patrol activity and one or two small raids were attempted, but generally no incident of outstanding importance took place worthy of special mention. The 1/6th had 1 officer—2nd Lieutenant Dodson—killed on the 27th.

Early in July all three Battalions moved back to training areas, the 1/4th on the 3rd to Blairville, the 1/6th on the 4th to Hendecourt and the 1/5th on the 4th to Bellacourt.

---

[1] The Battalion detailed to co-operate in the attack (East Lancashires) was commanded by Lieut.-Colonel E. W. Lennard, an officer of the 1/6th Gloucester Regiment.

CHAPTER XXVI

THE GERMAN ATTACK ON NIEUPORT,
10TH–11TH JULY

IT had been agreed between the Allies that French troops
should take part in the Flanders Offensive of 1917 and extend
the left flank of the British beyond Boesinghe. Accordingly
the relief of French troops on the Belgian coast, from St. George's
to the sea, took place about the middle of June. But the appearance of British troops on the coast appears to have alarmed the
enemy, not without good cause perhaps, and he later launched
a small counter-offensive against the 1st and 32nd Divisions
which had relieved the French.

The positions taken over from our Allies included a narrow
strip of boulder and dune some 2 miles long and from 600 to 1,200
yards deep, lying on the right bank of the Yser Canal between
the Passchendaele Canal, south of Lombartzyde, and the coast.
Half-way between the latter Canal and the sea the positions were
divided into two parts by a dyke known as the Geleide Creek,
which flows into the Yser south-west of Lombartzyde.

The 1st Division held the sector adjoining the sea. The
trenches were on the eastern side of the Yser and were reached
by two or three bridges across the Canal : they were very
susceptible to shell-fire.

The 1st Gloucesters were still in Juriac Camp, when early
on the morning of the 10th July the enemy began an intense
bombardment of the positions held by the 1st and 32nd Divisions.
All back areas were also subjected to heavy fire and as the day
wore on the shell-fire became intense. The defences, consisting
chiefly of breastworks built in sand, were soon flattened, and all
the bridges across the Yser below the Geleide Creek, as well as
across the Creek itself, were destroyed.

At 6.30 p.m. the German infantry attacked and the isolated
garrisons north of the Creek, consisting of the 1st Northants
and 2nd K.R.R.C. of the 2nd Brigade, 1st Division, after an
obstinate and most gallant resistance, were overwhelmed, only
some 70 men and 4 officers from both Battalions succeeding in
swimming across the Yser to their own lines.

At 9.15 p.m. the Gloucesters were attached to the 2nd Brigade and A and D Companies were sent, under the command of Captain Lavender, to Nieuport Bains, a watering-place at the mouth of the Yser. The Welch and South Wales Borderers were already holding trenches on the coast between Nieuport Bains and Coxyde Bains, while the Royal Munster Fusiliers were holding the line of the Canal south of the former place.

The following day D Company returned to Juriac Camp, A Company remaining in cellars at Nieuport Bains, but returned to camp on the 13th and by the 14th the affair had simmered down. During its course, however, the Gloucesters had lost 4 officers wounded, one of whom—2nd Lieutenant C. C. T. Clayton —died of his wounds. The other officers wounded were Captain E. D. Chamier (who belonged to the 3rd Lincolnshire but had served with the 1st Gloucesters since January, 1915, and had done most valuable work), Captain C. E. W. Lavender and 2nd Lieutenant F. T. Howell. One man was killed.

The 28th continued at Juriac Camp attached to the 2nd Brigade. Only Battalion Headquarters with A and D Companies were, however, present, for B and C Companies (under Captain K. A. R. Smith) had been despatched to an ' unknown destination'.

On the 17th July the 2nd Brigade was relieved by a brigade of the 66th Division and marched (the Gloucesters with it) via Coxyde, La Panne and Adinkerke to Leffring Houck, south of the Furnes—Dunkirk road and about 4 miles from Dunkirk.

Owing to the fact that no billets had been provided for them the Gloucesters did not get under cover till late that night. The following day the march was resumed and the Battalion, having reached Petit Synthe, about 2½ miles west of Dunkirk, came again under the orders of their own Brigadier.

CHAPTER XXVII

THE 'HUSH CAMP' ADVENTURE

THE story of the ' Hush Camp ' on the Belgian Coast, in which the 1st Gloucesters spent about three months, is one of the sidelights on the war in France and Flanders which cannot be omitted from the History of the Regiment.

The high ground which stretched from Messines and Wytschaete and ended in the Passchendaele Ridge, was not the only objective of the fighting in Flanders which began with the Battle of Messines, 1917. The German submarine campaign had become such a menace to communication between England and France that the capture of the Belgian coast and the enemy's submarine base thereon was also one of the intentions of the Allies. The British Admiralty considered that the submarine danger would never be overcome until enough ground had been gained on the coast to enable our heavy guns and howitzers to bring Zeebrugge under more or less continuous fire. A landing on the coast was therefore planned and the 1st Division was selected to carry it out. The landing was contingent upon the Fifth Army reaching Staden after the Battles of Ypres had opened on the 31st July. The place chosen for training was among the sand-dunes near the hamlet of Le Clipon, about 7 miles west of Dunkirk. Here a camp was to be built.

The preparation of this camp was begun early in July. On the 3rd of that month the Diary of the 1st Gloucesters contained the following cryptic statements : ' B Company sent on detachment to unknown destination and working under C.R.E., 1st Division.' Two days later C Company also was sent on detachment to the same place, which finally turned out to be Le Clipon.

On the 19th, Battalion Headquarters, with A and D Companies, set out from Petit Synthe on the march to Le Clipon where they were rejoined by C and B Companies. The Gloucesters were now in the celebrated ' Hush Camp'.

The plan of attack was as follows : the 1st Division was to land at dawn behind the German line while the XVth Corps made a simultaneous attack from Nieuport and Nieuport Bains in a north-easterly direction.

216

The enemy's heavy batteries defending the coast were at Raversyde, 2 miles west of Ostend : his lighter guns, employed in the defence of the line, were mainly about Westende, 2 miles east of the Yser.

It was essential that the landing should be sufficiently near to the Raversyde batteries so as to neutralize the sea batteries, and similarly the troops should be in a position to prevent the guns of the defence from opposing the advance of the XVth Corps. One brigade of the 1st Division was to be landed at Westende Bains, one at Middlekerke Bains and one between those places. On the right, the projected landing at Westende Bains would be level with and in rear of the defensive gun positions. The left landing at Middlekerke would be a little more than a mile from the nearest Raversyde battery. Immediately the landings had been effected the troops were to advance inland, those on the right about half a mile beyond the Nieuport—Bruges Canal, and those on the left but little beyond their landing-place. They were then to consolidate and push out strong patrols, while a flying column from the brigade, landed at Middlekerke, was to seize and destroy the Raversyde batteries. Thus, if the landings were successful, the destruction of the Raversyde batteries would prevent the enemy firing on ships approaching the coast, while the guns opposing the advance of the XVth Corps would be neutralized. If the whole operation succeeded our super-heavy artillery could be sited so as to subject the submarine base at Zeebrugge to continuous fire.

As the sea near the coast was shallow the troops were to be conveyed inshore in monitors which, being of light draught, were able to approach close in and use heavy calibre guns, with which they were armed.

Each brigade was to be transported by a pair of monitors, steaming abreast and having lashed between them a pontoon 200 yards long and 10 yards wide—surely strange craft. The guns, stores, hand-carts for stores and ammunition, three tanks and the two leading battalions of each brigade were to be on the pontoons and the remainder of the troops on the monitors.

The embarkation was to be carried out at Dunkirk, the monitors having arrived the previous day for the purpose of getting their pontoons in position and stores aboard the pontoons. The troops were to embark at dusk and the flotilla sail so as to land at dawn : it was to be preceded by small craft which were to produce a dense smoke cloud all along the coast as far as the Dutch frontier. Under the smoke cloud the monitors were to push their pontoons ashore and then open an intense bombardment with their 12-inch and 6-inch guns. The two leading battalions were to rush ashore, preceded by tanks, and form a bridge-head to protect the landing of the stores by the other two battalions. As soon as all were ashore the advance was to continue to the final objective.

The Gloucesters were to be one of the leading battalions of their brigade, but were never informed which of the three landing places was to be theirs.

For three months every phase of the operation was most carefully practised and everyone was keen on it, for its novelty appealed to all ranks : it was at least a change from ' going over the top ! '

The camp at Le Clipon was pleasantly situated among the sandhills, quite close to wonderful stretches of sandy beach. It was surrounded by a fence and only those who were actually to take part in the landing were allowed inside the fence. Rations and stores were brought up to the camp by the regimental transport of battalions which were kept outside the camp, no horses were to accompany the landing force, and the transport men conveying the goods were not allowed to communicate with anyone inside the camp. Excepting for the fact that leave was permitted to England, the utmost secrecy was observed. ' No one objects to getting leave,' said Colonel Pagan, ' but although every man going on leave was personally warned by his commanding officer never to mention where he was or why he was there, yet human nature being what it is, how could the average soldier refrain from telling his mother all about it ? '

The Gloucesters worked very hard in the ' Hush Camp ' and they also played very hard, for it was necessary to get everyone fit, and games were organized for that purpose.

Battalion drill was carried out nearly every day on the sands from 7 a.m. to 8 a.m.   Then, after breakfast, until 1 p.m. training in the various phases of the landing was performed. Whenever the weather was favourable the morning's work was terminated by the whole Battalion going into the sea together, which gave everyone an appetite for their midday meal. These bathes were very enjoyable, excepting on two occasions when jelly-fish took a hand in the entertainment !

The training for the landing was interesting. A certain number of battalion and brigade operations were carried out on ground similar to that over which the brigade would have to advance after the landing had been completed. The main portion of the training was, however, confined to perfecting the method of embarkation, disembarkation and getting a footing ashore. Plans of the monitors and pontoons were marked out on the sand and were used for the above purpose. An exact model of the sea wall was erected in the camp and everyone had, daily, to scale it wearing the equipment which he would wear for the actual operation. It was soon discovered that boots with new nails in the soles were the ideal footwear for this amusement and arrangements were made for every man's boots to be freshly nailed immediately before embarking for the landing operation.

Brigadiers and commanding officers were taken in destroyers to the monitors which were to carry out the landing. These monitors were anchored off the mouth of the Medway, and during the visit the pontoons were actually lashed in position and the monitors steamed for some distance pushing the pontoons before them.

The crews of the monitors were treated more in accordance with the needs of the situation than were the troops concerned. The Naval authorities were taking no chances of leakage of the projected operations, and in consequence the crews were never allowed to leave their ships and the only communication between them and the rest of the world was the destroyer which daily brought them their rations. Later, the naval men were conveyed in batches to spend a few days in the ' Hush Camp ' as guests of the various regiments. Needless to say they thoroughly enjoyed themselves and parties of them were taken up to see the Battles of Ypres, then in progress.

Sport in the ' Hush Camp ' was greatly encouraged and the Gloucesters were, as usual, well to the fore in Rugby and Association Football. They won the Brigade Association Competition but were beaten in the semi-final of the Divisional Tournament. They also won the Brigade Rugby and got into the Divisional Final which they would undoubtedly have won had it been played, but their opponents, the 6th Welch, had to leave camp before the final could be played. At boxing, however, the 28th did no good.

Their greatest achievement was in winning the Brigade long-distance running competition. This was for a cup presented by the Brigadier, whose idea was to discover which Battalion was physically the most fit. The race was over about 4 miles of the roughest, heaviest country imaginable, and was run in ammunition boots. The winner of the race counted one point for his unit as did every other runner who finished within 25 per cent of the winning time, i.e. if the winner took twenty minutes everyone who finished in twenty-five minutes counted one point. The percentage of points obtained (of the total strength of the Battalion on the day of the race) was then taken and the Battalion with the best percentage was declared the winner. Of the Gloucesters only two officers and about half a dozen men did not run. They beat the South Wales Borderers in the first round and the Royal Munsters in the final, though the latter had thirteen out of the first fourteen home.

The Regimental Sports were carried out during the second and third week in August. The number of entries was enormous —one hundred for the cross-country race, twenty-seven heats in the 100 yards and over fifty for the high jump.

The inter-company cup was won, as it was in 1916, by D Company.

On the 10th August the Final of an inter-section Association Football Competition, which had been begun on the 29th May, was won by No. 4 Section of C Company.

Thus work was combined with play, everyone being expected to work hard until 1.30 p.m. and keep himself fit in the afternoon by games : a sensible idea of the Brigadier's.

The 1st Division remained in the ' Hush Camp ' from the 19th July until the 20th October, by which date a decision to abandon the enterprise had been arrived at owing to the failure of the Fifth Army to advance sufficiently to render the operations feasible.

About the third week of October, therefore, the ' Hush Camp ' began to break up, and on the 20th of that month the Gloucesters marched to Eringhem, a village 9 miles south of Dunkirk, and billeted there for the night. The next day they marched to billets in the neighbourhood of Rubrouck, 4 miles farther south, where they remained until the 25th. On that date they marched to billets near Houtkerque, about 6 miles north of Poperinghe, remaining there until the 5th of November.

The 1st Division, after its extraordinarily easy summer, was in a very high state of efficiency. Everyone was in good condition and full of energy and it was unfortunate that it was necessary to plunge such a fine fighting force into the hopeless mud and morass at Passchendaele. But such was its fate, for the Higher Authorities had decided to put the 1st Division into the Battles of Ypres.

Nevertheless the ' Hush Camp ' will long remain in the memory of those who came through the War.

The Battles of YPRES, 1917

and trenches held by 1st Bn. Gloucestershire Reg

Dec., 1917 – April, 1918

Scale of Yards

1000   0   1   2   3   4   5   6   7   8   9

Heights in metres

Approx. Allied Line. 6th June, 1917 —————— Approx Br
"   "   "   31st July, "   — ∙ — ∙ — Approx. Allied Line. 20th Sept, 1917 .... " Alli

HOUTHULST

FOREST

A

B

C

Bixschoote

St Jansbeek

Steembeek

Poelcappelle

Langemarck

Triangle
Tileult
Charpentier Wd.
Wood

Pilckem

St Julien

Boesinghe

Elverdinghe

Kitchener
Park

Zo

Brielen

Wieltje

Frezenberg

St Jean

Potijze

Vlamertinghe

YPRES

Bellewaarde
Lake

Weschpek

POLY
WOO

Hooge

INVERNESS
COPSE

Lake

Zillebeke

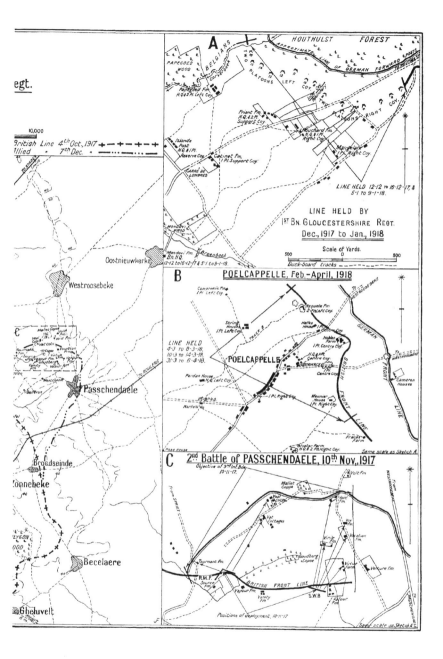

egt.

British Line 4th Oct., 1917 +·-+·-+·-
·Allied · 7th Dec. ·····

A

HOUTHULST FOREST

LINE HELD BY
1st Bn. Gloucestershire Regt.
Dec., 1917 to Jan., 1918

Scale of Yards.
500   0   500

Duck-board tracks --------

B   POELCAPPELLE, Feb.–April, 1918

POELCAPPELLE

LINE HELD
4·3 to 8·3·18.
10·3 to 14·3·18.
31·3 to 6·4·18.

Same scale as Sketch A.

C   2nd Battle of PASSCHENDAELE, 10th Nov., 1917

Objective of 3rd Inf. Bde.
10·11·17.

BRITISH FRONT LINE

Positions of deployment, 10·11·17   Same scale as Sketch A.

Oostnieuwkerke

Westroosebeke

Passchendaele

Broodseinde

Tonnebeke

Becelaere

Gheluvelt

CHAPTER XXVIII

THE BATTLES OF YPRES, 1917

WHILE the Senior Battalion of the Regiment was in training in the 'Hush Camp', the three Territorial Battalions, having spent a short period out of the line at Blairville (1/4th), Bellacourt (1/5th) and Hendecourt (1/6th), moved during the fourth week of July north, to the Ypres Salient, for the 48th Division had been ordered to take part in the Battles of Ypres, 1917.

Sir Douglas Haig's despatch, dated the 25th December, 1917, should be read for the general plan of campaign to be pursued by the Allied Armies during 1917. That plan (subsequently modified to meet the request of our Allies the French) ' comprised a series of offensives on all fronts so timed as to assist each other by depriving the enemy of the power of weakening any one of his fronts in order to reinforce another'. Attacks east of Arras, on both sides of the Scarpe, and south-west and east of Ypres were to take place on the British front.

The Vimy Ridge and the enemy's forward defences on both banks of the Scarpe were intended as the objectives in the Battle of Arras, after which the offensive was to be transferred to Flanders, the capture of the Messines—Wytschaete Ridge preceding the general attack on the high ground east of Ypres, of which the Passchendaele Ridge was the final objective.

Circumstances necessitated a continuance of the offensive at Arras beyond the time originally intended, and it is probable that had Sir Douglas Haig been permitted to break off the attack on that front and transfer his activities to the Flanders operations, we should have made greater progress, for the condition of the ground would have been better.

But it was mid-July before preparations for the Allied offensive east of Ypres were far enough advanced and the 31st of the month before the first of the Battles opened. In this operation (The Battle of Pilkem, 31st July–2nd August) neither the 1st, 1/4th, 1/5th nor the 1/6th Gloucesters were engaged. The 1st Division was on the Belgian Coast and the 48th Division had only a few days previously arrived in the neighbourhood of

Ypres, and on the 31st was in XVIIIth Corps Reserve, both the 144th and 145th Brigades being in the St. Jans Ter Biezen area.

The general results of the operations of the 31st July were that the Fifth Army had carried the German first system of trenches south of Westhoek. Westhoek Ridge was ours, though we had only won as far as the outskirts of the village. The capture of the Ridge robbed the enemy of observation over the Ypres plain. Farther north the enemy's main line, as far as St. Julien, had also fallen into our hands, while north again of that village we had passed beyond the German second line and held the line of the Steenbeek to our junction with the French on the farther side of the Ypres—Staden railway.

THE BATTLE OF LANGEMARCK, 1917 : 16TH–18TH AUGUST

The second attack was launched east and north of Ypres at 4.45 a.m. on the 16th August on a front extending from the north-west corner of Inverness Copse to south of St. Jans Hoek, where we joined up with the First French Army.

The 48th Division was in the left centre of the attack, having the 36th Division on the right and the 11th Division on the left.

The 145th Brigade was to assault the enemy's positions, the 143rd and 144th Brigades being in reserve to assist the 145th or act on its flank if necessary.

There were three objectives, i.e. Green, Red (or Pink as it is called in the Brigade orders) and Blue Lines.

The Brigade was to attack with three Battalions in the front line, i.e. 1/5th Gloucesters (right), 1st Bucks Battalion (centre) and 1/4th Oxford and Bucks (left) : the 1/4th Berkshires were in support (in artillery formation) in rear of the Gloucesters and Bucks Battalion.

The first objective—the Green Line—followed roughly the Winnipeg—Langemarck road : the second objective—Red Line —was the line of German trenches beyond the above road : the third objective—Blue Line—ran from Clifton House, thence Tirpitz Farm, Stroppe Farm, Hubner Farm, Flora Cott and the point about 350 yards south-east of New Houses.

Each battalion was to attack in four waves on a two-company front, each company on a two-platoon front.

Under cover of troops of the 143rd Brigade, located 150 yards east of the Steenbeek, the first two waves were to deploy east of the stream, the remaining two waves between the stream and a line 250 yards west of it.

For the first time the Territorials were to come up against a new form of defence which Sir Douglas Haig in his despatches described as follows :

'The difficulty in making deep, mined dug-outs in soil where water lay within a few feet of the surface of the ground had compelled the enemy to construct in the ruins of farms and in other suitable localities a number of strong points or " pill boxes ", built of reinforced concrete often many feet thick.

'These field posts, distributed in depth all along the front of our advance, offered a serious obstacle to progress. They were heavily armed with machine-guns and manned by men determined to hold out at all costs.'

There were several of these ' pill boxes ' along the 145th Brigade front, there were also a number of old gun-pits which had been adapted to hold machine-guns.

The 1/5th Gloucesters (who had already spent a short time in the front line from the 5th to 8th August) moved up on the night of the 15th/16th first to St. Julien and then to their positions of deployment.

C Company was on the right and A on the left, forming the first and second waves : D Company on the right and B on the left formed the third and fourth waves. The latter Companies were in artillery formation.

At 8.45 p.m. on the night before the battle the enemy's guns opened fire and continued in bursts up to zero hour on the 16th. This shell-fire fell heavily on the whole area between the Blue Line and the Steenbeek and did not improve the conditions under which the troops assembled for the attack. Heavy rain had already turned the ground almost into a morass and the ' going ' was likely to be difficult.

However, the Brigade succeeded in deploying west of the Steenbeek with practically no losses. Tapes for deployment had been laid out west of the stream and others had been put down to certain bridges to guide the advance. The original intention was to lay tapes east of the stream, but the Royal Engineer officers reported the enemy too close to permit of that being done.

Just before zero the leading waves moved across the stream and punctually at 4.45 a.m. the advance began.

Under an excellent artillery barrage the 1/5th Gloucesters reported that Border House and Gun Pits on the north and south side of the St. Julien—Winnepeg road were soon gained, but the attack was then held up by machine-gun fire from, and in rear of, Janet Farm. From a house on the St. Julien—Keerselare road also, heavy fire was opened on the attackers, but the latter, using rifle grenades and with Lewis-gun fire, silenced the enemy and occupied the house.

The check to the Battalion was caused by ' pill boxes ' from which, untouched by our artillery fire, hostile machine-guns raked the advancing infantry with cross and flank fire. By the time a fresh advance was attempted the barrage had got too far ahead and all that could be done was to dig in on the ground gained. The enemy then launched a small counter-attack which was broken up immediately by Lewis-gun and rifle-fire.

On the right of the Gloucesters the 36th Division had failed to come up and a defensive flank had to be formed, reinforcements from the 1/4th Berkshires being sent up to the former Battalion for that purpose.

The 145th Brigade dug in on the line Border House—Jew Hill—Gun Pits—eastern edge of northern part of St. Julien—Hillock Farm—100 yards west of Mon du Hibou. No further advance was made from this line throughout the 16th and when, during the evening of the 17th, the 8th Warwicks arrived and took over the line, the Gloucesters still held their positions.

The Battalion had been heavily sniped, which added further to the heavy casualties already suffered.

On relief the 1/5th Gloucesters moved back to Dambre Camp, stopping for a hot meal *en route* at Reigersburg Camp. They came out of the line having lost 1 officer killed, 1 missing and 6 wounded : their losses in other ranks were 209 killed, wounded and missing. Only 4 officers, exclusive of Battalion Headquarters, survived this battle. Many new N.C.O.s had to be made.

Neither the 1/4th nor the 1/6th were engaged in this action : the former was at Reigersburg Camp from the 16th to the 18th August, while the latter was at Reigersburg Camp on the 16th, on the Canal bank on the 17th and in support trenches in the old German line on the 18th.

In the interval between the Battles of Langemarck and the Menin Road, three minor operations of considerable local importance took place in the neighbourhood of St. Julien. Although under the most unfavourable conditions of ground and weather, positions were captured with some hundreds of prisoners and our line advanced about 800 yards on a front of over 2 miles.

In these three attacks, made on the 19th, 22nd and 27th August, the 48th Division was engaged, though neither the 1/4th, 1/5th nor 1/6th Gloucesters took part in the operations on the former date. On the 22nd August two Companies of the 1/6th Battalion attacked the enemy.

Battalion operation orders stated that, in conjunction with troops on the right and left, the 1/6th were to attack and capture the line Winnepeg—Poelcapelle road from Springfield (exclusive) to the road junction south-east of the Cockcroft where a post was to be established to join up with the 33rd Brigade (11th Division) which was to have a post on the cross-roads a little farther north. The attack was to be made by tanks supported by infantry who, after the capture of the line, were to consolidate and hold it.

D Company of the 1/6th Battalion was ordered to attack on the right, B on the left, the objective being Springfield—Vancouver and a point on the Winnepeg—Poelcapelle road just short of the road junction already mentioned.

D Company was to follow up the barrage, keeping touch with the 1/7th Warwicks on their right, and establish a post at the dug-outs and cross-roads north-west of Springfield. B Company was to occupy Vancouver and establish a post to connect up with the 33rd Brigade on the left.

Two platoons of C Company were to be in support at Mon du Hibou and two just west of the Steenbeek, A Company remaining in reserve at Alberta (about 500 yards north-west of St. Julien).

There is no account of the operations with the Diary of the 1/6th Gloucestershire Regiment, and the narrative as contained in the Brigade Diary is distinctly ' sketchy '.

Apparently the two attacking Companies of the 1/6th moved to the attack at 4.45 a.m., close on the heels of the barrage. At 6.30 a.m. they reported being within 50 yards of Springfield road and in touch with troops of the 143rd Brigade. The tanks were then dealing with Vancouver, which was still strongly held by the enemy with machine-guns, but could not leave the road. At 8.15 a.m. a report was received at Brigade Headquarters that Vancouver had been captured but that we had been driven out again by a fierce counter-attack from the right where the enemy had massed in an old gun-pit. The final result, according to Brigade Headquarters, was that ' we are back midway between the Springfield road and our old positions. All objectives gained on both flanks of the Division '.

At 12.30 p.m. orders were issued that the 1/4th Gloucesters were to relieve the 1/6th during the night of the 22nd/23rd, but the former Battalion before going out of the line was to establish one post on the Springfield—Poelcapelle road to connect with the 33rd Brigade on the left, and another at the cross-roads just south of Vancouver, and to push up and connect with the 143rd Brigade on the right.

The 1/6th established the posts as ordered and were relieved

15

by the 1/4th, the relief being completed by 1.30 a.m. on the 23rd August. The former Battalion moved back to Canal Bank.

In the attack which took place on the 27th the 1/6th Battalion was in support of the two attacking battalions of the 144th Brigade, while the 1/5th Battalion carried out similar duties on the 145th Brigade front.

The casualties sustained by the three Territorial Battalions during August were as follows: 1/4th—1 officer (Captain E. L. Andrews) and 9 other ranks killed, 4 other ranks died of wounds, 67 other ranks wounded and 1 officer and 13 other ranks ' gassed '; 1/6th—20 other ranks killed, 1 officer and 11 other ranks died of wounds, 5 officers and 91 other ranks wounded, 68 other ranks ' gassed ' and 1 other rank missing. The 1/5th were by far the heaviest losers: 2nd Lieutenant N. Steel and 67 other ranks killed, Captain Conder, Captain Hollington, Captain McDowall, Lieutenants Winterbotham and Cornish and 2nd Lieutenants Wagland, Gullick, Grubb, Lake, Bretherton, La Trobe and 249 other ranks wounded, 2nd Lieutenant Bamberger and 15 other ranks missing.

In the Battle of the Menin Road Ridge, which opened on the 20th September and closed on the 24th, the Territorials were not engaged. The 1/4th spent the whole month out of the line, i.e. from the 1st to the 17th at School Camp (St. Jan Ter Biezen), and from the 18th to the 31st at Nielles. The 1/6th similarly passed the first seventeen days of the month at School Camp, then moved to Zutkerque for the remainder of the month. The 1/5th were at Roads Camp, St. Jan Ter Biezen, until the 16th, then moved to the Licques area for divisional training, where on the 24th D Company won the Divisional Field Training Competition in Field Firing. On that date also the 1/5th moved to Bonninques and to Reigersburg Camp on the 25th, moving the next day to the familiar Canal Bank where they were in reserve to the 58th Division, which was attacking Aviatik Farm.

THE BATTLE OF POLYGON WOOD, 26TH SEPTEMBER–3RD OCTOBER

The 1/5th sent two Companies up to California Drive at the disposal of the 175th Brigade (58th Division).

The front of attack in this Battle extended from the Ypres—Comines canal, north of Hollebeke, to the Ypres—Staden railway, north of Langemarck. The 58th Division attacked from the front line originally held by the 48th Division and made good progress which took them to the forward slope of the Gravenstafel Ridge.

The two Companies of 1/5th Gloucesters made no attack on

the enemy, but on the 27th the whole Battalion relieved the 2/10th London Regiment in the front line, which on this front ran from Clifton House to the road south of Quebec Farm.

The German guns heavily shelled the line, and on the 28th Lieut.-Colonel W. Adam, the C.O. of the 1/5th, was ' gassed '. On the 29th the Battalion was relieved by the 1/4th Berkshires and moved back to support positions near Cheddar Villa.   Major A. B. Lloyd-Baker assumed command of the 1/5th on this date, the Battalion on the following day marching back to Canal Bank.

The Battle of Polygon Wood ended on the 3rd October, but the Gloucesters were not again in the front line during the operations.

The Battle of Broodseinde, 4th October

In this battle neither the 1/4th nor the 1/6th Gloucesters were engaged, but the 1/5th Battalion, having been placed in reserve to the 143rd Brigade (who carried out the attack from the front of the 48th Division) moved first to California Drive, with Battalion Headquarters at Cheddar Villa, and were afterwards drawn into the fight.

There are no operation orders either with the Brigade Headquarters or Battalion Diaries, but apparently the 1/5th moved up from Reigersburg Camp on the 3rd in readiness for the attack to take place at 6 a.m. on the 4th October.

At 3.30 p.m. that afternoon the Battalion was ordered to move up to Arbre in close support.   These orders were followed by others to attack at 5 p.m.

B, C and D Companies, in that order from right to left, were to attack Adler Farm, Inch Houses and Vacher Farm respectively : A Company, with Battalion Headquarters, were in reserve at Albatross.

The attacking companies formed up just south of Winchester Farm in two waves of two lines, the forming-up operations being completed by 4.55 p.m.

Conditions were beastly—a heavy rain was falling and the ' going ' heavy.   When the attack started the barrage was falling too far ahead and the enemy's machine-guns were free to fire on the Battalion as it struggled forward through mud and water to reach its objectives.   All that could be done was to consolidate a line about 300 yards east of Winchester Farm and this the Gloucesters did.   The Battalion Diary states that : ' casualties were light ', but 2 officers killed, 4 wounded and 125 other ranks killed, wounded and missing, is not a negligible total.

The 5th October passed with C and D Companies holding the

front line, B in support and A still in reserve, until relief came on the 6th when the Battalion moved back to Reigersburg Camp.

The 1/4th and 1/6th (according to Brigade Headquarters Diary) each supplied two platoons as stretcher bearers, prisoner guards, etc. The former Battalion during the morning of the 4th was warned to be ready to move at an hour's notice and at 1 p.m., followed by the 1/6th Gloucesters at 2 p.m., marched to Canal Bank.

THE BATTLE OF POELCAPELLE, 9TH OCTOBER

On the 9th October the general attack was resumed on a front of over 6 miles, extending from a point east of Zonnebeke to the junction of the British and French north-west of Langemarck. Zero hour was 5.20 a.m.

Both the 1/4th and 1/6th were engaged in this Battle, the 1/5th remaining at Dambre Camp, though supplying large parties for carrying duties, escorts for prisoners and as stretcher-bearers.

The Diaries of 144th Brigade Headquarters and the 1/4th and 1/6th Gloucesters all contain narratives of this Battle.

The 7th Worcesters were to attack on the right, the 1/6th Gloucesters in the centre and the 1/4th Gloucesters on the left. There were two objectives : (i) The Green Dotted Line which ran from north of Yetta Houses, on the right, thence in a north-westerly direction just east of Inch Houses and Oxford Houses to the Lekkerboterbeek where the left of the 144th Brigade joined up with the 11th Division ; (ii) The Green Line from just east of Wallemolen, thence just east of Varlet Farm and Berks Houses to the Lekkerboterbeek.

The attack was not easy, for before reaching the first objective there were several fortified buildings and strong points which had to be overcome and which the enemy had done his best to fortify very strongly. Moreover, the ' going ' was truly terrible, through mud and water and across soft, spongy ground which impeded the advance and made the keeping of any sort of formation an extremely difficult matter.

The 1/6th (Lieut.-Colonel H. St. G. Schomberg) were to attack with A (right) and B (left) Companies forming the first wave, C (right) and D (left) the second wave. The two first-named Companies were to capture the first objective, paying special attention to Vacher Farm, Burns House and the Cemetery and several old gun-pits which had been fortified by the enemy : C and D were to move in support of A and B and finally capture the second objective.

The 1/4th (Lieut.-Colonel J. H. Crosskey) were to attack with A Company on the right, D on the left to capture the first objective, B on the right and C on the left, the second objective.

Three hours before zero the 1/6th Gloucesters were in position on taped-out lines, the first wave extended along the front tape and the remainder of the Battalion in section columns in depth.

About half an hour before zero the enemy shelled the Winchester line fairly heavily, but the shells fell mostly behind the second wave and only 4 casualties occurred.

At zero the first wave got away well with the barrage, followed by the second wave about 300 yards in rear.

At once the raucous rat-tat-tat of machine-gun fire broke out from all along the German line: shell-holes belched flame and a storm of bullets met the attackers as they advanced as rapidly as their boots, clogged with mud and clay, would allow them. From shell-holes in front of ' 2 Mebus ' and from a trench on the right boundary of the 1/6th this fire was particularly heavy.

Keeping in close touch with B Company on the left, A Company met with considerable opposition from the trench already mentioned. Two officers were wounded during the advance— Lieutenant A. G. Poole, the Company Commander, and 2nd Lieutenant W. C. Townsend. The right platoons entered the trench (being joined later by a part of C Company) and bombed up it towards the 7th Worcesters on the right. They captured 20 prisoners and 4 machine-guns, a great many more prisoners being taken by the Worcesters. The platoons in the trench were commanded by Sergeants Wilcox and Courtier.

The left platoon, with some of the Worcesters who, in an unaccountable way had got on to that flank, advanced against Vacher Farm, though the buildings had been so knocked about that the farm could not be recognized. On they went, suffering heavy casualties, but it is not clear what happened. One officer, 2nd Lieutenant Southgate, with part of a platoon keeping touch with B Company on his left, eventually formed a post between Burns House and Vacher Farm.

Up to this period the losses of A Company, besides the 2 officers stated, were 59 other ranks.

On the left of A Company, B Company cleared the Cemetery which was held by snipers and a machine-gun team : the latter was wiped out completely. They next met with considerable opposition from machine-guns firing from shell-holes just in front of ' 2 Mebus '. But the shell-holes were charged and when the attackers got close up the Germans threw up their hands : about 20 prisoners and 3 machine-guns were taken here.

War has its tragic happenings which crop up on every side :
a party of Germans in the near distance was seen to kill an officer
who was trying to rally them.

B Company lost in this attack 1 officer and 45 other ranks.

Owing to the strong opposition encountered by the first wave
and the heavy state of the ground, the second wave was close
behind the first as the latter reached Burns House—Vacher
Farm road. The second wave then pushed through the first in
order to keep up with the barrage.

The front line of C Company (2nd Lieutenant B. A. Tussaud)
advanced in conjunction with D on the left through Vacher
Farm, but the second (2nd Lieutenant A. S. Hill) lost direction
and went too far to the right. Lieutenant Hill was killed early
in the advance and Captain R. G. Titley [1] was missing until
three days after, when he was brought in by the 9th Division.
This Company probably reached a point about 200 yards north-
east of Burns House—Vacher Farm road.

The casualties of C Company were 2 officers (Captain R. G.
Titley and 2nd Lieutenant A. S. Hill) and 55 other ranks.

On the left of the second wave D Company assisted B Company in capturing the ' 2 Mebus ', then advanced against a ' pill
box ' on the eastern side of the road strongly held by machine-
guns.

The Germans in this redoubt continued firing until the Gloucesters were close up, then ran out with their hands up, also surrendering four machine-guns. But having captured the redoubt, D Company came under heavy cross-fire from Oxford Houses, in the
area of the 1/4th Battalion. The latter had, apparently, been
unable to capture this strong point and were held up. Captain
J. A. Fletcher (O.C. D Company) therefore formed a defensive
flank on his left before attempting any further advance. He
threw out posts to the left, nearly to the County Cross-Roads,
where he afterwards obtained touch with the 1/4th Battalion.

The two platoons of C Company, under 2nd Lieutenant
Tussaud, and 2nd Lieutenant Southgate's platoon gained touch
from Burns House with the mixed force of A and C Companies
under Sergeants Wilcox and Courtier on the right, the 7th
Worcesters being on their right.

At about 3.20 p.m. the enemy was observed in artillery formation about Banff House, while a line of skirmishers was seen
advancing from east of Berks Houses. Lewis-gun and rifle-fire
was at once opened on them and they withdrew. Two further
attempts made by the enemy to advance were similarly driven

[1] Died of wounds in hospital, 13th October, 1917.

back while a barrage, which had been called for, fell at 3.40 p.m.
and must have increased the enemy's losses.

No further movement was observed.

At nightfall on the 9th the line of the 1/6th Battalion followed
closely the Vacher Farm—Burns House road, the northern half
being east of the road and the southern half west of it.

About 70 prisoners and twelve machine-guns had been captured by the 1/6th, but the losses of the latter totalled 242 all
ranks.

The 1/4th had not been as fortunate as the 1/6th in getting
forward. Along their front the enemy resistance was particularly
strong and he had many defended areas which defied capture.

During the evening of the 8th the 1/4th Gloucesters had been
brought up in motor-buses as far as Admiral's road, whence they
proceeded over duck-boards via Alberta Track and along the
Poelcapelle road in rear of the front line. They were then to
be met by guides from the Bucks Battalion, who were to guide
them to Tweed House by a taped track via Bavaroise House.

The Battalion arrived at the point where they were to meet
the guides, but there was no sign of the latter. After waiting
for some time the C.O. decided that it was best to 'turn about'
and move up via the board track and Hubner Farm, which route
he was to some extent acquainted with. This he did and arrived
at Tweed House at about 1.45 a.m., only to discover that the
three rear companies and about one platoon of the leading company had lost touch.

Those who knew not the Ypres Salient (or for that matter any
part of the line) on a pitch black night, with its utter desolation,
wide expanse of shell-torn ground pock-marked by craters and
huge gashes made by mining operations, or of the great difficulty
in finding one's way about, having to keep to muddy, slippery
duck-board tracks, to leave which (though they were under heavy
shell-fire) meant tumbling into craters full of water, will hardly
appreciate the reason why these companies and a platoon went
astray. The fearful conditions of the line, added to the fact that
companies and platoons had to move only at intervals, i.e. sometimes as much as 100 yards separating one from the other, were
responsible.

Having discovered that he had practically only three platoons
with him, the C.O. sent out runners to look for the missing
Companies, while C—the leading Company—was guided to the
' jumping-off ' point.

It was about 4.30 a.m. when A and B Companies and two
platoons of D were brought up to Tweed House and were at

once taken on to their 'jumping-off' line. They were just forming up along the tape when the Divisional barrage came down and the Battalion began the attack less two platoons of D Company and a few men of A and C. Only B Company was complete.

As the barrage fell A Company, on the right, and D, on the left, started off at once and were able to get within 50 yards of the barrage before the first lift. The second wave—B Company on the right and C on the left—moved forward a few minutes after A and D.

At the first lift the barrage was lost owing to the sodden condition of the ground and was never again caught up.

Immediately the advance began a crescendo of machine-gun fire broke out from the Cemetery and all along the line. A hostile machine-gun in a post south of Oxford House, two more firing from a breastwork in front of the latter, and another gun near the Lekkerboterbeek from behind the enclosures of Terrier Farm, raked the 1/4th as they struggled to get on. Snipers, from the large rectangular hedge along the road bounding Oxford Houses, from the houses themselves, from Beek Houses and other points north of the Lekkerboterbeek, impeded the advance.

The bulk of the Battalion was held up approximately on a line about 150 yards east of County Cross-Roads, though a party consisting of one officer and six men, the remains of a platoon, pushed on nearly to Oxford Houses. Another small party, under a sergeant, got into the enclosure about the Houses and fortified a shell-hole, from which they proceeded to fire on every German seen. On the left of the Battalion [1] the attack appeared to make no headway and C Company, therefore, formed a defensive flank facing north with three posts and a Lewis-gun post.

As already stated, the machine-gun in the Cemetery was silenced almost at once by the 1/6th Gloucesters. All that could be done was to keep down movements by the enemy, and whenever a German showed himself he was fired on. The two hostile machine-guns in the breastwork in front of Oxford Houses were dealt with by rifle grenades.

At 5 p.m. a Company of the 8th Worcesters, supported by another Company, attacked Oxford Houses but were unable to capture them as they were under fire from both flanks and the front.

The few men of the 1/4th Gloucesters who had got near Oxford Houses were compelled to withdraw owing to a Divisional barrage put down to assist the Worcesters.

[1] Presumably in the area of the 11th Division.

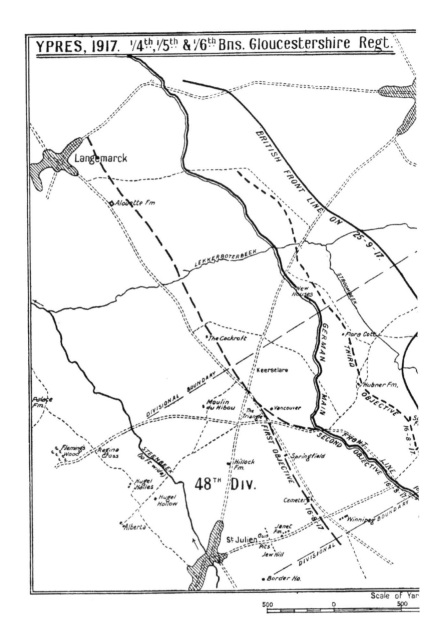

YPRES, 1917. 1/4th, 1/5th & 1/6th Bns. Gloucestershire Regt.

Langemarck

Alouette Fm.

LEKKERBOTERBEEK

BRITISH FRONT LINE ON 25-9-17.

STROOMBEEK

New Houses

The Cockroft

Keerselare

Flora Cott.

THIRD OBJECTIVE

Hubner Fm.

Palace Fm.

GERMAN MAIN

Maulin du Hibou

The Triangle

Vancouver

DIVISIONAL BOUNDARY

Fleming's Wood

Regina Cross

STEENBEEK (10 ft. wide)

FIRST OBJECTIVE

Springfield

SECOND OBJECTIVE 16-8-17

FRONT LINE

16-8-17

Hillock Fm.

48TH DIV.

Nugel Halles

Nugel Hollow

Cemetery 16-8-17

Winnipeg BOUNDARY

Alberta

St Julien

Janet Fm.

Gun Pits

Jew Hill

DIVISIONAL

Border Ho.

Scale of Yards

500   0   500

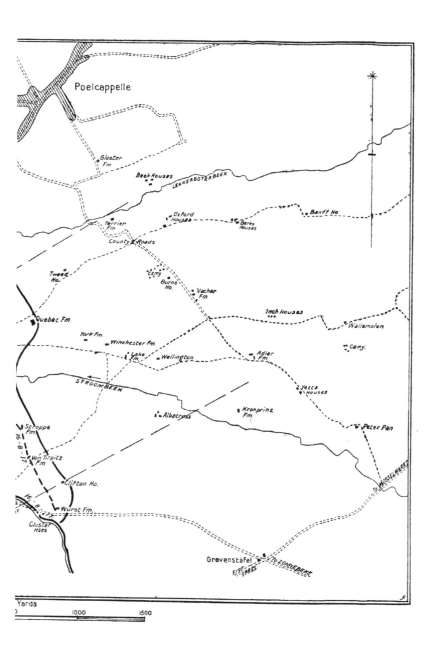

Poelcappelle

Gloster
Fm.

Beek Houses

LEKKERBOTERBEEK

Oxford
Houses

Banff Ho.

Terrier
Fm.

Berks
Houses

County Roads

Tweed
Ho.

Cemy.

Burns
Ho.

Vachar
Fm.

Inch Houses

Wallemolen

Quebec Fm.

York Fm.

Winchester Fm.

Cemy.

Lake
Fm.

Wellington

Adler
Fm.

STROOMBEEK

Yetca
Houses

Stroppe
Fm.

Albatross

Kronprinz
Fm.

Peter Pan

16·8·17

Von Tirpitz
Fm.

Clifton Ho.

16·8·17

MOSSELMARKT

Wurst Fm.

To

Cluster
Hses.

Gravenstafel

To ZONNEBEKE

To
YPRES

Yards

0   1000   1500

F

The 1/4th lost in this attack 4 officers killed and 6 wounded, and in other ranks 31 killed, 102 wounded, 3 died of wounds and 31 missing (probably killed).

Failure to reach their objectives did not rest with the gallant battalions of the 144th Brigade. They had fought splendidly, but the barrage moved too quickly, for the terrible nature of the ground would not permit of a rapid advance.

No change took place on the 10th. At night the Brigade was relieved by the 26th Brigade (9th Division) and the worn-out battalions moved back in stages to Siege Camp.

As already stated, beyond furnishing carrying parties and stretcher-bearers, the 1/5th took no part in this Battle.

THE SECOND BATTLE OF PASSCHENDAELE : 26TH OCTOBER–10TH NOVEMBER

In the First Battle of Passchendaele, fought on the 12th October, the Regiment was not engaged. The attack, made at 5.25 a.m. between the Ypres—Roulers railway and Houthulst Forest made progress along the spur and higher ground, but the valley of streams which run westward from the main ridge could not be passed : the attack was then broken off until a more favourable opportunity presented itself.

' By this time,' records the official despatches, ' the persistent continuation of wet weather had left no room for hope that the condition of the ground would improve sufficiently to enable us to capture the remainder of the ridge this year (1917). By limited attacks, made during intervals of better weather, however, it would still be possible to progress as far as Passchendaele, and in view of other projects [1] which I had in view it was desirable to·maintain the pressure on the Flanders front for a few weeks longer.'

From about the middle of October there was a temporary improvement in the weather and local attacks east of Poelcapelle, and within the southern edge of Houthulst Forest, took place. Then on the 26th the Second Battle of Passchendaele opened, when at 5.45 a.m. the enemy's line from the Ypres—Roulers railway to Poelcapelle, as well as his trenches south of the railway (the subsidiary attack) were assaulted.

The Canadians, advancing astride the main ridge, established themselves securely on a small hill south of Passchendaele. North of the Rhuebeek (a small stream flowing south-westwards from Passchendaele) they also captured the Bellevue Spur : in the subsidiary attack Gheluvelt was entered and Polderhoek Château, with a number of prisoners, recaptured, but mud

[1] Of these ' other projects ' a surprise attack at Cambrai was one.

choked the men's rifles and when a strong German counter-attack developed, having nothing with which to defend themselves, they were obliged to withdraw. On the 28th our Allies (French and Belgian troops), on the left, completed the capture of the whole of the Merckem peninsula.

The general situation at this period is interesting and worthy of brief mention. It is probable that had Sir Douglas Haig been free to follow his plan of operations the Battles of Ypres, 1917, would have ended before ' Passchendaele '. But the position of the Allies at the end of October was far from secure. In France and Flanders the British Army was carrying almost the whole burden of attack upon its shoulders : the French Army had been seriously affected by the mutiny which was the outcome of Nivelle's failure : in Italy, the German-Austrian forces had launched a powerful offensive in the Julian Alps, and our Allies in that country had been compelled to fall back : in Russia the Bolsheviks were engineering a *coup d'état* in Petrograd, while the Germans had already begun to transfer large forces of men and a great number of guns from the eastern front to France : Palestine was the one bright spot. Allenby's advance was making fine progress. It was, therefore, of paramount importance for the British Army to continue hitting the enemy hard, thus compelling him to concentrate his forces opposite our line in the Ypres Salient : at all costs he had to be prevented from gaining the initiative.

But what a dreadful scene the Ypres Salient presented : a desolate, water-logged country, deep in mud, pitted with shell-holes and mine craters, bare of any living thing, save the poor fellows who, holding the line, clung desperately to their positions despite the fact that they stood, sat or lay in muddy, icy-cold water which chilled their bones to the marrow. On ground too soft and spongy to permit of the digging of trenches, fortified shell-holes took the place of sandbagged posts such as would have been built had it been possible : ' pill boxes ', those concrete forts which the enemy had been compelled to construct, seeing that he also found it impossible to dig and establish ordinary trenches, even when captured from the enemy were frequently half under water : the ruins of what had once been smiling farms and hamlets offered only partial shelter amidst the bricks and rubble from the storm of shells which swept on and over them at all hours of the day and night : if some were fortunate to ' live ' in cellars, they only did so with the floors inches deep in mud, foul of atmosphere and sharing them with rats and vermin. The only routes to and from the front line lay along slippery duck-board tracks, with rudely-constructed bridges over numerous shell-holes, full of water, or across the swollen streams of which several crossed the Salient. Of roads there were only one or two, the remainder being semi-obliterated by the guns of both sides. All the duck-boarded tracks had been marked down by the German artillery and they were shelled frequently and very heavily, for the enemy knew that we had no other approach to the front line. To go overland meant slipping into shell-holes, feet deep in water, and not a few lost their lives by drowning in this manner. Few dared to show themselves on these tracks by day, for any movement drew almost instant fire from the enemy.

At night the Salient took on an even more dreadful appearance than in the daytime. Véry lights soared into the air and threw their fitful glare over the mournful scene : sharp stabs of flame spouted from the darkness, there was a constant roaring, moaning and whistling in the air as shells from the opposing artillery passed eastwards and westwards.

When darkness had fallen reliefs began, ration and working parties got on the move, transport and ambulance wagons warily made their way along the special tracks prepared for them : even the guns (during an advance) were moving after getting bogged to the wheel axles. Imagine man-handling guns across ground deep in mud, in absolute darkness and shell-holes all around.

Reliefs took anything from six to twelve hours—almost incredible. But look at the lines of silent, heavily-weighted men moving in single file, Companies ' in distance ' as they trudged hour after hour feeling their way almost step by step on the duck-boards, checked often by the necessity for keeping touch and held up frequently by a hostile barrage, or the fact that the enemy had the track under a constant rain of shells, causing casualties which in turn caused more delay until the stretcher-bearers had come up and had carried off the wounded. The guides leading an incoming battalion up to the front line frequently lost their way and only by the Grace of God would the unfortunate unit at last reach the battalion to be relieved, then probably dawn was breaking, bringing with it the usual heavy shelling which heralded the beginning of another day of torture. Under such circumstances men might be forgiven for desiring the bitterness of death sweet compared with the untold misery of living : and it was small comfort to them that the German was in no better circumstances.

If officers and men drained the cup of despair almost to its depth, there were yet two things which kept their bodies and souls alive. It was not the rum ration (though that often was a God-send) nor a drink, nor full meat ration. No ! the thing which kept the British soldier ' going ' was first his indomitable pluck and then his extraordinary optimism, his never-failing cheerfulness under the most appalling conditions.

In that spirit he faced ' Second Passchendaele '.

In that operation also (the last of the Battles of Ypres, 1917) the 1st Division took part, though it was the 10th November before the Division attacked the enemy.

On the 30th October and on the 6th November short advances had been made, Passchendaele passing into our hands : south, north and west of the village the high ground had been wrested from the enemy, no less than five strong counter-attacks being beaten off in one day. ' Pill boxes ' in the northern end of the village, around Mosselmarkt, and on the Goudberg Spur were also captured.

Finally, four days later (on the 10th November), in vile weather, British and Canadian troops attacked from Passchendaele and Goudberg and, after heavy fighting, captured further ground on the main ridge.

On the 5th November the 1st Division was ordered to move forward and take over on the night of the 7th/8th the front held by the 63rd Division and part of the left division of the Canadian Corps. The 3rd Brigade (plus one battalion of the 2nd Brigade) was to carry out the relief.

The 1st Gloucesters were last mentioned as occupying billets in Houtkerque on the 5th November. On that date Lieut.-Colonel A. W. Pagan assumed temporary command of the 3rd Brigade, Major W. A. Baillie Hamilton (who had joined the Battalion on the 3rd) taking over command of the Battalion. The following day the Gloucesters moved to billets in Dambre Camp, north of Poperinghe, having already received orders concerning the relief of troops of the 63rd and Canadian Divisions in the front line.

The 2nd Welch Regiment, on the right, and the 2nd King's Royal Rifles (2nd Brigade), on the left, were to take over the front line from Valour Farm, on the right, to point V.21.C.1.1., on the left : the 1st Gloucesters to be in support in Kronprinz Farm and the 1st South Wales Borderers in reserve.

These moves took place on the 7th/8th as ordered, one other rank of the Gloucesters being wounded during the relief. Battalion Headquarters were duly established in Kronprinz Farm, a ' pill box ' about 2 miles due west of Passchendaele, with the companies grouped around it in the mud.

Brigade Headquarters were in a strong but diminutive ' pill

box ' at Kansas Cross where the Ypres—Roulers and Lange-marck—Zonnebeke roads crossed each other. It was well that the ' pill box ' *was* strong because direct hits on it were scored daily by the German gunners. But it was a terrible place to write in and so small that when it was necessary to examine a map all its occupants but two had to clear outside.

On the 8th operation orders for the attack to take place on the 10th were issued from Brigade Headquarters. The original intention had been to employ the 2nd Welch (then holding the front line) in the attack, but as Colonel Pagan said, ' it became obvious long before November the 10th that troops which had been living for four days under the conditions endured by the Welch would be unfitted to attack anything.'

The line then held by the Welch was indeed a terrible spot : companies were located in a collection of broken-down ' pill boxes ' and mud holes—' Line ' was a misnomer. The support line held by the Gloucesters was little better, for Kronprinz Farm lay just east of the Stroombeek which, like other streams in the Salient, had overflowed its banks, flooding the surrounding country.

The objective of the attack was the capture of the Goudberg Spur, running south-west from the Passchendaele—Westroosbeke road and to give a still farther footing on the Passchendaele Ridge. It may be noted *en passant* that previous failures to gain the whole of the Ridge was responsible for the abandonment of the landing scheme for which the Gloucesters had been trained in the ' Hush ' Camp.

On the Second Army front the Canadian Corps was to attack on the right and the 1st Division on the left. The 2nd King's Royal Rifles were to hold the left of the Divisional front while the 3rd Brigade (1st South Wales Borderers, on the right, and 2nd Royal Munster Fusiliers, on the left) were to attack the enemy. The Gloucesters were to be in reserve and the Welch were to continue to hold their line.

The objectives on the Divisional front ran approximately from Void Farm to Veal Cottages, thence to Tournant Farm.

Owing to the state of the ground the attacking Battalions had to start with a considerable interval between them.

As a sidelight on the difficulties attending troops moving forward to take up their assembly positions, across seas of mud and water and along duck-board tracks, ' Instructions for move to forming-up positions ' are interesting. After stating that attacking battalions should be ready formed up to start half an hour before zero, and ordering the 2nd Welch to ' stand to '

' under cover ' (save the mark !) ' in their present position ', half an hour before zero and the 1st Gloucesters to do likewise, the ' Instructions ' then detail the routes to positions of assembly :

> ' 1st South Wales Borderers via Gravenstafel—Bellevue road to Meet-cheele and thence by duck-board track to Valour Farm . . . 2nd Royal Munster Fusiliers via Mousetrap Track to Wallemolen and thence by duck-board track to Source Farm.'

' Mousetrap Track ' will be picqueted by O.C., 1st Gloucester-shire Regiment, from its commencement to Wallemolen, also the road through Wallemolen to the start of the duck-board track to Source Farm.

> ' *Every place where a wrong turning could be taken must be guarded.*
> ' O.C., 2nd Royal Munster Fusiliers, will arrange that one officer marches behind his Battalion to inform the picquets when the whole Battalion has passed. Picquets will then withdraw.'

The 9th November was a fine but threatening day. At night rain began to fall and fell continuously, with incessant violence, throughout the 10th.

On the afternoon of the 9th November the attacking battalions began their long move forward to their forming-up positions. One took eleven hours to complete the move and the other rather less. But what of their condition after that agonizing approach march ?

Zero hour was 6.5 a.m., at which hour in pelting rain the attack began :

> ' On the right the South Wales Borderers never reached their objec-tive : on the left the Munsters got to theirs but were unable to hold it. The German barrage was very severe and from 9.30 a.m. until dark the shell-fire was intense. This was partly accounted for by the fact that our counter-battery artillery was unable to move up within range owing to the state of the ground.' [1]

The condition of the ground also was responsible for robbing the attacking troops of the support of the Stokes guns, the Brigade narrative stating that ' it was impossible to move the guns owing to the state of the ground '.

By 9.30 a.m. the attack had definitely failed and there was a danger that the enemy might even occupy the Brigade front line. One Company of the Gloucesters (D) was therefore sent forward at that hour to assist the Munsters. A little later A, B and C Companies were hurried up to help the South Wales Borderers. By the evening the Gloucesters were holding the whole front, rather in advance of the original line, with the Munsters and South Wales Borderers in rear.

[1] Colonel Pagan.

There was, however, a large gap between B Company, on the right (supported by A and C) and D Company, on the left, but during the 11th touch was gained, the gap filled and the line consolidated.

During the night of the 11th/12th November the 28th were relieved by the Loyal North Lancs and moved back to dug-outs on the bank of the Yser Canal.

Although the conditions had been execrable and the shelling very severe, the casualties were far less than might have been expected. One officer (2nd Lieutenant C. R. Harman) was killed, and another (Captain C. L. Priestley) died of wounds.

Lieut.-Colonel Pagan who, during the afternoon of the 10th, was proceeding towards Tournant Farm to clear up the situation, was wounded, as also were Captain B. R. Brewin, Lieutenants F. C. Davies and J. K. George. Four other ranks were killed and 45 wounded.

*   *   *   *   *

Until the 13th the Gloucesters remained on the Canal Bank, on which date they marched back to Dambre Camp, remaining there until the 22nd. From the 18th to the 22nd, however, two Companies, first A and C, then B and D, went forward to Wurst Farm (situated about 200 yards south-west of Kronprinz Farm) in order to support the 1st Brigade which was holding the line. In Dambre Camp several casualties were incurred from the enemy's long-range, high-velocity guns.

On the 23rd November the Battalion moved from Dambre Camp to Schools Camp, remaining there until the 27th, when yet another move took place, on this occasion to Proosdy Camp, north of Proven. In this village training was carried out until the 5th December. Even here, far beyond the front line, several casualties were suffered from the German long-range guns.

The 5th December found the Gloucesters on the march to a hutted camp near Eikhoek, about 5 miles north of Poperinghe. This camp was comfortable enough and the weather fine and frosty, but discomfort was caused by the almost nightly visitations of hostile bombing aeroplanes. Only two days were spent here and then the 28th marched to a very comfortable collection of dug-outs and huts scattered among the remains of a wood about 2,500 yards north-east of Woesten.

But on the 11th they once more turned their faces towards the trenches and that night moved up to reserve positions in a portion of the front line facing Houthulst Forest.

To reach the reserve positions the Gloucesters crossed the Yser Canal just north of the Lockkeeper's house at Het Sas, about

1,000 yards south of the point where the main Ypres—Dixmude road crossed the Canal. Here a bridge had been thrown over the Yser by the Sappers, and a road had been made on the western side connecting the bridge with the main road.

On the eastern bank of the Canal the bridge joined up with a road running east, thence just west of north from the Lock-keeper's house to the village of Bixschoote.

The reserve positions were about this road, Battalion Head-quarters being at the cross-roads named Bosche Cross-Roads, situated about a mile from the Canal. One company was on the Canal bank, another in a wood (known as Triangular Wood, adjoining Bosche Cross-Roads), the third and fourth companies each occupying a copse situated south-east of the Bosche Cross-Roads and known as Woods 14 and 16 respectively.

The accommodation was poor, the men being quartered in shelters and in old German ' pill boxes ', mostly full of water. It was, therefore, probable that when orders came to relieve the 10th Gloucesters in the line on the 12th December, they were not unwelcome.

The 1st Division was at this period holding a portion of the line opposite Houthulst Forest, immediately on the right of the Belgians. One brigade was in the line, the Gloucesters occupy-ing the left sub-sector, next to our Allies. The ground was very waterlogged and the front line consisted of a number of section posts. The Battalion held the front with two companies in the line, each with two platoons in the front line and two in support. The men in the forward posts lived in extreme discomfort. They were unable to move at all in daylight and the weather was cold and wet.

Right company headquarters with one platoon were in ' pill boxes ' at Houchard Post and the remaining platoon of the company in ' pill boxes ' at Mangelaare.

The left company headquarters with two platoons were at Papeguoed Farm, also in ' pill boxes ' situated on the edge of the valley of the Corverbeek Brook, the dividing line between the 1st Division and the Belgians.

Interpolated between the headquarters of the companies holding the line was another group of ' pill boxes ' named Friant Post : here also were the headquarters of the support company with two platoons.

At Catinat Farm, on the ridge about 500 yards in rear of the support line, was another platoon of the support company.

The reserve company was grouped in various posts on the left flank in line with, and in rear of, Catinat Farm : headquarters were at Islande Post with two platoons at Gourbi Farm and two at Victory Post : the remaining platoon of the support company was at Gourbi Farm.

These posts were far more comfortable than were the forward posts. Some of the ' pill boxes ' which had been erected by the Germans inside existing buildings were roomy and nearly all were watertight.

Battalion Headquarters were in a magnificent edifice called Mondovi Farm, farther to the rear and almost in the centre of the position.

But if these posts were comfortable the surrounding country was dismal and desolate in the extreme. The ground was practically impassable, excepting the roads, but there was a very complete system of duck-board tracks. The Steenbeek, which had originally run immediately to the west of Mondovi Farm, had broken its banks owing to the incessant shell-fire and had flooded large tracts of country. The expanse of water had been bridged whenever a duck-board track crossed it. North of Mondovi Farm and between the farm and Catinat there was a very large lake spanned by a wide bridge.

Active patrolling was carried out on each night and on the 13th December a strong fighting patrol from C Company advanced for a quarter of a mile into Houthulst Forest, but met none of the enemy.

This patrol was under the command of Captain K. A. R. Smith, who had served with the Battalion for nearly two years. He was enthusiastic and full of energy and did excellent work while he was with the 28th. He was a subaltern in the Special Reserve when the War began and before he joined the 1st Gloucesters served with the 2nd Battalion in 1915.

The 28th remained in the line until the 16th December, when they were relieved by the Munsters and withdrawn to the same reserve positions they had previously occupied.

Colonel Pagan records that ' during this period in the line no casualties were incurred, a thing which had not happened since the Le Rutoire Farm days in the summer of 1915 '.

The Battles of Ypres, 1917, ended on the 10th November, but Passchendaele remained (and still remains) a dreadful memory. The awful conditions of the ground put an end for the time being to offensive operations, and well it did for both sides were practically exhausted after nearly four months of bitter fighting amidst seas of mud and water. Of the gallant troops under his command, whose efforts were almost superhuman, whose courage and tenacity and cheerfulness were beyond all praise, Sir Douglas Haig said :

16

'They advanced every time with absolute confidence in their power to overcome the enemy, even though they had sometimes to struggle through mud up to their waists to reach him. So long as they could reach him they did overcome him, but physical exhaustion placed narrow limits on the depth to which each advance could be pushed, and compelled long pauses between the advances. The full fruits of each success were consequently not always obtained. Time after time the practically beaten enemy was enabled to reorganize and relieve his men and to bring up reinforcements behind the sea of mud which constituted his main protection.'

And from the other (the German) side it is evident that our enemy suffered as much, if not more, than we did :

'Enormous masses of ammunition, such as the human mind had never imagined before the War, were hurled upon the bodies of men who passed a miserable existence scattered about in mud-filled shell-holes. The horrors of the shell-hole area of Verdun were surpassed. It was no longer life at all. It was mere unspeakable suffering. And through this world of mud the attackers dragged themselves, slowly, but steadily, and in dense masses. Caught as they advanced by one of our hails of fire they often collapsed and the lonely man in the shell-hole breathed again. Then the mass came on again. Rifle and machine-gun jammed in the mud. Man fought against man and only too often the mass was successful.' [1]

For 'the mass' read British Infantry.

The 1st Gloucesters remained in reserve until the 16th December, on which day they moved to billets about a mile north of Woesten, thence on the 20th to a hutted camp near Crombeke. The following day they marched to another hutted camp— Zuidhuis Camp—2 miles north-west of Woesten where they remained until the 28th December. During the greater part of this period a hard frost covered the ground which improved conditions considerably : this frost continued with slight breaks until the middle of January. On the 26th December snow fell heavily. Zuidhuis Camp was very comfortable and here the Gloucesters enjoyed their Christmas dinner. The kind folk in England had again sent out an unlimited supply of turkeys and plum puddings, and with a goodly issue of beer all ranks had a really happy Christmas.

On the 28th December the Battalion moved to the comfortable collection of dug-outs and shelters now known as La Bergerie Camp, where a good deal of training was carried out and large working-parties were also found nightly to carry stores up to the front line.

When they reached camp on the 11th October the three Territorial Battalions—1/4th, 1/5th and 1/6th Gloucesters—had

[1] General Ludendorff in *My War Memories*, 1914–18.

(though they did not know it) seen the last of the front-line trenches in the Ypres Salient. For on the 13th and 14th they entrained at Houpoutre for the First Army area, the 48th Division having been ordered to relieve a Canadian division east of Vimy.

The 1/4th and 1/6th reached Villers-au-Bois on the 15th, and on the 17th the former took over front-line trenches from the 29th Canadian Regiment, while the 1/6th relieved the 28th Canadians in support. The 1/5th were at Camblain L'Abbé, but moved to Villers-au-Bois on the 19th.

The remainder of October was uneventful, neither during the three weeks in November that the 48th Division held the line at Vimy was there any incident of outstanding importance. In this part of the line also offensive action had, for the time being, ceased, and the opposing sides were busily engaged in making an uncomfortable existence as comfortable as possible.

During the fourth week, however, the Division entrained for Italy.

In October the Italians had suffered a severe reverse, the Austro-German armies having launched a great offensive on the 23rd in the Julian Alps. Gorizia and Udine were taken by the enemy and British and French divisions were despatched to assist our Allies : the 48th Division was one of them.

In half-battalions the 1/4th, 1/5th and 1/6th Gloucesters entrained at Tinques and Ligny on the 23rd and 24th November. The train journey, via Paris, Lyons, Marseilles, Cannes, Nice, Monte Carlo, Menton and well-known Italian towns, such as Parma and Bologna, Turin and Milan, was a pleasant experience, and by the 30th the 1/4th (Lieut.-Colonel A. C. Williams) were settled in billets in Pojana, the 1/5th (Lieut.-Colonel W. Adam) at St. Gregorio, and the 1/6th (Lieut.-Colonel H. St. G. Schomberg) at Villaraspa.

At the close of the year the 1/4th were at Bressanvido, the 1/5th at Stroppari and the 1/6th at Sandrigo. The first few days of the month were spent in making final moves and the remainder in training and the supply of working-parties : but front-line trenches were not taken over until the New Year.

CHAPTER XXIX

SALONIKA : II

' ALL quiet ' is the report of the 2nd Gloucesters in Salonika on the 1st January 1917. The Battalion on that date was located in Jeni Mah with an outpost Company (A) at Kakaraska. The line had been withdrawn south of the Meander Stream for the winter, though the northern banks were patrolled frequently.

At about 4 p.m. the outpost company saw clouds of smoke ascending away on the right front between Bejlik Mah and Arabadzik Mah : the enemy had fired the reeds and bushes, but the wind was blowing the wrong way and the fire did no damage.

Cold weather, rain and mist heralded the New Year—the beginning of the Gloucesters' second year in Salonika. There was ' little doing ' during the winter months, patrol encounters being the only excitement which fell to the lot of the Battalion.

On the 8th the Turks fired Bejlik Mah and Arabadzik Mah. At 8.30 a.m. a Gloucester sentry observed a mounted Turk riding towards No. 3 Post, Kakaraska, whom he shot and killed.

Several days passed without incident and then on the 13th a wire to 82nd Brigade Headquarters stated that on the 14th, as the Bulgarian New Year approached, action on the part of the Turks was probable. Divisional Headquarters also suggested that some small offensive action on our part should take place.

This offensive action, so far as the Brigade was concerned, appears to have been the re-occupation of Bejlik Mah, for which purpose D Company of the Gloucesters, in conjunction with Yeomanry and cyclists, occupied that place at 10.30 a.m. One platoon of D Company had been left behind at Kakaraska Bridge as a guard. About 11 a.m. a strong Turkish patrol of about forty was seen advancing towards the bridge.

The enemy was about 200 yards from the bridge when fire was opened. The Turks then made off leaving one dead, two wounded and two unwounded prisoners in the hands of the Gloucesters. Work on the defences continued, and on the 15th it is recorded that the weather was " hot in afternoon '. The diary also mentions the departure of a first leave-party to England.

Another small encounter took place on the 18th. B Company
had relieved D Company at Kakaraska, when at 8.30 a.m. a party
of between thirty and forty Turks again attacked the village, but
were driven off by rifle-fire. The enemy retired dragging his
wounded with him. At dusk that evening four dead Turks were
discovered in the mealies in front of Kakaraska by a screen of
men who had been pushed out to protect a wiring party working
in front of the village.

During the evening of the 20th B Company captured a Turk,
one of a patrol.

Towards the end of January the Struma began to overflow
its banks and floods were becoming a serious problem. The
construction of a new line of posts further back from the river
was begun. The G.O.C. Brigade also proposed that Kakaraska,
Kispeki and Aba should be temporarily evacuated in order to
entice the enemy to enter them : the villages were then to be
surrounded and the enemy captured. This operation was to take
place on the 7th. But before that date there is an interesting
entry on the 2nd February in the Diary of 82nd Brigade Headquarters : ' Brigade Commander tested an invention of
2nd Gloucestershire Regiment for covering wire more effectively
than at present possible by Lewis guns.' On the 4th also another
test was carried out, but unfortunately there are no details in
either the Battalion or Brigade Diaries, the former not even
mentioning it.

The advanced posts in the three villages were successfully
withdrawn during the 7th, but the wily enemy was not to be
enticed and by the 13th the posts had again been occupied by us.

February generally was a quiet month.

On the 1st March two companies of Lovat's Scouts and
Yeomanry with a section of machine-guns were in position before
dawn between Beglik Mah and Arabadzik to intercept hostile mealie
pickers, the Gloucesters also being ordered to ' stand to '. But
rain was falling and no enemy were seen and all troops were
withdrawn by 12 noon. The following day the Battalion again
' stood to ', as the 10th Division and the 81st Brigade were
carrying out an artillery and infantry demonstration, but again
nothing occurred to necessitate the employment of troops of the
82nd Brigade.

On various occasions throughout the month the Gloucesters
were called upon to be ready at short notice to assist other units
if necessary, and there are several entries in the Diary of such
and such a company having to sleep in equipment to be ready if
called upon. But apart from these small excitements there

is little in the Battalion Diary for March of outstanding interest.

The somewhat dull round of existence was relieved for an hour or two on the 18th (a Sunday, when work and parades were not usual) when a ' Rugger ' match took place between the 2nd Gloucesters and Lovat's Scouts. The former, keeping up the fine record of the Regiment for sport—especially Rugby—won by 15 points to 8.

Two Bulgarian deserters gave themselves up to a post of the Gloucesters on the last day of March.

Fine, warm weather heralded the month of April, but for days on end the records begin ' Work on defences continues ', until about the middle of the month the Gloucesters relieved the 2nd D.C.L.I. as ' offensive battalion ' and took over Ago Mah with Battalion Headquarters at that place and posts at Kakaraska and Kispeki. Two Companies (A and C) took over the first line of positions while the remaining companies continued training.

On the 22nd an officer and fourteen other ranks of A Company took up position north-west of Pheasant Wood at 3 a.m. At 6.45 a.m. a patrol of the enemy deployed from the north-west of the Wood, leaving nine men guarding their flank. The leader of the patrol was mounted. He was shot and another of the enemy was hit while approaching one of the Gloucesters' posts. Fire was opened on the party of nine guarding the hostile patrol's flanks, four men falling, the remainder scattering into the Wood. The Gloucester patrol then withdrew to Kakaraska.

On the 25th April the first raid of the year took place. The intention was to rush a hostile post and secure identifications. But the noise (unavoidable) caused by the men walking through the long grass warned the enemy, who bolted : one man was slightly wounded and another was missing as the outcome of this attempt.

Another raid—the raiders again returning empty-handed—took place on the night of the 2nd/3rd May. The Derbyshire Yeomanry had reported having located a hostile trench about a mile west of Seres Station and 400 yards of the railway, and Colonel Davie decided to raid it. For this purpose he selected a night when the moon would give a suitable light. C Company was detailed to make the raid which was to take place between the hours of 1 a.m. and 2 a.m. on the 3rd May. The raiders numbered 1 officer (2nd Lieutenant S. C. Hemming) and fifteen picked N.C.O.s and men. Two flanking parties, each of twenty-five men and an officer, were also detailed to protect the flanks of the raiders : these parties were under the command of 2nd

Lieutenants Weller and Cahusac. The O.C. B Company was to take over temporary command of the front line and the remainder of C Company, not engaged in the raid.

Second Lieutenant Hemming and his men successfully located the enemy's posts and rushed them but found them unoccupied. The raiders then waited in hiding for an hour to see if the enemy would return, but nothing happened. They then went to look for him. Two woods in the neighbourhood of the posts were searched and patrols went to within 200 yards of the Station, but no enemy was seen or heard. By this time it was 3 a.m. and getting light and the raiders withdrew.

Another raid took place on the night of the 9th/10th May, on a Bulgar post in the neighbourhood of Kuli Bejkoi.

B Company was detailed for this operation, which was to be in the nature of a surprise. Operation orders stated : ' The enemy post must be raided and the enemy attacked with the bayonet. Every endeavour must be made to take prisoners, or articles from the dead for purposes of identification.'

B Company was to move from Kispeki on its objective via Salmah and Scot Ford and was to withdraw to Kispeki before daylight by the same route.

Twenty picked men under an officer were to form the raiding party. Covering parties were to protect both flanks of the raiders, while another strong party was to be in support in rear of the raiders.

The raid was to take place between 11 p.m. and 12 midnight, 9th May.

Second Lieutenant R. E. Culverwell was in charge of the raiders.

Kuli Bejkoi was a small farm on the Seres road, some 2,000 to 3,000 yards north of Scot Ford.[1] The approach to the place was difficult. Across country there was only one narrow track to the farm, there were many bunds full of water and thistles abounded everywhere. These thistles were of an extraordinary height and strength and formed a very formidable obstacle.

The raiders set out, 2nd Lieutenant Culverwell advancing slowly along the track with Sergt. Gathern and six men on his right as flank guard and Sergt. Walkley and six men on the left. These unfortunate flank guards had to negotiate the thistles which took time as everyone was advancing with cat-like tread, fearing lest the slightest sound should warn the enemy.

A Bulgar advanced listening-post was first encountered and,

[1] Scot Ford over the Meander Stream was about 3,000 yards east of Kispeki.

after making a short reconnaissance, the raiders advanced on the post, two of the enemy having been seen in it.   Very silently they crawled along : Lieutenant Culverwell in the centre, Sergt. Gathern closing up on the right.   But Sergt. Walkley was stopped by a bund which he could not cross without showing himself and without a certain amount of splashing in the water.   He, therefore, lined the bund with his party and waited events.

When the main party got within 20 yards of the post they were seen and the order was given to charge, Lieutenant Culverwell leading.   The latter engaged the first Bulgar and, as he would not surrender, forced him to his knees with the intention of making him give in.   Sergt. Gathern, evidently thinking the officer was in danger, rushed across and, calling out ' Leave him to me, sir,' drove his bayonet through the Bulgar, two or three other men bayoneting the unfortunate man at the same time.

The other Bulgar made off for his main position by the path but was chased and caught up by Sergt. Gathern and his party : the latter ran straight on, but the N.C.O. turned off to the left in close pursuit of the enemy.   The Bulgar turned and showed fight, whereupon Sergt. Gathern gave him a ' jab ' in the throat and, having also received two more ' short points ' in the stomach, this man also fell dead.

The noise of the scuffle and the fight brought some sixty or seventy Bulgarians out of the farm who, seeing the raiders, advanced on the latter, spreading out fan-wise to take them in rear.   This new force of the enemy was almost immediately reinforced by sixty others.   The Bulgarians as they advanced fired their rifles from their hips.

Seeing there was a danger of being cut off, 2nd Lieutenant Culverwell gave the signal to withdraw to the rallying point where the supports were waiting.   On reaching this point Véry lights were sent up as a signal to the guns at Kispeki to put down a barrage.   The barrage fell almost immediately and the Bulgars ceased fire and fell back rapidly on the farm, evidently leaving wounded behind as cries were heard.

The raiders then withdrew unmolested to Kispeki.

On the 11th the 2nd Gloucesters left Ago Mah for Jeni Mah, though two companies remained in the former village in Brigade Reserve.

The remainder of May passed without incident of more than ordinary interest.   The weather had become very hot and as a consequence mosquitoes were once more assuming aggressive action, being a horrible pestilence.   Flies too were more than a nuisance.   From May to September the sun was very powerful and the heat almost tropical. Topees were issued and all ranks wore shorts during the hot weather.

Admissions to hospital from fever were now frequent and for medical reasons it was decided to withdraw all troops from the low-lying Struma plain to the hills, immediately south of the river. The withdrawal began early in June.

In accordance with orders the Gloucesters evacuated the villages of Kakaraska and Kispeki and A and C Companies set out on the march via Anogudeli, Gudeli, Apidje and Nigoslav to a camp on the side of a hill 2,000 yards south of the latter village.

Battalion Headquarters and B and D Companies remained in Ago Mah awaiting orders to withdraw to the new camp. On the 13th the whole Battalion was once more united and all companies were hard at work. The new camp was promptly named Gloucester Camp, and for some days after, working parties were busy improving accommodation as well as making a rifle range.

On the 18th July, however, two companies of the Gloucesters relieved the 10th Hants on the River Line which ran along the southern bank of the Struma. A Company took over from Gudeli Bridge to F.19, the latter being almost opposite Zouave Island in Zouave Wood, and B Company from F.20 to Komarjan.

On the 28th July No. 4 Platoon won the Brigade Platoon Shooting Competition, the Battalion Snipers being placed second in the Brigade Snipers' Competition.

At night, or rather at 1 a.m., on the 29th, D Company with one sub-section 82nd Machine-Gun Company crossed the Gudeli Bridge and marched to old Brigade Battle Headquarters, whence platoons moved off to Jenimah Wood with the intention of lying in wait for a Bulgar patrol, which the Yeomanry reported visited the Wood. Two Bulgars entered the Wood and, evidently suspecting something, fired as though to draw fire. Shortly after a party of six more of the enemy was seen in the distance, and the Gloucesters at once fired with Lewis and Vickers guns, but it was uncertain as to whether the enemy suffered casualties. At dawn a platoon pushed forward to Jenimah, but found the village unoccupied. The platoon withdrew and the whole force returned via Gudeli Bridge at 10 a.m.

During this period the Battalion had two companies in the Reserve Line and two in the hill camp, reliefs taking place at short intervals as the heat was almost tropical. August was a quiet month, spent mostly in work and training, though patrols frequently crossed the river in order to keep a strict watch on the enemy.

The life of the 2nd Gloucesters during these seven months

appears to have been spent more in keeping themselves fit in a beastly climate rather than in active operations, which, for the time being, were quiescent. Sickness, produced by heat, fever spread by mosquitoes, the abominable and ever-present myriads of flies were much greater enemies than the poor Bulgar who scarcely showed his grizzly face.

The severity of the hot weather was shown on the 23rd August when, owing to the shortage of water, ' washing parades ' became necessary. Companies paraded for washing between 4 and 7 p.m., drawing water at Wells 10 and 11 (east of Nigoslav). Each man was rationed to one gallon per man per day for all purposes, washing, cooking, drinking.

The rigour of discipline was, however, never relaxed and the Battalion was always to the fore when a test of skill, or evidence of good training, were called for. On the 29th (as an instance) a team of sixteen other ranks, under Lieutenant Russell from A Company, won the Brigade Wiring Competition. Fifty yards of wire fence, single span both sides, with French wire on one side, were put up in eighteen minutes, the next battalion's time being twenty-four minutes. In Salonika, as in France, the Regiment was always adding to its laurels.

Early in September the weather grew cooler and on the night of the 10th heavy rain fell, continuing during the morning of the 11th. In fact it spoilt ' an offensive stunt ' carried out on the night of the 13th/14th against Jenimah.

At 7 a.m. on the 13th A and D Companies marched down to Suhabanja and rested there until 8 p.m. They then moved off towards the Struma, which they crossed at 11 p.m. and reached Jenimah at 3.30 a.m. on the 14th. They then got into position and lay in wait for hostile patrols from north-east of the village. But the ground had been burnt bare by the enemy and the rain of two days before had made it soft and spongy, which showed the wily Bulgars the footmarks of those lying in ambush. The scheme proved abortive and the two companies withdrew to Gudeli at 6.30 a.m. on the 14th and, crossing by the Gudeli Bridge, they reached Camp Apidje, where they rested until the evening. They then returned to camp.

On the last day of the month the Battalion won the Divisional Wiring Competition, beating their own previous record by one and a half minutes, i.e. completed the task in 16½ minutes.

October began with a good deal of hard work. On the 1st C and B and half of D Companies were at work on a Decauville light railway, preparing ground and laying metals between Cereskojk and Gudeli Bridge. This railway work as well as work on the defences kept the 2nd Gloucesters busy until the second week of the month.   On the 8th, however, work was begun on the construction of a bund on the right bank of the Struma with a view to minimizing the floods in winter and spring.   The Battalion at this time was located in Marian Camp.

On the 13th it was announced that the 81st Brigade was going to raid Homondos and the 82nd Brigade was to move forward and take up a forward line on the left bank of the Struma.   In view of this operation the Gloucesters left Marian Camp at 10 p.m. and crossed the Gudeli Bridge at 11 p.m., bivouacking for the night in the following positions : A Company on the sites of Nos. 1 and 2 Redoubts of the forward line, B Company occupying sites of Nos. 3 and 4 Redoubts, C and D Companies in Brigade Reserve in Hampshire Copse and Battalion Headquarters in Dzami Mahale.

Throughout the daylight hours of the 14th all companies remained as quiet as possible, but at 6.30 p.m. began work on the redoubts.   The new forward line was to consist of a chain of all-round defence redoubts with lines of tactical wire beneath each. The weather was very bad, much rain had already fallen and was falling when the Gloucesters began their task amidst the greatest discomfort.   There were no shelters for fear of disclosing the whereabouts of the Battalion to the enemy.

Outposts covered the working parties (working in two shifts) who kept hard at their cheerless tasks until dawn appeared.   They were then permitted to rest until 6 p.m. on the 15th when their work was resumed.

By the 21st the redoubts were almost finished and the Battalion on that date was relieved by the 2nd D.C.L.I., and A, B and C Companies moved back to a bivouac camp on the Marian— Apidje road, about 500 yards east of the latter village : D Company remained in Gudeli Bridge Camp.

The Gloucesters had been ordered to take part in a night raid on the enemy and for this purpose practised night-marching on a compass bearing.   On this date also Lieut.-Colonel Davie was appointed Brig.-General.

Heavy rain fell on the 23rd amidst which preparations were made for the forthcoming operations which were to take place on the night of the 24th/25th.   Extra S.A.A., bombs, wire cutters, etc., were issued.

The raid was to be quite a big ' show '.   The enemy's outpost line, comprising the villages of Sal Mahale, Kispeki and Ada, were to be raided by the 82nd Brigade, while the Corps Mounted Troops were to carry out a similar operation on Kakaraska.   The object of the raid was to kill or capture the garrisons of the villages.

From captured documents it was found that the villages of Beglik Mahale, Kakaraska, Sal Mahale, Kispeki and Ada were regarded by the enemy merely as an outpost line and that the enemy's intention, if strongly attacked, was to withdraw rather than defend the line.   Kakaraska, Sal Mahale and Kispeki were each held by a company of Bulgars with machine-guns, but Ada was garrisoned by one or two platoons only.

The assaulting troops were to be divided into two columns, Column A, consisting of the 2nd Gloucesters and $1\frac{1}{2}$ companies of the 10th Hants, Column B of Lovat's Scouts, $2\frac{1}{2}$ companies of Hants and a sub-section of the 82nd Machine-Gun Company.

Column A was to cross Gudeli Bridge at 11 p.m. on the 24th and move via a gap in the wire, north of No. 3 Redoubt, to an old road north-east of Osman Kamila.   From this old road the Column was then to move to a point north of Ada.   The crossing of the Meander Stream was involved in this movement.   The operation orders are made difficult for the ordinary reader by the insertion of various co-ordinates which cannot be given but, briefly, the Column was to be in position north of Ada with its eastern flank in such a position as to lend assistance to Column B, which had to assault the other villages.

Lieut.-Colonel Davie, who had originally been ordered to command Column A, left the Gloucesters on the morning of the 24th after parading the Battalion and wishing all ranks good-bye. The Column was, therefore, placed under the command of Lieut.-Colonel Beckett, O.C., 10th Hants, the actual attacking troops being commanded by Major Owen Symons, 2nd Gloucesters, who had succeeded Colonel Davie in command of the Battalion.

At 10 p.m. the Gloucesters with Column A set out for the raid, crossed Gudeli Bridge at 11 p.m., reached Osman Kamila at 12.15 a.m. and by 1.30 a.m. had reached a pre-arranged point on the Meander Stream.

The Battalion Diary, however, gives no details of the actual raid : the following narrative is taken from the Brigadier's report in the Diary of the 82nd Brigade.

' Movements of Column A.   The Column reached the old work (G.17) north-eastern corner of Osman, at 00.45 hours (12.45 a.m.) on 25th October, Osman having been occupied previously by a company of the 2nd D.C.L.I. and a section 82nd Machine-Gun Company.   The head of the Column reached point 1909/1678 on the Meander at 01.30 hours (1.30 a.m.), the whole Column clearing this point by 02.30 hours (2.30 a.m.).   Up to the time of crossing the Meander good progress was made, but the onward march to point 1920/1690 proved very slow, delay being caused by many ditches and thick undergrowth.   The tail

of the Column left point 1920/1690 on the pivotal compass bearing at
04.30 hours (4.30 a.m.), the head at that time being at about point
1926/1687. The portion of the march as the enemy's line was
approached proved exceedingly difficult, the country being very thick
with hedges, briars and undergrowth, while several streams, rendered
marshy and boggy by the recent rain, had to be negotiated. In spite
of frequent halts to enable the Column to close up, it was found exceedingly difficult to maintain touch throughout the length of the Column,
and at times this was lost, necessitating halts of considerable duration.

' At 05.00 hours (5 a.m.) the leading company came into contact
with the enemy covering the line which ran almost due north from Ada.
These enemy posts opened fire, one from the immediate front and one
from either flank. The post in front was rushed, but a heavy fire was
brought to bear by the infantry posts on the flanks and to their rifle fire
was shortly added machine-gun fire from the Ada side, and an artillery
barrage. The flank posts were apparently some 200 yards from the
Column, and it was therefore difficult to rush them at once : but as a
considerable volume of effective fire was being directed from them it
was decided that they could not be ignored, especially as they were
close to the spot where the troops detailed for the assault of Ada were
to form up.

' Owing to the darkness and difficulty of movement amongst ditches
and scrub, it was some time before any of our troops reached the posts,
and when they did so the enemy had withdrawn from them. During
this time touch was lost temporarily between the leading troops and the
remainder of the Column, and when the whole Column was finally
closed up it proved too late for it to take up the blocking position from
the north of Ada to the bend in the Meander (1,000 yards north of Sal
Mahale) in time to conform with the pre-arranged programme.

' The assault on Ada was, however, carried out and troops pushed
along the northern edges of the village, the Column joining hands with
Column B as the latter moved through Kispeki.

' By this time the majority of both the Kispeki and Ada garrisons
had withdrawn towards Nihor, but a few casualties were inflicted on
the enemy in Ada and on isolated parties attempting to escape in a
north-easterly direction.

' The advance was made in column of route as far as the north-eastern
corner of Osman, after which the troops moved in file.

' Column A commenced to withdraw at 08.50 hours (8.50 a.m.) and
Column B at 09.30 hours (9.30 a.m.).'

The Gloucesters' own account of this raid is :

' Crossed Gudeli Bridge at 23.00 hours (11 p.m.), reached Osman
Kamila at 00.15 hours (12.15 a.m.) and arrived at our arranged post X
on Meander Stream at 01.30 hours (1.30 a.m.). Column A Head-
quarters at Point X, the attacking troops being after that under Major
Symons, 2nd Gloucestershire Regiment. In conjunction with Lovat's
Scouts, attacking from the east and south-east, raid was successful,
Ada being captured at about 07.15 hours (7.15 a.m.). Returned to
camp via No. 3 Redoubt, arriving back at 12.30 hours (12.30 p.m.).
Casualties—1 officer wounded,[1] 5 other ranks killed, 22 wounded. D
Company returned to Gudeli Bridge.'

---

[1] 2nd Lieutenant Jenkyn.

After this little excitement the Battalion resumed work on the forward line.

At the end of October the weather became very cold, winter was setting in, though many fine days favoured the working parties, whose labours seemed never-ending.   As it would not be long before the Struma began to rise dangerously, work on the bund was continued.

Odd entries are to be found in the official diaries at times. Mention of football matches and recreational training often creep into them : they were, indeed, part of the life of the Army, but on the 3rd November there is an entry in the Diary of the 2nd Gloucesters which might be more fully explained, i.e. ' beer issued to A and B Companies '.

On the same day the 2nd Gloucesters had played the Xth Corps Cyclists at ' Rugger ' and had beaten them by 2 tries to nil.

Battalion Headquarters moved to Dzami Mahale on the 8th, companies being billeted in the village and in Ago Mahale. Work on the redoubts and the bund was continued.

Very heavy rain fell on the 13th and two days later the Struma was very high and the ground near the river slightly flooded. Thereafter rain was frequent.

Apparently the troops in the redoubts were housed in huts, for on the 19th the Battalion Diary has the following interesting entry : ' The platoons in occupation of the redoubts worked on their respective redoubts, B Company cutting and collecting brushwood for making *wattle and daub walls for the huts.*'   Several days later it is recorded that ' the first of the wattle and daub huts at Battalion Headquarters came into use ', proving very successful.

One day was much like another now that the winter had settled in and the flooded condition of the Struma Valley hindered, if not entirely prevented, offensive operations by either side.

On the last day of November the 2nd Gloucesters were relieved and moved back, Battalion Headquarters to No. 2 sub-sector north of Marian, B Company in No. 3 Camp sphere, A Company in Dzami Mahale, C and D Companies in Ago Mahale.

Lieut.-Colonel A. C. Vicary joined the Battalion on the 3rd December and assumed command.

During the first week of December the 82nd Brigade changed areas with the 80th Brigade, the former taking over the southern portion of the line between the Gulf of Orfanu and Lake Tahinos.

Battalion Headquarters and A and B Companies of the Gloucesters moved off first, arriving at Nigrita at midday on the 4th : on the 5th they continued the march to Dzindzos, on the 6th to Kukos

and on the 7th to Bluff Camp where they were joined by C and
D Companies on the 10th.   Brigade Headquarters were now
established at Ano Krusoves.

Work and training now occupied the Gloucesters until the end
of the year.   Their Diary contains little of oustanding interest.

On Christmas Eve rain fell nearly all day, and although the
Battalion was given a holiday no sports were possible.   The
weather improved during the night and Christmas Day was fine.
Excellent sports were held during the afternoon and all ranks
enjoyed their Christmas dinner, the Diary recording a ' free issue
of beer and E.F.C. (Expeditionary Force Canteen) goods '.   On
Boxing Day there was an issue of plum puddings, kindly provided
by friends of the Battalion at home (Mrs. Budgett, Mrs. Power
and Committee).

Thus ended the year 1917 in Salonika.   It was all very well to
say that the gallant fellows who held the front in this comparatively
quiet part of the world war did little.   They did their job and
did it well, and all the while they were fighting disease and
discomfort.

CHAPTER XXX

THE LAST WINTER IN THE TRENCHES : JANUARY TO APRIL 1918

WITHOUT any signs or any hope that 1918 was to be the last year of war in France and Flanders, dawn broke on the 1st January in bitterly cold weather. ' Stand to ' usually took place as daylight was breaking and stout indeed was the heart of any officer or man who could produce a cheery smile and wish another a ' Happy New Year ' under such conditions.

The 1st Gloucesters were in La Bergerie Camp and it was not until the 4th that they moved forward to reserve positions, relieving the 8th Royal Berks. Battalion Headquarters were again at Bosche Cross-Roads, A Company in Triangular Wood, B Company on the Canal Bank, C in Wood 16 and D in Wood 14. But the Battalion spent only twenty-four hours in reserve, for on the 5th the 28th relieved the 10th Gloucesters in the front-line sector (left of the Brigade front), B Company on the right, C on the left, D in support and A in reserve.

The Brigade Diary gives the following pen picture of the sector :—

' The front line is merely held as an outpost line by a series of disconnected posts of about half a section each. No continuous trenches of any sort. By day men sleep in small shelters in the posts, by night they are largely employed in repairing the wire. The main line of defence is also a series of posts running through Papegoed and Hill 20. No continuous trenches at all. An immense amount of wire has been put out, as continuous lines in front of the various lines of resistance and always designed to be enfiladed by our machine guns.'

Heavy snow lay on the ground and the weather was bitter, nevertheless it was preferable to rain and mud, and everyone was keeping fit. Much patrol work in Houthulst Wood was carried out and useful information concerning the enemy's defences obtained. On the 9th the Gloucesters were relieved and withdrew into reserve about the Bosche Cross-Roads. Again no casualties had been suffered during the tour.

During the period in reserve very large working parties were

256

found day and night. They were employed mainly in carrying wire and other stores to the front line and, after dark, in putting up wide belts of entanglements in front of the various posts. The modern methods of defence in depth and of the use of wire to shepherd the attackers into areas swept by artillery and machine-gun fire, were at this period being evolved.

On the 12th the Gloucesters marched once more to La Bergerie Camp and on the 13th to a hutted camp just north of the village of Crombeke where training was carried out until the 20th. While in this camp R.S.M. Brain was awarded the Military Cross. This Warrant Officer was severely wounded on the Somme and had done magnificent service throughout the War.

The weather at Crombeke was of the vilest description. In-cessant heavy rain fell, with gales of wind which tore the roofs from several huts. During this period the 28th played a Belgian regiment at ' soccer ' and beat their opponents by 5 goals to 2.

On the 20th the Battalion moved to dug-outs and shelters in the east bank of the Yser Canal. These billets extended for some hundreds of yards and were, for the most part, comfortable and warm. They were situated south of the Lockkeeper's house at Het Sas and of a bridge over the Canal known as ' J. I. Bridge '.

The Gloucesters remained in these comfortable quarters in the Canal Bank until the 9th February.

During their stay in this area they, with other troops, were at work on the ' Army Battle Zone'. The entire Battalion was at work daily in large parties scattered over a wide area. For several days A Company was detached and employed in making deep dug-outs some distance north of Langemarck. They were thus located in the area in which the 28th did their earliest (and splendid) fight-ing during the Battles of Ypres, 1914. But how different the country was now ! Gone were the fields, trees, hedges and farm-houses which had made that part of Flanders so like the English country-side. There remained only a mud heap, scarred with shell-holes, derelict trenches and wire, traversed by duck-board tracks, and relieved alone by uncouth ' pill boxes ' and the splintered trunks of trees. The journey from Battalion Headquarters to A Company and back took five hours to complete.

The weather during this period in the Canal Bank was as pleasant as that at Crombeke had been beastly. There was a distinct touch of spring in the air, the days were warm and sunny and the country showed signs of drying up.

On the 9th February the 28th moved back to a hutted camp (Caribou Camp), nearly 2 miles west of Elverdinghe. Here they remained until the 19th and did useful training, very necessary

17

after nearly three weeks' employment as navvies. The weather continued to be delightful and quarters were comfortable.

The new Brigade Commander—Brig.-General Morant—inspected the Battalion on the 15th. While in this camp the Belgian Croix de Guerre was awarded to two very gallant N.C.O.s, who had done splendid service with the 28th. They were No. 8062 C.S.M. H. Eyers and No. 9380 Sergt. J. Read.

At this period the British Army was undergoing reorganization. Owing to the falling off of reinforcements from home and severe losses during the heavy fighting in 1917, it became necessary to disband some battalions and distribute their personnel among divisions to bring them up to strength. The number of infantry battalions in a division was therefore reduced to nine (plus the Pioneer Battalion). The 10th Gloucesters of the 3rd Brigade were disbanded and a number of their officers and men were transferred to the 28th. The reorganization also necessitated some battalions being sent to other divisions and, to the great regret of the Gloucesters, the 2nd Royal Munster Fusiliers were transferred from the 3rd Brigade, 1st Division, to the 16th Division. The Munsters had served in the 3rd Brigade since they replaced the Queen's in 1914. They were good comrades of the Gloucesters and had fought alongside them in many a hard struggle with the enemy. No one who knew him will ever forget their Regimental-Sergeant-Major, Mr. Ring, who was the soul of the Regiment. Their going was a great blow to the Gloucesters.

In mid-February the 1st Division took over a new sector of the line extending from Poelcapelle southwards, and on the 19th the Gloucesters paraded at 5 a.m., marched to a light railway, and proceeded in funny little trucks to the reserve area. Their billets were at Kempton Park—a hutted camp adjoining the Ypres—Langemarck road, about 2,000 yards west and a little south of St. Julien. While in this position (in reserve) the Battalion was to work once more on the 'Army Battle Zone'. On arrival at Kempton Park, therefore, the 28th dumped their kits and began work at once. They worked all day, though at noon heavy rain fell. Everyone was wet and tired when at last the Battalion turned into its new home about 6 p.m. It had been impossible to settle in before as its former occupants did not leave till that hour. Thus the place had to be cleaned and tidied up and everyone knew what that meant.

The Gloucesters remained in reserve until the 4th March, the whole Battalion working daily on the 'Army Battle Zone'. This was a magnificent line consisting of concrete emplacements, dug-outs and trenches, and had it ever been finished would have been impregnable : that it was not finished was due to events which took place further south in April. For it was abandoned when our line at Ypres was withdrawn in consequence of the German offensive on the Somme and on the Lys in March and April. The actual portion on which the Gloucesters were engaged was that running immediately south-west of Kitchener's Wood, and about a mile from the Steenbeek.

The Battalion at this period was commanded by Lieut.-Colonel A. W. Pagan, with Lieutenant J. Stevenson as Adjutant, Captain Green having left to become a Brigade Major in the 32nd Division. Major J. R. Guild was second-in-command and companies were commanded as follows : A—Captain E. Handford, B—Captain P. Mallett, C—Captain K. A. R. Smith, D—Captain A. Seldon.

During this period in reserve Captain T. R. A. Morris was awarded the Military Cross. This officer joined the 28th on the 2nd October 1914, and served with it continuously until the end of the War. He commanded a platoon of B Company until September 1915, when he was appointed Transport Officer.   In this rôle he did wonderful work. His transport was always as good as any in the Division and he never let the Battalion down. On many occasions, particularly on the Somme in 1916, it was far more pleasant to be in the line than to come up nightly to the line with the transport. Captain Morris never failed throughout the War to bring the transport up under his personal command, with rations and stores, whatever the conditions, when the Battalion was in the trenches.

On the 4th March the Gloucesters relieved the Cameron High-landers in the front line in the Poelcapelle sector. This was one of the most interesting sub-sectors of the front ever held by the Battalion.

The line was held by posts arranged in depth and supporting each other. The main feature of the defences was the village of Poelcapelle, which had been developed during the course of the War into a concrete fortress. Every house of any size in the village had been, so to speak, lined with concrete by the Germans. The outer coating of the houses had been removed by our guns, and later by theirs, and there remained instead of the village a series of massive concrete mounds which were nearly impervious to shell-fire. The principal fort was an enormous concrete building which had formerly been a brewery.

A number of outlying farms and buildings near Poelcapelle had been similarly treated by the Germans and formed admirable platoon posts.

The line was held by three companies with one in support. The centre company (C) held Poelcapelle with its headquarters and one platoon in the brewery : another platoon was in a forward post on the southerly Poelcapelle—Westroosebeke road : a third at Helles Houses on the northerly road and the fourth platoon at Noble's Farm. On the right A Company had its headquarters and two platoons at Gloster Farm, about 800 yards south-east of the brewery. One platoon was at Meunier House, 500 yards south of the brewery, and one near the site of Poelcapelle Church, the church having long since disappeared under the storm of shell-fire from the opposing guns.

On the left D Company Headquarters were located at Ferdan House, 200 yards north of the Poelcapelle—Langemarck road and about 500 yards from the village. Two platoons were at Requette Farm, a forward point some 400 yards north-west of Helles Houses. The remaining platoons were at String Houses and Compromis Farm, posts forming a second line respectively 500 and 800 yards north-west of the brewery.

Pheasant Trench served as headquarters for B Company in support. This trench ran north-west from the Ypres—Poelcapelle road from a point about 1,500 yards south-west of the village. The platoons of this Company were distributed in posts in and near the trench.

Battalion Headquarters were at Norfolk House on the Poelcapelle—Langemarck road and about 500 yards from the former village.

The Gloucesters, therefore, were distributed over a very wide area, but by this period the means of communication were excellent. Duck-board tracks led to most of the posts and cross-tracks were numerous. The enemy, of course, was aware of the positions of these tracks and dosed them frequently with machine-gun fire and shelling at inconvenient moments, principally at night when he knew that relieving troops or ration parties were moving up to the front line.

During this spell in the line the weather was gorgeous and such green things as still existed showed signs of the new life of spring.

Early on the morning of the 6th March the enemy attempted to raid a post at Meunier House. First he put down a heavy bombardment of 4·5-inch and 5·9-inch shells on the post. At the time a proportion of the garrison was at work on the defences and the Platoon Commander—2nd Lieutenant I. J. Warren—was mortally wounded and died on the 8th. Three men were killed and 4 wounded. The remainder of the platoon manned the defences and waited for the enemy, and as the latter approached the post gave them a warm reception and drove them back to their own lines.

The Battalion had been ordered to raid the enemy and during this tour the objective of the raid, i.e. a German post named Cameron Houses, situated just south of the Poelcapelle—West-roosebeke road and about 900 yards from the brewery with its approaches and surroundings, were reconnoitred nightly by patrols.

The 28th were relieved by the 2nd Welch on the 8th March and moved back into support. In this position A and B Companies were on the extreme right of the Divisional sector in Dimple Trench, which ran just south of the Langemarck—Gravenstafel road, its right flank beginning where the St. Julien—Gravenstafel road joined the former road. C and D Companies were on the extreme left of the Divisional sector in Pheasant Trench.

On the southern bank of the Steenbeek, and centrally situated between the half battalions, was a collection of low, flat-topped ' pill boxes ', termed Hugel Hollows : here Battalion Head-quarters were situated.

Only two days, however, were spent in support, for on the 10th the Battalion again went into the front line, taking over the same sub-sector from the 2nd Welch.

The proposed raid, which was to have been carried out on the 12th by B Company, did not take place. For on the 11th a patrol of C Company surprised a small German post on the Poelcapelle —Westroosebeke road and captured a sergeant-major and two men who supplied the necessary identifications : the raid was thus cancelled by a sensible ' higher authority ', who did not believe that raids were essential in order to keep the troops in good spirits. Would there had been more of the same mind, for many valuable lives were frittered away in raiding.

The line at this period was very quiet and on the 14th March the Gloucesters once again returned to Hugel Hollows, companies taking over the same positions. Two days later they marched back to Kempton Park Camp in reserve, though B Company was left behind in support in Pheasant Trench and in a post called Cat House. Until the 28th the Battalion remained at Kempton Park, the forward company being relieved every three days. During this period very large working parties were found, prin-cipally for the purpose of burying cables : little training could, therefore, be carried out.

On the 24th March, Lieut.-Colonel A. W. Pagan left to take over command of a brigade of the 61st Division. Excepting a

period of two months in the autumn of 1916, when he was away
wounded, Colonel Pagan had commanded the 28th from the
28th July 1915 until the 24th March 1918. In his own words :
' A good example of successful self-preservation.' [1]

Four days later Lieut.-Colonel J. L. F. Tweedie joined the
28th and assumed command : the 1st Gloucesters on that date
relieved the 2nd King's Royal Rifle Corps in the support battalion
area, moving on the 30th into the front line in the same sector
(Poelcapelle defences) as before. On the 31st active patrolling
took place with a view to carrying out a raid. During the night
(31st March/1st April) 2nd Lieutenant A. N. Gould took out
a reconnoitring patrol. While the reconnaissance was being made
Corpl. H. Glover and Privates Hunter and Austin were wounded.
The latter was able to walk back, but 2nd Lieutenant Gould and
Corpl. Glover had to assist Pte. Hunter, who was seriously
wounded, back to within 50 yards of the Battalion front line.
At this point, however, Corpl. Glover became exhausted and
2nd Lieutenant Gould went back to the trenches for stretcher-
bearers, finally bringing in both Glover and Hunter. For his
personal gallantry and successful reconnaissance 2nd Lieutenant
Gould was subsequently awarded the Military Cross.

During this tour in the line A Company was on the right
(Company Headquarters in Gloster Farm), B in the centre (Headquarters, Brewery), D on the left (Headquarters, Ferdan) and
C in support (Headquarters in Delta House). Battalion Headquarters were in Norfolk House.

The raid took place on the night of the 2nd/3rd April, the
raiding party consisting of 2nd Lieutenants Gould and Hampson
and 26 other ranks.

The objective of the raid was a German post on the Poelcapelle
—Spriet road. Brigade orders stated : ' The object of the raid
is to secure an identification and the importance of bringing back
a prisoner at the earliest possible moment will be impressed on
all ranks.'

The raiders were divided into two parties, each of one officer
and thirteen other ranks. Under an artillery barrage, which fell
at 10 p.m., the raiders ' went over '. Second Lieutenant Gould
with his party reached their objective and captured three prisoners:
2nd Lieutenant Hampson and his men also reached their objective,
but found it deserted. However, the latter officer later captured
a prisoner and shot another who had adopted a threatening

---

[1] From this date Colonel Pagan's notes on the 28th in France and
Flanders cease, and the story of the 1st Gloucesters must, therefore,
be rather less intimate.

attitude.   In all four prisoners were brought back, the Gloucesters' casualties being nil.

The success of the raid drew a message from the Army Commander (General Plumer), who wired his congratulations, the
identifications secured being very valuable.

On the 3rd April Corpl. Giles of B Company wounded a German
who was pinned to the ground during the whole day.   Every time
he attempted to move accurate rifle fire forced him to withdraw
to his shell-hole : at night he was captured.   The following
message was later received from the G.O.C., 1st Division :

' The credit for the capture of a German prisoner by the 1st Gloucestershire Regiment on April 3rd, 1918, lies with Corpl. Giles for his good
shooting, 2nd Lieutenant L. A. Denton for smartness in concerting all
measures and his promptitude in going out sufficiently early, and to the
sentries who kept such a close watch on the spot.'

On the night of the 6th/7th April the Battalion was relieved
by the 2nd Royal Irish Rifles and moved back to billets at Siege
Camp.

Though they were unaware of the fact the Gloucesters had
served their last tour in the Ypres Salient, for on the 8th April the
1st Division was transferred from the IInd Corps, Second Army,
to the Ist Corps, First Army.   On that day the 3rd Brigade
entrained at Peselhoek for the Fouquières area.   The Brigade
detrained at Chocques and Fouquereuil, the 1st Gloucesters
marching to Beuvry where they were billeted with the 1st South
Wales Borderers : the 2nd Welch were in Bethune.

The 1st Division was now disposed immediately south of the
La Bassée Canal (where the 2nd Brigade held the front line),
Marles-les-Mines (1st Brigade) and Vendin-lez-Bethune (3rd
Brigade).   Only the first-named Brigade held front-line trenches.
On the left of the 1st Division, and north of the Canal, the 55th
Division held the Givenchy—Festubert sector.

CHAPTER XXXI

THE GERMAN OFFENSIVE IN FLANDERS: 9TH— 29TH APRIL 1918

AT about 4 a.m. on the morning of, the 9th April the German guns opened with a bombardment of the greatest intensity, along practically the whole of the front between Lens and Armentières: it was the beginning of the second phase of the Great German Offensive of 1918.

Foiled in his first attempts on the Somme, from the 21st March to the beginning of April, the enemy had now turned his attention to our northern front, where he hoped to accomplish what he had failed to do a fortnight earlier farther south.

From south to north, when the Lys offensive was launched on the morning of the 9th, our line between the La Bassée Canal and Hollebeke (immediately south of the Ypres—Comines Canal) was held by the 55th, Portuguese, 40th, 25th, 19th and 9th Divisions. The enemy's first infantry attack was made at about 7 a.m. in thick fog (which made observation impossible), against the left brigade of the Portuguese Division. He broke into the trenches of the latter and, turning north and south, attacked the flanks of the 55th and 40th Divisions, which he endeavoured to roll up. With their inner flanks uncovered the two latter Divisions were forced to fall back, though the 55th Division on the first day of the battle lost only the outpost line in front of the left brigade.

At 10 a.m. a message was received at 1st Divisional Headquarters stating that the enemy had attacked Givenchy and had entered portions of our front line there. The 3rd Brigade was, therefore, ordered to ' stand to ' and the 1st Brigade was placed at ' one hour's notice to move '.

C and D Companies of the Gloucesters moved at 10.30 a.m. to the neighbourhood of Le Preol (Le Preol Bridge—Le Preol Keep—Tuning Fork) and at 2.30 p.m. A Company was sent off to Vauxhall Bridge and B Company to Westminster Bridge, two crossings over the La Bassée Canal, east of Le Preol. In these positions the 28th remained until, on the night of the 15th/16th April, they relieved the Liverpool Scottish of the 55th Division at Festubert, holding the village line: the 1st South Wales

Borderers were on the left, the Gloucesters holding as far north as Le Plantin. On the 16th the 1st Infantry Brigade took over the Givenchy sector on the right of the Gloucesters : the 2nd Brigade remained south of the La Bassée Canal.

On the 16th the Gloucesters captured one prisoner : 2nd Lieutenant J. E. Fearn and 1 other rank were wounded, otherwise the day was uneventful.

The following day Festubert and the Tuning Fork were heavily barraged by the enemy and the Gloucesters' casualties were 5 other ranks killed and 4 wounded. Another prisoner was captured— a German sergeant-major—from whom valuable information was received ' concerning intended attack on the 18th '.

THE BATTLE OF BETHUNE, 18TH APRIL

Hitherto the enemy's main attack had been directed towards practically the centre of a line north of the La Bassée Canal : his efforts at Givenchy and Festubert had been repulsed with heavy losses. But, having forced back our line to just west of Merville, Merris and Bailleul, he launched a great attack on the 18th against the southern flank, hoping no doubt to break through and gain possession of the La Bassée Canal and Bethune, which would have entailed a withdrawal of our line south of the Canal.

The official despatches record this attack in the following words :

' On the 18th April the enemy made a fresh effort to overcome our resistance on the southern flank of his attack. After a heavy bombardment, which at Givenchy is reported to have exceeded in intensity even the bombardment of the 9th April, his infantry attacked on nearly the whole front from Givenchy to west of Merville. At Givenchy and Festubert they succeeded at certain points in entering our positions, but after severe and continuous fighting lasting throughout the day, the troops of the 1st Division, under the command of Major-General E. P. Strickland, regained by counter-attack practically the whole of their original positions. Elsewhere the enemy failed to obtain even an initial success, being repulsed with exceedingly heavy loss at all points by the 4th and 61st Divisions.'

The 1st Gloucesters held the line from Le Plantin running due north to Cailloux, at which point a defensive flank had been thrown back in a westerly direction towards Route A Keep. A gap existed between Route A and the left of the Battalion. Thus any attack made upon the 28th would be from three sides. Companies were disposed as follows : A (Captain Handford) from Le Plantin to a point between the Dressing Station and the Piggeries ; B (Captain P. Mallett) held the works Festubert Central, Festubert Support and Festubert East ; D (Captain A. Seldon) held Malmahon Trench and Cailloux Keeps, north and south, with one platoon forming the defensive flank thrown back in the direction of Route A Keep, in which was the extreme right post of the South Wales Borderers ; C Company (Captain K. A. R. Smith) was in reserve at Battalion Headquarters, a small house about 150 yards south of Festubert on the road to Gorre.

The Lys Valley at this period of the year (April) was often wrapped in a thick mist which at times lasted all day. In April 1918, just as on the Somme in March, mist and fog had favoured the enemy's attack and had hidden the front line from our observers, blotting out even S.O.S. signals. It was seldom possible to see more than a few hundred yards and often not as much as 50 yards. Aeroplanes experienced the greatest difficulty in locating our and the enemy's trenches : in fact they sometimes bombed and machine-gunned friend as well as foe.

In confirmation of the warning given by the German sergeant-major captured on the previous day, the enemy's guns opened with an intense drum-fire of gas shells on the back areas and gun positions. Without intermission this continued until 6.30 a.m., our guns suffering severely.

' Knowing what was coming,' said Colonel Tweedie in his excellent report of this action, ' final arrangements were hastily run over, company commanders warned as far as possible, prominent works were temporarily evacuated for more advanced positions, and all ranks warned of what was coming. But for the impenetrable mist, we had a clear field of fire, plenty of ammunition, and all ranks were cool and confident of their ability to deal with the opposing infantry.'

' The amount of gas fired by the enemy was enormous, mostly " yellow cross ", and what with the added inconvenience of the mist, and dirt from falling buildings, coupled with the deafening noise, some anxious hours were spent by the Battalion.

' At 6.30 a.m. the enemy's gunners shortened their range and came down on the village line, Festubert Village, Battalion Headquarters and the roads leading to Gorre. Fortunately our trenches were in splendid condition—the village line had been in existence since 1914, and having been worked on, repaired and strengthened over years, both parapet and parados of the breastworks were from 6 to 8 feet thick, so that even 5·9's falling in the soft earth just short or just over did little material damage.

' About 8.15 a.m. the leading infantry attack commenced, the Huns swarming out of their front line. As a guide to their own artillery the leading wave kept a chain of Verey lights going, and long before the infantry were visible these lights, seen dimly through the mist, heralded their approach. Long ere this stage had been reached all telephonic communication had been cut and we were dependent for inter-communication on our runners, a picked body of men who may have been equalled but can never have been surpassed for gallantry or sustained devotion to duty. Several had been lost in attempting to get through to Battalion Headquarters, but shortly after 9 a.m. two gallant fellows gained Headquarters through a tornado of shell with a note from Captain Mallett saying the Germans were making no headway and that the " Old Braggs " had got their tails well up.

'That the Germans had made no headway was true as regards B and D Companies, but unfortunately opposite A Company, in Le Plantin, where the Le Preol Wood comes right up to the village, the enemy had met with a certain amount of success. A serious breach had occurred in A Company's line. Here a patrolled gap of 80 yards had been enlarged by shell-fire to some 200 yards, cutting A Company in two. Captain Handford was left with two platoons on the right of the gap. Lieutenants Hall and Dobson with the remaining two platoons on the left. Meanwhile the Company had suffered severely, Lieutenant G. M. Vaisey [1] having been mortally hit.

'Although subjected to a hot fire the advance could not be checked and a number of Germans got through the gap and gained the orchards and buildings in Le Plantin, but Lieutenant Hall promptly organized his line, threw back a defensive flank and prevented all reinforcements from reaching the Germans who had penetrated the gap in the first rush. Soon after the hostile infantry attack opened the fog lifted and, as the ground was devoid of all cover, they suffered severely. Meanwhile as soon as the Germans realized that their infantry were not progressing they ran up some guns into the open immediately behind the old British line and, firing over open sights, came into action against our works and the village of Festubert.

'Opposite the Cailloux Keep, where D Company were in position, the leading wave was within 150 yards of our wire before the fog, lifting, disclosed them and here they made no further headway. Festubert East was blown to bits. When 2nd Lieutenant Hudson was left with only eight men of his platoon, he ordered them to fall back on Festubert Support. Second-Lieutenant Hudson managed to find his way to Headquarters. A couple of minutes later he was killed by a shell. His Platoon Sergeant (Newman) had been killed and the Vickers team destroyed.

'Meanwhile B and D Companies continued to do sterling work. With their Lewis guns and with Vickers guns belonging to the 55th Division, they repulsed all attacks. No Germans succeeded in getting within 100 yards of their works. During this period our expenditure of ammunition was very great. Each man carried 175 rounds, and yet one platoon of B Company, with its Lewis guns, exhausted the contents of no fewer than eight boxes.

'The enemy, who had penetrated into La Plantin, now had command of Quinque Rue which we were compelled to use. Machine-gunners, runners and stretcher-bearers were shot down as fast as they appeared on the road. A house with a tower, occupied by the Battalion Scouts, was brought down and all the scouts imprisoned in the cellar. A German officer, who presented himself at the door, revolver in hand, was himself blown to bits by a shell before receiving a reply to his demand to surrender.

'The Dressing-Station was penetrated by a 5·9-inch shell which killed and wounded several of the medical staff, and Lieutenant Weir, who suffered a fractured skull. Lieutenant Fairey, Medical Officer,

---

[1] Died of wounds 19th April 1918.

who was inside at the time and partially buried, only reported this contretemps when the action had been brought to a successful close.

' Turning to Battalion Headquarters and our extreme left we come to the most critical time. A clear view of the enemy was presented, swarming down our Route A, close under their own barrage, and though three platoons of C Company were pushed well out into shell holes in the open to render what assistance they could, the enemy were seen to gain the Keep, thereby getting well in our left rear. This, with their occupation of Le Plantin, practically cut off the Battalion, for the open road to Gorre was under fire from both flanks. No sooner had the Germans captured Route A Keep than they at once commenced to work across into the rear of D Company. Lieutenant Cox, in command of the platoon forming the defensive flank, was killed, and shortly before 11 a.m. Sergt.-Major Biddle of D Company succeeded in getting through to Battalion Headquarters to ask for support. No men could be spared. Lieutenant Gosling, with his platoon (C Company), had been sent off to counter-attack Le Plantin and, in co-operation with Lieutenant Hall, to clear the Germans out at all costs. The remaining three platoons of C Company were heavily engaged with the enemy advancing from Route A. All that could be done was to scrape together twenty men of Battalion Headquarters consisting of Signallers under Sergt. Cole, cooks, orderlies and batmen. This party, under the command of Captain Smith, was ordered out to occupy the north end of Festubert and, facing east, to check the German advance. Working their way through the gardens at the back of the village, they gained their position and checked the hostile advance, but it cost the party the life of the Signalling Sergeant—Sergt. Cole, D.C.M.—a gallant soldier who had done splendid work for the Battalion.

' At this stage no runner had succeeded in getting through to Brigade Headquarters or, if they had, they had failed on their return journey. So Lieutenant Stotesbury, Signalling Officer, was ordered to find his way to a brigade headquarters (55th Division) at Le Preol and report the situation. This he succeeded in doing.

' Our casualties at this stage amounted to 8 officers and some 150 other ranks and, though not crippling, were sufficiently serious, taken in conjunction with the situation on both flanks. The mist had cleared and enemy planes, flying very low, were busy bombing us and shooting up the various keeps in the line. All this pointed to a further effort. The Adjutant, Captain Stephenson, who had been wounded but had remained with the Battalion, was sent down the line with a carrying party to confirm the report previously despatched by Lieutenant Stotesbury. Unfortunately he (Captain Stephenson) was again wounded on his way down, but succeeded in gaining Brigade Headquarters at Le Preol and giving a clear account of the situation.

' Battalion Headquarters was by now being subjected to very severe shelling by 5·9's, coupled with a severe machine-gun fire from the direction of Route A. As there seemed a likelihood of Battalion Headquarters having to vacate their quarters and join the companies in the line, all Orderly Room records and material were destroyed and the last two pigeons released. The first pigeon went off well, but unfortunately in the direction of La Bassée, the second was blown to bits by a shell before it had flown 50 yards. Before any further decision was made reports were received from D Company that the attack on our left had evidently failed as large bodies of the enemy could be seen retiring in disorder along the Neuve Chapelle road.

' In the meantime a report was received that Route A had been recaptured and that our left was secure. The report was incorrect but, owing to the enemy's retirement, there was no cause for further anxiety on this flank.

' The situation at Le Plantin was still obscure and unsatisfactory. A considerable number of the enemy were known to be in the village and orchards and their snipers made it impossible for runners to get through. The enemy had to be cleared out before nightfall, so the C.O. made his way back to Preol Wood and found a company of the 2nd Welch occupying the Tuning Fork trenches. On the situation being explained to the officer in command, Captain Simms, he at once agreed to advance and clear Le Plantin. Lieutenants Gosling and Hall, however, had the situation in hand and a company of Camerons had arrived in support of Le Plantin. Lieutenant Gosling's party, working their way through south of Le Plantin, accounted for many Germans, including the snipers who had taken heavy toll of men crossing the Quinque Rue, and finally the remnants of the party were found hiding in a large shell-hole.

' Almost the worst part of their failure was now experienced by the Germans. By midday they appeared to realize their attack had failed and that they could not hope for reinforcements. As soon as the fog lifted large numbers, who had taken cover in the shell-holes between the village line and the old British line, now attempted to crawl back, but were shot in scores in the act of crossing from one shell-hole to the next. Very few prisoners were taken, not more than a dozen, and these were mostly wounded. One lucky individual, a German-American, succeeded in getting into Cailloux Keep. Taking his courage in his hands, he suddenly loomed out of the mist, hands in his pockets and a large cigar in his mouth, and announced to our nearest men that he " was thoroughly fed up ".

' By 5 p.m. the action was over, and but for some desultory shelling of Festubert by 8-inch guns, all was quiet. About 10 p.m. the 2nd Welch Regiment was sent up from Gorre to relieve the Battalion. With them came our Echelon B men, as the Welch had suffered severely from shell-fire whilst in support at Gorre.

' In this attack the enemy made no attempt to advance in mass formation or successive lines, but tried the method of infiltration by groups. These groups consisted of machine-gun teams and parties of five or six men (infantry). One-half were armed to fight, the remainder carried blankets, boots, ammunition and three days' rations. Every soldier carried a map giving him his line of advance and his final objective—in this instance Bethune.'

The relief was satisfactorily carried through but casualties continued to occur, 2nd Lieutenant Gould being badly hit after B Company had arrived in their billets in the outskirts of Gorre.

The magnificent fight of the 1st Gloucesters on the 18th April drew special thanks and praise from all commanders in the field from Sir Douglas Haig downwards. Their own Brigadier (Brig.-General H. H. Morant) wrote to Colonel Tweedie as follows :

' I wish to express my admiration of the gallant defence put up by your Battalion yesterday. The tenacity with which they held their positions when attacked in front, flank and rear by four regiments (as officially stated by the Corps) has earned the praise of commanders of all grades. Under the peculiar circumstances of the sector you held, it was fortunate that a battalion, which had previously fought under similar circumstances, should have been in the line.

' All ranks fought as though mindful of the emblem they wear and fully justified the wearing of it.

' I trust your casualties are not as heavy as might have been expected.'

The Battalion had indeed repeated (though under modern conditions) that splendid incident at Alexandria in 1801 when they fought back-to-back and for which they were specially granted the privilege of wearing the Regimental Badge at the back as well as in the front of their headdress.

The casualties suffered by the 1st Gloucesters in this gallant repulse of the enemy were : 2nd Lieutenants G. B. Hudson, L. J. Cox and G. M. Vaisey killed : Captain Stephenson and 2nd Lieutenants Fearn, Calvert-Fisher, Weir and Gould wounded. In other ranks the losses were 53 killed or missing and 123 wounded.[1]

The official despatches state that for nearly a week following the failure of the German advance on the 18th April there was fighting on the Lys front, but the attack gradually died down, though in the neighbourhood of Festubert some sharp actions were fought. The strong point known as Route A Keep changed hands several times, but the Gloucesters were not involved in these actions, for on the 21st the 3rd Brigade was relieved by the 166th Brigade (55th Division) and moved south of the La Bassée Canal.

---

[1] The following decorations for gallantry during the battle were subsequently awarded : Bar to D.S.O., Lieut.-Colonel J. L. F. Tweedie ; Military Cross, Captain F. Seldon, Lieutenant G. N. Gosling, 2nd Lieutenants J. L. Hall and A. W. Dobson ; D.C.M., No. 9795 Sergt. W. Corbett, No. 32165 Pte. A. Mitcham ; Bar to D.C.M., C.S.M.s W. Biddle and W. Reece. The Military Medal was awarded to 24 N.C.O.s and men.

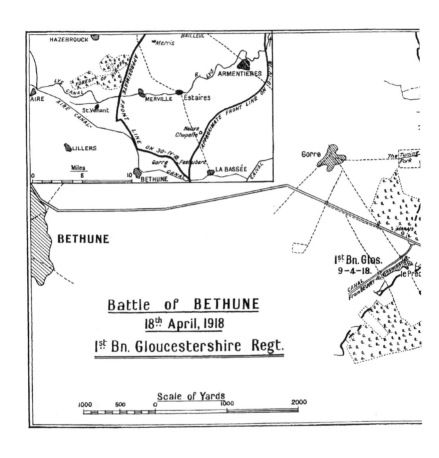

Battle of BETHUNE
18th April, 1918
1st Bn. Gloucestershire Regt.

Scale of Yards

1000   500   0   1000   2000

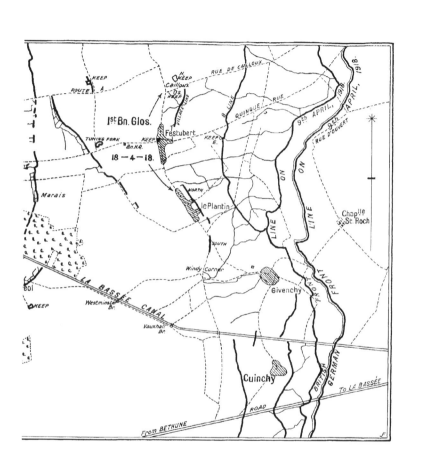

KEEP

ROUTE A

N. KEEP
Cailloux
D5 KEEP

RUE DE CAILLOUX

1st Bn. Glos.

VILLERRINE

B LINE

QUINQUE RUE

9th APRIL 1918.

9th APRIL 1918.

TUNING FORK
KEEP
Bn. H.Q.

Festubert

KEEP E.

RUE D'OUVERT

18—4—18.

Marais

NORTH

le Plantin

Chap.lle St. Roch

SOUTH

LINE ON

FRONT LINE ON

NORTH

Windy Corner

Givenchy

BRITISH GERMAN

Eol

LA BASSÉE CANAL

KEEP

Westminster Br.

Vauxhall Br.

Cuinchy

To LA BASSÉE

ROAD

From BETHUNE

CHAPTER XXXII

THE PERIOD OF ACTIVE DEFENCE

THE 1st Gloucesters, after being relieved by the 1/10th Liverpool Scottish of the 55th Division, marched back to billets at Sailly-la-Bourse : they had taken their part, and had done it splendidly, in helping to stem the flood-tide of the grey masses which had threatened to overrun the southern portion of the Lys battlefield.

' The Old Braggs ' had come out of the struggle with their ' tails right up '—to use a war expression. They rested on the 22nd and went to the baths, then on the 23rd the Battalion relieved the 5th Sherwood Foresters in the Cambrin sector south of the La Bassée Canal. But it was only a twenty-four hours' tour, and on the 25th the Gloucesters were once more at Sailly-la-Bourse undergoing training.

On the 28th they went into the Hohenzollern sector, but the tour was uneventful and on the 6th May, having been relieved by the 2nd Welch, A, C and D Companies moved to Annequin in Brigade Reserve, while B Company moved to the Grenay—Noyelles line, attached to the Welch.

By the end of April the German onrush had been stemmed for the time being, though the situation on the British front was still critical. Practically the whole of the British Armies in France and Flanders had been used to resist the immense weight of the enemy's attacks during March and April, and as a result the former were greatly weakened. Reinforcements from England, and considerable bodies of troops from other theatres of the War, were being hurried to France, but they took time to arrive and even then they had to be trained, to become acclimatized to the conditions in France, or if they were new drafts to become assimilated with their various units. But still the Armies were weak and at the beginning of May no less than eight divisions were reduced to cadre strength and their personnel transferred to those divisions which needed bringing up to establishment. In all, there remained available for operations on the British front some forty-five British infantry divisions, most of them below establishment. Three-fourths of them had already been heavily engaged and were urgently in need of rest and they contained a large proportion of youths, partially trained and totally inexperienced recruits.

The French had not suffered nearly as heavily as we had, nevertheless they had been obliged to employ a substantial proportion of their reserves in the fighting south of the Somme and north of the Lys.[1]

The American Army, though rapidly increasing in numbers, was not yet ready to take the field in sufficient numbers to materially affect the situation.

The enemy still possessed sufficient superiority in force to retain the initiative, but if he wished to turn that superiority to good account he would have to act in a comparatively limited time.

Faced by this situation, therefore, the Allies set themselves to preserve their front unbroken until August, by which time there would be a reasonable chance of regaining the initiative.

' The policy governing the actions of the forces under my command was the maintenance of an active front, whereby our line might be preserved unbroken while every opportunity was taken to rest and train our sorely-tried divisions. As the strength and efficiency of our divisions were restored, minor operations of gradually increasing scope, but with limited objectives, could be carried out with greater frequency. These would serve to keep alive the fighting spirit of the troops and could be used to effect local improvements in our line where such improvements were considered necessary either for defence or for attack.' [2]

The despatches then state that :

' At the outset of this period the most pressing need after that of filling up the gaps in our divisions, was to close the breaches which the German advances had made in our successive defensive systems.'

Although the 1st Gloucesters were not actually in a part of the line which had been broken by the enemy's advance, they were none the less busily engaged on the defences when out of the front line. On the 8th May they were at work at Annequin, south of the La Bassée Canal. The enemy was expected to attack on the 10th and all was ready for his reception, but no attack materialized. A Company lost its commander (Captain E. Handford) on this date, wounded, whilst conducting a reconnoitring party of the 1st Northants, who were to relieve the Gloucesters on the 12th. On relief Battalion Headquarters and B Company proceeded to Nœux-les-Mines, while A, C and D Companies, under Major

[1] On the 26th March, Marshal Foch had assumed command of the Allied Forces in France and Flanders.

[2] Official Despatches.

J. R. Guild, moved to Cambrin where they were attached to the
1st Infantry Brigade : these companies rejoined Battalion Headquarters on the 16th. Several days' training followed during
which the 3rd Brigade sports were held. On the 20th, however,
the Gloucesters returned to the front line. The next day the
Brigadier (Brig.-General H. H. Morant) was wounded and
Colonel Tweedie assumed temporary command of the Brigade,
Major Guild commanding the Battalion.

The Battalion Diary now begins to show the worrying tactics
which were eventually so successful in keeping the enemy continually on the alert, as well as causing him increasing casualties.
The enemy's guns were only spasmodically active. On the 21st
there was, during the evening, a considerable amount of gas
shelling, both on the sector held by the Gloucesters and on their
left. But the 27th was quiet. At night a patrol, consisting of
2nd Lieutenant W. C. Hampson and 9 other ranks, found two
dead Germans in No-Man's Land, whose papers and identity
discs were brought in. On the 23rd Colonel Tweedie returned
to the Battalion, as Brig.-General Sir W. A. I. Kay had arrived
on appointment to command the 3rd Brigade.

At 12.30 a.m. four hundred drums of gas were projected on to
the enemy's line, while the 60th Rifles, on the right of the 28th,
raided the enemy and brought back five prisoners. The same night
2nd Lieutenant T. H. Barnard, patrolling No-Man's Land, found
a position on the reverse slope of a crater from which observation
of the enemy's line could be obtained. Lieutenant Barnard,
taking out one man with him, occupied the post all day and whilst
reconnoitring a disused trench at 5 p.m. encountered an enemy
post.

The spell of fine weather broke on the 24th and heavy rain fell
during the morning. Company reliefs took place. In the evening the enemy was treated to another dose of gas, two hundred projectors being discharged on to the enemy's lines at
Auchy.

At 7 a.m. on the 25th 2nd Lieutenant Barnard and 10 other
ranks went out to capture the post discovered on the 23rd, but
in the meantime it had been heavily wired and the attempt was
abortive.

On the 30th the C.O. decided to raid the enemy's trenches on
the 4th June, and for this purpose D Company was relieved by
a company of the Welch and moved back to Cambrin to train
for the operations.

Hostile aerial and artillery activity increased towards the end
of the month, largely due, no doubt, to our own activities.

18

The Battalion Diary for the 1st June admirably sums up conditions in the line :

'The present tour in the line is quiet. Enemy artillery is inactive and does not respond to the activity of our guns and trench mortars which are engaged on wire cutting. There are occasional trench-mortar duels at dawn and dusk.'

During the afternoon of the 4th D Company from Cambrin relieved C Company in the left front line of the Battalion sector, C Company moving back to left support in order to take over the line held by the attached company of 2nd Welch.

The raid took place during the evening on the enemy's outpost and support lines west of Auchy. Artillery, trench mortars and machine guns co-operated and in addition a smoke barrage was put down by a special company of Royal Engineers, while dummy projectiles were fired on to suspected enemy headquarters. Feint barrages put down on the right and left flanks of the raid were also adopted in order to deceive the enemy.

The raiding party consisted of Captain C. F. L. Templer, 2nd Lieutenants Mayell and Pullen and 100 other ranks. Twelve men of the Royal Engineers with mobile charges for destroying dug-outs accompanied this party, and 2nd Lieutenant Barnard and 6 other ranks of C Company were ordered to deal with an enemy post lying in front of their lines. In order that the raiders could ' go over ' in the twilight and return in darkness zero hour was fixed at 9.30 p.m.

At zero the artillery barrage (described in the records as ' perfect ') fell and the raiders left their assembly positions in two waves, the second wave leap-frogging the first on the first objective, which apparently was the post lying out in front of the enemy's lines. The first wave (under 2nd Lieutenant Barnard) captured the post with great dash and thoroughness. The second wave then leap-frogged the first, but owing to the smoke clouds from the north and the dust created by bursting shells drifting down on to the area and blinding the raiders, about one-third of the second wave lost touch and direction. The remainder, however, reached their objective, bombed the dug-outs in the enemy's second line and returned with two prisoners of the 209th R.I.R., having also killed many Germans.

Fortunately the enemy's artillery was prevented by the dust and smoke from seeing the S.O.S. signals sent up from his own front line and when his barrage did fall it was both light and wild. Captain C. F. L. Templer was unfortunately killed by a stray shell whilst on his way back across No-Man's Land : 2nd Lieutenant Barnard was slightly wounded.   One other rank was killed, 6 wounded and 1 was missing.

In connection with this raid the following decorations were subsequently awarded : C.S.M. W. Biddle the Military Cross, L/Corpl. E. Gregory bar to the Military Medal and Military Medals to Corpl. H. J. Hook, L/Corpl. F. Powis and Pte. C. Leach.[1]

On the 5th the Gloucesters were relieved and moved back to rest billets in Nœux-les-Mines, but with the exception of the ' three days fever ' or ' P.U.O.' which broke out in the Battalion on the 6th and caused many ' casualties ', there is little of further interest to record during the remainder of the month.   The Battalion went into a new sector—Hohenzollern right sub-sector —on the 17th, but the enemy was even more inactive than he had been in the Auchy line.

All units now, when out of the line, were training hard and indeed it was almost a rest to go into the forward trenches, though occasionally the enemy took it into his head to put down heavy bombardments.   On the 17th July, for instance (the Gloucesters being then in the Cambrin right sub-sector), the German trench mortars heavily bombarded posts held by the front companies. The garrisons of the posts had, however, been withdrawn as our guns were engaged in wire cutting.

At 4.30 a.m. the next morning Sergt. Roberts took out a patrol and discovered three German posts, all occupied.   Leaving the remainder of his patrol to watch the two outside posts, Sergt. Roberts and Pte. Gaffney bombed the central post and afterwards shot its occupants.   For this little exploit Roberts and Gaffney were each awarded the Military Medal.

B Company made a small raid on a post on the 20th, but it was unoccupied.   Nothing else of importance transpired during July.

August the 1st found the 1st Gloucesters billeted in Nœux-les-Mines, where training occupied the Battalion for a week and more. During the evening of the 3rd the final of the Divisional Rugby Cup was played, the 1st Gloucesters being pitted against the 6th Welch.[2]   The latter won after a close and exciting game.   In the Divisional Horse Show, which took place the next afternoon

---

[1] In the King's Birthday Honours List the following awards were notified : Captain T. R. B. Moir the Military Cross ; L/Corpl. A. Froud the D.C.M. ; Sergt. R. E. D. Brasington the Meritorious Service Medal and Pte. H. Preston the Long Service and Good Conduct Medal.

[2] This was the final which should have taken place in Le Clipon Camp in October 1917.   By this time the Gloucesters had lost at least half their team.

and evening, the Battalion Transport obtained second prize. On the 9th the whole Battalion marched to Bois d'Olhain, near Barlin, for tactical training. The next morning the Brigade Inter-Company Football Final took place. The opposing teams both belonged to the 1st Gloucesters, i.e. C. and D Companies ; C Company proved the victors. In the afternoon the Battalion relieved the 1st Black Watch in support in the Hohenzollern sector, at Annequin. One more tour in the front line followed, then on the 21st, after relief, the Gloucesters ' embussed ' near Barlin and proceeded to Tangry, near Pernes, arriving at their destination at about midnight. The whole of the 1st Division had now been relieved by the 16th Division for the purpose of training and rest, the 3rd Brigade being located in the Pressy-les-Pernes—Tangry—Hestrus—Sachin area.

This training period lasted only about nine days, for at 1 a.m. on the 31st the Gloucesters received a warning order to be ready at very short notice to move from Tangry. Subsequently orders were received at 4.30 p.m. and the Battalion marched to Pernes and entrained for Arras. The 1st Division was now attached to the Canadian Corps. On arrival at Arras, at 4.30 a.m. on the 1st September, the Gloucesters marched to billets at Achicourt.

The strength of the Battalion was now 32 officers and 871 other ranks, with Lieut.-Colonel J. L. F. Tweedie in command and Major J. R. Guild second-in-command.

The Gloucesters rested throughout the 1st September, but at night (at 8.30 p.m.) marched out of Achicourt towards the front line, as the 1st Division was the reserve division in the Canadian Corps. The 28th halted for the night in trenches in front of Wancourt.

CHAPTER XXXIII

THE SECOND BATTLE OF ARRAS, 1918

THE BATTLE OF THE DROCOURT—QUÉANT LINE, 2ND–3RD SEPTEMBER

AFTER four months' trench warfare the 1st Gloucesters were now about to take part again in major operations, for the great advance had begun and the British Armies were moving forward along the whole front from east of Amiens to south of Ypres.

While the 1st Division was engaged in stationary warfare between Lens and the La Bassée Canal the enemy further south was being heavily attacked and driven back with enormous losses in prisoners and war material. First he had been forced out of his positions east of Amiens on the 8th August, which General Ludendorff called ' the Black Day of the German Army ', whereby the Paris—Amiens Railway was gained : the enemy lost in this battle 22,000 prisoners and over four hundred guns as well as ground to a depth of 12 miles. Next he was attacked on a front of about 33 miles from our junction with the French at Lihons to Mercatel (The Battle of Albert, 21st–23rd August) with great success, thousands of prisoners and more guns falling into our hands as well as extensive gains of ground. On the 31st August the Second Battle of Bapaume, 1918, opened and by the 3rd September Péronne, St. Quentin and the old Somme Battle-field of 1916 were in our hands with the Germans in retreat to the Hindenburg Line.

By the 25th August our advance had formed a salient of the German positions opposite Arras and the moment had arrived for the First Army to extend the flank of the attack to the north. By driving eastwards from Arras, covered on the left by the Rivers Scarpe and Sensée, the First Army was to turn the enemy's positions on the Somme Battlefield and cut his railway communications which ran south-westwards across their front.

On the 26th, therefore, the Canadian Corps attacked the enemy's positions astride the Scarpe River, and Wancourt and Guémappe and the hill and village of Monchy-le-Preux fell into our hands. The following day Chérisy, Vis-en-Artois, the Bois du Sart, Rœux and Gavrelle were taken and by the end of the month the high ground east of Chérisy and Haucourt, Eterpigny and the area between the Sensée and Scarpe Rivers west of the Trinquis Brook had been cleared and occupied. North of the Scarpe we held Plouvain.

The progress on this front had now brought us to within assaulting distance of the powerful trench system running from the Hindenburg Line at Quéant to the Lens defences about Drocourt (known as the Drocourt—Quéant Line), the breaking of which would turn the whole of the enemy's organized positions on a wide front southwards.

It was for this operation and the storming of the Drocourt—Quéant Line that the 1st Division had been put into the battle to support the Canadian Corps.

The Battalion Diary of the 1st Gloucesters records that at 5.30 a.m. on the 2nd September (the attack actually began at 5 a.m.) a general attack began. The Canadians attacked on a front of about 4½ miles south of the Trinquis Brook.

The 1st Gloucesters, being in support of a Canadian division, moved forward during the day as the attacking troops advanced and took up a position with the Arras—Cambrai road on their left and Cachencourt Wood on the right flank. In this position the Battalion remained until the afternoon of the 3rd when, with the remainder of the 3rd Brigade (1st Division) the 28th moved up to support the 1st and 2nd Brigades who had relieved the 4th British Division in the front line, the Gloucesters being in front of Vis-en-Artois and behind Rémy. They were shelled during the afternoon and evening and 4 other ranks were wounded.

The Drocourt—Quéant Line was broken and the Hindenburg Line stormed, the enemy being thrown into precipitate retreat on the whole front south of it. By nightfall the British line had been pushed forward to a depth of over 3 miles along the Arras—Cambrai road and had reached the outskirts of Buissy ; Cagnicourt, Villers-lez-Cagnicourt and Dury were captured. Eight thousand prisoners and many guns had been taken.

Throughout the 4th and 5th the Gloucesters remained in front of Vis-en-Artois, shelled occasionally by long-range guns. On the 6th the Battalion moved to trenches about 4 kilometres east of Arras where bivouacs were constructed. In this place the 28th stayed until the early morning of the 8th when they paraded and marched to billets in Noyelle-Vion, arriving there during the early afternoon.

But the 1st Division was again transferred to another part of the front and the Gloucesters, marching to Aubigny early on the 10th, entrained and arrived at Villers-Bretonneux near midnight, where they were billeted in ruined houses in the town. The 1st Division was now in reserve to the IXth Corps, Fourth Army, commanded by General Rawlinson.

CHAPTER XXXIV

THE BATTLES OF THE HINDENBURG LINE:
12TH SEPTEMBER—9TH OCTOBER

EPÉHY, 18TH SEPTEMBER

AFTER the successful storming of the Drocourt—Quéant Line, the results of the Battles of Amiens, Bapaume and the Scarpe now became evident, for on the night of the 2nd/3rd September the enemy fell back rapidly along the whole front of the Third Army and the right of the First Army. When darkness had fallen on the 2nd September he had taken up positions along the general line of the Canal du Nord from Péronne to Ypres, thence east of Hermies, Inchy-en-Artois and Ecourt St. Quentin to the Sensée River east of Lécluse. On the 3rd he began to withdraw also from the east bank of the Somme south of Péronne, and by the night of the 8th held the general line Vermand, Epéhy, Havrincourt, thence along the eastern bank of the Canal du Nord.

The official despatches thus describe the Hindenburg Line, in the capture of which the Gloucesters subsequently took part :

' From the neighbourhood of Havrincourt, southwards, the enemy's main line of resistance was the well-known Hindenburg Line which, after passing through that village, ran south-east across the Beaucamp, La Vacquerie and Bonavis Ridges to the Scheldt Canal at Bantouzelle, whence it followed the line of the Canal to St. Quentin. In front of this trench system strong German forces held formidable positions about Havrincourt and Epéhy, which had to be taken before a final attack on the Hindenburg Line could be undertaken. By successful operations carried out during the second and third weeks of September these different defences were secured and our line advanced to within assaulting distance of the enemy's main line of resistance.'

The Battle of Havrincourt was fought on the 12th September, in which that village and Trescault were taken by the Third Army and positions secured, of considerable importance in view of future operations.

On the right of the Third Army the IXth Corps and Australian Corps (Fourth Army) continued to push forward with light forces to positions from which to attack the Hindenburg Line on their

front.   By the evening of the 17th September they had captured
Holnon Village and Wood and Maissemy and were approaching
Le Verguier and Templeux-le-Grand.

In the operations of the IXth Corps the 1st Gloucesters took
part.

On the 12th September the Battalion ' embussed ' at Villers-
Bretonneux and were carried to Tertry on the St. Quentin front,
the 1st Division on the 11th having taken over the left half of
the front from the 32nd Division between Attilly and Vermand.

The long, perfectly-straight road from Villers-Bretonneux,
which crosses the Somme River at Brie and continues its way
to Vermand, was not unknown to the 28th.   The Battalion, as
this history shows, had not been involved in the March Retreat,
1918, but about a year previously, during the time we were
hurrying the enemy back to the Hindenburg Line, the 1st
Gloucesters were well acquainted with the road from Villers-
Bretonneux to the Somme and the Villages of Cérisy, Morcourt,
Chuignes, Proyart, Foucaucourt, Assevillers, Brie and a score more.
And now they were being carried along that very same road for
the same purpose, hurrying the enemy back eastwards and, for
the last time, across the old Somme battlefields.

But on this day of September, 1918, how many were there
with the Battalion who had been with it in February and March,
1917 ?

On the 11th the Fourth Army Commander had reported
that as a result of the operations of the early days of September,
his troops on the 11th were close up to, and in the centre had
occupied, part of the old British Reserve Line of March, 1918,
including the localities of Holnon, Maissemy, Jeancourt, Hesbe-
court and St. Emilie.   But east of this line the enemy was very
strongly posted.   He held five distinct lines of defence, the first
of which contained the important tactical localities of Fresnoy-
le-Petit, the high ground south of Berthaucourt, Le Verguier,
Grand Priel Woods, the high ground north and south of Hargicourt, Ronssoy, Basse-Boulogne and Epéhy-Peizières.   These
positions the enemy held during the time he was withdrawing
to the Hindenburg Line in 1917, and they had been held by us
as our main line of resistance in March, 1918.   They were all
naturally-strong positions but had been made still more formidable with wire, trenches and dug-outs, and they were now held
by the enemy who showed every intention of hanging on to them
as long as possible.   Some stiff fighting, therefore, lay before
the Gloucesters, whose first efforts were to be made against
Maissemy.

On arriving at Tertry the Battalion marched to the neighbour-hood of Villeveque, where they relieved the 16th Lancashire Fusiliers. The 28th were then disposed as follows : A Company along the bank of the Omignon Brook, near a wood ; D Company (front Company) was established on the railway embankment near Marteville, with C Company in support near Marteville Cemetery ; B Company was in rear of C in a sunken road. The whole of the 3rd Brigade was now in the front line : 1st Gloucesters on the right, 1st South Wales Borderers on the left, 2nd Welch Regiment in support. Nothing of interest happened during the remainder of the day, but one officer (Lieutenant G. F. Pullen) and one other rank were wounded.

On the morning of the 13th, D Company took over the front line from a battalion of Manchesters of the 32nd Division, A, B and C Companies taking up positions in the railway embank-ment immediately south-east of Marteville.

Early on the 14th patrols from D Company pushed forward to a sunken road near the Keeper's House,[1] Vermand, and the ridge east of it. Later C Company, on the right, B in the centre and D on the left, advanced under an artillery bar-rage and captured the Maissemy Ridge. The enemy counter-attacked heavily with bombs, but was repulsed. Captain A. Seldon and Company-Sergeant-Major W. Biddle were, how-ever, both severely wounded. Soon after dark A Company relieved D.

At 5.30 a.m. the next morning A, B and C Companies again attacked under an artillery barrage with a view to gaining the high ground.

This attack was splendidly carried out and resulted not only in the capture of all objectives, but nine prisoners and ten machine guns as well : in addition many of the enemy were killed. The enemy's snipers were particularly annoying throughout the day and caused many casualties in the Battalion. When darkness had fallen the Gloucesters (as a result of the day's operations) had lost Lieutenant E. Richardson, 2nd Lieutenant W. H. Lam-bert and Lieutenant G. E. Birkett, R.A.M.C., wounded, 13 other ranks killed and 47 wounded.

The Corps Commander (Lieut.-General Sir W. Braithwaite) wired his congratulations to the Battalion on the capture of ' some very important ground '.

[1] Close to Keeper's House and just inside Holnon Wood was a small quarry. During this attack the 28th found in this quarry a field kitchen belonging to the 2/6th Gloucesters which had evidently been destroyed during the German offensive in March 1918.

The Gloucesters were relieved and moved back into Brigade Reserve near Vermand.

Positions had now been gained along the front of the Fourth Army from which to attack the first of the enemy's defensive systems, and on the evening of the 17th all arrangements had been completed to attack the enemy at 5.20 a.m. on the 18th.

The 1st Division attacked with the 1st Brigade on the right, 2nd on the left and 3rd in reserve, at Vermand. The 1st Gloucesters, therefore, saw none of the fighting, though the Battalion was moved up to the Maissemy Ridge in support of the 1st Brigade. Battalion Headquarters were hit by a shell during the day and the new Medical Officer (Captain Kirkland), who had only arrived on the 17th to take the place of Lieutenant Birkett, was killed. Another Medical Officer—Captain Montgomery—joined the Gloucesters on the 19th.

Throughout the 19th, 20th, 21st and 22nd the Gloucesters remained on the Maissemy Ridge and, with the exception of light shell-fire, the period was uneventful.

The general results of the battle on the 18th had been to penetrate the enemy's defences to a depth of 3 miles, the greatest advance being along the centre of the Fourth Army front. The 1st Division had captured the first and half of the second objectives : but the left of the IXth Corps had been held up. For several days following the 18th isolated attacks went on along the Army front.

On the 21st 3rd Brigade Headquarters issued orders for an attack on Fresnoy-le-Petit (which had not been completed on the 18th). The attack was to be carried out by the 3rd Brigade in conjunction with a brigade of the 6th Division, on the right, and the 2nd Brigade on the left.

The 2nd Welch were to attack on the right and the 1st Gloucesters the village, on the left.

At 8 p.m. on the 23rd the 28th moved off to take up their assembly positions west of Fresnoy and east of Cartenoy Wood. A Company (Lieutenant J. S. M. Carnon) assembled north of the Fresnoy—Gricourt road in two lines, two platoons in each line. Two platoons of B Company, under Captain P. Mallett, acted as ' moppers up ' in support of D right front Company. C Company (Lieutenant G. E. Chaney) was in reserve.

At 5 a.m. on the 24th before it was light, under a creeping barrage, the attack began, the three companies of Gloucesters advancing as formed up on the 23rd. The Battalion's right flank was on Bugeaud Trench and its left along the northern edge of Marronniers Wood. The final objective was Cornouillers Wood and a trench running south to Bugeaud Trench.

The right front Company (D) went straight through, under the barrage, to its objective, the two platoons of ' moppers up ' clearing up the southern side of Fresnoy and a strong point in the Cemetery and immediate neighbourhood from which four German officers (including a Battalion Headquarters [1]) and about 160 other ranks, five trench mortars and several machine guns were captured. The ' moppers up ' with two Vickers guns then garrisoned the Cemetery.

On the left, however, the advance made little headway. Several belts of uncut wire barred the way and numerous cleverly-concealed machine guns opened a deadly fire on A Company as officers and men strove gallantly to get forward.

An attempt was made to charge the enemy's front-line trenches. This resulted in the enemy sallying forth with bombs. A hand-to-hand encounter took place in which severe casualties were inflicted on the enemy, twenty Germans being captured. But now the enemy in the trenches turned his machine guns on to friend and foe alike, shooting down his own men as well as the Gloucesters, though the latter eventually brought back eight prisoners.

As it was now light no further movement was possible. The Company, very much reduced in strength, remained pinned to its position all day until darkness had once again fallen, when it was withdrawn man by man. All attempts at communication during the day failed : volunteers to carry back messages were shot down immediately, the ground being open and commanded by deadly snipers. As soon as it was evident that no further assistance could be derived from A Company, the O.C. ' mopping-

---

[1] Lieut.-Colonel J. L. F. Tweedie adds the following amusing story concerning the capture of the German Battalion Headquarters : ' The enemy Battalion holding this portion of the front had its Headquarters in some deep dug-outs on the edge of the Cemetery. Our attack was unexpected and we arrived on the scene close behind the barrage, before the occupants of the dug-outs could man their machine guns. The dug-outs were known to be occupied but there was no response to a summons to come out, finally a missile of sorts set alight a store of Verey lights stocked at the bottom of the main entrance of the shaft. When the lights went off the garrison poured out by another entrance. The German Battalion Commander was loud in his complaints against his own divisional staff for omitting to warn him of the coming attack and cursed them all for letting them be caught napping. This C.O. had a packet of about fifteen Iron Crosses which had been sent up for distribution and he was probably thinking of a ceremonial parade suitable to the occasion when we arrived and took over the coveted Crosses.

up ' platoons on the right was directed to move up into the right half of the final objective, and the O.C. Company already installed there, ordered to sidestep to his left, capture Cornouillers Wood and get into touch with the 2nd Infantry Brigade (on the left of the 3rd). Strong opposition was encountered in the laddered trench (i.e. the trench between Cornouillers Wood and Bugeaud) but it was eventually cleared by a bombing party and the necessary connection made soon after midday.

During the afternoon the Battalion was ordered to prepare to advance through Gricourt under a creeping barrage and capture and hold Alsace and Beauvraignes Trenches, which ran round the eastern outskirts of the village.

Zero hour was 5.30 p.m.

This attack was entirely successful, Gricourt was captured and cleared and the two trenches occupied.

At 7.45 p.m. the enemy launched a heavy counter-attack supported by light trench mortars.

The junction of Beauvraignes and Alsace Trenches was immediately north-east of Gricourt Village, and east of the junction was a small network of trenches called the Three Savages. Down the latter the enemy advanced in large numbers, but his attack was smashed by rifle and Lewis-gun fire without it being necessary to call upon the artillery for support. Lewis guns were pushed forward and some sixty Germans captured.

After this costly repulse the enemy remained quiet. During the night two platoons from each front-line company were formed up on an outpost line and the remainder of the force was withdrawn to the laddered trench which the Battalion was ordered to hold as its main line of resistance.

Meanwhile the strong point in Fresnoy was still holding out, but only two platoons of the Reserve Company (C) were available, for the other two had been ordered up to the laddered trench to cover the attack on the second objective by overhead fire, Gricourt lying in a valley.

It was, however, absolutely essential to deal with the strong point without further delay, for the enemy's snipers in it had caused nearly 90 per cent of the casualties and they maintained that percentage all day.

The two platoons ordered to attack this place were commanded by Lieutenants W. T. Danahy and G. N. Gosling. Fresnoy Village was divided into two portions by a long, direct straight road which ran from west to east. By determined bombing the southern side of the village was cleared, but all attempts to cross the road to the north-western corner, which formed the strong point, were frustrated by numerous cleverly-concealed bombing-posts, machine guns and snipers, hidden among the ruined houses.   Progress from the east having failed, an attempt was then made to attack the strong point from the north, but here again bombing posts and machine guns rendered the Fresnoy—Arbousiers Wood road impassable.   Lieutenant Gosling [1] was wounded and after several casualties had been incurred the attackers were withdrawn and picquets established north and east of the strong point.

The grim tragedy of war was never more evident than during the hard fight for that strong point.   Throughout the day, on several occasions during the attack, parties of the enemy made repeated attempts, by holding up their hands, to surrender. But they were shot down or bombed by their own officers.

The two platoons of C Company were now withdrawn to a safe distance and the guns were ordered to bombard the strong point.   As nearly as possible the co-ordinates of what were thought to be headquarters in the strong point were given to the gunners, but it was impossible to locate the headquarters dug-out with any degree of exactitude.   Howitzers then opened fire, but the shells fell about 50 yards too much to the south-east.

At dusk an orderly succeeded in crawling out to A Company and withdrawing one of the officers.   Lieutenant Danahy was also called away and a plan was formed to storm the place from three sides at 10.30 p.m.

It was at this stage that fourteen of the enemy succeeded in evading their officers and escaped and surrendered to Lieutenant Danahy's platoon.   The position was explained to them.   One German volunteered to go back and try to induce his comrades to surrender.   He was permitted to do so.   Meanwhile Lieutenant Danahy was ordered to form the remainder of his platoon into two parties and get into position to storm the strong point at 10.30 p.m.   Second-Lieutenant T. H. Barnard was to work up Villemay Trench to the trench junction on the northern side, while another party was to work round to the north and attack along the trench running along the northern side of Marronniers Wood, so as to capture the machine guns in a sunken road on the western face of the Wood.   A Company was to make a

[1] This very gallant young officer joined the 28th in November 1916, at the age of 17, and continued with it until he was wounded on this occasion.   After the Armistice he went to North Russia and was murdered during the mutiny of the Russian Regiment in which he was an officer near Troitsa, about 300 miles south of Archangel, on the 7th July 1919.

simultaneous attack from the position in which they had been pinned all day.

The signal for the attack to begin was to be a hurricane bombardment by trench mortars for five minutes, one Véry light being fired simultaneously with the last shell.

On officers returning to their units, Lieutenant Danahy found that Lieutenant G. E. Chaney had already deployed his platoons for an attack.

All parties moved forward to their objectives, rifle men along the parapet and parados, bombers in the trench. The enemy at once began to fall back to his dug-outs. As soon as the position of the latter had been located parties were told off to deal with each one. No opposition was encountered and as the northern and western parties pushed on, the enemy retired to his dug-outs. The latter were then rushed, many of the enemy were wounded and the remainder surrendered and were allowed to come out. This had to be done as it was certain that several wounded men of the Gloucesters were in the dug-outs.

The captured Germans said afterwards that they intended to fight if the Gloucesters fired or bombed the dug-outs, but had agreed that if the attackers advanced without bombing they would fall back on dug-outs and surrender as their position was hopeless.

A pre-arranged signal was then fired to warn the other parties that the operation planned for 10.30 p.m. was ' off ' : this signal went up only ten minutes before zero.

The captures in this little affair included one 6-inch trench mortar, five light trench mortars, twenty-four heavy machine guns, 5 German officers and 114 other ranks unwounded and walking wounded and 8 severely wounded. Four men of the Gloucesters, all wounded, were found in the dug-outs. During daylight 16 Germans (two machine-gun teams) had been captured and about 30 killed.

On the 25th a few more prisoners were captured, but generally the day was uneventful. The two front companies were relieved by the 1st South Wales Borderers and moved back to support. The following day troops of the 6th Division relieved the Gloucesters and the latter moved back to reserve positions in the neighbourhood of Villeveque.

On the evening of the 26th September the Fourth, Third and First British Armies (from right to left), between the neighbourhood of St. Quentin and the Scheldt Canal, held a line running from the village of Salency (west of St. Quentin) to Gricourt and Pontruet, thence east to Villeret and Lempire to Villers Guislain and Gouzeaucourt (both exclusive). North of the latter village the line continued to Havrincourt and Mœuvres, thence along the western side of the Canal du Nord to the floods of the Sensée River at Ecourt St. Quentin.

On the British front the operations had reached a most important stage, for a great assault upon the Hindenburg Line had been planned to open on the 27th.

The rôle of the British Armies, in encompassing the final defeat of the enemy in France and Flanders, has so often been questioned that it is necessary to point out here that unquestionably the operations in which the Fourth, Third and First Armies took part were of paramount importance in the whole scheme of the final Allied offensive.

After the Battle of Epéhy it was decided that as soon as possible four converging and simultaneous offensives should be launched by the Allies, (i) by the Americans west of the Meuse in the direction of Mezières, (ii) by the French west of Argonne in close co-operation with the American attack and with the same general objectives, (iii) by the British on the St. Quentin—Cambrai front in the general direction of Maubeuge, (iv) by Belgian and Allied forces in Flanders in the direction of Ghent.

It was expected that as a result of these attacks the German forces opposite the French and Americans would be pressed back upon the difficult country of the Ardennes, while the British thrust struck at their principal lines of communication.

But the results to be obtained by these different attacks depended in a peculiarly large degree upon the British attack in the centre, for it was here that the enemy's defences were most highly organized : here also the enemy had massed the greater number of his troops. If the defences were broken the threat directed at his vital system of lateral communication would of necessity react upon his defence elsewhere.

It is very necessary to re-state the above points, for from a regimental point of view those gallant battalions who stormed the Hindenburg Line and broke the power of the enemy so that he was no longer able to withstand their terrific blows—theirs was the glory of that final advance to victory.

If any doubts exist that it was so they can be set at rest by the following words written by Sir Douglas Haig in his despatches : ' *I was convinced that the British attack was the essential part of the general scheme and that the moment was favourable.*'

Space must also be given to quote the admirable official description of the Hindenburg Line as it existed just prior to the great attacks which began on the 27th September and in which the Gloucestershire Regiment took part:

'Between St. Quentin and the village of Bantouzelle the principal defences of the Hindenburg system lie sometimes to the west but more generally to the east of the line of the Scheldt Canal.

'The Canal itself does not appear to have been organized as the enemy's main line of resistance, but rather as an integral part of a deep defensive system, the outstanding characteristics of which were the skill with which it was sited so as to deny us effective artillery positions from which to attack it. The chief rôle of the Canal was that of affording cover to retiring troops and to the garrisons of the main defensive trench lines during a bombardment. To this end the Canal lent itself admirably and the fullest use was made by the enemy of its possibilities.

'The general configuration of the ground through which this sector of the Canal runs produces deep cuttings of a depth in places of some 60 feet, while between Bellicourt and the neighbourhood of Vendhuille the Canal passes through a tunnel for a distance of 6,000 yards. In the sides of the cuttings the enemy had constructed numerous tunnelled dug-outs and concrete shelters. Along the top edges of them he had concealed well-sited concrete and armoured machine-gun emplacements. The tunnel itself was used to provide living accommodation for troops and was connected by shafts with the trenches above. South of Bellicourt the Canal cutting gradually becomes shallow, till at Bellenglise the Canal lies almost at ground level. South of Bellenglise the Canal is dry.

'On the western side of the Canal, south of Bellicourt, two thoroughly and extremely-heavily wired lines of continuous trench run roughly parallel to the Canal, an average distance from it of 2,000 and 1,000 yards respectively. Except in the tunnel sector the double line of trenches, known as the Hindenburg Line proper, lies immediately east of the Canal and is linked up by numerous communication trenches with the trench lines west of it.

'Besides these main features, numerous other trench lines, switch trenches and communication trenches, for the most part heavily wired, had been constructed at various points to meet local weaknesses or take advantage of local command of fire. At a distance of about 4,000 yards behind the most easterly of these trench lines lies a second double row of trenches known as the Beaurevoir—Fonsomme line, very thoroughly wired and holding numerous concrete shelters and machine-gun emplacements. The whole series of defences, with the numerous defended villages contained in it, formed a belt of country varying from 7,000 to 10,000 yards in depth, organized by the employment of every available means into a most powerful system, well meriting the great reputation attached to it.'

The operations which began on the 27th September are called by Sir Douglas Haig the Battle of Cambrai—a much better title than the two titles given the operations by the Battles Nomenclature Committee, who divided the operations into two actions (i) The Battle of the Canal du Nord, 27th September–1st October, and (ii) The Battle of the St. Quentin Canal, 29th September–2nd October : the two operations were obviously one battle.

The scheme of attack provided that the Third and First Armies on the 27th September were to assault the strong enemy positions covering the approaches to Cambrai between the Nord and Scheldt Canals, including the section of the Hindenburg Line itself north of Gouzeaucourt. In this sector the enemy's trenches faced south-west and it was desirable that they should be taken in the early stages of the operation so as to render it easier for the artillery of the Fourth Army to get into position. The heaviest attack was to be made from the Fourth Army front on the 29th. Along the fronts of all three Armies the enemy's positions were to be heavily bombarded on the night of the 26th/27th and this, followed by the attacks of the Third and First Armies, would (it was hoped) deceive the enemy as to where the main attack was to fall.

The latter attack was a great success and by the night of the 29th September the Third and First Armies had reached the line Gouzeaucourt, Marcoing, Noyelles-sur-L'Escaut, Fontaine-notre-Dame, Sailly and Palluel : at Marcoing posts had been established on the eastern bank of the Scheldt Canal, while on the northern flank our troops had entered Aubencheul-au-Bac.

THE BATTLE OF THE ST. QUENTIN CANAL, 29TH SEPTEMBER–2ND OCTOBER

The Fourth Army at 5.50 a.m. on the 29th launched its attack against the enemy's front from Salency to Vendhuille. On the right of the attack the IXth Corps attacked from Salency to near Buisson Gaulaine Farm. The main attack of the IXth Corps was made against Bellenglise and the Canal north of it by the 46th Division, supported by the 32nd Division. The 1st Division operated between Gricourt and Bellenglise, while south of the 1st Division the 6th Division, though not actually engaged in the main attack, endeavoured to gain ground eastwards.

The 1st Division, at zero hour on the 29th, disposed in the front line the 3rd Brigade on the right and the 1st Brigade on the left. Of the former Brigade the 1st Gloucesters were on the right and the 1st South Wales Borderers on the left : the 2nd Welch were in reserve.

Operation Orders issued by 3rd Brigade Headquarters may be summarized briefly, for the original orders are somewhat extensive :

The 1st Division was to detail a detachment to advance with the right of the 46th Division (on the immediate left of the 1st, and attacking due east) and in the first instance form a defensive flank north-east of Ste. Hélène : the 1st was also to attract the attention of the enemy south of the Canal and east of Pontruet, especially on the high ground north-east of Gricourt, or, in other words, the Germans holding Faucille and Forestier Trenches and the trench system in rear. ' Later ', states the orders, ' the Division will probably be required to cross the Canal at Le Tronquoy.'

The 1st Infantry Brigade was to supply the detachment mentioned above, form the defensive flank and push forward on the southern bank of the Canal.

The 3rd Infantry Brigade, on the right, was disposed as follows : Right—the 1st Gloucesters with one section of the 1st Battalion Machine-Gun Company and two guns of the 3rd Trench-Mortar Battery attached, held a north and south line from immediately north of Gricourt—a front of about 1,200 yards ; D Company on the right, A Company in the centre, C on the left, B Company in support in a trench running north-west from Cornouillers Wood, and Battalion Headquarters in Maguet Wood ; Left—1st South Wales Borderers.

Orders to the Gloucesters were as follows :

' The 1st Gloucestershire Regiment by active patrolling will try to ascertain enemy's dispositions on high ground in M.17 (Faucille and Forestier Trenches). If strong enemy resistance is encountered a fire fight with rifles and machine guns is to be commenced, only sufficient force will be employed in the first instance to keep the enemy fully occupied. On receipt of information that the 46th Division are across the Canal pressure can be gradually increased and artillery will be available to co-operate after zero hour plus two hours thirty minutes. As soon as enemy resistance weakens or if patrols meet with no resistance, Faucille Trench in M.17.b and 11.d will be captured, a defensive flank being thrown back to Alsace Trench.

' The 1st Gloucestershire Regiment will make a further advance to trenches in M.12.C (Forfait Alley and Foreats and Glu Trenches) at any time after 1st South Wales Borderers have come up in line with them on the previous objective in accordance with part C above ' (the previous objective was Faucille Trench which the South Wales Borderers were to occupy on the left of the Gloucesters).

The Diary of the Gloucesters states that three objectives were given to the Battalion : (i) Faucille Trench, (ii) Foreats Trench and Forfait Alley, (iii) Glu Trench as far south as the trench junction Forestier and Fumistes Alley. They also record that the final objective of the South Wales Borderers was Thorigny and Talana Hill.

At 5.45, patrols sent out by the Battalion reported the first objective strongly held by the enemy with machine guns.

The early morning of the 29th was foggy, though fine, just such another as had witnessed the great attack on the 8th August. But, owing to recent rains, the surface of the ground was soft and slippery. All the attacking infantry were assembled in their jumping-off positions and waiting for the signal to advance. Some held trenches, other shell-holes in No-Man's Land, while numbers were sheltered in sunken roads. The guns, which had not ceased firing, were still battering the enemy's positions.

At 5.55 a.m. (zero hour) the noise was appalling—1,500 guns of all calibres, from field-guns to the great howitzers, put down a barrage 200 yards only in front of the infantry, and was steadily moving forward though it could not be seen owing to the thick mist. Only flashes from the shell-bursts were visible. Tanks rumbled forward, becoming enveloped in fog, the air was filled with shrieking shells, the whistle of bullets and bursting of shrapnel shells.

At 9 a.m. when the barrage fell the thick mist still covered the battlefield. The roar of the British guns, to which was now added that from the enemy's artillery, produced such an appalling din that the troops, waiting to advance, unable to do so for fog, were also unable to distinguish the barrage fire. The consequence was that they did not advance. But by 11.40 a.m. the mist had cleared and there was brilliant sunshine : the smoke barrage which had been falling on the left of the Gloucesters also ceased. At that hour the creeping barrage opened and two companies of the Battalion (A Company on the right, under Captain Merrick, and C Company on the left, under Captain Chaney, supported by B Company, under Lieutenant Greene) advanced to the assault, the South Wales Borderers on the left having orders not to advance until the 28th had gained the first objective.

But the enemy's shell and machine-gun fire was terrific and no advance on a general front could be made, though in places sections worked forward.

At 3 p.m. the situation was as follows : the front-line troops were held up about 250 yards from the first objective : Lieutenant Forbes with the leading platoon of the support company was working round the left flank of the front line.

Shortly after 3 p.m. the South Wales Borderers attacked and gained their first objective with little opposition, and subsequently their second objective.

By 5.30 p.m. Lieutenant Forbes, assisted by the South Wales Borderers, had also reached the first objective. He worked up Faucille and then bombed a German machine-gun nest still holding out on the top of the ridge. The Germans here, however, did not stay long but withdrew: some, going by way of Forestier Trench, escaped, but those retiring by way of Forfait Alley were forced to surrender to the South Wales Borderers, who had gained their second objective.

When darkness had fallen on the 29th the Gloucesters had captured all their objectives at a cost of 8 other ranks killed and 47 wounded. One German officer and 22 other ranks had been captured.

On the 30th companies reorganized and the positions were consolidated, dispositions being : D Company centre, A left, C on the line of the third objective, with B Company in support in Faucille Trench.

On the 29th the 46th Division had captured Bellenglise and the 32nd Division, passing through, had reached a line east of Le Tronquoy, Lehaucourt and Magny-la-Fosse.

' Not so dramatic perhaps,' states *The Story of the Fourth Army*, ' but almost equally difficult and important in its results was the work of the 1st Division on this day, as the safety of the right flank of the Army depended on the success of its advance, which the enemy opposed throughout the day with the greatest determination. The sector which had been considered in some ways the most formidable part of the Hindenburg Line on the Army front had been captured at small cost on the whole of the IXth Corps front.'

The 1st Division again attacked on the 30th September, the 3rd Brigade on the right advancing against Thorigny and Talana Hill, the 1st Brigade co-operating by moving along the low ground with its left resting on the Canal. Thorigny and Talana Hill were captured during the morning with but little opposition, and early in the afternoon the 3rd Brigade linked up with the 14th Brigade (32nd Division) on the Le Tronquoy tunnel : the 1st Brigade, crossing the Canal, then relieved the 14th Brigade between Le Tronquoy and Levergies.

During the morning of the 1st October the 1st Gloucesters moved from the right south-east of Pontruet, which they had captured on the 29th September, to an area south of the St. Quentin Canal opposite Lehaucourt : in this area the Battalion remained throughout the 2nd.[1]

THE BATTLE OF THE BEAUREVOIR LINE : 3RD–5TH OCTOBER

The Fourth Army was now within easy striking distance of the Beaurevoir—Fonsomme Line. The breach in the Hinden-

[1] The Battalion was commanded by Lieut.-Colonel Tweedie with Major J. R. Guild second-in-command and Captain A. Jarvis as Adjutant. The Battalion strength was 19 officers and 618 other ranks.

burg Line on the 29th September had been widened and the enemy's defences from Le Tronquoy to Vendhuille captured. South of the Fourth Army the French had occupied St. Quentin and had reached the line of the Canal. The Third Army, on the left of the Fourth, had captured Masnières and secured the crossings of the Scheldt Canal between that place and the out-skirts of Cambrai. It was considered, therefore, that one more determined attack would result in the capture of the Masnières —Beaurevoir—Fonsomme Line on the whole of the Fourth Army front, turn the enemy's defences in front of the right of the Third Army and on the south enable the French to advance east of St. Quentin.

Operation orders were then issued for an attack to take place by the Fourth Army on the 3rd October from Sequehart to Le Catalet.

Zero hour was 6.5 a.m., at which hour the 32nd and 46th Divisions, on the left of the 1st Division, atttacked the enemy: the 1st Division (1st Brigade holding the front line with the 3rd Brigade in close support) made no direct attack but was to keep touch on the flank. The 32nd took Sequehart and the 46th Division the Beaurevoir—Fonsomme Line on its front, then Ramicourt. At night the 3rd Brigade was attached to the 46th Division, and took over the Beaurevoir—Fonsomme Line, i.e. 2nd Welch on the right and 1st South Wales Borderers on the left : the 1st Gloucesters moved to Joncourt, in support, occupy-ing the village and the eastern outskirts.

On the 4th the 3rd Brigade came under the orders of the 137th Brigade (46th Division) and the Gloucesters moved from Joncourt to the Beaurevoir—Fonsomme Line in front of Preselles.

During the morning the G.O.C., 3rd Brigade (Brig.-General Sir W. A. I. Kay) and the Brigade Major, whilst reconnoitring the line, were killed by a shell and Colonel Tweedie assumed command of the Brigade.

At 6 a.m. on the 5th the Gloucesters were ordered to attack Mannequin Hill, which lay some 2,200 yards east of Preselles. The Hill had been taken but lost again in a heavy German counter-attack.

The jumping-off line was about 250 yards west of the Hill. Dispositions of companies were A Company on the right, C Company in the centre and D on the left : B Company was in support.

Detailed narratives of this attack are not to be found with the documents, but in the Battalion Diary it is stated that

' A and C Companies reached the objective, but D Company was heavily enfiladed by machine-gun fire and had to withdraw. Severe casualties were inflicted on the enemy, twenty-six prisoners and six machine guns were captured and four enemy machine-gun teams were entirely wiped out. Our casualties were Lieutenant K. Ford wounded, 3 other ranks killed and 13 other ranks wounded.'

At night the 1st Gloucesters were relieved by the 1st King's Shropshire Light Infantry and marched back to the area south of the St. Quentin Canal occupied before moving up.

In this battle another battalion of the Regiment—1/5th Gloucesters—was also involved in the operations of its Division, i.e. the 25th.[1]

The 25th Division was one of those unfortunate divisions reduced to cadre strength in June 1918. The Division proceeded to England, where in July the cadre battalions were made up with drafts. In August the Division made up a full-strength brigade for service in North Russia and the remaining battalions were broken up. Divisional and Brigade Headquarters returned to France in September 1918 and the Division was again reconstituted with nine battalions withdrawn from Italy, the 1/5th Gloucesters, from the 48th Division, being one of them.

The Diary of 75th Brigade Headquarters records that on the 17th September (the Brigade being then at Gapennes) the 1/5th Gloucesters and 1/8th Worcesters arrived from Italy and were billeted respectively at Domvast and Argenvillers (Abbeville area).

The reconstituted 25th Division consisted of the 7th, 74th and 75th Brigades and the three battalions forming the latter were the 1/5th Gloucesters, 1/8th Worcesters and 1/8th Warwicks.

On the 21st the Gloucesters were inspected and commented favourably upon as to their turnout, general steadiness on parade, completeness of their equipment and the good condition of the transport.

Training was carried out until the 27th when the Battalion marched to St. Riquier and entrained for Albert. It was midnight when the latter place was reached and 2.30 a.m. before the Gloucesters arrived at Warloy (a 6-mile march) and billeted in the village. On the 29th they ' embussed ' for Montauban where they were accommodated in Nissen huts and dug-outs. Owing to a shortage of men the Battalion on the 30th reverted to a three-platoon-per-company formation.

The 75th Brigade moved to Combles by march route on the

---

[1] The story of the 1/5th Gloucesters in Italy will be found under the heading of Italian Operations.

1st October, the Gloucesters sheltering in Leuze Wood near the village. On the 2nd the Battalion moved to Nurlu (9 miles).

The Battle of the Beaurevoir Line being in progress the whole Brigade ' stood to ' on the 3rd and moved in the late afternoon to St. Emilie, arriving at 8 p.m. There was no accommodation for the Battalion but in a field under ground-sheets. The night was fine though cold.

The Battle was still raging on the 4th and the 75th Brigade ' stood to ' from 7 till 11 a.m., and at 11.30 a.m. moved forward to the outpost system of the Hindenburg Line (in our hands) and billeted in Quennemont Farm south-west of Bony.

The 25th Division formed part of the XIIIth Corps, Fourth Army. The Division had relieved the left of the 2nd Australian Division on the night of the 3rd October and on the 4th, under a barrage, in a dense fog which continued until a late hour of the morning, had attacked in the direction of Beaurevoir. This attack had been carried out by the 7th Brigade in conjunction with Australian troops on the right and left, but was unsuccessful. It was, therefore, decided to continue the attack on the 5th and to capture the village together with the high ground between La Sablonnière and Guisancourt Farm, while the 2nd Australian Division was to attack Montbrehain.

On the night of the 4th the 74th Brigade had been moved into the line on the left of the 7th Brigade while the 75th Brigade was concentrated in close support in the neighbourhood of the Masnières—Beaurevoir Line.

On the morning of the 5th the Gloucesters ' dumped ' greatcoats and packs and set out in fighting order for the Masnières—Beaurevoir Line : B Echelon moved back to Hargicourt. The destination of the Battalion was Lormisset—a 4-mile march via Grand Court (south of Mont St. Martin). On passing the latter place they came under salvoes of 5·9s, during which five men were wounded. The disposition of the 75th Brigade was then 1/8th Warwicks and 1/5th Gloucesters in Lormisset (which was in the actual trench system of the Masnières—Beaurevoir Line) and Worcesters in Mont St. Martin.

At 3 p.m. orders from Divisional Headquarters were received at 75th Brigade Headquarters to attack and capture Beaurevoir, the 74th Brigade clearing up the situation at Guisancourt Farm (nearby Beaurevoir). The attack was to take place at 6.30 p.m. after a preliminary bombardment at 6.15. A line was to be consolidated at least 200 yards east of the village and touch obtained on the right and left flanks with the 7th and 74th Brigades respectively.

Personal orders were issued by the Brigadier to all three
C.O.s. The 1/5th Gloucesters were to attack on the right, 1/8th
Worcesters on the left. The two Battalions were to form up on
a two-company frontage on a north and south line just short of
the ridge on which stood Beaurevoir Mill.

The Gloucesters by 3.30 p.m. had taken up a position in
sunken roads, in support of the 1/8th Warwicks who had just
captured Beaurevoir Farm overlooking Beaurevoir. The 1/5th
were ordered to capture the southern half of the village and the
Worcesters the northern half. Companies formed up—B on the
right, A on the left, with C as ' moppers up ' and D in reserve.
At 6.15 p.m., under cover of the barrage and machine-gun fire,
the Battalion moved into its assembly positions.

At zero hour the Gloucesters advanced immediately. West
of Beaurevoir there was a railway embankment which the leading
companies, keen to get at the enemy, reached before the barrage had actually lifted from it. Although suffering casualties
from their own barrage, A and B Companies surprised a
machine-gun nest, the German gun crews of which were still
taking cover. Eleven machine guns were taken from this
position. The Battalion pushed on into the village and through
it, meeting with very little opposition except from isolated
machine guns and snipers. The village was, in the meanwhile,
being ' mopped up ' by C Company while the forward companies
were establishing the line 200 yards east in conjunction with the
Worcesters on the left.

Night fell on the 5th with the two Battalions holding a line
from the south-eastern and eastern exits of the village, thence
in a north-westerly direction to (and including) Bellevue Farm.

This highly successful operation (the first since the Battalion
arrived in France from Italy) cost the 1/5th Gloucesters 1 officer
(2nd Lieutenant C. F. Hussey) and 9 other ranks killed, Lieutenant Seago and 42 other ranks wounded and 1 other rank
missing.

Between the hours of 7 p.m. and 1 a.m. on the 6th not a shell
or a machine-gun bullet was fired at the Gloucesters, thus giving
the Battalion ample time to consolidate the position.

The general result of the fighting on the 5th October was that
Montbrehain, Beaurevoir and Guisancourt Farm had been
captured and the right Corps (Vth) of the Third Army was now
rapidly extending the front of attack northwards.

The capture of the Hindenburg defences, on which the enemy
had expended so much skill and labour, and which he had believed
capable of defying any assault by the Fourth, Third and First

British Armies, was the culminating point in the first phase of the British offensive. Sir Douglas Haig, in what is now known as his ' Victory Despatch ', stated :

' The enemy's defence in the last and strongest of his prepared positions had been shattered. The whole of the main Hindenburg Line had passed into our possession and a wide gap was driven through such rear trench systems as had existed behind them.

' The effect of the victory upon the subsequent course of the campaign was decisive. The threat to the enemy's communications was more direct and constant, for nothing but the natural obstacles of a wooded and well-watered country-side lay between our armies and Maubeuge.

' Great as were the material losses the enemy had suffered the effect of so overwhelming a defeat upon a *morale* already deteriorated was of even larger importance.'

Let the Regiment remember the great part it played in the splendid achievements described by the British Commander-in-Chief.

THE BATTLE OF CAMBRAI : 8TH–9TH OCTOBER

The enemy by now was approaching a state of desperation. His prepared defences were gone, he had lost enormous numbers of men and vast quantities of war material. Despair had already entered into his soul, though he still clung tenaciously to his positions as long as possible. With machine guns, placed in depth, he might hold us up for a while, but what then ? The Allies saw to it that there was no ' then'.

On the 8th October the second and concluding phase of the British offensive opened ' in which ', state the official despatches,

" the Fourth and Third Armies, and the right of the First Army, moved forward with their left flank on the canal line which runs from Cambrai to Mons, and their right covered by the French First Army. This advance, by the capture of Maubeuge and the disruption of the German main lateral system of communication, forced the enemy to fall back upon the line of the Meuse and realized the strategic plan of the Allied operations.

' The fighting which took place during this period, being in effect the development and exploitation of the Hindenburg Line, virtually falls into three stages, the breaks between the different battles being due chiefly to the depth of our advance and the difficulties of re-establishing communications.'

To the military student the concluding stage of the great thrust in a north-easterly direction, by the left of the First French Army and by the Fourth, Third and First British Armies, is of profound interest, for it broke the power of the enemy, cut through his communications and was the principal cause of his

debacle. There is no doubt about this. The German General
Staff had massed their greatest strength opposite the above
Armies—they knew where the danger was.

And it is due also to the gallant battalions, which fought their
way towards the Avesnes—Maubeuge—Mons Line, to place
upon record their splendid tenacity and courage in bringing
about the downfall of the enemy.

Fighting was now to begin in open country—Lord Haig called
it so in his despatches. Gone for ever were the old Somme
battlefields, with their blood-soaked trenches and ruined villages
many of which by this period were a mere rubbish heap of brick
and stone marked by a rough notice board bearing the grim
legend ' This is so-and-so ' : gone the scarred and broken country
east of Arras, the weird pylons at Loos, the awful dreariness of
the marshes of the Lys Valley : even the Second Army had left
the ghastly Ypres Salient and the bloody ridge of Passchendaele
far behind : the whole line was moving east—the German was
at last ' on the run '.

And what, perhaps, was even more dramatic, the British Army
was approaching the very ground over which it had fought at
so great a disadvantage (outnumbered both in artillery and men)
in August 1914.

In the next operation, to begin on the 8th October, the Fourth
and Third Armies were to attack on a front of about 17 miles
from Sequehart to south of Cambrai. On the right the First
French Army was continuing the attack as far south as St. Quentin.

On the 6th October the front of the Fourth Army ran from
Chardun Vert to Neville's Cross, just south of Montbrehain (IXth
Corps) with the 6th Division, reinforced by the 139th Brigade of
the 46th Division, in line, and with the 46th Division (less 139th
Brigade) and 5th Cavalry Brigade in support. American troops
held the line from Neville's Cross to the Torrens Canal. From
the latter, to about 1,000 yards south of Villers Outreaux (XIIIth
Corps) the 25th and 50th Division held the line, with the 66th
Division in support. The Cavalry Corps was in reserve near
the St. Quentin Canal.

The 1st Gloucesters were not engaged in this battle : indeed
the 1st Division as a whole was in Corps Reserve. On the 6th
a detachment from the Battalion, as buglers, attended the funeral
of Brig.-General Sir W. A. I. Kay, who was buried at Vaden-
court. On this date also Colonel Tweedie returned to command
the Battalion. On the 7th the Gloucesters were under orders
to move forward on attachment to the 46th Division, but the
orders were cancelled and the Battalion remained south of the

St. Quentin Canal, in training, not only during the 8th and 9th but until the 15th October.

The 1/5th Gloucesters of the 25th Division, however, took part in the battle.

On the morning of the 6th the 75th Brigade maintained its position 200 yards east of Beaurevoir, captured but a few hours earlier.

From 1 a.m. the enemy had shelled the western edges of the village, eventually opening spasmodic fire on the whole of it and the western approaches during the remainder of the day. After darkness had fallen a platoon of C Company, under 2nd Lieutenant Cox, with a platoon of the 1/8th Worcesters, attempted a raid on an advanced enemy post. But the raiders were met by heavy fire from five machine guns and were compelled to retire, the Gloucesters having suffered 2 other ranks killed and 3 wounded.

During the morning and evening of the 7th Beaurevoir was again shelled heavily, but the 1/5th were relieved by the South African Brigade of the 66th Division and at 1.30 a.m. on the 8th moved to a sunken road north of Estrées where they arrived at 4.30 a.m. without further casualties.

At dawn (4.30 a.m.) the Fourth and Third Armies launched their attack along the whole front, advancing about 5 miles. By 12 noon the 7th Brigade (attacking in front of the 75th Brigade) was on the line Prémont—Serain. The 75th Brigade moved forward at 2.20 p.m. to Poncheaux and later to Sonia Wood, remaining there during the night in the dry bed of the Torrens Canal.

During the night verbal orders were received for an attack to take place at 5.20 a.m. on the 9th on Maretz and Honnechy. The Worcesters were to be on the right and the Gloucesters on the left. These two Battalions were to capture a line from near Trou-aux-Soldats to a point east of Maretz and south of the Estrées—Le Cateau road. The Warwicks were to protect the Brigade's right flank facing Butry Wood. After the line had been captured and established the Worcesters were to pass through the Gloucesters, while a battalion of the 7th Brigade passed through the Warwicks, to take Honnechy, Honnechy Station and the main road to Busigny. The 74th Brigade was to be on the right of the 75th and the 66th Division on the left. The attack was to be made under a creeping barrage.

The Worcesters and the Gloucesters formed up on the line of the Serain—Prémont road, both Battalions being in their assembly positions by 4.15 a.m. D Company of the Gloucesters was on the right, C on the left, B had been detailed as ' moppers up ' and A was in reserve.

As the barrage fell at 5.20 a.m. both Battalions advanced in artillery formation.   On the right the Warwicks met with very little resistance and gained their objective.   A defensive flank was then established until touch was gained with the Americans. On the left the Gloucesters met with no resistance until they reached the eastern edge of Maretz, but the Battalion had had a difficult advance.   Under cover of the creeping barrage and closely supported by the Worcesters, the 1/5th advanced towards the village, but on the left troops of the 66th Division were not advancing in alignment, nor was there a barrage along the front of that Division until 5.45 a.m. and then it overlapped the 75th Brigade sector, causing several casualties among the Worcesters and the support and reserve companies of the Gloucesters.

By 6.30 a.m. a mist had fallen over the battlefield but it did not impede progress.   At that hour the ' Heavies ' lifted off Maretz and D and C Companies of the Gloucesters pushed forward and occupied the western outskirts of the village.   But again they came under the fire of the guns of the 66th Division, whose barrage was half an hour late, with the result that after C Company had suffered many more casualties, both Companies had to withdraw and wait until the screen of fire had lifted.   On the barrage lifting the Gloucesters again pushed on, meeting with very little resistance until they reached the eastern outskirts of the village, where they met with a stubborn resistance from machine guns and snipers.   But eventually, after some heavy fighting, Maretz was secured and a line consolidated some 200 to 300 yards east of it.   The 1/8th Worcesters and Cavalry subsequently passed through this line to attack Honnechy.

At 5.20 a.m. on the 10th the 75th Brigade continued the advance in artillery formation, battalions in the following order : 1/8th Warwicks, 1/5th Gloucesters, 1/8th Worcesters.   One mile east of Honnechy resistance was encountered which gradually stiffened as the Warwicks pressed on.   The latter Battalion halted, whereupon Captain R. de W. Rogers of the Gloucesters gallantly led his Company (B) through the Warwicks.   But heavy enfilade fire from machine guns brought the attempt to a standstill and, having lost all its officers wounded and many N.C.O.s as well, the Company was forced to fall back upon the Warwicks and dig in on a line west of St. Benin, where the night of the 10th/11th and most of the following day were spent.

Thus, so far as the 1st and 1/5th Gloucesters were concerned, ended the Battle of Cambrai, 1918.

CHAPTER XXXV

THE PURSUIT TO, AND BATTLE OF, THE SELLE, 12TH–25TH OCTOBER

DISORGANIZED bodies of infantry retiring steadily eastwards, roads blocked with troops, artillery, transport and ambulances, all the signs indeed of a beaten foe temporarily deprived of all resistance—such is a picture of the Eighteenth, Second and Seventeenth German Armies, the very same who had advanced so triumphantly across the Somme Battlefields in March, but now falling back before the Fourth, Third and First British Armies with the First French Army on the right.

The pursuit was vigorous, and so much so that it was impossible for the guns and transport and all the necessary impedimenta of war to keep pace with our infantry pressing resolutely upon the enemy as he fell back to the Selle River where (it was expected) he would make another stand.

On the night of the 10th October Le Cateau had been rushed and captured though the attacking troops were withdrawn to the western portions of the town. On the right of the Fourth Army the First French Army had reached as far east as Seboncourt, while the Fourth Army line ran east of Bohain, almost directly north to Le Cateau, embracing Vaux Andigny and St. Souplet : on the left of the Fourth, the Third Army had reached a line running from the high ground overlooking Neuvilly and Briastre on the Selle, due west to Quiévy, thence northwards to Hilaire-le-Cambrai and St. Aubert, though all these villages were still in the hands of the enemy.

The next battle—that of the Selle—had been planned for the 17th October. The Fourth Army was to attack first on a front of about 10 miles from Le Cateau southwards in conjunction with the First French Army operating west of the Sambre and Oise Canal. The Third Army was to follow with an assault on the line of the Selle River.

We left the 1st Gloucesters on the 15th October south of the St. Quentin Canal, opposite Lehaucourt, and the 1/5th on the 11th billeted in Honnechy.

On the 16th the former Battalion moved forward and bivouacked north of the road between Brancourt and Bohain. At 7.30 a.m. on the 17th another move forward was made, on this occasion to the outskirts of Vaux Andigny. The attack had then begun, the 46th Division attacking on the right and the 6th Division on the left, while the 1st Division, concentrated north and west of Bohain, was to pass through the 6th Division and capture the second and third objectives including the villages of La Vallée Mulatre (second objective) and Wassigny (third objective) after the 46th and 6th Divisions had secured the first objectives. The 3rd Brigade was, however, in Divisional Reserve on the first day of the attack, but on the 18th attacked through the 2nd Brigade.

The attack was carried out by the Welch on the right, South Wales Borderers on the left and Gloucesters in support.

The Gloucesters had moved forward to Molain at 2 a.m. where they remained during the attack on the high ground between Ribeauville and Wassigny. At 10.30 a.m., however, B Company received orders to form a defensive flank on the left of the Divisional sector and gain touch with the Americans on that flank. The Company then took up a line in front of the railway, north-west from Wassigny, and at 11.30 a.m. moved forward to the neighbourhood of Belle Vue Farm. Machine-gun and artillery fire met this advance all the way and several casualties were suffered.

At 6 p.m. B Company was ordered to clear Ribeauville, which was done. Opposition was not strong, though the enemy's machine-gun posts held on as long as possible until they were either knocked out or forced to retire. At 11.30 p.m. orders were received to rejoin the Battalion after finally clearing Ribeauville and assuring touch between the Americans and the South Wales Borderers.

The 3rd Brigade again attacked the enemy on the 19th, in the same order, and pushed the front line forward to the Rejet de Beaulieu—Cambresis road. At night the 1st Gloucesters relieved the 2nd Welch on the right of the Brigade front and took up a line along the road 800 yards from the Canal de la Sambre, A Company on the right, C on the left, D in support and B in reserve. Patrols were pushed out and posts established on the western banks of the Canal. Liaison was obtained with French troops on the right at Beaurepas.

The Gloucesters were now almost on what might be described as familiar ground, for Beaurepas is not far from Oisy where, on the night of August the 26th, 1914, the 1st Battalion, tired and worn after a long day of marching and fighting, bivouacked in wet fields during the Retreat from Mons. And a little farther off still, south of Oisy, in Etreux Cemetery, the gallant Captain Shipway, mortally wounded in the day's fighting, was buried early the next morning.

How many of the original ' Old Braggs ', who had trudged those weary miles back to the Marne in 1914, were with the Battalion on the 19th October, 1918 ?

On the 20th October the outpost line was pushed forward some 200 yards nearer the Canal and on the 21st B Company took over Cambresis from the French, on the right of A Company, but the latter was relieved by D Company and at night-fall the position was B on the right, D in the centre, C on the left and A in support. The situation during the 22nd was quiet but a vigilant watch was kept on the Canal.

Meanwhile the 1/5th Gloucesters of the 25th Division had also been engaged with the enemy.

The Battalion moved from Honnechy on the 12th October to Serain, but on the 75th Brigade being detailed as reserve to the 50th Division in the forthcoming attack on the 17th, the Battalion concentrated again at Honnechy. During the afternoon of the 17th the Brigade moved to the neighbourhood of Essarts Farm and occupied sunken roads.

On the 18th dense mist covered the battlefield until about 9 a.m. when the 75th Brigade received orders to move to St. Benin. The crossings over the Selle River had been won on the previous day, but even so in the early morning mist and with hostile shell-fire still heavy, the Battalion had difficulty in getting across.

The attack of the XIIIth Corps of the Fourth Army on the 18th was made by the 50th Division, having as its first objective the ridge 2,000 yards east of the Arbre Guernon—Le Cateau road : the attack was to be launched at 5.30 a.m. The second phase of the attack was to begin at 8.30 a.m. when the 75th Brigade of the 25th Division was to pass through the line of the 50th Division and attack the second objective, which consisted of Bazuel and roughly the line of the Bazuel—Baillon Farm road. The 66th Division, on the left of the 50th, was to push forward its right to the ridge east of Le Cateau and clear the Faubourg de Landrecies of the enemy.

The 75th Brigade was attacking with the 1/8th Worcesters on the right, 1/5th Gloucesters on the left and 1/8th Warwicks in support.

The Gloucesters were disposed as follows : B Company on the right, C on the left, A in support and D in reserve.

The attack of the 50th Division was completely successful and at 8.45 a.m. the 75th Brigade passed through and captured the second objective, the Gloucesters taking the railway and main Le Cateau—Bazuel road, immediately west of Bazuel. During the remainder of the day hostile machine-gun fire and sniping were heavy and at nightfall four casualties had been suffered by the Gloucesters, including 2nd Lieutenant S. V. Woodward (C Company) and 2nd Lieutenant H. H. Searle (B Company) seriously wounded.

The Scottish Horse relieved C Company during the night of the 18th/19th and the latter moved and occupied a line along the railway north of Bazuel and on B Company's right.

Rain fell during the night of the 18th/19th and when dawn broke on the 19th mist again covered the battlefield. At 8.20 a.m. A Company, under Lieutenant F. J. Lovell, tried to occupy the line of the River Richemont (500 yards north of B Company's front) by ' peaceful penetration '. But after an advance of 250 yards heavy machine-gun fire was encountered and eventually the Company had to fall back to its original line.

Excepting periodical shell-fire in the neighbourhood of Bazuel the situation throughout the 19th was quiet. During the night of the 19th/20th one company of the 21st Manchesters relieved part of B Company of the 1/5th Gloucesters in the front line, B and C Companies then closing to the right : C Company relieved a platoon of the 1/8th Worcesters.

At 7 a.m. on the 20th, under a creeping barrage, No. 15 Platoon of D Company, under 2nd Lieutenant V. Scroggie, with the 24th Manchesters on the left, made another attack on the line of the River Richemont. Stiff resistance was met with at first, but after stubborn fighting the enemy was compelled to withdraw from the objective, which the platoon then occupied and consolidated, two sections of A Company assisting. Throughout the day several patrol encounters with the enemy took place, sixteen prisoners being captured and several Germans killed and wounded.

At 8 p.m. the Battalion was relieved and marched back to St. Benin where billets were occupied in the factory and houses. In this place the 1/5th Gloucesters remained during the 22nd and until an hour before midnight on the 23rd.

On the 20th the Third Army had attacked the line of the Selle north of Le Cateau and, after heavy fighting about Neuvilly, Amerval, Solesmes and Haspres, had gained the high ground east of the river, pushing out patrols as far as the River Harpies : the First Army (on the left of the Third) had reached Denain,

20

had made progress on both sides of the Scheldt Canal and had reached the slopes overlooking the left bank of the Ecaillon River.

The Selle positions having been captured, operations of a more extensive character followed almost immediately : they were the attainment of a general line running from the Sambre Canal along the edge of the Forêt de Mormal to the neighbourhood of Valenciennes.

In the assault, which was to take place at 1.20 a.m. on the 23rd October, the front of attack stretched from east of Mazinghien to Maison Bleue, north-east of Haussy—a front approximately of 15 miles.

The attack of the Fourth Army was to be delivered by the IXth and XIIIth Corps, employing respectively the 1st and 6th Divisions and the 25th and 18th Divisions.

Thus the 1st and 1/5th Gloucesters were again to be involved, either in the direct attack or in support or reserve.

Taking the IXth Corps attack first—the rôle of the 1st Division was to gain ground towards the Canal and drive the enemy across it, south of Catillon, while the 6th Division, conforming to the advance of the 25th Division (on the left), was to form an ever-lengthening defensive flank facing east as the latter Division gained ground.

The 1st Division was to attack with the 2nd and 3rd Brigades in line, the 1st Brigade in reserve. The task allotted to the Gloucesters (if it did not involve a direct infantry attack it was nevertheless important) was to establish forward posts with observation over, and control of, the Canal de Sambre along its front.

On the XIIIth Corps front the attack on the first objective (the Pommereuil—Forest road) was to be carried out by the 7th Brigade, 25th Division, with one battalion of the 75th Brigade attached : the strength of the 7th Brigade was at this period under seven hundred rifles. The second objective (Tilleuls Farm—Vert Baudet road) was for the 18th Division only : the third objective (a line along the north-eastern edge of L'Eveque Wood and the western edge of Bousies) was allotted to the 75th Brigade : the 74th Brigade was to attack the fourth and fifth objectives which, however, need not be detailed seeing that they do not materially affect the story of the 1/5th Gloucesters.

The records of both the 3rd Brigade Headquarters and 1st Gloucesters are very brief concerning the operations on the 23rd. The former merely states that ' It was successful but casualties heavy owing to the intense barrage put down by the enemy'.

The Gloucesters state that : ' Whole objectives gained. Casualties 7 killed, 14 wounded.'

On the 24th the 3rd Brigade was relieved and moved back to Vaux Andigny in Divisional Reserve, the 1st Battalion being billeted in that village.   In this position the 28th remained until the 30th of the month.

The 1/5th Gloucesters formed up for the attack with A Company on the right, C in the centre and D on the left : B Company was in reserve.

The Battalion advanced in rear of the 7th Brigade. Mist again covered the battlefield and there was a certain loss of cohesion among the attacking troops. But the first objective was carried without much difficulty. The second objective being for the left division of the XIIIth Corps only, the 75th Brigade then advanced through the 7th to capture the third objective, a line along the north-eastern edge of L'Eveque Wood and the western edges of Bousies.

After advancing some 300 yards the 1/5th met with resistance in the centre from hostile machine-gun nests which had not been ' mopped up '. For five hours heavy and stubborn fighting ensued until, by the splendid gallantry of one single man— No. 17324 Pte. Francis George Miles of C Company—the enemy's resistance was completely broken down.

' Pte. Miles, alone and on his own initiative, made his way forward for a distance of 150 yards, under exceptionally heavy fire, located one machine gun and shot the man firing the gun. He then rushed the gun and kicked it over thereby putting it out of action. He then observed another gun firing 100 yards further forward. He again advanced alone, shot the machine gunner, rushed the gun and captured the team of eight. Finally, he stood up and beckoned on his Company which, following his signals, was enabled to work round the rear of the line and to capture sixteen machine guns, one officer and fifty other ranks. The courage, initiative and entire disregard of personal safety shown by this very gallant private soldier enabled his Company to advance at a time when any delay would have seriously jeopardized the whole operation in which it was engaged.' [1]

Pte. Miles was very deservedly awarded the Victoria Cross.

The enemy machine-gun opposition broken down, the advance went ahead, but C Company had been so delayed that it now went into reserve.

D Company met with resistance first at Jacques Mill and later at Garde Mill, but after stubborn fighting was able to ' mop up ' and proceed to the assembly positions along the Forester's House

[1] *London Gazette*, 6th January 1919.

—Flaquet Brifaut road where B Company took the place of C Company.

B and C Companies,[1] endeavouring to get into position with a view to ' mopping up ' L'Eveque Wood towards the north-eastern edge, met with strong machine-gun resistance from the flanks, but after several hours' fighting managed to get to their assembly positions, where orders were received to attack in a south-easterly direction.

The attack took place at 4.45 p.m., but there was little resistance and a line was established along the road running north-east from Forester's House to Malgarni.

' A ' Company also had stiff fighting along the road running south-west from Forester's House to Bazuel. Not being able to reach the assembly positions at Forester's House this Company received orders to move to Battalion Headquarters and thence proceed along the road towards Forester's House (which by that time had been ' mopped up ') and take up a position in support of B and D Companies.

During the night of the 23rd/24th the line was heavily shelled, but at 9.15 a.m. on the 24th the 1/5th Gloucesters were relieved and withdrawn to, and concentrated at, Flaquet Brifaut, moving thence to Pommereuil where the Battalion remained in billets until the 31st.

At the close of the 23rd the line of the Fourth Army ran from La Louvière—Catillon Halt—western outskirts of Ors—through L'Eveque Wood to within 500 yards of Malgarni, then east and north of Bousies to the south-eastern edge of Vendegies Wood. On the 24th the line of the Army objective was pushed still further north, Malgarni and Robersert fell and the final objective on the north of the front had been gained. The Third Army had pushed its line forward to the western outskirts of the Forêt de Mormal, capturing Vendegies.

During the next three days local attacks yielded Englefontaine and advanced our line well to the north and east of the Le Quesnoy—Valenciennes railway, from the outskirts of Le Quesnoy, past Sepmeries and Artres to Famars, but, as already explained, the 1st and 1/5th Gloucesters were out of the front line until the end of the month.

[1] The Diary says ' C Company ', but D Company is probably meant, as shown later : C was in reserve at this period.

CHAPTER XXXVI

THE BATTLE OF THE SAMBRE,
1ST–11TH NOVEMBER [1]

BY the end of October the enemy's *morale* had been practically broken : here and there his infantry and machine-gunners put up a stout resistance, but their staying power had gone—the old tenacity of the German soldiery had disappeared. A further 20,000 prisoners and 475 guns had been captured in the Battle of the Selle and thirty-one German divisions beaten by twenty-four British and two American divisions.

Upon Germany's Allies also disaster had fallen : Turkey and Bulgaria had capitulated and Austria was on the verge of collapse : the German Nation was, therefore, faced with an impossible position. Nevertheless, if she could withdraw her Armies to shorter lines and so prolong the struggle through the winter, she might hope for better terms when the time came to capitulate—for to win the War was obviously impossible. To prevent her thus baulking the Allies of the full fruits of victory, it was essential to attack the enemy immediately and in a vital centre, i.e. the line Maubeuge—Mons. A necessary preliminary was the capture of Valenciennes, accomplished on the 1st and 2nd November. On the 3rd, as a result of this fresh defeat, the enemy withdrew on the Le Quesnoy—Valenciennes front. Arrangements for the principal attack were then completed.

On the 4th November the Fourth, Third and First Armies, at various hours from 5.45 a.m. to 6.15 a.m. attacked the enemy on a front of about 30 miles from the Sambre, north of Oisy to Valenciennes.

The 1st Division was on the extreme right of this great attack, the official despatches referring to it in the following terms :

' On the right of the attack the 1st Division of the IXth Corps, under the command of Lieut.-General Sir W. P. Braithwaite, starting at 5.45 a.m., captured Catillon and proceeded to pass troops across the Sambre

---

[1] The official report of the Battles Nomenclature Committee gives the date as the 4th November, but it is quite obvious that the battle was of more than one day's duration and the 1st to the 11th November is a more comprehensive period.

at this place and at the lock some 2 miles to the south of it. This difficult operation was accomplished with remarkable rapidity and skill and by 7.45 a.m. the 1st Battalion Cameron Highlanders and the 1st Battalion Northampton Regiment were east of the river. Bois L'Abbaye, Hautrève [1] and La Groise were captured in turn and, though held up for a time at Fesmy, our troops took this place also in a renewed attack at 4 p.m., subsequently advancing well to the east of it.'

The scheme of attack by the 1st Division was simple : the 2nd and 1st Brigades (right and left respectively) were to capture the crossings over the Canal south of Catillon : the 3rd Brigade was to attack and capture Catillon and form a bridgehead east of the Canal obtaining touch with the 32nd Division, on the left of the 1st Division.

Catillon was to be captured by the 1st Gloucesters who were also to form the bridgehead on the eastern side of the Canal.

The 28th had remained billeted in Vaux Andigny until the 30th October [2] and had then moved into the front line northeast of Mazinghein. On the 1st November A Company's posts were attacked by the enemy and, although he was repulsed with casualties, the Gloucesters lost Lieutenant A. R. Skemp and 6 other ranks killed and 1 other rank wounded : 4 other ranks were wounded later.

On the 2nd the Battalion was holding an outpost line roughly 2,000 yards in length, west of the Sambre—Oise Canal and a mile south of Catillon. At 10 p.m. on the night of the 3rd the 28th were relieved by the 1st Camerons, 1st Loyal North Lancs and 1st Northants, and moved to their assembly positions for the attack to be launched the following morning.

It may be that a paraphrase of the narrative of the Battle of the Sambre, contained in the Diary of the ' Old Braggs ', would give the story in more flowing language, but its historical value would be small compared with that of the Gloucesters' own record of their final fight with the enemy in the greatest war the world has ever known.

The record begins with the words ' Attacked Catillon ' and the story continues as follows :

' The Battalion's objectives were to seize that part of the town of Catillon which lies east of the road running north and south through the Church (Square) inclusive : secondly, to force the crossing of the Canal at the broken bridge, M.19.b.6.6. (on the north-eastern exits of Catillon), press forward to the road junction M.20.a.7.7. (600 yards east of the broken bridge and Canal), form a bridgehead and there await

[1] The 1st Division War Memorial stands at the cross-roads at Hautrève.
[2] On the 25th October Lieut.-Colonel J. R. Guild had assumed command of the 28th from Lieut.-Colonel J. L. F. Tweedie.

arrival of the 1st Infantry Brigade and 32nd Division. The remaining portions of the town of Catillon were also to be " mopped up ".

' The following co-operated with the Battalion under the orders of the Commanding Officer : two tanks of 10th Battalion Tank Corps, one section 26th Field Company, R.E., one section D Company, 1st Battalion, Machine Gun Corps, and two Stokes guns from 3rd Trench Mortar Battery.[1]

' The Battalion was in its assembly positions, from road junction R.30.a.3.0 (about 600 yards south of Catillon and nearly 800 from the western bank of the Sambre Canal) eastwards to the Canal, at zero minus thirty minutes (zero was 5.45 a.m.). Dispositions were as follows : C Company right front-line company, D Company left front-line company, B Company " moppers up " and to move behind D Company. A Company in reserve. One section D Company 1st Battalion M.G.C., two Stokes mortars and one section 26th Field Company, R.E., were attached to C Company and followed that Company in the advance : Battalion Headquarters at R.35.C.5.3. (La Louvière Farm).

' The left flank was the flank of direction, the road south from Catillon Church through R.30.a.4.1 (one of the cross roads previously mentioned) being taken as a guide.

' Zero hour. The Battalion, moving under a creeping enfilade barrage of artillery and machine guns, made excellent progress northwards towards Catillon although, owing to a very dense fog, it was difficult to keep direction. The left Company overcame three machine guns in the orchards and then worked straight for the Church. Near this point they were overtaken by a tank and together they turned right at the Church and worked around the southern portion of the town into the street on the eastern outskirts of the town. Several machine guns were encountered and the crews captured. This Company then pushed east towards the bridge and reconnoitred the Canal crossings. The right Company advanced, taking as their right the road running north and south about 100 yards west of the Canal. They encountered heavy machine-gun fire from the hedgerows and orchards and eventually captured nine or ten machine guns with their teams. Reaching the town they pushed on to the bridge and here a careful reconnaissance revealed a heavy machine gun in a house nearby. They communicated with the tank co-operating with them and it pushed forward close to the bridge, engaged the gun and succeeded in putting the whole crew out of action.

' By this time our barrage was falling on the Canal, but the Company Commander considered it worth while to work round the barrage and gain the eastern side before the lift. This they managed to accomplish although they had some difficulty in overcoming a formidable obstacle

---

[1] Being so near the scenes of their actions with the enemy in 1914, and but a few hundred yards only from the La Groise—Oisy road down which they had retired in August of that year during the Retreat from Mons, one's thoughts turn naturally to the progress of warfare in those four years and more : and this list of units attached to the 28th for the last battle brings strongly to the mind the extraordinary difference between our Army in August 1914 and in November 1918. We had no tanks, no battalions of a machine-gun corps, no trench-mortar batteries in those early days.

in the shape of a number of farm implements piled together and entwined with barbed wire.

' Immediately our barrage lifted the enemy began to scramble from the cellars only to be received by our men. This haul furnished about 100 prisoners and a number of machine guns. The left Company then swung out to the left, guarding the left of the bridge and facing north-east, while the right Company did similarly on the right, but facing south-east. Having formed this bridgehead the two Companies, taking the *Route Nationale* as their guide, pushed forward in the face of heavy machine-gun fire and reached the road junction of the final objective.

' Touch was gained at this point with the 1st Infantry Brigade on the right and later with the 32nd Division on the left.'

Platoons of the reserve Company then reinforced the front line and the Diary gives the final dispositions, but gives them in co-ordinates, which interpreted meant that they were disposed on a north-west to south-east line astride the road running east from the Canal and 200 to 300 yards from the latter. One Company was pushed on a further 200 yards eastwards along the road.

' Simultaneously the " mopping-up " Company had worked systematically through Catillon, capturing many prisoners and machine guns.

' The captures of the Battalion included about 450 prisoners and a number of trench mortars and machine guns.

' Our casualties were Lieutenant W. G. Tunnicliffe and 2nd Lieutenant W. Barnett wounded, 4 other ranks killed and 26 other ranks wounded.'

At 5 p.m. that night the Battalion marched back to billets in Vaux Andigny, thence on the 5th to Bohain and on the 6th to Fresnoy-le-Grand : the 28th were still billeted in Fresnoy when at 11 a.m. on the 11th of November the Armistice came into force.

On the left of the IXth Corps the plan of attack of the XIIIth Corps entailed an attack through the southern portion of the Forêt de Mormal, the forcing of the Canal Crossings at Landrecies and capture of that town—a total advance of about 10 miles.

The 25th Division was on the right of the Corps front and had been allotted the difficult task of forcing the crossings over the Canal, capturing Landrecies and pushing on to the Corps' intermediate objective which included the capture of Maroilles.

The initial attack of the Division was to be carried out by the 75th Brigade, the 74th and 7th Brigades ' leap-frogging ' the first-named Brigade on the first objective (the Red Line)—a north and south line on the eastern edges of Landrecies. The 32nd Division was on the right of the 25th (between the 25th and 1st Divisions).

The 75th Brigade was to attack with the 1/5th Gloucesters on the right, 1/8th Warwicks on the left and the 1/8th Worcesters in support. On the right of the Gloucesters two companies of the 21st Manchesters were to attack and capture Happegarbes.

Zero hour was 6.15 a.m. on the 4th.

The first three days of November were unpleasant : the enemy's artillery was active and on the 1st the 1/5th Gloucesters, who were still in the line in front of Malgarni, had seven casualties. On the 2nd the Brigade on their right attacked and advanced the line slightly. In the hostile bombardment which followed the right front company (B) of the Gloucesters lost four or five more men. The enemy counter-attacked later during the day and B Company, which as a result of the morning attack by the brigade on their right, had formed an advanced post, were obliged to relinquish it again in order to conform to the Lancashire Fusiliers on the right who had fallen back. The reserve Company (A) also came in for heavy shell-fire and suffered seven casualties. On the 3rd the neighbouring brigade on the Gloucesters' right again attacked the enemy and gained its objective. During the attack the enemy's gun-fire was negligible, but later in the day it was considerable.

When zero hour dawned on the 4th the dispositions of the 1/5th Gloucesters for the attack were as follows : A Company on the right, C on the left, D Company ' moppers-up ', and B in reserve.

To the 1/5th (Territorial) Battalion of the Gloucestershire Regiment also the actual story of that last fight with the enemy in France, as written at the time, is of historical interest : it is, therefore, given in full :

' Objective was to reach the bank of the Sambre Canal and, if possible, to bridge and cross it. The attack started in a thick mist, which at first caused a little confusion owing to the close country and A Company became somewhat split up, but B Company moved up to the front line and the attack progressed successfully right up to the Canal bank where a few of B Company crossed. The Worcesters then came through us, crossed the Canal and advanced through Landrecies, followed by the Battalion which, after successfully crossing, formed a defensive flank facing south. The Battalion in this operation captured about 350 prisoners, three anti-tank guns, one field gun, one motor ambulance, one horse ambulance complete, and numerous machine guns. Our casualties were Captain F. S. Hill (4th Battalion) and 2nd Lieutenant V. Scroggie (1st Battalion) killed : 2nd Lieutenant Jackson, Lieutenant Gilshenan, 2nd Lieutenant Powell and Captain G. Hawkins were wounded : twelve other ranks killed and forty-nine wounded.

' In this operation we were protecting the flank of the 74th Brigade which had passed through us early in the evening. The 32nd Division was on our right.

' Between 20.00 and 22.30 hours (8 p.m. and 10.30 p.m.) three enemy patrols were seen to be approaching A Company's posts. These were at once dealt with in a satisfactory manner and, as a result, the enemy lost four prisoners and four machine guns captured.'

At ' stand down ' the next morning A Company withdrew to the Landrecies—Maroilles road and at 10 a.m. the Territorials, as rear Battalion of the 75th Brigade (advancing in rear of the 74th Brigade) moved off and two hours later reached the cross-roads one kilometre south-east of Le Preseau. Here the Gloucesters halted and were billeted in houses near by. The 6th was spent in this position.

At 4 a.m. on the 7th the Battalion moved off in column of route to the outpost line which lay one kilometre east of Marbaix. On passing through this line at 8 a.m. the Gloucesters formed an advanced guard, B and D Companies in the van, A and C Companies as the main body, to the Brigade. The objective was the main road from Avesnes to Maubeuge on the north-western outskirts of the former town. A mile east of St. Hilaire the advanced guard was held up by a strong line of hostile machine guns. At dusk an outpost line about 2,000 yards in extent was formed with B Company on the right, D in the centre and C on the left, A being in reserve. Touch was obtained with the 32nd Division on the right and the 7th Brigade on the left. The 1/5th were relieved by a battalion of the King's Regiment and moved back into billets at Marbaix.[1]

But the Territorials were not destined to be in the Corps front when the War ended, for at 9 a.m. on the 9th the Battalion sent off an advanced party of 1 officer and 7 other ranks on bicycles to Preux-au-Bois and at 10.30 a.m. the Battalion followed, marching again through Landrecies where the civilian inhabitants showed their gratitude for their release from German domination ' by distributing tricolour flags and flowers to the troops '—the last human ' touch ' in the Diaries of the 1/5th Gloucestershire Regiment.

At Preux accommodation was poor and crowded. The 9th was given to cleaning up and resting : the 10th being a Sunday, there was a Church Parade and light duties afterwards.

Commonplace in the extreme was the work of the Battalion on the last day of the terrific struggle between the Nations which had raged for four long years and more. Roads in the neigh-

---

[1] Every survivor of the 1st Battalion who took part in the Retreat from Mons in 1914 will remember Marbaix : also le Grand Fayt, not far off.

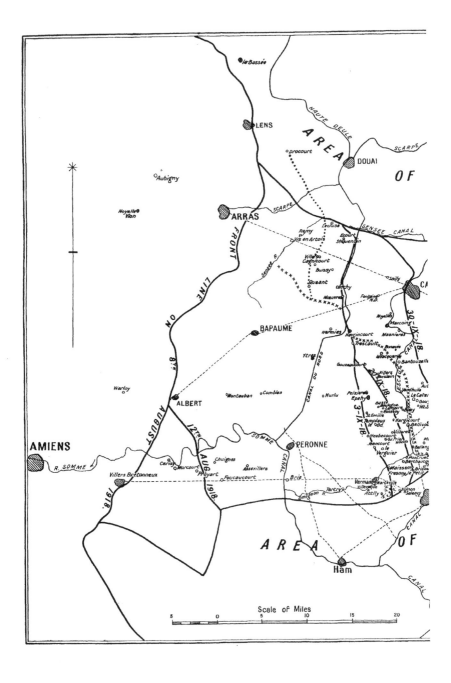

la Bassée

AREA

LENS

OF

Aubigny

Drocourt

DOUAI

SCARPE

Noyelle Vion

ARRAS

SCARPE

SENSEE CANAL

Ecluse

Remy
Vis en Artois

Ecourt
St Quentin

Villers
Cagnicourt

Bursoy

FRONT

Senree R.

Quéant

Dinchy

CA

LINE

Maurres

Fontaine
N.D.

30·IX·18

Noyelle

Marcoing

8th

BAPAUME

Ivermies

Hargincourt

Masnieres

Ytres

Trescault
Bonavis

Flesquieres
Bantouzell

AUGUST

Warloy

Montauban
Combles

Gouzeaucourt

Nurlu

Villers
Guislain

CANAL DU NORD

Aut

Vendhuile
La Catea

ALBERT

Pelziere
Epehy

le Gou
Mc.

Bass
Hamel
Honnsley

Epey

3·IX·18

ESCAUT CANAL

St Emilie
Templeux
Od.

Hargicourt
Bellicou

12TH

AMIENS

SOMME CANAL

PERONNE

Nillere
Jeancourt
le
Verguier

Wood

R. SOMME

Cerisy
Morcourt

Chuignes

Proyart

Asseviliers

AUGUST 1918.

Foucaucourt

Brie

Vermand
Marteville
Villeveque

Attilly

Pontruet

Berthauco

Maissem
Fresnoy
le Petit

1918.

Villers Bretonneux

Amignon R.

Tartcry

Holnon

Selency

AREA

OF

Ham

CANAL

CANAL

Scale of Miles

5   0   5   10   15   20

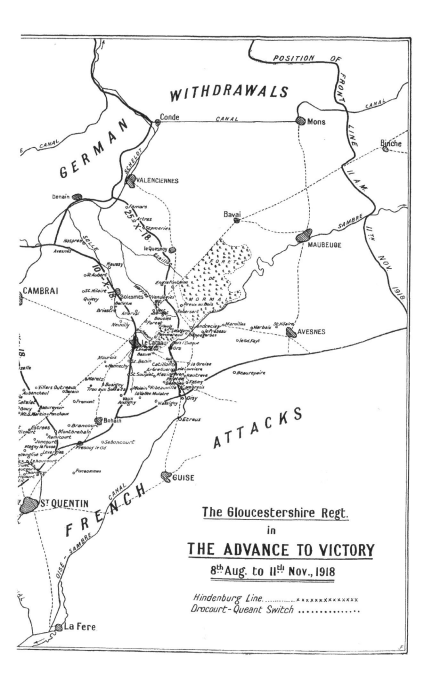

The Gloucestershire Regt.

in

THE ADVANCE TO VICTORY

8th Aug. to 11th Nov., 1918

Hindenburg Line............ xxxxxxxxxxxxx
Drocourt-Queant Switch ....

bourhood of the camp were cleared, the Signalling Sergeant gave instruction to the Signallers, a new draft was inspected by the C.O. and guard-mounting was practised. Then at the very end of the Diary, cramped in between the lines, there are these words : ' News of Armistice received, very little interest—a few Véry lights let off in the evening. A.A. guns dismounted.'

Thus the 1/5th Gloucesters ended their part in the Great War in France and Flanders.

CHAPTER XXXVII

SALONIKA : III

THE momentous year 1918 opened in Macedonia with the usual climatic discomforts. No changes had taken place in the dispositions of the four battalions forming the 82nd Brigade (27th Division) and the 2nd Gloucesters (Lieut.-Colonel A. C. Vicary commanding) were still at Bluff Camp on the 1st January. Bluff Camp was not a tented camp but a collection of bivouacs and dug-outs, occupied by the Battalion in Reserve to the Brigade holding the Neohori bridge-head. To mark the advent of the New Year a day's holiday was given all ranks and in the afternoon there was a football match between the officers and the sergeants of the Battalion : the result is not recorded.

The Diary of the 61st for January is a record of work and training carried out under all sorts and conditions of weather and circumstances. There were fine days, wet days and days when the snow lay so thick upon the ground that no outside work was possible. The construction of a Decauville railway necessitated work at night. There were days when the assault was practised, others when the building of huts and dug-outs claimed attention.

On the 23rd January the Diary records that Captain S. B. Swan and 2nd Lieutenant H. R. Power were awarded the Military Cross.

Little happened during the first half of February and it was not until the 16th that the Gloucesters moved from Bluff Camp and relieved the 10th Hants in the left centre, sub-sector (K.C.) of the Brigade front line.

There is with the April Diary an account of the period 17th February—30th April inclusive, which may be quoted verbatim as it explains in the Battalion's own words life in the front line between those dates :

' This period in the trenches has been marked with no incident of great importance, but there has been plenty to do, and the Battalion has left its mark on the line, and the strength of the positions has been considerably increased.

' As the trenches run along the crest of the first ridge on the left bank

316

of the Struma there is no depth to the bridge-head position at all, and should the enemy penetrate and capture our one line of trenches the garrison, if any were left, would unquestionably have to retire across the river.

' To counteract the lack of depth in the positions as far as the nature of the ground permitted, a strong advanced line was constructed as it was impossible to make a support line close in rear of the main trenches.

' The existing line of night posts was chosen for this line and the posts were strengthened, good dug-outs for the garrison were made and the wire in front of them considerably thickened.

' The key to the advanced line is Sniper's Knoll, a hill about 400 yards in front of the left sphere in the main line. This hill was tunnelled [1] through and a Lewis-gun position made which sweeps the whole of the front of the advanced line.

' Finally, another line of wire was run out from Sniper's Knoll northwards to the river across the Drama road, and a post made on the Drama road where the river crossed it.

' This completed the strengthening of the advanced line and it can safely be said that such a line would give great annoyance to an enemy attack and quite possibly stop it altogether.

' Having strengthened the advanced line and provided a certain amount of depth to the position the main line of trenches had to be considered. As there were not enough Vickers guns to cover the front of the position, a barrage of Lewis guns was arranged. To start with the Lewis guns were all mounted in positions on the parapet, and in only two or three cases could good fields of fire be obtained. Accordingly it was decided to make tunnels out under the parapet and strike up from thence to selected positions where a good field of fire could be obtained. This was done with eight gun positions and proved very successful. A mounting was devised and night lines laid out for the guns to sweep the whole front very thoroughly.

' The main line of wire was then increased and some new tactical switches run out. The main wire is now about 25 yards thick and presents an almost impassable obstacle.[2]

' Having provided for the defence of the position more securely the protection of the garrison during bombardment was considered and galleries, cut out into the rock of the hill, were made for the entire garrison. Some of these had already been made before the Battalion came into the line. It is not known what stopping power they have, as no direct hit on top of them has yet been obtained, but as they are at least 6 feet thick in the roof, nearly all of which is rock, they should keep out shells up to 5·9-inch howitzers.[3]

' In view of the coming fever season, the mosquito preparing work was pushed on with, and all the galleries and many selected dug-outs were made mosquito proof. Terraces were also prepared on which mosquito-net barricades would be pitched.

' From a fighting point of view the period spent in the line was quiet.

---

[1] The tunnel was 200 yards long, through rock, and was constructed by the Gloucesters without any extraneous assistance.

[2] This wiring was carried out in the form of inter-platoon competition : prizes were awarded by the Commanding Officer.

[3] Each gallery was connected with the front line trench by a tunnel.

One raid was carried out by the Battalion on a small enemy post at Picket Bank and a separate account of this has been prepared and is attached.[1]

'The 40th Bulgar Regiment is holding the line in front of the position and they showed very little enterprise.   Latterly, however, there has been a marked increase in the enemy's patrolling activity and it is possible that a new regiment of Bulgars has arrived.   Owing to the very large tract of country over which patrols had to work, it is very hard to lay an ambush for the enemy who is, furthermore, exceedingly wary. The hostile artillery is not very active and we had only three casualties from shell fire.   Considering the number of shells fired this is extraordinarily few.   No gas shells have been used as yet by the enemy on this front.

'The sickness has not been excessive, an average of thirty-five a day from the Battalion, and of these an average of nine go to hospital each week.'

On the 18th March Captain H. J. Hammond was seriously wounded by a ' blind ' enemy shell and died in Stavros on the 23rd.

The Diary for the 24th March records that the ' days are beginning to get hot ', but thoughts of summer were apparently premature, for a few days later there was a heavy fall of snow and the last day of the month—it was Easter Sunday—was cold.

Ptes. Nos. 8853 and 8718, Davis and Legg, were awarded the Military Medal on the 19th March, for the raid on Picket Bank.

The Battalion held K.C. sub-sector throughout the whole of April.   On the 13th the 82nd Brigade held its sports at Asprovalta, in which the Gloucesters won two first events and two seconds : competitors in these sports were allowed to leave the line to attend them.   On the 19th a considerable increase in fever cases is mentioned, and a few days later there is another entry to the effect that ' khaki drill will not be issued this year '.

Major Owen Symons left the 61st on the 27th to go to France : he was liked by all ranks and the Diary records that ' everybody was sorry to lose him '.

By the 30th the 2nd Gloucesters had been relieved by the 10th Hants and were back again in Bluff Camp, a portion of A Company going to K.A. sub-sector and D Company to Tasli.

---

[1] No separate account is with the Battalion or Brigade records, but this incident is described in the Diary of the 61st in the following words : ' Party under Lieutenant Collins raided enemy post on Picket Bank, leaving Drama road post at approximately 24.00 hours (12 midnight). The operations were quite successful and at least eight of the enemy were killed.   Our casualties were two other ranks wounded, one wounded and missing.'   This raid took place on the 7th March.   Lieutenant Collins was subsequently awarded the Military Cross for gallant conduct during the raid.

Sun-helmets and shorts were issued on the 2nd May—summer had begun.

The life of the Battalion was now divided between training and work. A Rifle Club was brought into existence on the 18th and 'went very well', and near the camp on the same night the 'Follies' gave a show.

Dust and rain storms were part of the summer weather which towards the end of May is written down as 'exceedingly hot'. Fortunately the enemy's activity was practically nil, and it was not until the 30th that the Bulgars showed any inclination to disturb the comparative peace. On that date, however, the French were attacking on the Vardar and the enemy, possibly fearing attacks all along the line, threw bombs till nearly midnight.

On the last day of the month the Diary contains an entry which shows how, even on the Macedonian front, France and Flanders seemed not so far distant : ' Heard news of another big enemy attack in France.'

Little of outstanding importance happened during June.[1] On the 10th orders were received to relieve Lovat's Scouts who were leaving the Brigade in K.B. sub-sector. The relief began the following night and by the 12th was complete. On going into the line, however, the Gloucesters were told that Greek officers and some other ranks would shortly be attached to the Battalion with a view to taking over the line.

Two Greek officers per company and Battalion Headquarters arrived at 10.30 p.m. on the 13th : also about twenty Greek N.C.O.s. On the 15th the 5/42nd Euzone Regiment, 1st Battalion, was ordered to relieve the Gloucesters, but the operation was postponed, as the enemy opened desultory shell-fire, obviously with the idea of interfering with the relief. It was not until the night of the 22nd that the Greeks began to take over the line. On the night of the 24th the 61st were back in Bluff Camp where they were to stay one night, march down to Tasli the next day and move by train to camp at Vrasta.

The tour at Vrasta, where sea-side camps had been erected on the shore of the Gulf of Orfanu, was one of the brightest spots in the life of the 2nd Gloucesters during their long period on the Macedonian front—and they deserved it. Leave to the United Kingdom had been in force some time, nevertheless it worked out at once in three years for the men and there were some who had no leave at home at all.

---

[1] On the 3rd the *London Gazette* announced the award of the Meritorious Service Medal to No. 8491 Sergt. Clements and No. 7777 C.S.M. Stenner.

An advanced party, under 2nd Lieutenant James, had been despatched to Vrasta to prepare a camp on the seashore east of the town, and by the time the Battalion arrived on the 26th June the camp was practically completed. The Battalion Diary on that date states that ' the time to be spent in this camp is to be a rest period as far as possible ', and it *was*. Various duties and necessary things had to be carried out of course, the first being to dig shelter trenches to be used in the event of an air raid. This work began on the 27th, by which time ' all ranks are now settled down in camp and the place is very popular, the sea bathing being very much appreciated '.

Twelve days were spent thus happily, on the shores of the Gulf, but towards the end of that period rumours were afloat that, on returning to the line, a new sector was to be taken over. These rumours proved to be true, for orders were received by the 2nd Gloucesters to entrain on the 8th for Guvesne, whence the journey was to be resumed to an ' unknown destination ', which eventually turned out to be west of the Vardar, the 27th Division having been ordered to relieve the 122nd French Division in a sector immediately west of the river and south-west of Doiran.

The 61st therefore spent the 7th in cleaning up and getting ready for the move. In three parties they entrained on the 8th and proceeded by the Decauville railway to Sarakli, where they changed to standard-gauge train and continued their journey to Guvesne Camp.

The night of the 8th was spent in this place in tents, the men being very comfortable. On the 9th, at 4 and 4.30 p.m., the Battalion in two parties entrained and went on to Salmah where the trains joined up and proceeded thence to Kilo 67 Station. The Gloucesters then detrained and marched to another camp, everybody being in by 3 a.m. on the 10th, but the darkness hid the surroundings.

The camp in which the Battalion spent the night of the 9th was, on inspection on the 10th, found to be extremely dirty and unsanitary.

The Gloucesters were now in Divisional Reserve, occupying the third line : Brigade Headquarters were in the neighbourhood of Dreveno. The 10th Hants and 2nd D.C.L.I. had taken over the second line which ran along the Kara Sinanci—Mayadag Ridge, the former Battalion from the northern bank of the Vardar to Kara Sinanci (inclusive), the D.C.L.I. thence to the Ravine des Poilus (inclusive).

By the 13th the Gloucesters had straightened up their camp and had begun work on the ranges. The weather was hot and precautions against malaria and sand-fly fever were necessary. Leave parties for England continued and by this date the fighting strength of the Battalion was only 438 all ranks.

To the end of July there is little of outstanding interest in the Battalion and Brigade Diaries : training was almost impossible owing to the constant need for supplying large working parties.

On the 1st August there was a violent thunderstorm which flooded the men out and made things very uncomfortable. But there was one characteristic about rain storms in Macedonia : the soil was porous and quickly absorbed water.

The month began with training and the usual supply of working parties. Lack of time for adequate training was, however, a considerable source of anxiety to the C.O., for the strength of the Battalion was extremely low, so that he was constrained to issue stringent orders on the method to be adopted :

' With the numbers now available,' state these orders, ' it is clear that any company attack training on the old lines of company in normal formation is at present impossible. It must be the chief object, there-fore, of company commanders to make real experts of the few men they have left and this, by careful organization and supervision and use of the good instructors which are available, they should be able to do.

' Later on reinforcements will undoubtedly arrive and the training by companies can commence under the few men who have already had the individual training for building up the company. This individual training requires great personal effort, not only on the part of the com-pany commanders but also on that of all officers and instructors. A bad instructor is worse than no instructor at all, as the men get bored and lose interest. If any company is short of instructors for any par-ticular subject, application should be made to Battalion Headquarters for one. Officers will be used as instructors whenever possible and great care must be given to the checking of faults which is one of an instructor's chief duties. It is absolutely essential to avoid waste of both time and men. Punctuality is, therefore, a most important feature and everybody in the company must undergo training, the majority during the whole day and the few necessarily.employed men during either the morning or the evening.'

This order was issued on the 6th August. On that date Colonel Vicary had been informed by the Divisional Commander (Major-General Sir G. Forestier-Walker) that it intended to seize by a surprise attack the Roche Noir Salient, as a preliminary to opera-tions on a larger scale by the whole of the Allied Army.

The primary object of the attack was to deceive the enemy into believing that the main attack of the Army was to be in the direction of Guevgeli, up the Vardar Valley, thereby drawing off the Bulgar reserves and especially artillery from other parts of the front to this area, thus weakening the front against which the main

21

attack of the Allies was to be launched.   A secondary object was to deprive the enemy of the Roche Noir Salient as a threat to Guevgeli and as an observation post.   This salient overlooked the whole of the front held by the 27th Division and a large area in rear.

As will be seen later the 2nd Gloucesters had been allotted the position of honour in the attack.   This may have been known to Colonel Vicary when he issued the above training order.   In any event the knowledge that an attack *was* to take place was circulated in an order of ' Preliminary Instructions ', issued on the 15th. This order stated that the 27th Division was to undertake offensive operations at an early date ' with the following preliminary objects :

' (i) Of attacking and holding the enemy salient Trenchees du Yatagan, Mamelon [1] aux Buissons, La Table, La Roche Noir, Dos de Mulet, Trenchees des Roches and Les Deux Roches.
" (ii) of advancing our present line to approximately the line of the enemy's outposts between the River Vardar and M. du Yatagan (exclusive).
' The above with a view to the ultimate capture of the Dzeov La Mitre position.'

The 82nd Brigade was to carry out (i), the 81st Brigade (ii) and the 80th minor enterprises.

The 2nd Gloucesters and 10th Hants were to carry out the principal attack.

With this knowledge, therefore, the Battalion set to work to train hard and make all the necessary arrangements, while the C.O. on the very day these orders were issued reconnoitred the forming-up ground in Alcah Mah and selected assembly trenches in Hadzi Mah for companies.

Battalion Preliminary Instructions were issued on the 16th, but for the moment it will suffice to note down what happened during the period intervening between that date and the attack which took place on the 1st/2nd September.

Practice attacks over ground dug in exact imitation of the actual trenches to be attacked took place as frequently as possible. Special bombing and Lewis-gun courses were introduced, and the formation of the inevitable Battalion Dump began.   The latter was no light task, for by the time it was completed—on the 24th—no less than over two hundred mule loads of stores had been moved by the Transport to the front line without having a man or a mule hit—a very creditable performance.

On the 29th the Battalion Diary records the issue of Preliminary

---

[1] A French military expression denoting ' a rounded mound '.

Instruction No. 5 and adds the following significant words :
' Remains, only operation orders now.'   A slight change in orders
necessitated the issue of Preliminary Instruction No. 6 on the
30th, but on the 31st Operation Orders were issued which may
be summarized thus :

The 2nd Gloucestershire Regiment was to capture and hold the
Tr. du Yatagan and the Mamelon aux Buissons (which, being
fifty feet higher than any other part of the salient, was the key
to the position), comprising the following works—Tr. D'Alcah
Mah, Novelle Tr. du Sommet, Tr. du Sommet, Boyeau de la
Couronne, Trench C.118 and Points C.102a, C.103a, C.103c,
D.361 and 5033.   The 10th Hampshires were to capture and hold
the remainder of the salient, which comprised La Table, Les
2 Roches, La Roche Noire, Dos de Mulet and Tr. des Roche.
The Gloucesters were, therefore, to be on the right and the Hants
on the left.

The former Battalion was, shortly before X Day, to take over
the camp of the 2nd D.C.L.I. at La Dent and the upper Pactol,
and two nights before the attack were to assemble in Hadzi
Bari Mah, remaining there until they advanced to carry out the
attack.

Companies were to be formed up for the attack as follows :
Right Company—D under Captain Russell ; Centre Company—
C under Captain Whitcomb ; Left Company—B under Captain
Collins ; Headquarters Lewis-gun section under Lieutenant
Palmer : Battalion Reserve—A Company under Lieutenant
Jenkyn.

The Battalion was to attack in four waves preceded by a thin
line of scouts and guides on a front of 200 yards with 30 yards
distance between waves.   Each wave was to consist of $1\frac{1}{2}$ platoons,
i.e. two sections of each of the three assaulting companies who
had been organized on a two-platoon basis.   The Headquarters
Lewis-gun section was to move with the fourth wave behind the
Centre and Left Companies and the one platoon of A Company
as a fifth and sixth wave behind the right company.

Each company wave to consist of two columns in single file
(strength eight to ten other ranks) at 25 yards interval.

With the Battalion Diary for September 1918 there is a ' Narrative of Attack ', and as it gives a very excellent account of the
training given each company prior to the operations, incidentally
mentioning the objectives allotted to each, an extract is given
which may help to a clearer understanding of what the Battalion
actually accomplished when the assault took place :

324 THE GLOUCESTERSHIRE REGIMENT [1918

'Each company practised their share of the attack over ground on which a model of the trenches had been marked out: D Company taking the Boyeau de la Couronne and the Mamelon du Yatagan: C Company Trench C.105 and the eastern half of C.108 and B Company taking Trench C.104 and the western half of Trench C.108 and down to D.360 and 361 and the Boyeau du Danube exclusive. Headquarters Lewis-gun section occupied C.108b and C.105b to bring covering fire for troops on either flank.

'The attack was practised daily by all companies in fighting order, each man carrying his haversack and small kit on his back, four sand bags rolled in the belt, two bombs, 170 rounds S.A.A. and a certain proportion picks and shovels and wire cutters (first wave). Each Lewis-gun team carried twenty-eight magazines into action and each bomber eight No. 5 or rifle bombs.

'By the end of August,' said Colonel Vicary, 'the Regiment was probably at a higher scale of efficiency, especially in the handling of light automatics, than it had been since 1914. In spite of secrecy it was obvious that all ranks were convinced that the Regiment was to carry out an important attack. *It was almost unbelievable that after nearly four years of war officers and men could have been so extraordinarily keen.*'

All preparations were completed by the 30th. This had entailed very careful camouflaging and screening of the assembly trenches, the cutting of communication and assembly trenches and the arrangement of dumps for ammunition, material for consolidation and supplies in the front-line trenches. Practically the whole of the work was done by the Gloucesters at night from Divisional Reserve.

The screening and camouflaging was carried out by 2nd Lieutenants Sibley and James with a party of twenty-four men, who lived in a mulberry grove at the eastern end of Hadzi. The formation of the dumps was done by the Quartermaster, Captain E. H. Dinham,[1] Transport Officer, and 2nd Lieutenant Sibley. The cartage from Dreveno down to the dump was all done by mules.

Wire cutting was carried out by the 'Heavies', Colonel Vicary indicating the gaps required.

At last all was ready and at 9.30 p.m. on the 31st August the Gloucesters set out on the march down to the front-line trenches at Hadzi Bari Mah. The enemy's suspicions had some time since been aroused and during the past few days his artillery had been increased on the front to be attacked. All precautions were therefore taken to guard against casualties from artillery fire before the assault opened. The Battalion marched in the order A, B, C, D, Headquarters. An interval of ten minutes was allowed

---

[1] He was Quartermaster to the Battalion throughout the whole War, and never failed to be at the right place with the right stuff at the right moment.

between platoons and half an hour between companies. There was some delay for about ten minutes caused by C Company, owing to the darkness, missing the track when nearly in Hadzi. Apart from this small misadventure all went smoothly and by 3 a.m. the Battalion was concentrated in the front-line trenches at Hadzi. Three times during the night the enemy put down an intense barrage over Meunier, Parallel 3 and Hadzi, but by remarkable good luck only one man of the Gloucesters was slightly grazed.

During the morning of the 1st September companies drew from the ' complete-for-action ' dump their final requirements of bombs, ammunition and aeroplane flares.

Zero had been fixed at 5.36 p.m.

The assembly position of the 2nd Gloucesters was on the uneven slope of a small hill in ' No-Man's Land ', just south-west of the ruined village of Alcah-Mah, and was approached by carefully-camouflaged communication trenches leading out of the re-entrant in the front-line trenches at Hadzi. The attack was planned to take place in daylight, in order to allow sufficient time for hasty consolidation of the captured positions before darkness fell, but insufficient time for the enemy to organize a counter-attack on a big scale before night had fallen.

No artillery fire was to support the attack as far as the enemy's first-line trenches, speed and surprise being relied upon to carry the attack thus far before the enemy had time to bring down his artillery barrage. From thence on to the final objective the advance was to be carried out under a timed or lifting artillery barrage.

CAPTURE OF THE ROCHE NOIRE SALIENT : 1ST–2ND SEPTEMBER

At 5 p.m. C and D Companies moved out of their billets followed at 5.10 p.m. by B Company, and lined up the Sallypost, B behind C Company in X Trench and D Company in Y Trench.

At 5.20 p.m. companies moved out to their forming-up places in good order, without being observed. The enemy fired a few chance shells which fell near the Sallypost just at this period, but they did no damage. By 5.29 p.m. all companies were formed up ready to advance, everything having worked exactly to programme in spite of hostile shell-fire.

The three assaulting companies, D, C and B (right to left), were led respectively by Lieutenant J. Vicary, 2nd Lieutenant D. L. Bateson and Lieutenant P. H. Hadida : the pace and direction of the attack was to be set by Lieutenant Vicary's company. A Company was in Battalion Reserve.

'At 5.36 p.m., Zero Hour,' states Colonel Vicary, 'the Gloucesters rose as one man and made for the enemy's trenches. The first line was captured before the enemy realized an attack had been made.'

The artillery barrage then fell on the enemy's 'Nouvelle Trench du Sommet' and the assaulting companies advanced to within 50 yards of it. The barrage lifted and companies charged down on the trench.

At this stage it is preferable to let each Company tell its own story of the attack which followed the first lift of the barrage :

D Company : ' Reached and crossed the Bulgar front line at about Point C.116 without opposition, losing one man as they crossed the trench. Point C.102a was reached without any live Bulgars being met with and, leaving a Lewis gun at this point (G.3a) the Company turned east and cleared the Yatagan, also C.100, C.101 and East Post from there to the east. Shelling was heavy but only six casualties occurred up to this point. Wiring and other material came up as soon as it was dark and by dint of hard work, under heavy fire, a very fair fence was put up round the G.1 and G.4 works before dawn. About 04.30 hours (4.30 a.m.) 2nd September, the Company handed over the post to C Company and withdrew to Butoir.'

C Company : ' C Company, moving in the centre, crossed the Alcak Trench without loss and lay down 50 yards behind our barrage on the Nouvelle Trench du Sommet. No opposition was met with during the advance and it was not until the Company reached the Sommet Trench that the enemy shortened their range and casualties began to occur. The front wave pushed forward (to) C.103a behind our barrage, and a covering party was sent out and consolidation began. This was greatly impeded by heavy enemy shelling, but a considerable amount of work was got through nevertheless and this undoubtedly saved many lives when the enemy bombarded at 04.00 hours (4 a.m.) and sent his patrols forward. Company Headquarters was established in a dug-out in trench C.107.

' As soon as it was dark a strong patrol, under 2nd Lieutenant Berry, was pushed out to gain contact with the enemy in the vicinity of the Trench des Loups, which it did, being heavily fired on, and killing one Bulgar without any casualty itself. Enemy was found to be holding Trench des Loups in considerable strength both at this time and again at 03.45 hours (3.45 a.m.) when the patrol went out for a second time.

' As soon as the enemy shelling died down a little, which was about 04.45 hours (4.45 a.m.) the Company took over the Yatagan from D Company, and together with B Company took over the defence of the Buissons also, Company Headquarters being established at 4G.2, reinforced by the Battalion Lewis-Gun Section which had then withdrawn to 4G.1 and 4G.2.'

B Company : ' The whole Company had crossed the Trench D'Alcak before the enemy barrage fell. Our own barrage then came down on the Nouvelle Trench du Sommet and the Company advanced to within 50 yards of it and then, as soon as it lifted, charged the trench, meeting no opposition. The line then advanced to the barrage and as soon as it lifted for the second time the front wave charged down upon the dug-

outs round D.361 and D.360 where about twenty Bulgars were visible.
The majority of these ran for their second line and about six of them
were shot as they ran.   The dug-outs were then bombed out, L/Corpl.
Edwards and Corpl. Collins doing good work here, and several enemy
were killed, though the exact number is not known.

'Having cleared these dug-outs the front platoon withdrew to its
consolidation posts 2G, 2G2, 2G2a and 3G1, the move being completed
just before the enemy barrage shortened and came down on top of the
Buissons.

'During the consolidation the advanced posts lost heavily, having 75
per cent. of their effectives wounded or killed.   The consolidation work
was greatly impeded by heavy enemy shelling but a good deal of deepen-
ing trench was possible, and when at about 04.00 hours (4 a.m.) the
enemy opened an intense bombardment and sent forward patrols, they
were easily repulsed and the work which had been done reduced the
casualties very considerably.

'Owing to the weakness of C Company it was found necessary to
keep both B and C Companies in for the whole of the 2nd inst. and
not withdraw B Company as was intended.   At about 21.00 hours
(9 p.m.), however, on the 2nd of September, B Company withdrew,
being relieved by A Company.   The following men of the Company
did remarkably good work, besides those who were awarded the Military
Medal or recommended for award in the gazette : L/Corpl. A. H.
Webber, Ptes. S. Haslum, G. Millet (all three since killed), Sergt.
Whiting, L/Corpl. Fisher and L/Corpl. Sallis.'

A Company : 'A Company remained in Meunier and the Trench
D'Hadzi during the assault and about 18.15 hours (6.15 p.m.) the Company moved up carrying wire and ammunition to the various posts.
On its arrival at C.116 the material was distributed and one section was
sent to each 4G.1 and 4G.2 to help consolidate, the remaining six being
employed in carrying material from the dump formed by the mule loads,
etc., just behind 4G.1, up to the various posts.   This went on all night
and about 04.45 (4.45 a.m.), when the enemy shelling was less severe
for the time, the Company came back to Meunier and rested there for
the day.'

Battalion Headquarters : 'Moved forward at 18.15 hours (6.15 p.m.)
having received information from the advanced headquarters at C.116
that all objectives had been gained.

'Signal wires were constantly being cut and it was only very rarely
that the telephone could be used.   Lamp signalling was not found
practicable owing to the thick dust and smoke.   At 05.00 hours (5 a.m.)
on the 2nd Battalion Headquarters withdrew to Butoir where it remained
until it was relieved.'

From the above it is possible to obtain something of the battle
from every point of view in the Battalion area.

The carrying parties (fifty men of the 4th Rifle Brigade as well
as the party of twenty-four of the 2nd Gloucesters under 2nd
Lieutenant Sibley) did splendid work.   The dump itself, from
which the stores were drawn, was supervised by Captain Dinham,
who organized the details for all the carrying parties.

At 3 a.m. on the 2nd hot teas were carried up to all ranks of

C Company on the Buissons. Considering the heavy shell-fire, practically all the time, this was a very creditable performance on the part of the carriers.

At no time during the operations was there a serious shortage of any material.

The attack had been successful in every detail and the Gloucesters had had the honour of opening the final battle of the campaign which ended in the complete collapse of Bulgaria.

The casualties suffered by the Battalion (14 other ranks killed, 4 officers and 71 other ranks wounded) were practically all caused during the enemy's subsequent bombardment of his lost posts. The ground was hard sandstone, rendering consolidation difficult and causing splinters of rock and stone to fly from high-explosive shells, and dense clouds of smoke. Under such conditions the difficulty of maintaining communication was almost insuperable, added to which the whole of Battalion Headquarters personnel, with the exception of the C.O. and Adjutant, were killed or wounded during the early stages of the attack.

Throughout the night of the 1st/2nd September the enemy's shell-fire continued, but under cover of darkness, with the assistance of A Company, the position was put in a state of defence. A series of machine-gun and Lewis-gun posts were formed in depth, mutually supporting and cross firing : for this purpose the Regiment went into action with thirty-eight Lewis guns. The forward slopes of the Buissons were not occupied, but dummy trenches constructed to draw the enemy's fire, this part of the position being in reality defended by machine guns and Lewis guns, carefully sited well back on either flank.

All other troops were withdrawn to the Meunier or as Battalion Reserve ready to be launched in an immediate counter-attack should the enemy succeed in penetrating the defences on the Salient.

In the early hours of the 2nd September the enemy suddenly increased his artillery fire, and a few minutes later his infantry advanced to the attack. On reaching the forward slopes of the Buissons the enemy came under fire from the Lewis-gun posts and the attack failed hopelessly.

Shortly afterwards the Bulgars repeated their attack, but it was broken by the Gloucesters' fire before it could mature.

* * * * *

On the night of the 4th September the Battalion took over the whole of the Roche Noire Salient, the 10th Hants withdrawing to another part of the line.

With the casualties suffered in the attack and on defences of the Buissons and Yatagan, the ranks of the Gloucesters had been sorely depleted.[1] The holding of the whole Salient, therefore, threw a great strain on all ranks, who were subjected to constant shelling by day and night. Night after night the Battalion was working on the defences as well as harassing the enemy with strong patrols.

Excepting for raids by means of patrols, all of which were repulsed, the enemy made no further attempt to recapture the position.

The splendid work of the Battalion did not pass without due reward by General Headquarters. On the 16th September the British Commander-in-Chief (General Sir G. Milne) sent for and decorated at 27th Divisional Headquarters the following officers and other ranks of the 2nd Gloucesters in recognition of their gallantry and devotion to duty in the field during the attack and defence of the Roche Noire Salient : Bar to D.S.O., Brevet-Major (Acting Lieut.-Colonel) A. C. Vicary, D.S.O., M.C. ; Second Bar to M.C., Lieutenant J. Vicary,[2] M.C. ; Military Cross— Lieutenant (Acting Captain) J. F. Russell ; Military Medal— —6761 Corpl. Hunt, 9206 L/Corpl. Toop, 8904 L/Corpl. Edwards, 10347 Pte. Carter, 20328 L/Corpl. Major, 16328 Pte. Rudge.

In addition to the above awards Lieut.-Colonel Vicary was also rewarded with the order of Chevalier of the Legion of Honour, Captain E. H. Dinham was promoted Major, Captain C. E. Whitcombe was awarded a bar to his Military Cross, Captain H. R. Power the Greek Military Cross, 2nd Lieutenant D. L. Bateson the Military Cross, and 8898 Sergt. Walkeley, 9287 Sergt. Whittern, 5013 C.S.M. Webb, 8071 C.Q.M.S. Sharpe, 7861 L/Corpl. Maddox, 9217 Pte. Jeynes, 16388 Corpl. Collins and 8852 Pte. Hoxley the Meritorious Service Medal.

Apart from those who received awards the following are mentioned in the records as having shown great gallantry— 6281 Sergt. A. E. Fry, 8588 (killed) Sergt. A. Arnold, 8439 Sergt. C. Connock, 8282 Pte. A. Mortimer (stretcher bearer), 27286 Pte. J. Haddow (stretcher bearer), 2272 Pte. A. Clark and 266528 Pte. J. Alford.

---

[1] The Battalion Diary on the 4th gives the casualties to date as 20 other ranks killed, 87 wounded.

[2] Lieutenant Vicary, owing to wounds received on the 1st September, could not attend. Although badly wounded in the thigh he remained at duty for several days. This devotion to duty nearly cost him his life and he was incapacitated from taking any further part in the campaign.

THE BATTLE OF DOIRAN, 1918 : 18TH–19TH SEPTEMBER

On the 12th the 2nd D.C.L.I. relieved the Gloucesters, the Diary recording that 'enemy pleasantly quiet and whole night very favourable for good relief'. The Battalion then moved back to reserve positions at Molaire. Cleaning up and the replacement of kit occupied the 61st on the 13th and 14th, and then on the 15th came news of a big Franco-Serbian attack on the enemy on the left of the 27th Division. On the 16th preparations were made for a sudden move forward in case the enemy evacuated his positions. On the 17th orders were received to 'stand by' to move back to the Ravin des Poilus.

On the 18th came news of the Franco-Serbian advance. Previous to that date the two other brigades of the 27th Division, on the right of the Gloucesters, had been continually raiding and harassing the enemy. On the 18th the British attack on Doiran opened, but it is unnecessary to describe these operations as the 2nd Gloucesters were not involved in the battle. From that time, however, the effect on the enemy in front of the 82nd Brigade was visible, for he began to show signs of weakening. His artillery fire became more and more normal and it was obvious that he had been forced to withdraw his guns to meet the Franco-Serbian and British attacks. At night, in the Vardar Valley, loud explosions and tongues of flame shooting up into the sky told their own tale : the Bulgar was demolishing his supply and ammunition dumps and preparing to retreat.

On the 20th, at night, troops of the 80th Brigade relieved the 2nd Gloucesters and the latter moved to the Ravin des Poilus, but some idea of the condition of the Battalion may be gathered from the fact that twenty-seven men had to be left behind who could not march. During the relief the Battalion came in for a short but violent burst of shell-fire from the enemy. This turned out to be the last time the Regiment came under fire during the War, for that night the enemy began his retreat. As dusk fell, from their Headquarters Observation Posts, the Gloucesters saw clouds of dust and columns of troops on the hills, moving back from the Bulgar lines.

On the 21st the Battalion received orders to prepare to advance in pursuit of the enemy, who was in full retreat all along the front. The day was spent in collecting spare kit and overcoats and sending them back to the Quartermaster's Stores in the Ravin du Pactol. By 11 p.m. that night the Gloucesters were ready to advance with existing transport. It was not, however, until 11 a.m. on the 22nd that orders were received to march to Alcah Mah, which march was completed by 4 p.m., companies bivouacking in among the ruined houses. No wheeled transport, however, accompanied the Battalion as the roads were blocked with traffic. Emergency rations were drawn from Hadzi Dump.

At 9 a.m. on the 23rd the 61st left Alcah Mah and, marching a mile along the Yatagan track, bivouacked in the Ravin du Dos de Mulet.

In the Bulgar trenches at Zamade large quantities of S.A.A. and gun ammunition were discovered. At 2.30 p.m. the wheeled transport with the Quartermaster joined the Battalion.

The next morning at 7.30 a.m. the Gloucesters left the Ravin.

The Battalion marched first to Negorci, intending to proceed to Pardovika and cross the Vardar there, but owing to trouble with the bridge and the impossibility of crossing, a halt for the night had to be made at Negorci. The whole of the 25th was spent in this place. Twelve Lewis guns, with mules and harness complete, were returned to Kilo 67 Ordnance, as there were not sufficient men to man them. Indeed so weak was the Battalion that the four companies were amalgamated into two, A and D becoming No. 1, B and C No. 2.

On the 26th the 61st marched to Pardovika where a halt was called at 10 a.m. : at 4 p.m. the march was continued to a camp across the Vardar, one kilometre west of Bogdanci, which place was reached at 7 p.m. to everyone's relief. The day had been extremely trying. The dust was terrible on the road and during the time the Battalion halted, there being no shelter from the fierce sun, fever-wracked men became rapidly worse. Only some 330 all ranks were now on the ration strength of the Battalion.

The Gloucesters marched to a camp 300 yards north-east of Dedeli at 4 p.m. on the 27th—a distance of about 8 miles. The same trying conditions existed—dust, heat and congested roads, but only four men fell out.

The 28th was spent in this camp, in which no shade whatever existed. All that could be done was to rig up rough and ready cover with greatcoats. On this date the 82nd Brigade received orders to amalgamate the three battalions into one composite battalion to be called the 82nd Brigade Regiment. The Battalion was to consist of three companies, one from each battalion (2nd Gloucesters, 2nd D.C.L.I. and 10th Hants) and a machine-gun company : all transport being on pack mules, reduced to a minimum to allow rapid movement.

This Composite Battalion was formed to rush ahead and attack the Bulgar rearguards, but it was destined never to come into

action, for in crossing the Vatando Valley on the 29th a lamp
message was received—

'Stand Fast.'

The Bulgars had sued for an Armistice and hostilities had
ceased.

It was still dark when the news was circulated that the enemy
had capitulated, and the attitude of the troops may be gauged by
the remark of a Gloucestershire transport man :

' Just my —— luck, after all the trouble I had to get the ——
mule nicely loaded up ! '

The mule in question was notorious for its rooted objection
to being ' loaded up ', and those who have ever had anything to
do with transport mules will know well what that meant !

Hostilities ceased at 12 noon on the 30th September.

Thus, after nearly three years, the Bulgars had acknowledged
complete defeat, surrendering practically the whole of their Army.

The 2nd Gloucesters then billeted, or rather bivouacked, in
First Bulgarian Army Headquarters which, until a few days
previously, had been occupied by Field-Marshal von Mackensen.
For a few days the Battalion worked on the roads, clearing and
repairing them to enable the British Army to continue its march
into Bulgaria.

The story of the closing weeks of the War, so far as the 2nd
Gloucesters were concerned, may appropriately be told by
Lieut.-Colonel Vicary, whose narrative states :

' It was here that the First Bulgarian Army had suffered such heavy
casualties. The Bulgars, with their line of retreat up the Vardar Valley
cut off by the Franco-Serbian troops, had only one road over the Belachitza Mountains from Valandovo to Strumitza by which to retreat.
Here the whole Army, striving to get back into Bulgaria, were caught
by our Air Force who quickly turned the retreat into a rout and inflicted
terrible casualties. The road over the mountains was strewn with guns,
wagons, dead soldiers and animals. The smell was appalling, as the
weather was still hot, but as one good soldier remarked :

" It was the smell of victory."

' The Regiment then crossed the Bulgarian frontier to Strumitza.
Day after day the advance was continued along the Strumitza river,
north of the Belachitza Mountains to Petric and thence north up the
Struma Valley, through the Kresna Pass where the Bulgarian Army,
retreating from the Struma Valley, had been caught by our Air Force
and completely routed.

' In October the Regiment reached Dupnitza, where they received
orders to march north of Rila Dagh with a view to taking part in operations against the Turks in the direction of Adrianople. This advance
never materialized as the Turks capitulated. The Regiment then
received orders to march north to the Danube to take part in operations
against the Austrians. The disbanded Bulgarian soldiers were now

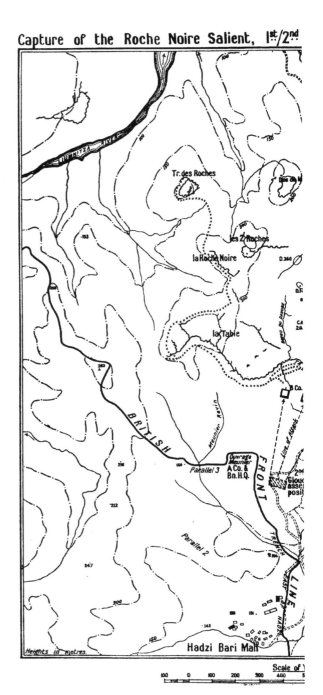

Heights in metres.

Scale of

100   0   100   200   300   400   5

2nd September, 1918

Mamelon Vert

Mamelle I.

R!! du Clos de Mulet

a du Mulet

C.103.a

C.103

C.102

C.101

D.54

B.104.a

C.104

C.108.b

2.6.2

Mon. Aux
Buissons

A.A.2.

A.A.1.

C.108

C.101

M!! du Yatagan

Alcak-Mah
(East)

B Co. C Co. D Co.

R!! des Buissons

Alcak-Mah
(West)

2nd Bn.
Gloucesters
assembly
position

LINE

Barakli-Mah

returning in numbers to their homes and they continually warned the
British troops :
" Finish all, finish Johnny."
' This proved correct, the Gloucesters' marching orders were can-
celled as the Austrians retired from the struggle.
' The Regiment then withdrew by rail and march route down the
Struma Valley through Marinopolje, the Roupel Pass to Demiraissar
and thence across the valley to Kopriva and Lahana and down their
old friend, the Seres Road, to Guvesne. From here the Regiment
entrained to Janes, south of Doiran.
' It was during this march that news of the Armistice with Germany
was received.
' Here the Regiment settled down in dug-outs and bivouacs to prepare for demobilization and await orders to embark for home. The
winter had set in and a bivouac is not a good house in snow and Vardar
winds. Once again the mules and chargers were formed into racing
stables and frequent race meetings were held. The Regiment once
more came to the front at Rugby football.
' Hopes of an early return home were, however, sadly dashed to the
ground, and on the 24th December orders were received to proceed
to South Russia.[1]
' The Regiment embarked at Salonika and proceeded via Dardanelles
and Constantinople to Batoum. Here the Regiment remained for a
few days before entraining to Tiflis.
' In spite of their disappointment at not going home (and many had
had quite sufficient of war), the behaviour of the men was beyond all
praise.'

---

[1] It is interesting to note that no less than eight officers of the 61st
commanded Battalions with the Salonika Force : viz., Lieut.-Colonel
K. M. Davie, 61st, Lieut.-Colonel F. C. Nisbet, 61st and 8th D.C.L.I.,
Lieut.-Colonel D. Burges, 7th S.W. Borderers, who won the Victoria
Cross whilst commanding that Battalion, Lieut.-Colonel J. L. F. Tweedie,
12th Lancashire Fusiliers, Lieut.-Colonel R. L. Beasley, 9th K.O.R.
Lanc. R., Lieut.-Colonel A. C. Vicary, 61st, Lieut.-Colonel H. F. L.
Hilton-Green, 10th Devons, Lieut.-Colonel J. Fane, 9th Gloucesters.

CHAPTER XXXVIII

ITALY

AT the end of December 1917 we left the 48th Division in Italy, the 1/4th Gloucesters at Bressanvido, the 1/5th at Stroppari and the 1/6th at Sandrigo. The Division was at that period in reserve, forming with the 5th, 7th, 23rd and 41st and five French divisions, a portion of the Second Italian Army, then holding the line roughly from Montello to the Brenta River above Bassano. The British sector was on the extreme right, i.e. the Montello Sector with the Third Italian Army on the right and two French divisions on the left. The Third and Second Italian Armies (in that order from right to left) lay along the left bank of the Piave up to a point south-west of Valdobbiadene, where the river turns north : the Italian line then ran almost due west crossing the Brenta, including Mount Grappa and Asiero, but on reaching the north-eastern edge of Lake Garda turned north-west and then north.

Hence, the sector of the line of chief interest to the Gloucestershire Regiment was first the Montello and later the Asiago sectors.

The situation when the British divisions arrived in Italy was disquieting : the Italian retreat had been arrested on the River Piave, but it was uncertain whether the Italians would hold that line. At first it was arranged that the British and French divisions should move to the hills north and south of Vicenza where a stand could certainly have been made. The British and French offered to take over sectors on the foothills of the Asiago Plateau, but snow was imminent and the Italian Higher Command considered that their allies would suffer losses and hardships from cold on the hills, especially as they were unaccustomed to such warfare, and to provide special mountain equipment was difficult. It was, therefore, suggested that the British should instead take over the Montello sector with the French on their left, and this was done.

General Sir Herbert Plumer, the Commander-in-Chief of the British forces in Italy, thus described the sector in his despatches, dated the 12th April 1918 :

‘ The Montello sector is a feature by itself and an important one. It acts as a bridge to the whole Italian line, joining as it does that por-

tion facing north from Mount Tomba to Lake Garda, with the defensive
line of the River Piave covering Venice, which was held by the Third
Italian Army.'

The arrival of British and French troops had an excellent moral
effect on the Italians and enabled the latter to withdraw troops
to train and reorganize after the strenuous time during the close
of 1917. Local attacks on and by the Italians were frequent
during December of that year. At Christmas-time the situation,
both on the Grappa and Asiago, was serious, but on the 30th the
French captured 1,500 Austrians in the Mount Tomba sector,
assisted by British artillery.

During all this period the British divisions holding the front
line carried out patrol work across the Piave.

' The Piave is a very serious obstacle, especially at this season of the
year, the breadth opposite the British front being considerably over
1,000 yards and the current 14 knots. Every form of raft and boat
has been used, but wading has proved the most successful : but the icy
cold water made the difficulties even greater. In spite of this there
has never been any lack of volunteers, both officers and men, for these
enterprises.'

The New Year had scarcely dawned ere the Third Italian Army
cleared the Austrians from the west bank of the Piave about
Zenson : the Fourth Italian Army on the 14th attacked Mount
Asolone and took four hundred prisoners : on the 28th the First
Italian Army carried out successful operations on the Asiago
Plateau, capturing some 2,500 Austrians.

Thus the Year 1918 began well, but the weather was bad, much
snow had fallen and conditions in the line were hard.

The 48th Division, however, did not go into the front line until
the end of February, having spent the intervening period between
moving up to reserve positions and taking over part of the Montello
sector, in training.

Of the three Territorial Battalions of the Gloucestershire Regiment, the 1/5th (Lieut.-Colonel W. Adam) went first into the
line, having marched up from Cusignana on the 27th February,
they relieved the 22nd Manchesters at night on that date on the
River Piave near Nervesa, the right sub-sector of the Montello
sector.

Patrol work began immediately. It was difficult. A party
from the 1/5th crossed a stream 4 feet 6 inches in depth and
60 yards wide on the southern end of Luvi Island, then crossed the
main stream of the Piave in order to reach the left bank. They
observed a trench with three good rows of wire and a group of
hostile troops : they then returned. This incident is mentioned

only as an instance of what patrolling meant on the Italian front. One man suffered from cramp as a result of immersion in the icy water. On the 3rd the Battalion was relieved—four days on end in the front line was quite enough for any troops. Four days in and four days out was the rule, though the 1/5th spent only two tours in the front line in March, for by the end of the month they had moved to Marsango, for by this period the 48th Division, with other British divisions, had been withdrawn from the Montello sector and were due to take over trenches on the Asiago Plateau.

In the meantime neither the 1/4th (Lieut.-Colonel A. E. Williams) nor the 1/6th (Lieut.-Colonel H. St. G. Schomberg) Gloucesters of the 144th Brigade had been into the Montello sector, but spent the period in training and in furnishing working parties in the Brigade area, which on the 1st January was Sandrigo and subsequently Sovernigo, Villa Rosa and Selva. By the end of March the 144th Brigade had also moved west and was in the Campos Martino area on the 31st, the 1/4th Gloucesters being at Curtarold and the 1/6th at Pieve.

During April and May there is little to record of outstanding interest. All three Battalions went into the front line during April, but beyond patrol work, with an occasional encounter with hostile patrols, there is nothing to record. The 1/4th and 1/6th were inspected by H.R.H. the Duke of Connaught on the 9th April.

Winter had given way to spring and there were rumours of another Austrian offensive against the Italians. In France all was not going as well with the enemy as had been expected. The Great German Offensive in March had not provided the result aimed at and it was necessary to create a diversion elsewhere. So in April there were signs of an enemy attack on a large scale, possibly astride the Brenta. In May it appeared probable that this operation would be combined with an attack across the Piave, and by the end of that month the enemy's attack was certain.

THE BATTLE OF THE PIAVE : 15TH–16TH JUNE

The Austro-Hungarian attack was originally fixed for the 11th June, but was subsequently postponed until the 15th. It was to begin with an advance at the Adamello on the West Tyrol Front, but the main attack was to take place in several groups between Asiago and the sea, directed on the Brenta, Montello and lower corner of the Piave, or in other words from S. Dona di Piave to Montello on the plains, and from Grappa to Canove in the mountains.

The whole of the British sector (held by the 23rd Division on the right and the 48th Division on the left) was involved in this attack.

Early on the morning of the 15th June a short, but violent, bombardment of the whole Allied line broke out, smoke and gas shell being freely used : the enemy then launched his attack. The 23rd and 48th Divisions were attacked by four Austrian divisions. On the front of the former the enemy was completely repulsed, but in the sector held by the 48th Division he succeeded in occupying some 3,000 yards of the front-line trench and subsequently penetrated to a depth of about 1,000 yards.

When this attack was made the 145th Brigade was holding the right sub-sector and the 143rd the left : the 144th was in reserve, but under orders to relieve the 145th on the 15th June. Of the first-mentioned Brigade the 1/4th Oxford and Bucks held the right sub-sector and the 1/5th Gloucesters the left.

The scarcity of trench maps and information concerning the Divisional front line make a full description of the line held by the Gloucesters impossible. The main line appears to have run from east to west just north of Buco de Cesuna and immediately south of the Ghelpac Ravine. The whole sector is thus briefly described by Captain C. E. Carrington,[1] from the divisional point of view :

' The 48th (South Midland) Territorial Division (Major-General S. R. Fanshawe) moved up to the hills on the 31st May and took over a new sector of 4,000 yards frontage, running from Boscon to the Ghelpac Ravine. On the right the bare forward slope of Mount Kaberlaba made a good defensive position with sufficient field of fire. On the left a wooded, rocky ridge ran forward from the village of Cesuna and fell steeply into the Ravine. Up the valley, between these two forward spurs, ran two roads leading south from the enemy's lines to Carriola and to Cesuna. The front line, well down the forward slope, was not much above the general level of the Plateau. Divisional Headquarters at Carriola were 1,000 feet higher. Most of the traffic to the front passed through the cross roads known as Handley Cross, where there was a great dump of ammunition. The 145th Brigade (Lieut.-Colonel Reynolds) held the right sector, the 143rd Brigade (Brig.-General Sladen) the left : in reserve was the 144th (Lieut.-Colonel Tomkinson), but for lack of accommodation two of his battalions were down on the plains. To reach the line they had to advance 10 miles, climb 4,000 feet up to Carriola, then down 1,000 feet to the level of the Plateau. . . . In this line there was no field of fire, there were no dug-outs and no strong points. In case of attack everything depended on the two unfinished trenches, Cesuna Switch and Lemerle Switch, forming a pocket into which an advancing enemy might be herded.'

The average strength of battalions was about 491 rifles, for

[1] In the *Army Quarterly*, July 1927.

early in June an epidemic of influenza had broken out and 30 per cent of all ranks were in hospital.

A general Allied attack had been planned on the Austrian positions and preparations were made from the 1st to the 14th June.

The advanced posts of the 1/5th Gloucesters [1] (consisting of one company) were north-west of Cunico Hill, north of the Ghelpac Ravine : the posts extended from south-west to north-east, being roughly opposite the centre of the village of Righe with Holla N behind Righe, and Holla S on the left front. The right of the Gloucesters and the left of the Oxford and Bucks were in touch at about Bassastoc.

A Company held the right and D the left of the main line : B Company held the outpost line and C was in support.

The enemy's bombardment began at about 2.45 a.m. on the 15th. His infantry were first observed on a hill overlooking the left front company headquarters. He then extended across the valley and took the left company in reverse. One platoon of the support company had been sent up to the front line at 6.40 a.m. in accordance with Battalion orders to push on to Hill 964. On arrival in the front line this platoon was heavily engaged with the enemy, who was then trying to pass through the Ravine : the platoon successfully kept the enemy out, a Lewis gun, manned by No. 13773 Pte. S. Pegler, doing great execution. A second platoon from the support company was pushed up the valley as soon as the enemy was observed on the hill first mentioned, in face of heavy machine-gun fire, with the intention of driving back the enemy and extricating part of the left front company. The whole of the Lewis-gun team of the second platoon, however, was knocked out. The enemy, in great strength, now pushed on along the ridge to the north of the valley and the two platoons of the support company were forced to retire. The left of these two platoons was ably extricated from a difficult position by 2nd Lieutenant G. F. Churchill. The two platoons then retired on a defensive line organized as follows :

' Left flank—remaining platoon of the support company, which had been pushed up on the ridge H.31.34 : a Lewis-gun section of left front company on western slope of valley : remains of other two platoons holding exits and eastern slope of valley up to Battalion Headquarters. Headquarters details and one platoon of outpost company and a few details of right front company forming a defensive flank on ridge above

---

[1] The Battalion in this action was commanded by Major N. H. Waller as Lieut.-Colonel W. Adam left for England on the 2nd June.

Battalion Headquarters back to Cesuna—Canove road about H.345.350. This line formed about 7.30 a.m.' [1]

The outpost company had retired, under Brigade orders, at about 4.30 a.m. to the hills north of the Ghelpac Ravine. About 6.30 a.m. they drove back enemy scouts, but on being threatened with envelopment by the main attack, retired across the Ghelpac, part to the remainder of the left front company, part to the right front company. The right company was still holding out, but the enemy succeeded in breaking through somewhere in the neighbourhood of X Track and in enveloping the right centre. The remainder of the right company, finding themselves isolated and the enemy coming in behind their right and along the front line from the left, managed to retire to the Cesuna—Canove road, their retirement from the front line being covered by No. 203325 Pte. G. H. Oliver who, with splendid devotion to duty, sacrificed himself and his Lewis gun in order that his comrades might get away. This company formed the right during the withdrawal.

In the second position the enemy was held up until 8.15 a.m., suffering heavy losses, particularly on the left flank where numerous bodies, including those of two officers, were found hanging on the wire in front of the Italian mortar position, when the line was retaken later. By means, however, of bringing up numerous light machine-guns, and the constant firing of rifle grenades, the enemy worked round the left flank and also advanced on the right between the defensive flank and that part of the front line which was still holding out. The line was then withdrawn behind Track H.32.33 [2] and the Cesuna—Canove road. The Battalion at this time consisted of two composite companies, the left, of the remains of the support company and Headquarters details, holding roughly from H.32.33 to the junction of the track with the road at H.355.360 : the right, formed from the outpost company and a few men from the right front company, held from the latter point to the railway line about H.39.36.

At about 9.15 a.m. the enemy was again working round both flanks and a further withdrawal became necessary. During this retirement touch was lost between the two composite companies, owing to the very thick woods and casualties. A new line was, however, formed running across and below the railway from H. 33.31 to H.345.310, thence for 200 yards along the railway to about H.39.33. But the enemy was pressing on in great force,

[1] Battalion Narrative.
[2] There is no other way in which to describe these positions, save by co-ordinates : the French system of co-ordination was used in this instance.

particularly on both sides of the Cesuna—Canove road and, as no communication could be established on the flanks, companies withdrew again to the line of the track connecting the road with Pelly Cross.   Good work was done during this retirement by the Battalion Signalling Sergeant (No. 240181 Sergt. R. A. Burton). This gallant N.C.O. also immediately laid a line to Brigade Headquarters when Battalion Headquarters reached Lemerle Switch a little later.

Eventually the line taken up by the 1/5th Gloucesters during the early evening was as given in the Battalion Narrative which stated :

' Our line was now reorganized and held by the remains of our support and outpost companies, with one platoon in support 300 yards up Mount Lemerle, and reserves, consisting of the remainder of two front-line companies and Headquarters details in Lemerle Switch.'

Touch was obtained later with the Berkshires on the right and Warwicks on the left.

The situation was saved by the action of Colonel Knox, commanding the Warwicks who were in support.   A week before he had been doing a tactical exercise with his unit over this particular bit of ground, the exercise consisting of a counter-attack on the front line which was supposed to have been lost.   Realizing what had happened and without waiting for orders, Colonel Knox set his Battalion in motion on the same lines as his tactical exercise, and this undoubtedly was chiefly instrumental in stopping the Austrian attack in this part of the line.

The remnants of the 1/5th remained in this position during the night of the 15th/16th June.

Meanwhile the 1/6th had come into action.

As already stated the 144th Brigade was about to relieve the 145th Brigade when the Austrian attack was launched.   The 1/4th Gloucesters were at South Dona, the 1/6th at Mount Serona.   At 11.30 a.m. the 1/6th, under verbal orders from the Brigade, having been issued with fifty extra rounds of S.A.A. per man, arrived in fighting order at Carriola.   At the latter place the Battalion was ordered to march to Casa Magnaboschi and to discover and restore the situation.   Moving via Pra Pelucco and Val Magnaboschi in single file, the 1/6th arrived at Casa Magnaboschi at about 1 p.m. and took up their position among the rocks, touch being gained immediately with the 1/7th Warwicks, the latter having already made one counter-attack earlier in the day. The latter Battalion was holding the enemy along the line C. Traversos—Villa Brunialti—Clo : the Lemerle and Cesuna Switch Lines were held by troops of the 145th Brigade.

The situation east and north-east of Clo was still unknown, but the left flank of the 1/4th Oxford and Bucks Light Infantry (145th Brigade) was believed to be in the neighbourhood of Pelly Cross. It was then decided that the 1/6th Gloucesters should prolong the right flank of the 1/7th Royal Warwicks north-east along the Clo—Pelly Cross track (Pine Alley) and counter-attack with two companies—B on the right and D on the left, A and C Companies remaining in reserve at Casa Magnaboschi. Battalion Headquarters were 200 yards south-west of Clo.

This counter-attack was launched at 5.30 p.m., in conjunction with the 1/7th Warwicks. After advancing about 150 yards through dense pine forest, the 1/7th Warwicks and D Company were held up by heavy machine-gun fire. B Company, which had lost touch with D, advanced north-east with little opposition to Pelly Cross but failed to obtain touch with the Oxford and Bucks. B Company then pushed on north-west with the intention of turning the enemy's flank, but on reaching the railway embankment N.35.34 they were attacked from front and both flanks and were obliged to withdraw to positions along Pine Alley, on the right of D Company.

At 7.30 p.m. the 1/7th Worcesters, with A and C Companies of the 1/6th Gloucesters in reserve, made an attack in conjunction with the 1/7th Warwicks and B and D Companies of the Gloucesters on the left. After advancing about 200 yards the attack was again held up by strong hostile machine-gun fire.

At 2 a.m. on the 16th orders were issued from Brigade Headquarters that the attack was to be resumed at 4.30 a.m. by two companies of the 1/6th Gloucesters and 1/7th Worcesters, in conjunction with the 1/8th Worcesters who would advance on both sides of the Handley Cross—Pelly Cross road. The left flank of the 1/7th Worcesters could not be located and this attack also was stopped by machine-gun fire.

At 7.30 a.m. the 1/8th Worcesters came into position astride the Handley Cross—Pelly Cross road, and a combined attack was arranged with a view to regaining the whole of the original position.

The following positions were then taken up : 1/8th Worcesters on the right, 1/6th Gloucesters in the right centre, 1/7th Worcesters left centre, 1/7th Warwicks left.

The whole line advanced at 8.30 a.m. and the Austrians, having by this time suffered heavy casualties and apparently being in no mind to put up any further resistance, withdrew, offering little opposition. On reaching the old front-line system considerable captures of prisoners and booty were made and patrols from the 1/6th Gloucesters were sent forward who recaptured the whole of the original outpost positions on Hill 972 and Cunico Hill and effected further substantial capture of prisoners and machine-guns. At 11 a.m. on receipt of orders from Brigade Headquarters, the 1/6th took over the left battalion sector with the 1/7th Worcesters in close support.

The 1/4th Gloucesters had moved in lorries to Carriola at noon on the 15th and at 6 p.m. marched to Casa Magnaboschi, where they remained in reserve throughout the 16th.

Thus, so far as the Regiment is concerned, ended the Austrian offensive of the 15th June—an inglorious affair in which the enemy lost more than he had gained, for the temporary lodgment in a small portion of the second British line was all the advantage he had gained for an exploitation of many lives and a large number of prisoners and many machine-guns left in our hands.

The losses of the 1/5th Gloucesters were heavy : Captain B. V. Bruton, Lieutenants G. P. Chutter and A. K. Stanley, 2nd Lieutenant G. S. Hayes and 24 other ranks were killed ; Captain R. F. Rubenstein, 2nd Lieutenants W. Pettigrew, R. R. E. Elcock, J. J. Ovenstone, J. Thomas, L. H. Frye and 114 other ranks missing ; Captain G. A. Lister, 2nd Lieutenants E. R. C. Ames, V. Scroggie, C. S. Stafford, R. F. Taylor, Captain A. T. L. Grear and 2nd Lieutenant G. L. Ovenden and 64 other ranks wounded.

At the end of the June Diary of the 1/5th Gloucesters there is a list of awards for gallantry in action : Captain C. R. Coote, M.C., the D.S.O.,[1] Captain the Rev. C. A. Clark and 2nd Lieutenant G. F. Churchill the M.C., No. 240181 Sergt. R. A. Burton the D.C.M., and the following N.C.O.s and men the Military Medal —240877 Sergt. H. Parker, No. 241942 Sergt. W. J. Pearson, No. 242523 L/Corpl. W. J. Tonge, No. 240890 L/Corpl. T. H. Whitehead and No. 13373 Pte. B. Pegler.

The Diary of the 1/4th Battalion does not mention any casualties.

The casualties of the 1/6th Gloucesters were 1 officer and 14 other ranks killed, 3 officers and 39 other ranks wounded and 1 other rank missing. The 1/6th captured 1 officer and 168 other ranks unwounded, 30 other ranks wounded, fourteen machine guns and one *flammenwerfer*.[2]

On the 16th the Divisional front was again completely restored and the repulse of the Austrians was followed by many weeks of

----

[1] The Diary also contains mention of the award of the D.S.O. to Lieut.-Colonel W. Adam.

[2] No names of officers are given in the Diary.

comparatively quiet operations in which raids and patrol work were the only exciting incidents.

During the remainder of June and throughout the whole of July little transpired of outstanding interest. In August, however, patrols became extremely active, keeping a close watch at night on the enemy's lines. Many raids were also made, during which the Austrians lost heavily, the raiding parties from the 48th Division taking prisoners who, in the aggregate, totalled hundreds. In these raids the Gloucesters took part.

It is, however, desirable to relate the doings of the 1/5th Gloucesters first, for that Battalion (as the previous narrative shows) left the 48th Division in September and returned to France.

After the affair of the 15th/16th of June the 1/5th Gloucesters moved back to Mount Pau on the 18th and on the 22nd to the Marziele area until the 2nd July. On the latter date they changed areas, i.e. to Cornedo where training was carried out until the 17th. On the latter date the Battalion began to move back to the forward area and on the 21st reached Granezza where they were in support until the 26th when they relieved the Oxford and Bucks in the front line as right battalion in the right sub-sector of the 48th Divisional front, south of Asiago.

With the exception of a small patrol encounter at S. Ave the tour was uneventful and the 1/5th on the 30th were relieved and returned to Granezza. Tours in the front line from the 13th to the 18th of August (during which active patrolling took place) and the 22nd to the 25th August, followed by a move back to Club Camp, near Granezza from the 26th August to the 2nd September, then a final tour in the front line south-west of S. Ave from the 3rd to the 10th September, closed the work of the 1/5th Gloucesters in Italy.

The 25th Division was being reconstituted in France and three Divisions (7th, 23rd and 48th) each supplied three battalions to form the infantry of the Division : the 1/5th Gloucesters were one and received orders to proceed to France on the 13th. Having entrained on the 14th they crossed the French frontier on the 15th and reached St. Riguer on the 17th, the Battalion marching thence to Domvast where they billeted in barns and roomy outhouses.[1]

The 1/4th were in Brigade Reserve at Granezza when on the night of the 28th August they supplied a raiding party of 2nd Lieutenant F. Alcock and 25 other ranks from C Company and 2nd Lieuten-

[1] For the further story of the 1/5th in France and Flanders see p. 295 *et seq.*

ant W. M. Shepstone and 25 men from A Company. The raid
was on the enemy's front line at Sec and resulted in three Austrians
being taken and many killed. The casualties of the raiders were
2nd Lieutenant Shepstone and 14 other ranks wounded.

The 1/6th raided the enemy on the night of the 8th/9th August,
the country south of Gaiga South and the western portion of
Norfolk Trench being the objectives. The raid was made by
three companies : B (under Captain S. F. Sullivan) carrying out
the attack on the western portion of Norfolk Trench and C, with
D in support (under Captain D. G. Stewart), raiding the cutting.
No prisoners were taken but many Austrians were killed. The
raiders had three other ranks killed and seven wounded.

Another raid was carried out by A Company on the night of
the 24th August. The raiders consisted of two parties, one of
18 other ranks under 2nd Lieutenant W. E. Marks, and the
other of 32 other ranks under 2nd Lieutenant D. W. Ware : the
O.C., raid, was Captain W. M. Lowick. The right party (2nd
Lieutenant Marks) met with opposition, but took three prisoners
and killed one officer and about six men : 2nd Lieutenant Ware's
party were held up by machine-gun fire. Only four casualties
(all wounded) were suffered by the raiders.

September, if one can believe the records, was bare of interest
save for ' offensive patrols '. October the 1st found the 1/4th
in Club Camp and the 1/6th at Granezza South. The 1/6th
took over the left front of the right sub-sector on the 3rd and the
1/4th the right front of the same sub-sector on the 4th. The
former were in the line until the 16th but the latter were relieved
on the 11th.

The Austrians at this period were showing signs of weariness :
the trend of affairs in France and Flanders had filled them with
despondency and already there were rumours of a retirement.
Patrol work was redoubled and a vigilant watch kept on the
enemy's front-line trenches.

About the middle of October the Allied Higher Command drew
up a plan for attacks on a large scale upon the whole Austrian line.
It is unnecessary to detail the scheme of attack other than to say
that, so far as the 48th Division was concerned, as part of the
Sixth Italian Army, its rôle was to hold its front until the Italians
with the 7th and 23rd Divisions (which had been detached from
the Sixth Army and sent over to the Tenth Army on the right)
had driven a wedge between the Fifth and Sixth Austrian Armies.
The 48th Division remained on the Asiago Plateau, attached
temporarily to the XIIth Italian Corps.

Before joining in the operations, however, the 48th Division carried out several big raids, i.e. on the 4th, 11th and 23rd of October : the latter was made by the 1/4th Gloucesters.

The point selected for the operation was the Ave area and practically the whole Battalion was engaged. The object of the raid was to kill or capture the garrison and capture war material. The French, on the right, and Italians on the left, were also to raid the enemy.

The march up from the support area and assembly in front of the picquet line was carried out without a hitch, the last 50 yards in front of the line being covered on hands and knees. A Company was on the right, B in the centre, C on the left : D Company furnished two platoons to attack the front line from Ave to Lone Tree House, the remainder of the Company providing a flank guard and Battalion Reserve.

At zero the whole Battalion moved forward and reached the enemy's wire before the barrage lifted. For four minutes the guns poured a heavy fire on the hostile trenches, then lifted, when the raiders entered. Several prisoners were captured in front of the wire just east of the Ave road.

The scheme of the raid comprised three separate company operations which were exactly carried out according to orders. The following narrative is taken from Major E. E. Wookey's report of the operations :

' C Company. Left—met with machine-gun fire and resistance from enemy front trench opposite Ave. This was soon overcome and a machine gun captured. Wire here new but not very thick. Company then attacked its further objectives. A few of the enemy were captured in the front line towards Silvegnar and twenty men, running away towards T. Ghelpac, were machine-gunned. Majority of prisoners obtained in Maxim dug-outs, seven of which were set on fire. These are connected by tunnels and have each two entrances. Two machine guns were also captured here. Total captures of the Company were three machine guns and about fifty prisoners.

' B Company. Centre—captured several enemy in shell holes in front of wire, found wire poor, passed straight to objectives. Quarry is apparently a headquarters of some kind. A large red signal lamp was burning and there is considerable accommodation : twenty prisoners captured here. B Redoubt has many dug-outs and had a large garrison who showed fight until outflanked from the rear : thirty to forty prisoners taken here. V-shaped trench was empty. Total captures—sixty prisoners, three machine guns.

' A Company. Right—went straight through to their objectives and cleared the Lowe dug-outs right up to those at the S. M. Maddalena cross roads. About one hundred prisoners and two machine guns were obtained from these.

' D Company. Two platoons attacked and occupied from line from Ave to Lone Tree House, the remainder provided a flank guard and a battalion reserve. This Company captured fifteen prisoners and two machine guns.

' Battalion Headquarters remained throughout the raid at Red Redoubt. Runner communication was maintained with companies and signal communication with brigade through the whole period in the enemy line.

' Withdrawal was effected at zero plus fifty minutes, area then being reported entirely clear of the enemy. Companies returned directly across Guardimalti Ridge and met with no casualties while doing so. All troops, except Battalion Headquarters, had re-entered our picquet line by zero plus seventy minutes. Battalion Headquarters returned at zero plus two-and-a-half hours, having sheltered in a gun pit on Ave Spur. Enemy barrage did not come down on his front line until after our departure. On picquet line and front line it was fairly heavy. It increased on picquet line after our guns ceased firing and continued till zero plus two-and-a-quarter hours. The valley in front of Silver Posts received special attention, also the western end of Guardimalti Ridge and the village itself.

' Total casualties—one killed, three wounded, three wounded (remained at duty), one Jugo-Slav [1] killed.'

Thus ended a very satisfactory raid, well planned and splendidly carried out.

Several days of rest and cleaning up followed this brilliant little operation and then on the 28th the 1/4th went back into the line, relieving the Warwicks in the right battalion sector of the left brigade sub-sector.

On the 29th October the enemy was reported to have retired. Daylight patrols from the 1/4th pushed forward to Tal and Campo Rovere and established posts on the high ground north of these two points : they rejoined the Battalion after dark. The 30th and 31st were quiet days, the Battalion carrying out trench routine. Their Diary for the 31st states : ' Enemy apparently in Mount Catz.'

On the left of the 1/4th the 1/6th Gloucesters, having relieved the 1/6th Warwicks on the 28th, settled down to trench routine, but it was evident that the Austrians were preparing to retire and on the 31st the Battalion pushed forward and established a picquet line in what had previously been the enemy's front-line. The entrance to the Val d'Assa, which formed the enemy's main line of retreat, was still strongly held.

On the right of the Allied line the attack had gone splendidly and the despatches speak of the enemy's defeat becoming a rout from the 30th October. But in front of the Sixth Italian Army and 48th Division on the left the enemy, as already stated, still clung to the mountains though his hold was distinctly precarious.

---

[1] A small number of Jugo-Slavs were with the 1/4th Gloucesters and did fine service.

In front of the 48th Division he was holding the line Mount
Catz—Bosco—Campo Rovere.

Very early on the 1st November the 1/4th and 1/6th Gloucesters
received orders to attack the enemy, zero hour being fixed at
5.45 a.m.

The 1/4th formed up on an east and west line through Capitello
—Mulche—Tal, C Company on the right, B on the left, with
D and A in support.

The 1/6th, on the left of their sister Battalion, disposed C
Company on the right, D on the left with A in the railway cutting
and B in the redoubt line.

The attack started well up to time. Of the 1/4th C Company
entered the enemy's line and captured Bosco, but A, B and D
Companies were unable to make progress owing to the heavy
machine-gun fire and failed to enter the enemy's trenches, finally
being forced to retire and take up positions in several old trenches
east of Lamara. C Company, being unsupported, was ordered
to retire in small parties, the last party falling back at about 2
p.m. At dusk the 1/4th formed a defensive flank to the 145th
Brigade on the right and on the left gained touch with the 1/6th
in the railway cutting.

The 1/6th also met with determined resistance on the slopes
of the Mount Interrotto—Mount Rasta Ridge.

At dawn on the 2nd November a further advance was made.
The 145th Brigade, which on the previous day had captured
Mount Catz, exploited their success and by 8 a.m. the Gloucesters
of the 144th Brigade had reached the top of Mount Interrotto.

The Val d'Assa was forced also on this day and the great
Austrian debacle had begun.

When darkness had fallen the advanced guard of the 48th
Division had reached Vezzena and the Division was, therefore,
the first British division to enter enemy territory on the western
front of the Italian battlefield.

On the 3rd the advance was continued, but the 1/4th and
1/6th Gloucesters had seen their last fight. The 1/4th (attached
to the 143rd Brigade) reached billets at Ischia, marching via
Vezzena and Caldonazza : on the 4th the Battalion reached
billets in Baselga de Pine and Fornace where four days were
spent, the 1/6th being at Cire.

At 3 p.m., when the Armistice came into force, the leading
troops of the 48th Division were on the line Miola—eastern
outskirts of Trent. The 1/6th were in the neighbourhood of
the latter, but entry to that coveted goal was reserved for the
Italians.

The part played by the 48th Division in this final historic battle cannot be over-estimated. The Duke of Braganza, commanding the 6th Austrian Cavalry Division, in surrendering his sword to General H. B. Walker, said : ' The advance of your 48th British Division will go down to history as one of the most splendid feats of the British Army.' And the official despatches stated :

' It must be remembered that the Division was attacking very formidable mountain positions with only a fifth part of the artillery that would have been at its disposal had the initial attack started over the Actipiano. Its performance, therefore, in driving in the enemy's rearguards so resolutely while climbing up to heights of 5,000 feet, is all the more praiseworthy.'

No less than 20,000 prisoners and 500 guns were captured by the 48th Division.

Thus ended the Italian Campaign in which the 1/4th [1] and 1/6th Gloucesters had splendidly upheld the high traditions of the Regiment and added fresh laurels to its honours.

[1] The Diary of the 1/4th Gloucesters for November contains the following list of Honours and Awards : Bar to Military Cross—Captain F. A. Browning ; Military Cross—Captain R. Lowe, Lieutenant W. J. Dutton, 2nd Lieutenant F. A. Webster ; D.C.M.—No. 201099 Sergt. C. Bees, No. 265502 Corpl. G. F. Fry, No. 200469 C.Q.M.S. A. Dyer, No. 200870 C.S.M. J. R. Wilcox, No. 38670 Pte. G. T. Collins, No. 201149 Sergt. G. Barnfield, No. 200617 Sergt. G. Lane, No. 38603 L/Corpl. W. H. Hopson, No. 200347 Sergt. W. Taylor, No. 201008 Sergt. T. Denby, No. 201943 Pte. A. Marchant, No. 200273 Sergt. W. Toplin, No. 265035 C.S.M. G. Blackbourne, No. 201780 L/Sergt. E. H. Sprague.

Italian Honours : Silver Medal for Valour—Captain E. W. Thompson, Major E. E. Wookey, Lieutenant C. H. Chaffer, R.S.M. J. S. Sanders ; Bronze Medal for Valour—No. 201431 Sergt. S. O. Sell, No. 20497 Sergt. T. Ashcroft, No. 23507 Pte. A. Blatchford, No. 202101 Pte. A. Hutchings ; Croce di Guerra—2nd Lieutenant R. B. Lambert, No. 201141 Sergt. A. James, No. 26632 Sergt. C. Dunster, No. 200504 Pte. H. Q. Weymouth, No. 201333 Corpl. W. Cryer.

In December the following awards were announced : Bar to Military Medal—No. 200379 L/Corpl. W. H. Hopson, No. 200065 R.S.M. J. S. Sanders, No. 240333 Sergt. C. H. Hayward, No. 200071 Corpl. W. Harris, No. 200482 L/Corpl. G. J. Radford, No. 21272 Pte. C. A. Arthurs, No. 202101 Pte. A. Hutchings, No. 38615 Pte. J. Reading ; D.C.M.—No. 202803 Pte. A. Smith ; Military Cross—Lieutenant G. C. Carter ; Italian Silver Medal—No. 33191 Pte. T. Hammond ; Italian Croce di Guerra—Lieutenant C. R. Failis.

In January Major E. E. Wookey was appointed Brevet-Major and Captain E. W. Thompstone and Lieutenant C. H. Chaffer were awarded the Military Cross ; No. 200489 C.Q.M.S. A. Dyer was awarded the Meritorious Service Medal.

No Honours and Awards List is with the records of the 1/6th Gloucesters.

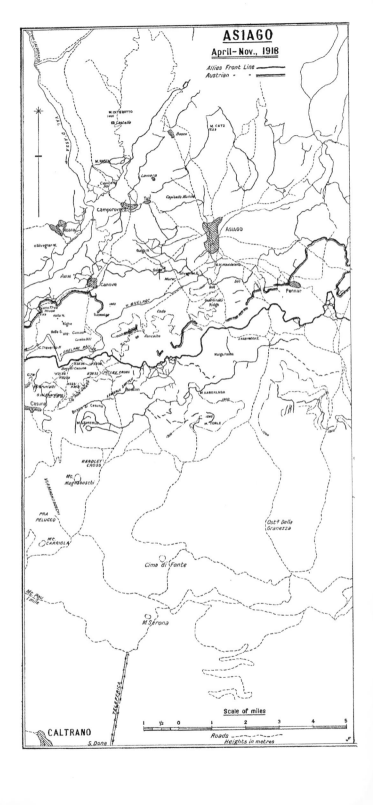

ASIAGO
April–Nov., 1918

Allies Front Line ———
Austrian " — · ———

Scale of miles

Roads — — —
Heights in metres

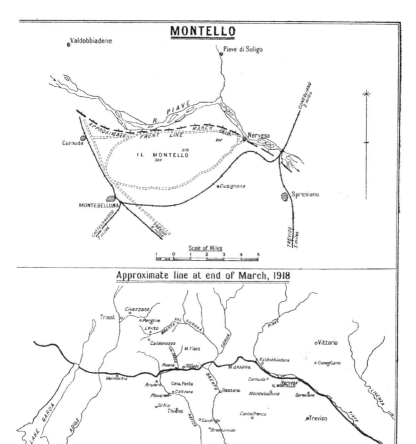

MONTELLO

Approximate line at end of March, 1918

ITALY

Illustrating the operations of the

¼ᵗʰ, ⅕ᵗʰ & ⅙ᵗʰ Gloucestershire Regt.

1917-1918

CONCLUSION

IN his despatch describing the Advance to Victory Lord Haig paid this tribute to the troops under his command :

' In our admiration for this outstanding achievement ' (he referred to the three months' epic fighting which finally brought the War to an end) ' the long years of patient and heroic struggles by which the spirit and strength of the enemy were gradually broken down cannot be forgotten. The strain of those years was never ceasing, the demands they made upon the best of the Empire's manhood are now known. Yet throughout all those years, and amid all the hopes and disappointments they brought with them, the confidence of our troops in final victory never wavered. Their courage and resolution rose superior to every test, their cheerfulness never failing however terrible the conditions in which they lived and fought. By the long road they trod with so much faith and with such devoted and self-sacrificing bravery we have arrived at victory and to-day they have their reward.'

The most wonderful thing when the Armistice came into force and all ranks ' stood to ' was the silence of the battlefields. Here and there along the long line of battle-worn and weary troops a cheer broke the stillness, but the records show that when hostilities ceased Peace fell amidst a hush almost painful in its coming. If, far away from the line of muddy, dirty trenches in France and Flanders, across the Channel, in every city, town and village throughout the United Kingdom (even throughout the world) people went mad with joy and forgot everything but that the black pall of war had been lifted and the sun shone once more, as if bursting through the dark clouds after a violent storm ; no such happenings took place in the front-line. It was impossible to forget in a moment the four long years and more of ' the terrible conditions in which they had lived and fought '. Impossible also to forget those brave messmates who had not come through, who in a soldier's grave somewhere between the Aisne and the tortured Ypres Salient lay silent for ever, asleep until the Judgment Day. To them the joy of living had been just as sweet : they too had left behind homes and wives and little children or aged parents to whom they one day hoped to return : and in the hour of victory the thoughts of all ranks turned first to those gallant dead who had given their lives :

' That *we* might live.'

349

In Fresnoy-le-Grand the ' Old Braggs ' stood to at 11 a.m.
In their ranks there was but a handful of those who had landed
in France in August, 1914 : who had known the torturous retreat
from Mons, the terrific struggles of ' Ypres '14 ', the bloody
fighting at Givenchy and then at Loos, by which time the Old
Army had largely disappeared.   Truly and well the 28th had
given of their best, and when the time came for the march into
Germany to begin, it was but right that the 1st Division should
be one of those selected to occupy the Rhine Provinces.   In
Cologne the 1st Gloucesters spent many months before they
returned to England.

The 25th Division did not march into Germany and the 1/5th
Gloucesters, therefore, remained in France until they returned
to Gloucester and were demobilized.

From Salonika the 61st, as already stated, with few regrets at
leaving that uncomfortable country, went on to Batoum and
Tiflis and did not return to the United Kingdom until 1919.

Of the 1/4th and 1/6th Gloucesters, the former moved to
Cornedo via Malo on the 15th November and remained in that
place until March, 1919, by which date the Battalion had been
reduced to cadre strength, i.e. 7 officers and 63 other ranks.
The date of the return of the cadre to Bristol is unknown.

The 1/6th recrossed the frontier into Italy on the 11th
November and proceeded to demobilization camps.   Further
service was, however, in store for the Battalion, for when the
remainder of the 48th Division proceeded homewards, the 1/6th
Gloucesters stayed behind for garrison duty in Albania and
Montenegro.   On the 8th May, 1919, they embarked for Egypt
and soon afterwards were encamped within a short distance of
the spot where in 1801 the 28th won the Regiment's famous
back badge.

It was only on the 25th March, 1920, that the cadre and the
Colours reached Bristol, the 1/6th having been abroad on active
service for five years seven months—surely a record for a
Territorial Battalion.[1]

---

[1] The 1/6th Gloucesters lost in killed 824 all ranks, including 40
officers, during the War.

APPENDIX

During the War, 1914–18, twenty-four battalions of the Gloucestershire Regiment existed.

These were :

1st Battalion	France	1st Division
2nd Battalion	France and Macedonia	27th Division
3rd Battalion		
1/4th Battalion	France and Italy	48th Division
1/5th Battalion	France and Italy	48th Division
,, ,,	France	25th Division
1/6th Battalion	France and Italy	48th Division
2/4th Battalion	France	61st Division
2/5th Battalion	France	61st Division
2/6th Battalion	France	61st Division
3/4th Battalion		
3/5th Battalion		
3/6th Battalion		
7th Battalion	Gallipoli, Egypt	13th Division
,,	Mesopotamia, Persia	,,
8th Battalion	France	19th Division
9th Battalion	France and Macedonia	26th Division
,,	France	66th Division
10th Battalion	France	1st Division
11th Battalion		
12th Battalion	France and Italy	5th Division
13th Battalion	France	39th Division
14th Battalion	France	35th Division
15th Battalion		
16th Battalion		
17th Battalion		
18th Battalion	France	16th Division

The 1/5th Battalion was taken from the 48th Division in Italy, in 1918, and sent to the 25th Division in France.

The 9th Battalion was taken from the 26th Division in Macedonia, in 1918, and sent to the re-organized 66th Division in France.

The 1st Battalion was attached to the 41st Division during the battle of Messines in 1917 and to the 46th Division during the Battle of Beaurevoir in 1918.

The 13th Battalion, as part of the ' 39th Division Composite Brigade ', was attached to the 9th Division during the battle of Kemmel in 1918.

The 18th Battalion was sent from England in 1918, to the reorganized 16th Division.

The 3rd, 3/4th, 3/5th, 3/6th, 11th, 15th, 16th and 17th Battalions did not serve overseas.

The battle honours gained by the battalions of the Regiment which served overseas are as follows :

1st Battalion   31 Honours
France and Flanders 1914–18
Mons
Retreat from Mons
Marne 1914
Aisne 1914
Ypres 1914, 1917
Langemarck 1914
Gheluvelt
Nonne Boschen
Givenchy 1914
Aubers
Loos
Somme 1916, 1918
Albert 1916
Bazentin
Pozières
Flers-Courcelette
Morval
Arras 1918
Messines 1917
Passchendaele
Lys
Estaires
Bethune
Drocourt-Quéant
Hindenburg Line
Epéhy
St. Quentin Canal
Beaurevoir
Selle
Sambre

2nd Battalion   8 Honours
France and Flanders 1914–15
Ypres 1915
Gravenstafel
St. Julien
Frezenberg
Bellewaarde

Macedonia 1915–18
Struma

1/4th Battalion   12 Honours
France and Flanders 1915–17
Ypres 1917
Langemarck, 1917
Somme 1916
Albert 1916
Bazentin
Pozières
Broodseinde
Poelcapelle
Italy 1917–18
Piave
Vittorio-Veneto

1/5th Battalion   16 Honours
France and Flanders 1915–18
Ypres 1917
Langemarck 1917
Somme 1916
Albert 1916
Pozières
Polygon Wood
Broodseinde
Poelcapelle
Cambrai 1918
Hindenburg Line
Beaurevoir
Selle
Sambre
Italy 1917–18
Piave

1/6th Battalion   11 Honours
France and Flanders 1915–17
Ypres 1917
Langemarck 1917
Somme 1916

Albert 1916
Pozières
Broodseinde
Poelcapelle
Italy 1917–18
Piave
Vittorio-Veneto

2/4th Battalion   4 Honours
France and Flanders 1916–18
Ypres 1917
Langemarck 1917
Cambrai 1917

2/5th Battalion   13 Honours
France and Flanders 1916–18
Ypres 1917
Langemarck 1917
Somme 1918
Cambrai 1917
St. Quentin
Rosières
Avre
Lys
Hazebrouck
Bethune
Selle
Valenciennes

2/6th Battalion   4 Honours
France and Flanders 1916–18
Ypres 1917
Langemarck 1917
Cambrai 1917

7th Battalion   10 Honours
Gallipoli 1915–16
Egypt 1916
Mesopotamia 1916–18
Persia 1918
Suvla
Sari Bair
Scimitar Hill
Tigris 1916
Kut 1917
Baghdad

8th Battalion   23 Honours
France and Flanders 1915–18
Aisne 1918

23

Ypres 1917
Somme 1916, 1918
Albert 1916
Pozières
Ancre Heights
Ancre 1916
Arras 1918
Messines 1917, 1918
Menin Road
Polygon Wood
Broodseinde
Passchendaele
Cambrai 1918
St. Quentin
Bapaume 1918
Lys
Bailleul
Kemmel
Hindenburg Line
Selle
Sambre

9th Battalion   6 Honours
France and Flanders 1915 and 1918
Macedonia 1915–18
Cambrai 1918
Hindenburg Line
Selle
Doiran 1917

10th Battalion   8 Honours
France and Flanders 1915–18
Loos
Somme 1916
Albert 1916
Bazentin
Pozières
Flers-Courcelette
Morval

12th Battalion   22 Honours
France and Flanders 1915–18
Italy 1917–18
Ypres 1917
Somme 1916, 1918
Albert 1918
Delville Wood
Guillemont

Flers-Courcelette
Morval
Bapaume 1918
Arras 1917, 1918
Vimy 1917
Scarpe 1917
Polygon Wood
Broodseinde
Poelcapelle
Passchendaele
Lys
Hazebrouck
Hindenburg Line
Epéhy
Canal-du-Nord

13th Battalion   9 Honours
France and Flanders 1915–18

Ypres 1917
Somme 1916, 1918
Ancre Heights
Ancre 1916
Pilckem
St. Quentin
Rosières
Kemmel

14th Battalion   5 Honours
France and Flanders 1916–18
Ypres 1917
Somme 1916
Bazentin
Passchendaele

18th Battalion   1 Honour
France and Flanders 1918

INDEX

BATTALIONS

OFFICERS AND V.Cs.

24

OPERATIONS

Printed in Great Britain
by Amazon